The
POLITICAL
DYNAMICS
of
AMERICAN
EDUCATION

THIRD EDITION

By

FREDERICK M. WIRT

University of Illinois, Urbana

and

MICHAEL W. KIRST

Stanford University

McCutchan Publishing Corporation
3220 Blume Drive #197
Richmond, California 94806

ISBN 0-8211-2280-0
Library of Congress Catalog Card Number 2005925789

Printed in the United States of America

Preface

This book is the third revision of the most widely used text in the politics of education, *The Political Dynamics of American Education*. The many new concepts and the extensive new content of this are reflected in the title, which symbolizes rapid changes in education politics. This revision places emphasis on current reforms, reflecting the political conflict and stress throughout the system. A concluding chapter focuses on the most recent reforms—choice schools and vouchers. The authors also expand on the political interactions within the local setting to address the current increase in bottom-up political activity. At the same time, the limits of both deregulation and centralized strategies are stressed as systemwide academic standards that confront complex local political reactions.

The most contemporary issues are treated: the debate over the decline of local control, the expanding role of state government in influencing policy direction, the growth of vouchers, and federal oversight of education. Across this range of conflict there has emerged new pressure groups from all parts of the political spectrum. As always, the latest school politics research and footnotes are included.

This text is designed in part for practitioners involved in education—administrators, teachers, state officials, and lay groups. The book will also be valuable to scholars of educational administration, political science, and sociology, because of its conceptual framework and extensive current research base. For students, the book provides an overview of the origins, nature, and historical evolution of the political forces surrounding and influencing schools.

The authors employ a conceptual framework to organize and chart the increasingly complex political web of American education. There are competing forces of challenge and steady state now affecting all levels of policymaking and administration. Combined, these forces constitute the "dynamic" nature of American education.

Finally, this book seeks to link the knowledge of scholarship with the practical needs of administration. There exists a "disconnect" between research and school-site practice. Even now, different branches of national government perceive different messages from voluminous educational research. Indeed, in 2005 a national research council is working to devise a new arrangement to produce useful knowledge for schooling. To this end, then, the authors seek to relate theory and behavior as they link to educational administration, teaching, and governing. Grasping theory enables one to understand current behavior and, furthermore, to test new ideas about schooling.

Contents

Part I:

CONCEPTS AND HISTORICAL PERSPECTIVES

1

Conflict, Politics, and Schools

Elementary and secondary education was a major national concern of voters as the twenty-first century opened. The political aspects of education have attained unprecedented visibility at all levels of government. Once there existed a "steady state" of education. Here, professionals controlled most aspects of schooling with only minor influence from citizens or elected politicians through school boards. In time, though, this professional, producer-oriented control faced a citizen, consumer-oriented conflict over what schools should do.

At the core of this book is an emphasis on politics and governance of the school system. Many education professionals believe politics should have no role in their work. For many citizens, though, their political action responds to dissatisfaction over their children's schooling.

THE THEMES OF POLITICS AND GOVERNANCE

It is important that we start with an understanding of the terms *politics* and *governance* before we discuss some of the challenges that now produce conflict in the schools. Two propositions about human behavior encompass these two terms. The first is that

3

politics is a form of social conflict rooted in group differences over values about using public resources to meet private needs. The second is that *governance is the process of publicly resolving that group conflict by means of creating and administering public policy.*

These broad concepts can be seen specifically in the issues presented in the profession's *Education Week.* In Table 1.1 we display the headlines for those stories that reflect concepts of politics and conflict. This listing tells us much about the currents of issues, parties, interest groups, and leadership that run through the political system of schools. From local to federal levels, from legislative to judicial arenas, from conflicting stands on current issues before the public—all these highlight the dominant political nature of educational politics. Moreover, the list also suggests the dynamic quality of politics that characterize a democratic nation. In addition, school politics is open to ideas that link leaders and the led, policymakers and citizens. Namely, all these attributes reflect a contest over public policy toward schooling.

To this competition there is added the weight of studies about the system's operations. In Table 1.2 we again use information from *Education Week* to highlight a range of surveys or polls reaching across the nation. What Table 1.2 shows are several qualities of a diverse school system where we find

- variety in many problems among the fourteen thousand school districts,
- challenge to reforms of education, and
- success for some students and failure for others amid calls for change.

Moreover, these studies reflect broad-scope problems developed by states, districts, or professionals. It is amid this challenge and defense that the current tensions in educational policies take place.

Diversity and Conflict

As we will see in the next chapter, political activity occurs as a result of the inevitable clash between groups with different values about many aspects of life. American society is composed of

Table 1.1
Story Headlines of Political School Issues

Spellings to Listen But Not Retreat on NCLB
Runoff Election Thrusts D.C. Union Critic Into Top Job
New School Board in San Diego Eroding Bersin's Reform Plans
Georgia Lawsuit Seeks Vouchers as Remedy to School Aid Disparities
Bush's Plan May Face Skepticism From the Left and Right
Much at Stake for Schools in Local Elections
Scouts' Ban on Gays Is Prompting Schools to Reconsider Ties
Polls Dispute a "Backlash" to Standards
Districts Accused of Shortchanging Workers
High Court to Referee Football Dispute
Abstinence Education Growing in Popularity
Future of School Leadership Open to Debate
In State Campaigns, Schools Emerge as Topic A

From *Education Week*, February, 2005.

Table 1.2
Studies of School System Operations

Certification Found Valid for Teachers [in] NBPTS Tests
Report Tracks "Crisis" Conditions in Special Education
Vouchers and Class Size: Not in the Same League
As Studies Stress Link to Scores, Districts Get Tough on Attendance
Extra Benefits Tied to [the] Extracurricular
NSBA Report Casts Critical Eye on Charter Movement
Panel Targets Hispanic Lag in Attainment
Children's Early Needs Seen as Going Unmet
Free High Schools from Traditional Borders, Panel Urges
Governance Report Calls for Overhaul [of board power]
Ten States Seen as Topping Rural Education Priority List
USDA Standard for Beef Has Schools Scrambling

From *Education Week*, September–November, 2000.

a diversity of groups that can generate social conflict. Some of this conflict is handled privately; if you don't like the new people in the neighborhood, or the prices of the local store, you can go elsewhere. In an historical example, American youth have left farms and small towns to seek in big cities new values and opportunities that were not found back home. Conflicts can also be resolved within existing social systems without recourse to violence. Thus, the church can help resolve class conflict among its members, the family can deal with generational differences, political parties can resolve ethnic conflict, and so on.

It is the political system that governs such conflict. How? It does so in the classic statement of David Easton, by "authoritatively allocating the distribution of values and resources,"[1] as its central characteristic. Note that this definition does not distinguish between democratic or authoritarian systems of government, or between presidential or parliamentary systems of democracy. Rather, the political system is a generic concept that applies to a variety of governing formats.

Conflict and Governing

We can get a sharper focus on both politics and governing if we examine how social conflict is resolved. The conflict potential inherent in value differences arises when a diverse population impinges on the political system. Leaders representing diverse groups seek new values and resources drawn from the political system. In that system, resolution of conflict takes the form of considering programs designed to deal with conflict. In considering such policy alternatives, controversy arises over such matters as the identification of the problem, the possibilities for implementing programs, and the analysis of their likely outcomes.

Once decisions are made to create public policy, then they must be carried out through organization, staffing, and financing through a process of "implementation." In time, implementation can lead to yet another policy stage—evaluating policy outcomes. In turn, the results of these evaluations may precipitate even more demands, more program alternatives, and so on. Governing was once defined sarcastically as doing nothing until someone complains, then adjusting to that complaint, then waiting for the complaint about that adjustment, and then adjusting to the complaint to the earlier adjustment.

All kinds of public policy, including education, are surrounded by these twin concepts of politics and governing. In this book we discuss how groups have differed over a long period of time on the issue of "schooling for what." For much of that history answers were provided by school professionals. These professionals were rooted in colleges, government agencies, and school administrations and teaching staff. They created a consistent pattern of operations we term "steady state." In recent decades, however, this condition has faced some challenges. These challenges may turn out to be more "tinkering," which has historically been the norm.[2] Both themes, persistence and challenge, appear throughout this book. In this first decade of the new millennium, it is still unclear how many of these challenges have changed the system.

Exploring Some Current Challenges

Later in this book there will be more details of persistence and challenge, but some current examples will highlight this conflict in the politics of school reform. Among the fourteen thousand school districts of the nation, it seems as if everyone is trying something new in the way of curriculum, organization, finances, and so on. However, the impression left to the observer is that of disorganized problems and hasty remedies. As Ernest Boyer, a veteran reformer, noted recently, "You could draw a 'Keystone Cops' image here of people charging off in different directions and bumping into one another. There's no overall sense of where the problem is and how we should work together to get there."[3] After completing a series of national opinion polls, the Public Agenda Foundation concluded, rightly or wrongly, that the public feels that the schools are no longer theirs, that they have been captured by teachers, by reformers, by unions—in short, by someone else. They see leaders and experts as being unresponsive to their concerns. As long as these concerns go unaddressed, public resistance will continue to stiffen, possibly leading them to abandon public education.[4] At the very least, the past forty years of reforms signals a long-term loss of confidence by some in their local school officials.

A DIVERSE POPULATION

One of the underlying challenges facing education today results from the impact of a diverse population. One measure of the diversity is the ethnic differences of our population.

New Migrants to America

The United States is a nation of immigrants. A chronicler of educational change once noted that 20 percent of U.S. senators in his time were grandchildren of immigrants, a claim that can be made by "no other nation . . . about its leading legislative body."[5] As the poet Walt Whitman wrote well over a century ago, the United States is truly a "nation of nations."

By the end of the twentieth century American society had transformed from one in which descendants of white Europeans were an overwhelming majority into another in which many more citizens are members of "minority" groups. This change in demographics is largely rooted in the history of U.S. immigration. In the first wave of immigration in the late-nineteenth and early-twentieth centuries, Europeans accounted for 85 percent of all immigrants. Since World War II, however, European immigration has been eclipsed by a "second wave" of immigration from Latin America and Asia, so that today European immigrants constitute only 10 percent of the total.

One political question raised by descendents of the first wave is the degree to which new immigrants can be absorbed into American society. Some indicators of that question are optimistic. For example, rates of home ownership among immigrants are equal to those of the general population, about 59 percent. Many Asians and Hispanics are moving to suburban area, another indicator of their entry into the middle class.

Because reproduction rates among white Americans are lower than those of other ethnic groups, the Census Bureau estimates that

- by 2010, blacks and Hispanics will be equal in numbers to whites.
- by 2025, half of American youth will be white and half "minority"
- by 2050, no one group will be a majority among adults, producing in the nation "a minority majority."

In the dilution of the traditional white majority, the potential for conflict also increases among an increasingly diverse people.

This could be a national crisis. However, such conflict will be focused in just a few states. Thus, 80 percent of all new migrants in 2000 lived in just six states—California, New York, Texas, Illinois, Florida, and New Jersey. California had the largest share, with 44 percent of the total. Moreover, federal agencies estimate that for every legal immigrant to that state there was one who was illegal. These immigrants are also seen as a threat by many citizens of the earlier waves who as taxpayers provide schooling and welfare for illegal immigrants. As a measure of this apprehension, in 1994 two-thirds of California's voters supported a referendum limiting public resources for illegal immigrants. Support for the measure was not restricted to whites—almost 60 percent of black and Hispanic Americans also supported the limitation.

There is an enormous impact on schools in this second wave of immigration. Languages other than English (mostly Spanish) are the dominant languages spoken in 31.5 percent of homes in California, and in 14 percent of homes in Illinois. Moreover, today's immigrants speak a broader variety of languages, thereby posing problems for school authorities. The proportion of "minority" teachers to students will decrease in states such as California , where the immigrant school population increased to 38 percent by the year 2000. Moreover, school graduates from the second wave of immigrant groups are applying for colleges, thereby placing pressure on the resources of higher education. There are already complaints that Asian-American students are "overrepresented" at the most prestigious campuses within the University of California system.

The school problems suggested here will affect all levels of educational governance, for questions will necessarily arise in the school district. Where can teachers be found for non-English-speaking students? Who should represent immigrants on local boards? Where will the local resources for expanding schools be found? There are other questions arising at the state level. Where will funds come from to supplement local resources, especially when white voters dislike paying for education of the children of immigrants? At the national level, how can the limited federal funds for education keep pace with the large number of immigrants? What changes in curriculum and instructional methods are appropriate? All these questions set off conflict and political decisions.

School Libraries and Censorship

Other sources beside ethnic diversity can generate school politics. For example, there has always been a surprisingly wide variety of groups that did not like some particular book in the school library. Any hint of profanity or irreligious attitudes was anathema to some, as witnessed by the decades-long criticism of Salinger's *Catcher in the Rye*. Business groups disliked books that were critical of free enterprise. Some in the South objected to being criticized for slavery in earlier times and for segregation in the modern era. Jews objected to anti-Semitic references in literature, as personified by the character of Fagin in Dickens' *Oliver Twist*. Blacks criticized racist terms, like "Nigger Jim" in Twain's *Huckleberry Finn*.[6]

Library protests of this type have grown in recent years. More groups have become critical of books that, in their view, derogated women, Indians, Hispanics, and so on. The American Library Association has documented a growing number of cases of censorship in the nation's schools since 1991.[7] Those who argue for banning school books always claim that their purpose is to protect the young. The supporters of free speech, however, believe that such measures reflect a lack of confidence in youth and thus charge that this is indeed censorship, pure and simple. Many of these attempts to ban books are instigated by conservative groups, often from the "religious right," who see some books as a challenge to the established order. Tennyson's theme of "The old order changeth" underlies this fear.

Both sides of this debate believe that families should have the right to decide what is best for their children. However, librarians want parents to exercise this right at home, while liberals and conservatives want the school board itself to intervene on the ground that no parent can read everything before determining what is acceptable for his or her child. Local actions find evangelical Christian clergy and families objecting to one or more books that they perceive as advocating such practices as homosexuality or Satanism (e.g., stories about witches or devils). Occasionally these efforts are made at the state level. In 1994 an Idaho referendum to ban materials that were represented as promoting homosexuality was narrowly defeated.

Church efforts against teaching evolutionary concepts of the earth's origins found support in a Kansas state board that left it up to the local district to eliminate evolution in texts. However, that effort was overturned when voters removed Kansas State board members who had supported that view. Critics of censorship claim that this effort of certain religious groups is only the beginning of a movement to assert citizen control over *other* kinds of books. Some school systems are bending to these new pressures by dropping "objectionable" materials from libraries. Teachers or librarians may come to doubt whether the inclusion of such books in their classes or reading hours is worth the parental resistance. That doubt leads to success by the challengers.

Sex Education and "Abstinence Only"

Diversity of thought is also reflected in controversies over curricula. A curriculum is based on an underlying philosophy of certain values and assumptions against which others may contend. Due to this, citizen groups, often religious in orientation, have challenged the content of specific curricular material or courses. For decades, challenges have been argued in the U.S. Supreme Court by those opposed to banning school prayers or Bible reading in public schools. The Court has held steady on this challenge. However, such protests have in the last decade become more overtly political, as local groups won seats on school boards and insisted that their values should or must be incorporated in the curriculum.

One example is sex education. Many of these challenges argue that in such courses sexual abstinence is the only acceptable method of birth control. A report found over two hundred cases of this issue.[8] More significantly, over twenty thousand schools subscribe to a three-volume guide advocating only abstinence. These critics argue that existing courses ignore abstinence and instead emphasize the use of condoms, thus implying that premarital sexual intercourse is acceptable. Supporters of the existing curriculum argue that promoting sexual abstinence is not enough. They point to statistics that most American youth are sexually active years before marriage. Supporters of existing sex education also refer to increasing rates of sexually transmitted diseases, including HIV, the virus that leads to AIDS. Against such a real danger among sexually active youth, supporters believe that education in the use of condoms is appropriate.

The tactics of both sides are extremely political in their efforts to match private values to public decisions. The strategy of each side precludes accepting anything on the other side totally—a-winner-take-all policy. As a result, both sides seek to influence the media by meeting with editors, by writing articles, or by seeking coalitions with churches, health organizations, and local businesses. Candidates from both sides run for school boards, hoping to influence local decisions. Losers at the local level can also take their cases to the courts, or they can challenge state laws. A recent Louisiana court cases overturned the prohibition of curricula that were deemed medically inaccurate or religiously based. In this case, supporters of an "abstinence only" curriculum had won.

Although censorship and sex education are relatively low-visibility issues, they reflect the conflict of values among groups who see schools as a forum for promoting a certain way of thinking. Such conflict has consequences for governance, primarily at the local level. Some school professionals see these parental pressures as a challenge to their own definition of what constitutes good education. From these clashes, the politics of value differences follows.

VALUE DIFFERENCES

As noted, core questions over value differences are relevant to educational policies. Two questions of critical and enduring interest always underlie such value conflict. What should be taught? Who should do it?

Enduring School Questions

What should children be taught? For much of our early history, the answer to this question was family and church. They provided the teachers who shared many of the same values. Instruction in both moral and practical lessons guided such teaching. The slow emergence of professional education late in the nineteenth century added new points of view, but teachers still focused primarily on moral and practical subjects. By twentieth century, new ideas emerged about what should be taught. Later, state law and regulations were promulgated to achieve curricular change. These changes originated from the judgments of professionals (e.g., the Carnegie requirements) and later from the judgments of interest groups (e.g., the celebration of the birthday of Martin Luther King, Jr., Lief Ericson Day, or Cinco de Mayo). Today, the centers of decision-making power on such issues are still relatively remote from most parents.

Challenges to established values in curricula has generated yet another conflict over schools. When an effort was made in the 1990s by Washington, D.C., to create national standards of history, public complaints followed. Whether conservative (criticizing absence of traditional subjects or emphases) or ethnic (reaction against not enough emphasis on "diversity" in history), few wanted it, so it was dropped.

Another continuing question of education lies in who should teach. For much of our earlier history, teachers were those—often women—with an interest in teaching and a certain level of education who were hired by family and church. In general, these teachers shared the values of those who hired them. Yet with the rise of "free public education" after 1840, formal instruction of teachers became the norm. Teachers were trained in "normal" schools, and over time, more education and training were required to teach. In the last of the twentieth century, teachers began to experience the pressures of two sets of values, one from the community and another from the profession, and often they were conflicting. Recently, national organizations like Teach for America contend that year-long teacher training is not needed for effective teaching.

The Issue of Multiculturalism

These general findings of the history of schooling have contemporary relevance. One question of conflicting values can be found in the current debates over "muticulturalism."[9] Beginning in the late 1980s minority educators and activists were appointed by the New York Department of Education to discuss the formulation of a new curriculum. In their 1989 report this group argued that minority groups "have all been the victims of an intellectual and education oppression that has characterized the culture and institution of the United States and European-American world for centuries." In light of the growing number of people of non-European descent in the nation, the report called for replacement of the "Eurocentric" curriculum by one that reflected the multicultural experiences of other Americans.

This agenda was criticized in the intellectual circles of universities and also generated questions in big-city schools. This new challenge sought to highlight not simply the contributions of minority groups to American life, but also the control by European-Americans over the curriculum. When elements of multiculturalism emerged in the mid-1990s in a report by a national commission on standards of teaching history, it was criticized by conservatives for its emphasis on minority groups and its allusions to European "oppression."

The response to the challenge of multiculturalism has taken several forms. Schools had traditionally smoothed over ethnic or religious differences in order to produce "Americans" who constitute a nation. Public schools are among the most common shared experience for most Americans, and the public school system has been crucial to the Americanization process. It was also argued that the role of minorities in creating and building a new and developing nation was adequately treated in the current curriculum. By the late 1980s a state like Mississippi, with its earlier repressive treatment of blacks, had already required textbooks that reflect the contribution of blacks and other ethnic groups. In another example, a world history text, widely used elsewhere, had separate chapters on Islamic, African, Latin American, and Asian histories. A high school civics text had a chapter explaining equality under law, the earlier inferior conditions of blacks and women, and their movements that changed the law. Similar references to these groups appeared in other chapters.[10] Criticism of the multiculturalists, on the other hand, insisted that the commonality of the heritage taught through the schools is what holds Americans together, not the innumerable divisions of the society. Emphasis on difference, it was argued, will drive groups apart, while a stress on commonality must underlie the concept of a nation.

THE AGENCIES OF GOVERNANCE

Yet at the heart of this conflict lie persons having legitimate authority who must make policy decisions at different levels. How do these agencies affect this conflict? Two recent incidents— school prayer and institutional change in Congress—highlight how conflict resolution by such public agencies is a primary function of governance in education.

School Prayer

The U.S. Supreme Court, in a series of decisions spanning several decades, has decided against the official requirement of school prayers in public schools.[11] Although its line of cases continues to confirm that decision today, more recently its once unified view has weakened. For example, in 1962 the Court overturned (6–1) New York's law encouraging daily prayer recitations. In this and in later cases the First Amendment's prohibition of government promoting or establishing religion was determinative. In 1963 the Court overturned (8–1) Pennsylvania and Baltimore laws requiring prayer and daily Bible recitations. Two decades later in 1985 the Court, composed of a new membership, overturned (6–3) an Alabama law authorizing a daily moment of silence instead of a prayer. The purpose of that Alabama law, the opinion said, was not secular but religious. In 1992 a much narrower split of opinion (5–4) banned a public school in Providence, N.J., from using a rabbi for prayers. School officials who arranged this practice, the majority opinion argued, had created an environment that was coercive to students.

The national context is important here. Much of the nation is rooted in a traditional religious culture, particularly in small-town and rural areas, where these judicial actions had sharply violated a basic proposition of community life. Public opinion polls showed that a majority of respondents believed that the schools should emphasize religious values, especially the right to pray. The Court has recently written that schools cannot forbid the use of school property for meetings of religious groups, if secular groups have similar access.

While the Court's stance has softened somewhat, its decisions to prevent prayer and Bible reading have generated political pressure from citizens' groups for passage of a constitutional amendment permitting such practices. However, despite the growing strength of conservatives in Washington since 1981, noted later, there have not been enough congressional votes to support the necessary two-thirds majority for passage of such an amendment.

The best hope for religious conservatives was a change in the Court's membership, which could bring about a change in constitutional standards. However, some districts are still trying new arrangements for prayers that could bypass the Court, for example, when the Court overturned prayers before football games if part of official school policy. Clearly, some of those in small-town and rural America ignored the First Amendment requirements from the Court. Support for the Court's views is rooted in civil liberties groups and major religious organizations—mainline Baptists, Presbyterians, Lutherans, and Jews.

The politics over prayer arises from differences in values. Conservative religious groups argued that education and prayer were linked through historical and traditional school practices. Defenders of religion in schools argued that religious values were being ignored in textbooks and in curriculum. Their frustration with the rejection of a traditional set of values led first to the movement to change state laws, and later to demands for constitutional change. Were a constitutional amendment to pass, it would be a useful illustration that political questions involving schools are rarely settled definitively. There are always other political arguments and other arenas in which these political fights can be carried out.

Elections

Elections represent a crucial means of influencing policy about school. They are the key to creating legitimacy in the agencies of democracy, and electoral victors assume the authority to implement a political agenda. Elections thus provide one of the most important means of translating public opinion into public policy. When there is considerable conflict over policy, elections can act to maintain or to challenge established practices. Schools directly experience effects of electoral politics in the form of school board elections and referenda. Superintendents and board members, who on an election night see a referendum that they supported has lost, know the authority of voters. Politics aside, however, such change has direct policy consequences. In 2001 George Bush, and majorities in both houses, passed new laws on federal policy toward schools. The No Child Left Behind law was 1,100 pages long, and as we will note later, expanded the federal role dramatically.[12]

SCHOOL POLICIES

Policies produced by schools are similar in two respects to those of any governance agency. They involve allocation of values and resources, and they all reflect a common process of policymaking. Almost all of the services provided in schools are regulated by a complex set of policies generated by constitutions, legislation, court decisions, bureaucracies, and elections. This book will later deal with many of these policies in a systematic way, but it would be useful at this point to indicate a few new currents within the realm of public policy that involve schools. This will serve to highlight various elements of politics and governance in the policymaking process that involves stages of initiation, implementation, and evaluation.

Criticisms and Reform "Waves"

Among the many national policy initiations within American education have been large-scale programs created in the 1980s to improve the quality (or "excellence") of schools. In the 1990s, however, these reforms centered around issues of providing "choice" through vouchers or accountability for parents. Such reform was directed against the steady state of education in all states with its pattern of routine activities by school professionals.

The background of change is relevant here. This steady state resulted from reform over the last one hundred years that was implemented by generations of professionals. A new feature, particularly after World War II, was the creation of large bureaucracies at the local and state level to oversee the administration of an increasing number of regulations regarding schooling. Again, this steady state existed in every local and state jurisdiction in the nation. Wherever one's children were schooled, there were much the same technique of teaching, curriculum, special services, and administration—altered, of course, by variations in local context and funding.

This steady state was controlled by a hierarchy of power within each school system. Superintendents, sometimes termed "benevolent autocrats," and their agents in management—the principals— occupied the top of this hierarchy. Until about 1960 teachers, lacking any collective bargaining power, had very little authority in the schools. In big-city schools a central-office bureaucracy dominated all decisions, including resource allocation. A seemingly democratic channel of popular views—the school board— was limited by its tendency to accept the definitions of problems and solutions offered by professionals. Parents had little interest in these matters, except to support the school's authority and discipline and to vote for school taxes. When they turned up at school, usually as members of an acquiescent PTA, parents focused only on side issues, like a cookie sale to provide a projector for third grade. And as for another constituency—the students—their closest contact in this organization came only from teachers, and that interaction was similarly controlled.

Beginning in the 1950s, however, public dissatisfaction over declining student achievement grew, reflected in opinion polls critical of schools.[13] Federal laws in the 1950s sought to improve science quality and teaching, and in the Elementary and Secondary Education Act of 1965 to improve the education of poor children. In the early 1980s most states sought laws involving a host of mandates to provide services for all school districts.

Yet these laws did not satisfy opinion, so even more change was debated about providing "choice" for parents by moving children within or between districts. Decentralizing authority to the school site was much discussed, but again, relatively few districts took such measures, despite the publicity given to the issue. Still, decentralization did appear in Dade County, Florida, and in Los Angeles. In 1989 in Chicago, over four hundred decentralized sites were created with local councils of parents, teachers, and the principal. There was little indication by 2005 that these changes had any major impact on student achievement. We review those results later.

Other large reforms were publicized, but little action had been taken as of 2005. Voucher plans, using public funds to enable students to attend schools of their choice, had been much discussed for several decades. Yet, little reform of this kind appeared; indeed, voucher referenda failed in three states (California, Colorado, and Oregon) in the early 1990s, and in California, Michigan, and Colorado in state referenda in 2000. However the Republican party's success in the 1994 election brought new GOP governors who were committed to vouchers, reviving hopes for this reform. When elected president in 2000, George W. Bush claimed support for vouchers, and even created a Department of Education subunit to further them. As seen later, the number of voucher and charter schools increased but still represent a small minority of school sites or students. Choice policy was weakened due to opposition from Democrats and teachers.

Another reform that found some supporters was "privatization" of public schools, which contracted school operations to private firms. A large-scale effort in Baltimore was later withdrawn. However, critics of these reforms, primarily teachers' groups, were numerous, although some elements of privatization, for example, contracting for outside technical services, appeared to have benefits.

Private foundations also funded the search for small-scale reform successes that might be translated into large-scale public reform. Those foundations that entered the field to improve schools included Ford, Carnegie, Pew, Annenberg, Gates, Lilly, MacArthur, and Mott. However, success in a few local cases ran into major problems when transformed into wider use, namely, the scaling-up problem. Much of this is the result of "partial implementation" in which political considerations, rather than professional criteria, operate.[14]

These challenges to the steady state of public schools were paralleled by assertions that schools had failed to teach students to meet even basic standards. A larger perspective would show, however, that such criticisms reach way back in history. In earlier periods there were complaints that students did not learn much, teachers were incompetent, and schooling cost too much. But by the early 1990s some analysis was questioning this charge of school failure as a "myth," claiming that the reforms were directed against a system that had not been broken, as critics claimed. For example, there were national reports of schools with fewer dropouts, higher test scores for both whites and minorities, and greater rates of college attendance by minorities. In 1995 the RAND Corporation reported academic gains, not losses, on standardized test scores over the two decades between 1970 and 1990. Those gains occurred despite such off-setting increases in percentages of teenage mothers, children in poverty, working mothers, or single-parent families.[15]

Reforms, often labeled as "waves" in recent decades, were more likely an artillery attack coming from many guns. But did they hit the target? Many reform ideas were never adopted, or if so, never implemented on a wide scale. Yet school policy, which had once been the province of the professional, had now entered a different political arena. More groups were involved, more effort was made across a wider front of governments, and more new practices were undertaken. However, it is still unclear whether any of these efforts have been successful in the first and primary goal—improving student achievement compared to those in public schools. Moreover, if recent analysis suggests that schools have not been doing as badly as the reformers had insisted, there may not be a need for a complete overhaul of the system. This debate continues through 2005.

IMPLEMENTATION OF SCHOOL POLICY

Programs approved within the political system are never self-executing and so must be implemented. To meet program objectives, an organization must be created, staff employed, managers appointed, funds provided and disbursed, services dispensed, and results evaluated. There is much controversy surrounding each of these topics. A few of these problems, related to politics and governance, are highlighted below.

Examples of the Politics of Implementation

Politics surrounding implementation often shapes the administration of school programs. For example, leaders of reform programs in Southeastern states have been unable to stay in place as administrators, so that incumbency turnover has weakened the thrust of change.[16] By 2000 there had been six superintendents in seven years in Dallas. On average, high-level state positions changed hands three times from 1983 to 1995. Consequently, policy initiatives were interrupted when state economies faltered or state leaders changed.

State mandates have been increasingly used to compel local compliance. This approach has generated a local challenge because state governments have failed to provide funds to carry out state mandates. All schools, localities, or municipalities are constitutionally dependent on the state for their own authority, but that dependency has been politically challenged by the local revolt. Not only do localities want to escape federal mandates, but they resist also mandates from the state capitol.

The result has been increasing political pressures on the superintendency, as a later chapter shows, thereby leading to greater turnover in office. The average term in several big cities is down from six years a few years ago to three years. Length of service is about twice that for smaller cities, but still less than in the recent past. Working in a world where laypersons are empowered has altered the superintendent's old role of "benevolent autocrat" to one of "politician." To undergo a role change in life generates much stress, leading to more change in administrative activity in which sharing, not dominating, prevails. More superintendents spend more of their time involved in public relations designed to generate public support for school programs, as well as preserving their own tenure. For many of them—as well as for principals—the result is often being fired or resigning, and many leave the profession; by 2004 a shortage of principals emerged in the United States.

PROGRAM EVALUATION

Implementation is not the end of the dynamic process of politics and governance. At some point there is evaluation, that is, the effort to deal with the pragmatic question, Did it work? This effort is often linked to "hard" quantitative measures of changing effects. But it is clear that evaluation has a "softer" and highly political quality. Group conflict arises over such matters in evaluation as the nature of research questions, the data needed to test them, the measurement methods employed, and their interpretation. Just such a review of charter schools is currently undertaken at the University of Washington. Evaluators, scholars, and public officials regularly differ over such questions. We can briefly view such matters in the cases of school desegregation and of teaching science.

The "Effects" of Desegregation

For example, how would we measure the "effects" of desegregation?[17] Many may ask whether the central evaluation question is: Do desegregated schools improve education for blacks? However, that evaluation is confounded by the realization that the Supreme Court in the basic case of Topeka and related cities in the 1950s did not judge that question to be the constitutional measure of desegregation. Rather, the judges unanimously agreed that the mere fact of segregation of resources was itself the central question, and that such segregation violated constitutional values. If segregation is the constitutional question, and not whether blacks learn more under desegregated conditions, other evidence must be used than just test scores.

What if the central research question were this: With resources now integrated, are more black students now obtaining more years of schooling than before? The question does not address the results of learning, but focuses rather on whether there has been an increase in school years for a specific minority group. By comparing only contemporary data—a method often used in testing desegregation effects—the researcher fails to ignore other improvements found in more schooling and the larger allocation of school resources for blacks. Clearly, the data that are sought can influence which questions are asked.

Now that ethnic groups understand the political quality of evaluation, many participate in assessing proposed school policies. In a short time these representatives have challenged the validity of tests, including standard IQ tests, and have sought to measure student outcomes other than just test scores. However, this sophistication in evaluation has not been applied to the consequences of desegregation after the *Brown* decision. Does mandatory desegregation actually contribute to a further segregation of races of students, not in schools but in residential areas? Is the white flight from urban centers creating a pattern of "apartheid" that results from changes in demographics within big-city school systems? Such a result would work against a notion of society that is free of racism. As always, schools reflect major aspects of the larger society in which they are embedded.

Knowing Science and Teaching Science

The pages of the journal *Educational Evaluation and Policy Analysis* and others closely evaluate the process and effects of school policies. One case will demonstrate how evaluation is affected by noneducational factors, even when professionals wish to do the right thing.

Since the 1950s the effort to improve the teaching of science has been backed by hundreds of millions of federal dollars. Hundreds of university-based scientists have been engaged in research to improve science curricula, and courses based on these curricula have been taught by unnumbered teachers in public schools across the country. By the end of the 1960s universities and scientific institutes had developed solid curricula in earth sciences, physical science, biology, chemistry, and engineering. By the mid-1970s, however, the adoption rate of these curricula had slowed. Worse, by 1983 national survey had found a fall-off in student science achievement in all subjects except biology. These results could stimulate a variety of questions, but our attention here is directed to the outcomes and evaluation of science education policy.[18]

In policy evaluation there are always major questions that must be addressed, but at the core of evaluation is the highly pragmatic American question: Did it work? In this case, were high-quality materials for curriculum developed? The answer is a definite yes. Scientists from the bet universities and from different fields created solid instructional materials. However, if the question is, Did more teachers use these materials? the results are disappointing. The most widely used curriculum (Introductory Physical Science) was adopted by no more than 25 percent of secondary schools (for at least one class), and other types of curricula had only a 15 percent adoption rate. One judgment made by the evaluators was that "other than content, length, and difficulty of class, little had changed."

Another evaluation question is "Were more students enrolled in science courses?" These results are also dismal. Schools often used these new science curricula as alternatives to but not replacement for existing courses, so fewer students took them. These courses also often received the stigma of being for "college-bound" students, hence they were regarded as elitist and avoided by most students. However, one ongoing effect has been the change in commercial textbooks. Many of these texts have incorporated some of the factual content and emphasized laboratory work found in these earlier science education projects. Nevertheless, national tests do not reflect any gains in student knowledge of science.

What are the causes of these failures in implementation? First, these curriculum projects were developed by scientists who rarely consulted with teachers. The curriculum developers, then, had little understanding of how teachers might adapt the content of these curricula to suit their own pedagogical styles. Second, few teachers had been trained in the "new" science. Not surprisingly, many found the new material too difficult to understand themselves, let alone to teach to their students.

Finally, the scientists who developed these curricula had little understanding of limitations within the school structure or their ability to adapt to the implementation of new curricula. These new science reforms required longer classes and more teacher preparation time. Moreover, many of the changes required by the new curricula were too complex to be handled within traditional teaching formats or in outmoded labs. Because of this, physical changes in the classroom and the school were needed, and these often entailed the construction of new laboratories. So teachers were often stuck with old textbooks and older facilities, and whatever new courses were offered focused on college-bound students.

The best thing we can find to say of these reforms is that science courses and books were updated, and a new generation of leaders within science education emerged. But the needs of the target group, the larger student body, were not met, and instructional materials had changed very little for most of them. The "political" quality of science curriculum, like many other aspects of curriculum reform, is due to the pressure of inertia within organizations. Added to this pressure was the unwillingness of teachers to accommodate to change, because, after all, teachers feel most comfortable with what they have already done. Efforts to induce change, through such means as salary increases as incentives to undergo course training in universities, often come up against the heavy pressure of inertia.

WHAT CONCEPTS HOLD TOGETHER SUCH DIFFERENT CASES?

In short, the origins, administration, and evaluation of school activities must be seen within the human context of professionals and laypersons who work daily within schools. Human interests and conflict shape all aspects of the political system, and it is ideas that move actors in politics and governance.[19] The variety of contemporary cases reviewed in this chapter may appear to be unconnected events. We now need to turn to a deeper examination of the evolution of school politics.

NOTES

1. David Easton, *A Systems Analysis of Political Life* (New York: Wiley, 1965). For a more recent theoretical overview see James March and Johan Olsen, *Democratic Governance* (New York: Free Press, 1995).

2. For major challenges see Diane Ravitch, *Left Back: A Century of Failed School Reform* (New York: Simon & Shuster, 2000); for the concept of "tinkering" see David Tyack and Larry Cuban, *Tinkering Toward Utopia* (Cambridge, Mass.: Harvard, 1995); and Tyack, *Seeking Comon Ground* (Cambridge, Mass.: Harvard University Press, 2003).

3. Ernest Boyer, quoted in *Education Week* (December 7, 1994): 13.

4. Deborah Wardsworth, Executive Director, Public Agenda Foundation, as

quoted in *California and Their Schools* (Menlo Park, Calif.: Ed Source, 1996), p. 6. See also Joseph Murphy, "Governing America's Schools," *Teachers College Record* 102, no. 1 (2000): 57–84.

5. Observations below are from Harold Hodgkinson, "A True Nation of the World," *Education Week* (January 18, 1995): 32.

6. David Post, "Through Joshua Gap: Curricular Control and the Constructed Community," *Teachers College Record* 93, no. 4 (1992): 673–96.

7. *Education Week* (November 10, 1994): 10.

8. Jessica Portner, "Grassroots Warriors Waging Battle Over Sex-Ed Curriculum," *Education Week* (October 12, 1994): 5.

9. The quotations below are from the critiques of multiculturalism in Willard Hogeboom, "Multiculturalism: Build on What Holds Us Together," *Education Week* (December 4, 1991); and from Diane Ravitch, "Standards in U.S. History: An Assessment," *Education Week* (December 7, 1994): 48; See also, Arthur Schlesinger, Jr., "The Disuniting of America," *American Educator* 15 (Winter 1991): 14–33. For a focus on "ebonics" controversy, see John Rickford, *Spoken Soul* (New York: Wiley, 2000).

10. The changing nature of this curriculum is evaluated in Frederick Wirt, *We Ain't What We Was: Civil Rights in the New South* (Durham, N.C.: Duke University Press, 1997), chaps. 5–6.

11. Reviewed in *Education Week* (December 14, 1994).

12. See Center on Education Policy, *From the Capitol to the Classroom: Year 2 of NCLB* (Washington, D.C.: CEP, 2004).

13. Polls are surveyed for a quarter-century in Stanley Elam, *How America Views Its Schools* (Bloomington, Ind.: Phi Delta Kappa, 1995). See also David Mathews, *Is There a Public for Public Schools?* (Dayton, Ohio: Kettering, 1996).

14. On vouchers, foundations, and business leaders see separate stories in *Education Week* (December 14, 1994); for privatization see the symposium edited by Richard Hunter and Frank Brown in *Education and Urban Society* 27 (1995): 107–228. On partial implementation, see Kathryn McDermott, "Barriers to Large-Scale Success of Models for Urban School Reform," *Educational Evaluation and Policy Analysis* 22 (2000): 83–89.

15. The "myth" claim is found in David Berliner and Bruce Biddle, *The Manufactured Crisis.* (Reading, Mass.: Addison Wesley, 1995). See also *Student Achievement and the Changing American Family* (Santa Monica, Calif.: RAND Corp., 1995).

16. Lynn Olson, "Rapid Turnover in Leadership Impedes Reforms, Study Finds," *Education Week* (January 11, 1995): 6.

17. These questions are pursued in Wirt, *We Ain't What We Was.*

18. These elements of the reform are developed in Gary Yee and Michael Kirst, "Lessons from the New Science Curriculum of the 1950s and 1960s," *Education and Urban Society* 26 (1994): 158–71; quotations that follow are from this source. For an evaluation of 1958 to 1970 math and science reforms, see Peter B. Dow, *Schoolhouse Politics* (Cambridge, Mass.: Harvard University Press, 1991).

19. For a historical review of research in education politics, see Jay D. Scribner, Enrique Aleman, and Brenda Maxcy, "Emergence of the Politics of Education Field," *Educational Administration Quarterly* 34: 1 (February 2003): 10-40. For an analysis of current research, see Bob L. Johnson, Jr., "The Nagging Headaches: Perennial Issues and Tensions in the Politics of Education Field," *Educational Administration Quarterly* 34:1 (February 2003): 41-67.

2

Overview of the Education Political System

INTRODUCTION

Was it just because old beliefs die hard? Was that why, when asked who has the most power to improve public schools, respondents in a 2002 survey by the Public Education Network and *Education Week* said it was local school boards?[1] The public has been told repeatedly, after all, how much the nation reveres local school control, told it even by those who have been taking away much of that control. Thus, Americans are largely unaware that local boards as well as local superintendents and individual schools have been losing influence over education programs for some time to state and federal officials and other interests. Indeed, some analysts even view local school boards as an endangered species.[2]

Historically, of course, American education has been rooted in local policy, local management, and local financial control, traditions deeply embedded in our political culture. Until recently, in fact, the public thought officials beyond their districts had acquired too much power over their schools. In 2000, for example, the annual Phi Delta Kappa/Gallup education poll reported that 61 percent of Americans wanted to reduce Washington's influence over local education programs.[3] Yet now No Child Left Behind (NCLB) has greatly expanded federal power instead. Gallup reported in 2002 that "57 percent of Americans believe the federal government's increased involvement is a good thing; 68 percent of Americans would go beyond the requirements of NCLB and require all fifty states to use the same nationally standardized test to measure student achievement, although not suggested by NCLB, 66 percent would go so far as to have a national curriculum."[4]

The country, which is struggling through another turning point in the history of education governance, clearly is having difficulty deciding which way to go. Does it want more centralized state and federal control, with even less discretion for local policymakers and teachers? Does it want little or no state or local voice in what is taught or tested, as would happen with a national curriculum and national exams, both of which the public has long supported in Gallup polls?[5] Does the nation want to scrap much of its democratically governed public school system and substitute a market-based system of school vouchers instead? Or do Americans want their local school boards and local educators to regain lost power? These are some major governance issues confronting U.S. schools, and the answers will tell a great deal about how Americans wish to educate their children. Changing how schools are governed, after all, long has been a backdoor way of changing broad education policies and priorities.

At the moment, there appears to be little to reverse the trend toward increased nonlocal power over schools. Indeed, the likelihood is that traditional local governance structures will be overwhelmed by this trend, a prospect that stems from several factors, including

- a loss of confidence by higher authorities in local decision makers, a phenomenon that began well before the 1983 publication of *A Nation at Risk* and its fears (some would say seriously mistaken fears[6]) about U.S. economic competitiveness;
- the intense economic rivalry among states, in which governors use education, as they use tax breaks and other lures, to help attract more businesses and jobs;

- changes in school funding pattern to enhance equity and limit local property tax spending; and
- the tendency of federal and state standards-based reform to centralize far more authority than it decentralizes.

The challenge today is to rethink the institutional choices Americans have been making—to analyze the schools' purposes, examine the likely effects of governance shifts on those goals, and decide who can best serve students. Federal or state officials, for example, often play crucial roles in the areas of civil rights and school finance; local politics typically preclude consensus on policies that significantly redistribute resources. On the other hand, the most appropriate balance of control over curriculum, instruction, and assessment policies—the pivotal issues in today's school reforms—is much less clear.

Some states and school districts, for example, have been centralizing these functions for more than twenty years, but student achievement has barely budged. The deadline for Goals 2000 came and went with the nation nowhere near fulfilling any of the education aspirations set by the White House and U.S. governors a decade before. Is there reason to believe that more state and federal centralization now will yield notable academic gains and achieve such goals? The current system is dominated by conflicting public desires and complex fragmented institutions in a federal structure. To address these and other questions, it is helpful to understand earlier turning points in U.S. school governance and to see how the historic evolution of the system resulted in today's complex and fragmented structure, in which everybody—and therefore nobody—appears to be in charge.

THE IMPORTANCE OF DISTRUST

At the heart of the questioning of institutional control is popular distrust of those who hold power, and America has come full circle on this matter with the loss of confidence in local school authorities. In the early days of the republic, Americans distrusted distant government and wanted important decisions made close to home, especially regarding education. Thus the U.S. Constitution made no mention of schools, leaving control of education to the states, and states then delegated a great deal of power to local school districts. While states always have been able to abolish school districts or take over their management, a power rarely exercised until recent years, the doctrine of local control of public schools has occupied a special place in American political strategy.

Evidence of distrust can be found today not only in declining confidence in local education officials but also in the reassertion of authority over school policy by governors, presidents, and mayors. Although few Americans realize it, the nation long has maintained one government for schools—comprised mainly of local and state boards of education and superintendents—and another for everything else. While the education government was strengthened particularly by school reforms adopted at the turn of the twentieth century, the two-government tradition dates back to 1826, when Massachusetts created a separate school committee divorced from general government, a practice that spread nationally.[7]

In early agricultural America, of course, schooling was a very different affair from the current one. Formal education for young people was by no means a universally shared goal. On the contrary, at the founding of the republic, when the principal purpose of education was religious training, many reasons existed for opposing the establishment of public schools. Echoes of some of these arguments are heard today among advocates of education vouchers or tuition tax credits, some of whom want public funding for private schools in the belief that school should be an extension of the home, where children encounter only values espoused by like-minded families.

The public school as we know it did not emerge until the 1840s with the advent of the common-school movement, a vast force that spread a basically similar institution across a sparsely settled continent. Determined to protect and improve what the founding generation had crated, common-school supporters had broad social purposes, from molding morals and fostering cultural unity to teaching citizenship responsibilities, spreading prosperity and ending poverty. The schools were to be vehicles for realizing a millennial vision of a righteous republic.[8]

As advocated by Horace Mann in Massachusetts, Henry Barnard in Connecticut, John Pierce in Michigan, and others, common schools were imbued with egalitarian and majoritarian values. Designed to produce literate, numerate, and moral citizens from all classes, sects, and ethnic groups, they were to be the "great equalizer," in Mann's phrase (though they certainly practiced the racial and sexual discrimination of their era). In general, laypeople built, financed, and supervised the schools, and young, untrained teachers instructed the pupils. Although theoretically nonsectarian and nonpartisan, the schools had a conservative and Protestant bent. This reflected the world view of their promoters, Victorian opinion shapers who were largely British American in ethnic origin, bourgeois in economic outlook and status, and evangelically Protestant in religious orientation.[9] Nonetheless, most citizens (with the exception of Roman Catholics) found the common schools' teachings inoffensive. (While Roman Catholics constitute a considerable exception, even by the late nineteenth century they made up only 10 percent of the population).

The Protestant-republican ideology embodied in the schools was vividly expressed by the *McGuffey Readers*, first published in 1836 and used by some 200 million schoolchildren from 1900 to 1940 (though their use began to fade in the 1920s). The *Readers*, which included selections from British and American literature as well as lessons in science, farming, history, and biography, were frankly moralistic. In story after story, good children were rewarded (soon after their deeds and with solid items like silver coins), while bad ones were punished with equal celerity. Honesty and industry were the leading values promoted, followed closely by courage, kindness, obedience, and courtesy. The *Readers* supported the temperance movement but were silent about efforts to abolish slavery and establish trade unions.[10]

By the Civil War, the common school had become the mainstream of schooling in the United States, thriving in hundreds of thousands of school districts from Maine to Oregon, financed largely by public taxes and controlled by local trustees. Creating this system was an undertaking of immense magnitude—arguably the greatest institution-building success in American history—though the result was not uniform in structure. Southern states developed county school districts, while the Northeast organized around small towns. Southwestern and Western school districts grew by annexation. Hence, San Jose, California, today has nineteen separate school districts within its city limits, as San Antonio, Texas, has twenty.

While the common-school movement established a fairly uniform education system, another nationalizing force—professionalism—was of greater consequence in this regard and over a longer period. The growth of professional standards for administration, teaching, curriculum, testing, and other elements essential to the system began drawing it together in the final decades of the nineteenth century. Before this process emerged, the fabric of American schools was still plaid, and a ragged plaid at that. Experience drawn from the testing of a jumble of ideas—transmitted through new professional journals and new training for the emergent profession—did more than the common school to instill uniformity in U.S. education.

Common-school reformers also created education agencies at the state level, but these generally were bare-bones units with scant power. As late as 1890, the median size of state departments of education was two persons, including the state superintendent. (By contrast, today the California State Department of Education has about 1,600 employees.) As for the federal government, it had no direct involvement in any of this. Washington long had given rhetorical support to education and had made a national commitment early on to use land sales to finance schools, formalized in the Northwest Ordinance of 1787. But it was not until after the Civil War, in 1867, that Washington created even a low-level Bureau of Education and gave it the modest chore of collecting education data and disseminating information about school organization and teaching methods.

TAKING EDUCATION "OUT OF POLITICS"

At the turn of the century (1890–1910), schools were placed under stronger control of local education governments, the result of reforms that followed disclosures of widespread municipal corruption in schools as well as in city offices. Muckrakers exposed textbook publishers and contractors who allied themselves with corrupt school trustees for common boodle in the common school. The spoils system frequently determined who won or lost teaching jobs. Leaders concerned about such practices gathered information from across the country. Their reports indicted every region of the nation.

A superintendent in one of the Eastern states writes: "Nearly all the teachers in our schools get their positions by political 'pull.' If they secure a place and are not backed by political influence, they are likely to be turned out. Our drawing teaching recently lost her position for this reason." One writes from the South: "Most places depend on politics. The lowest motives are frequently used to influence ends." A faint wail comes from the far West: "Positions are secured and held by the lowest principles of corrupt politicians." "Politicians wage a war of extermination against all teachers who are not their vassals," comes from the Rocky Mountains.

In Boston, the teachership is still a spoil of office. It is more difficult, at the present time, for a Catholic than for a Protestant young woman to get a place, but, nevertheless, some Catholics secure appointments, for "trading" may always be done, while each side has a wholesome fear of the other assailing it in the open board. A member said one day, in my hearing: "I must have my quota of teachers."[11]

The corruption was reinforced with a vengeance by the turn-of-the-century version of local control: a decentralized school committee system rooted in ward politics, which provided extensive opportunities for undue influence as school sought to cope with the immigrant waves overwhelming the cities. In 1905, for example, Philadelphia alone had forty-three elected district school boards, with 559 members. Little wonder that, while consolidation of school districts began in 1900, the nation still had more than 195,000 of them by 1917.

Reformers contended that, among other things, board members elected by wards advanced their own parochial and special interests at the expense of the school district as a whole.[12] What was needed to counter this, they believed, was election at large or citywide, without any subdistrict electoral boundaries. A good school system was good for all, not for just one part of the community.

Reformers also charged that the executive authority of the larger school boards was splintered because they worked through so many subcommittees. The 1905 Cincinnati school board, for example, had seventy-four subcommittees, while Chicago had seventy-nine. No topic, down to the purchase of doorknobs, was too trivial for a separate subcommittee to consider. The basic prerequisite for better management was thought to be centralization of power in a chief executive to whom the selection board would delegate considerable authority. The school superintendent would be controlled, but only on board policies, by a board respectful of his professional expertise. Only under such a system would a superintendent make large-scale improvements and be held accountable.

By 1910 a conventional educational wisdom had evolved among the "school folk" and the leading business and professional men who had spearheaded these Progressive Era reforms. They sought to use state legislatures and departments of education to standardize public education and consolidate one-room schools into larger township or regional schools. Essentially, they aimed to "take education out of politics"—often meaning away from decentralized control by certain lay people—to turn "political" issues into matters for administrative discretion by professional educators. Sometimes only a small group of patricians secured new charters from state legislatures and thereby reorganized urban schools without any popular vote. The watchwords of reform were efficiency, expertise, professionalism, centralization, and nonpolitical control. Taken together, reformers thought these ideals would inspire the "one best system."[13]

The most attractive models for this new governance structure were the industrial bureaucracies rapidly emerging during this era. The centralized power of the school superintendent, comparable to that of the plant manger, was intended to overcome the tangles and inefficiencies of school board subcommittee. The appeal of the industrial model came from another source as well—the reformers' social class and status. The financial and professional leaders who deplored the politics and inefficiency of the decentralized ward system had another reason for disliking that arrangement: It empowered members of the lower and lower-middle classes, many of whom were working-class immigrants. Reformers wanted not simply to replace bad men with good; they proposed to change the occupational and class origins of the decision makers.

That is indeed what happened: A classic 1927 study showed that upper-class professionals and big businessmen dominated the new centralized boards of education. After reforms were adopted in St. Louis in 1897, for instance, the share of professionals on the school board jumped from 4.8 percent to 58.3 percent, and the portion of big businessmen climbed from 9 percent to 25 percent. By contrast, small business owners dropped from 47.6 percent to 16.7 percent and wage earners from 28.6 percent to zero. The new professional and managerial board members delegated many formal powers to school professionals, giving educators the leeway to shape schools to meet the needs of the new industrial society, at least as defined by one segment of that society: chiefly prosperous, native-born, Anglo-Saxon Protestants.[14]

Some prominent concerns of that society would be familiar to Americans today. There were worries about global competition and worker training, which prompted Washington to enact the 1917 Smith-Hughes Act for vocational education, the first federal program of categorical aid for elementary and secondary schools. There were concerns about schools where children were taught in German or Polish and about the need for educators to provide health and social services for poor pupils, particularly in immigrant communities. There were worries about student achievement, triggered in part by the dismal performance of World War I recruits on newly created IQ tests and in part by complaints in the 1920s from such business groups as the National Association of Manufacturers that many high school graduates were awful at basic math and at expressing themselves in English.

Nonetheless, the period from 1920 to 1950 was a "golden era" for school superintendents, who had wide discretion to deal with these problems (and others that emerged during the Great Depression and World War II) and who had no teachers' unions to worry about. Whatever the problems, the federal government and the states were content to let most decisions rest with local education authorities.

After World War II, the curriculum adapted, as did society, to economic expansion and peacetime social changes, particularly the postwar baby boom.[15] School enrollments climbed, as did the percentage of students graduating from high school. The egalitarianism of the army encouraged egalitarianism in the schools, as it did in previously elitist institutions—private colleges and universities—as thousands of ex-soldiers enrolled with the help of Washington's GI Bill of Rights. However, the turn-of-the-century triumph of the doctrine of efficiency achieved through professionalism and centralization had attenuated the ties between school leaders and their constituents. Parent participation had little effect on the school policymaking. Until the 1950s, for example, Baltimore held its school board meeting in a room that could seat only 25 people. As the leading citizens' "interest group," the PTA considered its prime function to be providing support for professional administrators.

The weakened link between education leaders and constituents had been acceptable in the pre-World War II decades, when schooling made fewer claims on community financial resources and when professionals benefited from their own publicity about education as the sovereign key to success.[16] It continued to be acceptable in the two decades after the war, when the emphasis was on the rush to obtain schooling for all with expanded school systems and bureaucracies amid continued district consolidation. (From 130,000 school districts in 1930, the number declined to 89,000 by 1948, compared with fewer than 15,000 today.) But school politics and governance were about to change and in more than one direction. The efficiency of the centralized local administration was starting to lose its aura, and new waves of both egalitarianism and elitism were to trigger new turning points for education governance.

WASHINGTON AND THE QUEST FOR EQUITY

It was during the 1950s that confidence in local school boards and administrators began to weaken. In 1954 the Supreme Court's Brown decision outlawing statutory school segregation called attention to the disgraceful failure of Southern school systems to educate black students. The next year Rudolph Flesch's best-selling *Why Johnny Can't Read* bemoaned what it saw as a national literacy crisis stemming from a decline in teaching phonics, an issue that dates back to Horace Mann (who was closer to the whole language school) and that is debated again today. In 1957, after Moscow launched Sputnik, an angry chorus complained that the Soviet education system was surpassing our own. Such Cold War fears galvanized a more aggressive federal education role, embodied in the 1957 National Defense Education Act, which sought to improve math, science, and foreign-language learning (not that different from goals adopted in 1984 to deal with what was then believed to be a Japanese economic threat).[17]

The decline of confidence accelerated during the 1960s and 1970s, when the driving force was the quest to reduce unequal educational opportunities tolerated by state and local policymakers, a force set in motion by *Brown*. The centerpiece of that quest was President Lyndon B. Johnson's 1965 Elementary and Secondary Education Act (ESEA), which would transform Washington's role in education.

For a century, between 1862 and 1963, Congress had considered unrestricted general aid to schools thirty-six times and had rejected it thirty-six times. Opponents had long argued successfully that because the Tenth Amendment to the Constitution left control of schools to the states, Washington had no constitutionally defensible role in education. Although the Supreme Court by 1930 had supported a less-restrictive federal role, Washington's post-World War II school programs were still modest. In 1950, the U.S. Office of Education (USOE) was transferred from the Department of the Interior to what became the Department of Health, Education and Welfare. It had a staff of three hundred to spend $40 million (compared with the $20 billion the Department of Education disburses today for the No Child Left Behind Act and the $50 billion it spends overall). Focusing on such matters as mathematics, libraries, and school buses, USOE appointed specialists and consultants who identified primarily with the National Education Association (NEA). Federal grant programs operated in deference to local and state education agency priorities and judgments. USOE regarded state administrators as colleagues who should have the maximum decision-making discretion permitted by federal laws.[18]

In 1963, the year of President John F. Kennedy's assassination, the Department of Defense and the Veterans Administration spent more on education programs than the Office of Education and the National Science Foundation combined. But that was to change after President Johnson's landslide election victory in 1964, when Democrats as well won substantial majorities in both houses of Congress. Johnson made ESEA central to his antipoverty and Great Society programs. Rather than pursuing the unrestricted general aid that the slain Kennedy had sought in vain, Johnson tied education money to special-needs categories (schools with low-income and low-achieving pupils) that existed in every congressional district, thereby spreading the funds far and wide and thus winning lawmakers' hearts and minds. Johnson also began the federal role of stimulating innovation and experiments with new schools and teaching methods.

Amid growing racial and class strains, including big-city riots, ESEA steadily expanded, and programs for other neglected groups—children with disabilities, minority-language students, and others—were added, often following supportive court rulings. Federal courts in the 1970s led the way not only in the fight against segregation but also in establishing the right of disabled children to an appropriate free education, in requiring extra help for limited-English-speaking students and in combating sex discrimination, as measured by school expenditures and curricular opportunities. Federal courts, for example, ordered high schools to stop tracking women into sex-stereotyped training to become secretaries, waitresses, or nurses. Those rulings were a stimulus for Title IX of the Civil Rights Act, which is best known for expanding women's opportunities in intercollegiate sports but which prohibits sex discrimination in funding at all levels of education.

The mid-1970s also was the peak expansion period for new state court regulations on local schools, indicating that local schools could not be trusted to guarantee student rights or due process. The legalization of local education expanded through state education codes and through lawsuits increasingly directed at local authorities.[19]

If this era brought dramatic increases in federal activity, the basic mode of delivering federal services remained the same. This differential funding route sought bigger and bolder categorical and demonstration programs. The delivery systems stressed the need for more-precise federal regulations to guide local projects. Today's overlapping and complex categorical aids evolved as a mode of federal action on which a number of otherwise com-

peting education interests could agree. This collection of categoricals, which dominated national education politics from 1965
to the election of President Ronald Reagan in 1980, was not the
result of any rational plan for federal intervention but rather an
outcome of political bargaining and coalition formation.

The national movements behind such programs, moreover, often
spawned new local interest groups on such issues as civil rights,
women's roles, special education, students' rights, and ethnic self-
determination. Hence, atop Washington regulations, these new
forces began agitating locally for reforms. They sought black history
and bilingual education programs. They challenged the use of
IQ tests for pupil placement and tracking. They pressed for revised student suspension policies and for community control of
school boards. Indeed, big-city "decentralizers" in the 1970s sought
to reinstitute something resembling the old ward boards of education abolished at the turn of the century. They ended up winning partial decentralization through subdistrict board elections,
with tighter oversight of superintendents. All these efforts eroded
the power of local school authorities—and there was more to
come.

WHEN TEACHERS ORGANIZE FOR PAY AND POLITICS

In the 1950s teachers found themselves cut off from the school
board and the public Increasingly, business managers, administrative assistants, subject-matter coordinators, and department heads
were telling them how to conduct their classrooms. With the
postwar baby boom, however, came extraordinary growth in education spending, in teachers' ranks, and in pressure to give teachers
a greater voice. Between 1949 and 1970, the share of the gross
national product devoted to education more than doubled, from
about 3.5 percent to 8 percent. Where the nation had provided
only $2 billion in 1940, it spent $50 billion in 1970 and more
than $100 billion in 1980. With this massive injection of funds,
the teacher workforce grew from just over one million in 1940
to nearly 2.5 million in 1971. By the mid-1970s the country had
substantially more teachers than autoworkers, steelworkers, team-
sters, or doctors.

It was during the 1952s that the teachers' perception of their "proper professional role" began to change. Once viewed as submissive, they now began to form unions, to engage in collective bargaining, and—despite laws in many states barring public employee strikes—to walk picket lines. Indeed, teacher walkouts escalated annually, climbing from 35 in the 1955-56 school year to 114 in 1967-68 and to 131 in 1969-70. By 1980, the teacher drive for collective bargaining had spread to most U.S. regions, except the Southeast and Mountain states, resulting in a significant reduction in administrative dominance of local school governance.[20]

The outcome of collective bargaining is a written, time-bound, central-office contract covering wages, hours, and employment conditions. What happens to administrator authority, particularly among principals, when such contracts filter down through the loosely coupled school system? One major study found that some provisions tightly limit the principal's freedom of action, while others get redefined to fit the requirements at the particular school.[21] Having high standards and expecting much of teachers earns principals tolerance and even respect in interpreting the contract; for teachers, a good school is more important than union membership, close contract observance, or control of schools. As one administrator observed, "Teachers like to be part of a winning team." While the effects of central-office contracts vary widely by district and school, they nonetheless generally restrain the power of school boards and superintendents and force principals to react to centralized personnel policies.

Because teachers' unions negotiate districtwide accords, they also tend to be wary of school-based management (SBM), another force that has reduced local school board and superintendent authority. Indeed, the basic assumption of SMB, which has evolved into today's charter school movement, is that schools would do better if only they were not under the thumbs of boards, superintendents, and central offices, if power were decentralized to the school level. Although the concept has spread in various forms to numerous states and school districts, full-blown SBM has eluded most policymakers. Education reform has been characterized as "tinkering towards utopia," and SBM keeps inching forward, while state and federal mandates for academic standards, aligned curricula, and tests are having far larger centralizing effects.

Teachers organized not only to gain strong local contracts but also to obtain preferred policies through state and national political processes.[22] This led the NEA to give its first endorsement, in 1976, to a presidential candidate—the Democrats' Jimmy Carter—and to spend $3 million in support of federal candidates that year. The nation may have been fond of the Progressive-era myth that it could "keep education out of politics," but it clearly could not keep politics out of education.

Because of a closely divided Congress during his 1976-80 term, Carter could not expand the federal role much, as the NEA would have wished. Rather, he chiefly embellished and refined existing equity-driven programs while federal regulations and enforcement continued to expand, as they had under his Republican predecessors. It was President Richard M. Nixon, for example, who successfully pressed for large sums for school desegregation. It was President Gerald R. Ford who issued Title IX regulations that still stir controversy today.

Similarly, from the Nixon presidency through the Carter years, there was bipartisan support for aggressive enforcement of the ESEA requirement that Title I funds supplement, not supplant, local resources for disadvantaged children. Republicans did periodically attempt to decategorize programs by creating bloc grants to states and districts, but those efforts were defeated by Democrats who held majorities in both houses of Congress, as well as by the interest groups that benefited from categorical programs.

What Carter did achieve, in 1979, was to create a Cabinet-level Department of Education, which the NEA had greatly desired and which had been justified partly on the ground that it would consolidate scattered education programs in one accountable department. A number of groups, however, wary of seeing their programs in a department they presumed would be dominated by professional educators, successfully lobbied to keep them separate. As a result, the school lunch program is still housed in the Department of Agriculture, and the National Science Foundation still provides research and demonstration grants for secondary school science. Similarly, Head Start is part of the

Department of Health and Human Services, even though it is designed to help preschool children in their transition to kindergarten.

After the Carter years, Reagan tried but failed to reorient federal education policy. He proposed a tuition tax credit for parents with children in private schools, an idea pushed by some conservative lawmakers for decades but never before endorsed by the White House. While a Democratic Congress defeated the tuition tax plan, the Reagan endorsement did help keep federal aid for parents of private school students on the national agenda. Indeed, as part of his big 2001 tax cuts, President George W. Bush succeeded in enacting tax-free savings accounts that can be used for private school tuition. The Reagan administration also attempted to scale back federal education activity in general—it initially wanted to dismantle the Department of Education, a notion that went nowhere—and equity-driven education programs in particular, urging flexible bloc grants for the states instead. Equity concerns, however, remained Washington's principal education thrust—though the emphasis already had begun to change elsewhere in the nation

THE RISE OF STATES AND ACADEMIC CONCERNS

Among the important effects of greater federal involvement in education was the dramatic expansion of state education agencies (SEAs) and thus of SEA and state board of education capacity to intervene in local school affairs. Starting in 1965, Washington began funding additional state staff members to enforce local ESEA implementation and compliance. Thirty years later, in 1965, the General Accounting Office found that Washington had become the largest funder of a good number of state agencies, in some cases footing 70 percent of their budgets. Many states, moreover, mirrored the federal thrust by creating their own categorical aids for groups neglected or underrepresented in local politics. Thus by 2002, California had sixty-five state and federal programs for poor, disabled, limited-English-speaking, and other children.

Atop the expansion of state agencies came other developments that moved school power to state capitals. The main one was a rapidly spreading state school finance movement, based on state court rulings that local property tax bases were inherently unequal. Another, albeit inadvertent, development was the educational consequences of California's Proposition 13; by cutting local property taxes, that 1978 measure shifted most school funding and power to Sacramento. As a result of such developments, states became the nation's largest single source of school financing. In 1930, states provided only 17.3 percent of school funding. In the early 1970s, they contributed about 40 percent. By the late 1990s, the state portion had climbed to 48 percent, exceeding the 45 percent local share.[23]

With mushrooming school spending and enlarged SEAs, states increasingly asserted the control over local schools that was theirs by law but that they had only modestly exercised until then. During the nineteenth century, states concentrated on minimum standards for rural schools; the best systems were thought to be in big cities, and no state intervention was needed there. Until the 1970s, states mainly focused on such things as enforcing minimum standards for teachers and facilities, requiring a few courses and dispensing federal aid. Organizations of local administrators, teachers, and school board members dominated state policy agendas no longer. Local education authorities now were seen as the problem—and states as the solution. Indeed, despite Washington's greatly enlarged role, perhaps the most striking change in U.S. education governance in recent decades has been the growth of centralized state control and the ascendance of governors over school policy in most states.

The rise of governors often has put them into conflict with chief state school officers, usually called the state superintendent or state commissioner of education. The chiefs, after all, long have been accustomed to being administrative bosses of the state education government, providing some insulation between it and the general state government. This is especially true of elected chiefs, but appointed ones also view themselves as working for the state board of education, not the governor, just as local superintendents overwhelmingly work for local school boards, not mayors.

As governors grew more active in education, however, they wanted more direct control, whether by repealing the election of chiefs or overseeing the state boards that appointed them.

Since they rarely are members of the governors' cabinet, however, chiefs still tend to view themselves as quasi-independent voices for education, following some of their own policies unless governors appoint them or exert heavy pressure on state boards of education. In only fourteen states, however, are chiefs still elected today, down from thirty-three in 1930. Governors now appoint all state board members in twenty-five states and some members in fourteen states.

The growth of gubernatorial influence had its origins in state economic development strategies, in which improved schools are used to help attract businesses and jobs. Southern governors with uncertain economies and historically weak school systems led the way in the 1970s, and others soon followed. While Washington was expanding equity programs, governors and state legislators were impressed by arguments that local school officials had permitted academic standards to decline. Surely business would look favorably on state education systems that produced well-trained workers and good schools for employees' families by requiring a more-demanding curriculum, stricter requirements for teachers, minimum-competency tests for high school graduation, and other measures. Here, in state plant-siting competitions, were the seeds of U.S. education's new focus.

The growth of state and gubernatorial influence accelerated in the 1980s as a result of the 1980-82 recession and fear of increasing global competition, especially from Japan. That worry triggered a series of highly critical private and public studies, most notably *A Nation at Risk* in 1983, which assailed schools as producing a "rising tide of mediocrity" that threatened nothing less than "our very future as a nation and a people." Education suddenly became a leading electoral issue. Governors across the country proposed major reform packages, which, in the mid-1980s, began including higher standards for student learning. Then, as now, states differed in how strenuously they asserted control of education, ranging from highly aggressive states such as California and Florida to more decentralized ones such as Vermont and Iowa. The growing assertion of state education control, moreover, prompted local reactions by decentralizers, with the idea of charter schools—essentially much more independent public schools—beginning to gain attention in 1987-88. The main governance thrust, however, remained more state control, as reflected, for example, in state curriculum initiatives.[25]

Until the 1980s, most states left curriculum largely to local discretion, satisfied to specify a few required courses and issue advisory curricular frameworks for local consideration. States did respond to influential curricular lobbies, another force that impinges on the discretion of local school authorities. The most vigorous curricular lobbying often came from relatively newer subject areas such as vocational education, physical education, and home economics. Such subjects, introduced amid great controversy after 1920, had to rely on state laws to gain a secure place in the curriculum. Hence teachers of these subjects used state NEA affiliates to lobby state lawmakers, supported by manufacturers of hardware, such as sports equipment and home appliances, which are required for the classes. Teachers of driver's education make up a newer lobby than the others, but they have been so effective that almost all states now mandate that subject.

By contrast, teachers of such "standard" courses as English, mathematics, and science—subjects that did not require political power to ensure inclusion in the curriculum—have been more poorly organized at the state level. As a result, academic subjects were less frequently mandated by state law, creating some curious results. Until recently, for example, states required many high school students to take only one year of science or math but four years of physical education. That sort of anomaly was swiftly put to an ending starting in 1983-84. In just those two years, thirty-four states established high school graduation requirements in standard academic subjects. They were determined to focus schools on the kind of academic subjects that had prevailed in post-Sputnik days, only now with economic justification.[26]

Unfortunately, despite these and many other state reforms of the 1980s—financial incentive for teachers, more student tests for promotion or graduation, longer school days—there was little improvement in student performance. The result was growing impatience among business leaders, public officials, and others, and the birth of the more comprehensive standards-based reform movement, with overarching aims to foster student mastery of more challenging academic content and to increase the emphasis on its application. A standards-based reform bandwagon began to roll, with associations of business executives, governors, education policymakers, subject-matter specialists, and others jumping aboard. Everybody, it seemed, was interested in setting education standards, including the White House.

INCREASING FEDERAL CENTRALIZATION

Shortly after his election, amid continued economic concern and frustration at the snail pace of education progress, President George H.W. Bush invited the nation's governors to a 1989 education "summit" in Charlottesville, Virginia. With great fanfare, it was agreed there that what America needed was standards or goals, at the national level, six of which initially were issued. Clearly, states by themselves also could not be trusted to produce the desired education gains. So, to much applause in 1990, the White House and the National Governors' Association (NGA) declared that by 2000, the nation would meet such goals as ensuring all children begin school ready to learn and American students are to be first in the world in mathematics and science achievement.

The rest of the Bush years included support for more specific national student standards and assessments, but those ideas died in ideological crossfires that doomed the Bush education legislation. President Bill Clinton, however, whose political rise owed much to his education efforts and who had played a prominent role in Charlottesville, picked up the torch and in 1994 won enactment of Goals 2000, a measure that reinforced three key state education reforms spreading across the nation:

1. Creating challenging academic standards for what all students should know and be able to do in each subject area. By 2001, forty-six states had done this in most academic subjects, a remarkable shift in the historic state role.
2. Aligning policies—testing, teacher certification, professional development, and accountability programs—to state curricular standards. All states but Iowa had statewide student achievement tests in 2002, and most were addressing the other systemic components.

3. Restructuring the governance system, ostensibly to delegate to schools and districts the responsibility for developing specific instructional approaches that meet the academic standards for which states hold them accountable.

The 1994 reauthorization of the Elementary and Secondary Education Act, called the Improving America's Schools Act, also linked categorical programs such as Title I and bilingual education to standards developed under Goals 2000 and required schools to make state-defined annual progress toward meeting those standards. It is impossible to isolate the distinctive contribution of Goals 2000 legislation to the rapid spread of standards-based state and local policies.[27] It has helped, but how much is uncertain. Goal 2000 state-level funding added flexible state money for test and standards development, as well as for systemic initiatives that state categoricals rarely permit. But 90 percent of Goals 2000 appropriations, which never exceeded $400 million, went to local school districts, and the law's effectiveness is problematic.

The Clinton administration proposed to supplement Goals 2000 in 1995 with a voluntary national test. Although it would have been a logical successor to Goals, the fourth-grade reading and eighth-grade mathematics examination were blocked by a rare congressional coalition of conservative Republicans, African-Americans, and Hispanics. The Republicans were wary of excessive federal control from the voluntary test, while the minority Democrats worried about the lack of opportunity of students in low-income schools to learn the content of the federal test.

In his second term, Clinton changed his priorities from standards and testing to class-size reduction and school construction, issues that moved Washington closer to providing general aid for education. But as the nation approached the end of 2000, when George W. Bush was elected president, it still had not advanced very far toward the goals set for that year by Bush's father and the governors. So, with little attention, the 2000 goals faded away. Thus, since the 1970s, when states first zeroed in on academic concerns, relatively little progress had been made in U.S. student achievement, though much centralization of governance had occurred and much money had been expended. Just since the 1983 release of *A Nation at Risk*, for example, federal funding for elementary and secondary education had more than tripled.

None of this, however, discouraged the new President Bush. On the contrary, Bush, another former Southern governor whose political popularity rested heavily on education initiatives, had made education central to his White House victory. Once in office, then, he pressed hard for his No Child Left Behind (NCLB) act, the latest ESEA reauthorization, and signed that measure into law in January 2002. Thus, Republican presidents since Reagan had done an about-face, going from a desire to dismantle the U.S. Department of Education to Bush's dramatic expansion of Washington's education power.

While NCLB generally extends the approach of the 1994 ESEA, it compels states to comply with scores of stricter assessment, accountability, and performance requirements. States must test all students in grades three through eight each year in several subjects, starting with reading and mathematics and then adding science. They must develop "adequate yearly progress" objectives that result in all students becoming "proficient" in core subjects with twelve years. They must participate biennially in the state-level version of the National Assessment of Educational Progress (NAEP), as a check on the rigor of their standards and assessments. They must find "highly qualified" teachers for every classroom and much better prepared paraprofessionals for Title I schools. They must break down student assessments by poverty, race, ethnicity, disability, and English proficiency to determine progress in closing education gaps among student subgroups. They must issue a public school "report card," with basic aggregate and disaggregated information on assessment, graduation, teacher qualifications, and the identification of low-performing schools.

These mandates will require, among other thing, immense data gathering, analysis, and reporting by SEAs. A recent report by the Education Commission of the States noted that only fifteen states had the required testing programs and "most states do not have the infrastructure to support the level of data collection, disaggregation and reporting that the new law requires."[28] Congress recognized the burden of developing new assessments by including $380 million for five years to help states develop and implement new assessment tools.

BESIEGED LOCAL AUTHORITIES AND THE TURN TO MAYORS

This chapter has shown that, over the past four decades, many forces have squeezed the authority of local school boards and superintendents into a smaller and smaller space (see Figure 2-1). From the top, local discretion has been eroded by the growing education power of the states, the federal government, and the courts. Greater education influence also has accrued to business elites and other private interests, professional "reformers" (such as the Ford or Gates foundations), interstate organizations (such as NGA), and nationally oriented groups (such as the Council for Exceptional Children). From the bottom, superintendents and local boards have been hemmed in by such forces as teachers' collective bargaining, pressures from local offshoots of national social movements, and the growth of charter schools and related decentralizing forces. The declining population of students during the 1970s and the spreading resistance to increased school taxes further constrained local initiative and options.

Figure 2.1
Trends in Education Governance—1960–2004

(+ = increasing influence)

+ Federal
+ State
+ Courts
+ National Networks and Nonprofit Organizations
+ Private Business, Educational Testing Service, Business Roundtable

↓

* School Board
* Local Superintendent
* Local Administration

↑

+ Teacher Collective Bargaining
+ Community-Based Interest Groups
+ Charter Schools

The general public may think that school boards still have the most power to improve schools, but the reality is that boards have been greatly weakened. Indeed, if one projects current trends for twenty years, the threat of minimal local discretion becomes quite dramatic, raising the risk of declining voter and taxpayer support for local public schools that cannot respond to many of their grievances. Little wonder, then, that Assistant Secretary of Education Chester E. Finn in 1980 called the school board a "dinosaur left over from the agrarian past" or that Albert Shanker, the late president of the American Federation of Teachers, recommended a major overhaul modeled on hospital boards that meet less than once a month.

This does not mean local authorities are helpless. Rather, it means they have much less control over their agenda and policies than in the past. Superintendents and administrative staff now are frequently reactive forces trying to juggle diverse and changing coalitions across different issues and levels of government. They must deal, for example, with a small army of administrative specialists in remedial reading, bilingual education, child nutrition, and other areas who are paid by the higher levels of government. Indeed, the specialists' allegiance often is to the higher levels of education governance rather than to the local community. Similarly, superintendents must address policy items on local board agendas that are generated by external forces or are reactions to proposals from teacher organizations and other local interest groups, including parents organized to support federal equity-driven programs.[29]

If concerns have arisen about the effect of categorical programs on teacher practices, they have multiplied as a result of state and federal curriculum mandates. For example, new state requirements specifying the grade level at which particular mathematical concepts must be taught can create rigid timetables for teachers, conflicting with the autonomy that enhances teacher responses and professionalism. Teachers' unions, like a vocal minority of parents, are troubled by the growth of certain state tests and may form coalitions on the issue with those parents. At the district level, increasing centralization of instructional policy forces the curriculum function into the central office (whose growing control of information gives it more authority over other

Figure 2.2

Influence Directions for Instruction Policy from 1980–2004

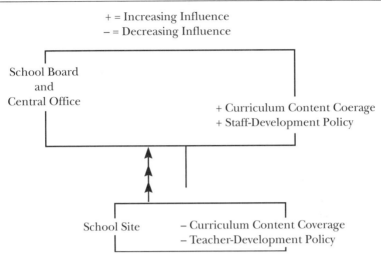

+ = Increasing Influence
– = Decreasing Influence

School Board
and
Central Office

+ Curriculum Content Coerage
+ Staff-Development Policy

School Site   – Curriculum Content Coverage
– Teacher-Development Policy

issues as well, at least in urban school systems), with a consequent loss of discretion at the school (see Figure 2.2).

Just as state economic competition prompted governors to assert
more control over education policy, so too did economic concerns drive city hall's involvement. Indeed, because of the growing belief among business leaders and others that improving deeply
troubled city schools is critical to urban economic development,
mayors no longer can avoid education-related issues. Mayors also
may be better able to integrate other children's services—health,
housing, police, arts, and recreation programs—with schools.
Moreover, mayors have financial incentives for becoming more
involved with education. Mayors want to control property tax
increases, and school boards can be a major factor in the city
tax burdens.[30] Thus, there are economic, social, and budgetary
reasons for mayors to seek greater school control.

Such mayors as Richard M. Daley in Chicago, Thomas Menino
in Boston, and Michael Bloomberg in New York have mustered
support at both the city and state levels for their efforts to assert
more control over education. In part, this is because of the belief that highly visible mayors are more likely than relatively
unknown school board members to be held accountable by vot-

ers for public school performance. In part, some city and state politicians also have political motives for shifting education control from an elected board that they cannot control, to a mayor over whom they may have some influence.[31]

There are limits, however, to the spread of mayoral involvement. Many cities, for example, are not contiguous with school districts. Remember that cities such as Phoenix, San Diego, and San Antonio have many school districts within their borders and that Southern cities are part of county school districts. A decline in teacher strikes, moreover, has removed one crucial trigger for mayoral takeover. Nonetheless, more efforts at mayoral control of schools seem likely. This would complete the cycle of putting politics firmly back into education, with councils, local and state school boards, teachers, and many others spinning an extensive political web around public schools.

This political web is what has led some to seek a virtual end to democratically controlled schools and to substitute market-based alternatives instead, a view that began receiving increased attention after *Politics, Markets and America's Schools* was published more than a dozen years ago.[32] John E. Chubb and Terry M. Moe contended in that book, "The specific kinds of democratic institutions by which American education has been governed for the last half century appear to be incompatible with effective schooling." Viewing school autonomy as a vital determinant of pupil performance, Chubb and Moe essentially argued that the political web surrounding schools was so complex, fragmented, and incoherent that it severely restricted such autonomy. In place of the gridlock they saw, they called for a version of school choice that included federal, state, and local deregulation, with students receiving scholarships that could be used to attend any public or private school that met minimal state standards.

WHO SHOULD BE IN CHARGE OF SCHOOLS?

On the question of who should be in charge of schools, the nation faces another kind of choice: picking a path through today's historic turning point in education governance. Do Americans want more or less centralization? Do they prefer greater control in Washington, the states, or local school districts? Should politicians, educators, or the marketplace rule schools? These are not easy questions, and there are no easy answers.

Governance and Student Achievement

Consider the goal of improving student achievement. Although this is not uppermost in the public's mind, U.S. elites have put it atop the education policy and governance agendas, with key teaching and testing decisions increasingly taken away from distrusted local school systems. Those decisions first moved to state capitals. When states, too, could not be relied on to meet achievement goals, more decision making moved to Washington, most recently with NCLB.

That law's implementation, however, will depend on strengthening federal-state partnerships and increasing SEA capacity to monitor and manage education progress and reform. Are Washington and the states likely to succeed in these undertakings? Margaret Goertz, professor at the University of Pennsylvania, prepared a matrix of instruments states use to influence local academic standards and overcome local resistance to state-imposed curriculum. She distinguished between state (1) *performance standards*, which measure an individual's performance through tested achievement observations, (2) *program standards*, which include curricular requirements, program specifications, and other state mandates affecting time in school, class size, and staffing, and (3) *behavior standards*, which include attendance requirements, disciplinary codes, and homework. Her fifty-state survey demonstrated dramatic increases from 1983 to 2001 in state specification and influence for all three types of standards.[33]

While the scope of state activity is wide, however, the effectiveness of state influence on local practice often has been questioned. Some think it is quite potent, while others see a "loose coupling" between state policy and local schools that leads to local symbolic compliance. Still others believe that worries about federal dominance of education are greatly exaggerated precisely because NCLB is unlikely to be implemented as intended.[34]

Then there is the question of student test motivation. Some state tests are of the high-stakes variety, used for promotion or

graduation, which is why they are the main ones stirring controversy. But no exams required by NCLB—neither the annual tests
in grades three through eight nor the biennial NAEP samplings—
carry direct rewards or punishments for students, only for per-
sistently failing schools and their staffs. It is reasonable to wonder
how much students will be motivated to do their best to raise
their scores on these tests.

There is similar reason to wonder how much weight the 88
percent of eighth-grade students hoping to attend a postsecondary
institution will give to state tests, beyond minimum passage of
examinations needed to graduate. Higher education authorities,
after all, generally pay no heed to state exams. Forty-nine states,
all but Iowa, now have K-12 content standards in most academic
subjects, and all but two have statewide K-12 student achievement tests. Almost all, however, have ignored the lack of coherence in content and assessments—the veritable Babel—between
K-12 and higher education standards.[35]

In light of all this, will the nation's big bet on centralized,
standards-based reform pay off in the significant student gains
(at least as measured by state tests or NAEP) that have eluded
the nation in recent decades? Unfortunately, nobody can say with
any confidence. The same question, of course, should be asked
of other governance arrangements. Can public charter schools
or market-based vouchers, for example, be expected to yield significant gains in student learning? The evidence so far is, at best,
ambiguous, as reviewed here in Chapter 14.[36] Are mayoral takeovers
likely to lead to improved classroom performance? There have
been slight to moderate test-score gains for elementary school
students under mayoral regimes in Boston and Chicago, for example, but no gains for secondary students.[37] But mayors are
just beginning to understand how to connect their control of
schools to improving classroom instruction, as discussed in detail in Chapter 5.

Citizen Influence and Policymaker Accountability

Another important goal one might consider is which level of
school governance promotes the most democracy (other than
market-based initiatives, which, of course, reject democratic gov-

ernance)? Is local school district control more democratic than federal or state control? Will citizens hold policymakers equally accountable at the federal, state, and local levels?

In general, citizens, for a variety of reasons, have more opportunity to affect policy in their local district than they do at the federal or state levels. Local policymakers serve fewer constituents than state or federal officials and are much closer to citizens psychologically, as well as geographically. (Indeed, local officials understand better than anyone else their community's zone of school policy tolerance.) It is difficult for most citizens to get to the state capital or to Washington. Local school board elections provide a much more direct means to influence local education policy than election of a state legislator, who represents many local school districts on a far wider variety of issues. In the thousands of small school districts in the nation, a significant portion of community residents personally know at least one school board member. Local media provide better information and can capture the attention of citizens more effectively than reports from distant state capitals.

This is by no means to suggest that local school politics approach the democratic ideal. While the Institute for Educational Leadership found strong public backing for the idea of local school boards as buffers against state and professional administrator control, for example, the public does not necessarily support its own local board and knows little about the role of school boards in general. Importantly, moreover, rarely do more than 10 to 15 percent of eligible voters even turn out for school board elections, in which about 95,000 board members are chosen for three- or four-year terms on a staggered basis.[38]

That is an important question, one that must be addressed by anyone interested in strengthening the American school board tradition and local education control in general. It also should be remembered, however, that the public scarcely holds state and federal officials responsible at all for education results. Although officials at all levels no doubt will claim credit if U.S. schools are seen as improving, for example, it is difficult to think of any president, governor, state legislator, or member of Congress who has lost an election because of U.S. education failures. Yet, these officials increasingly have been driving education policy in recent decades, with modest results to show for it. On the other hand, while local school board members, as well as superintendents, principals, and teachers, have less and less say over education, the public still holds them accountable for school results.

A POLITICAL FRAMEWORK FOR UNDERSTANDING SCHOOL TURBULENCE

Given the turbulence and complexity described in this chapter, it would seem hard to find patterns in what Henry James called the "buzzing, booming confusion of reality." These currents operate in over fourteen thousand school districts, erecting a truly indecipherable mosaic without some guide for explaining what transpires. What political framework of thought enables us to understand the nature of school turbulence? In short, is there a "theory" to describe and explain all this?

METHODS OF ANALYZING STEADY AND CHALLENGE QUALITIES

Theory involves suppositions and supporting evidence about the causes, consequences, and interrelationships of objects in reality. Causal theory of this kind is frequently found in the psychology of education and in the sociology of education, but seldom in educational administration before the 1970s. The most significant reason for the meager analysis of educational politics is probably the lack of theory and methodology. As political scientists pointed out thirty years ago, no single theory, simple or complex, guided it nor was there agreement on the methodology. Despite the flood of "politics of education" work done since the 1970s, no overarching general theory generated any hypotheses that could be tested by acceptable methods in the crucible of political experiences. The politics of education is certainly not orderly for those who prefer scholarship that explicates established truths, but it is exciting for those who prefer to innovate in the development of theory and hypothesis.[39]

Because scholarship, like life, is always some compromise with ideal requirements, we turn instead to one form of theory—heuristic. *Heuristic theory is not so much a predictive scheme as a method of analytically separating and categorizing items in experience.* It is a heuristic scheme or "framework for political analysis" that we employ in organizing the concepts and data of this book. This framework is termed *systems analysis,* from the ideas of David Easton who emphasizes a "conceptual framework" or "categories for the systems analysis of politics."[40] The utility of systems theory is that, like all other heuristic schemes, it enables us at least to order our information or hunches about reality. The use of systems analysis has limits, noted later, but explaining the current state of knowledge in the politics of education is our major purpose. For this, systems analysis provides an organizing principle to deal with the current turbulence in school politics.

THE SYSTEMS ANALYSIS FRAMEWORK

Easton's framework construes a society composed of major institutions or "subsystems"—the economy, the school, the church, and so on. Individuals interact with one another and these institutions in regular ways that constitute a distinctive culture. One of these institutions is the *political system.* It differs from the others because it alone is the source, in Easton's classic statements, of "authoritative allocation of values, [i.e.,] those interactions through which values are authoritatively allocated for society." This is the subsystem whose decisions are generally accepted as authoritative, that is, *legitimate.* The values this system allocates may be *material*—a textbook, defense contract, free land for constructing railroads, or dropout schools. Values allocated may also be *symbolic,* conferring status and deference on favored groups—for example, making Christmas or Martin Luther King's birthday a school holiday. Such an allocative system exists in every society, although its exact forms, inherent values, and public politics differ with place and time.

The link between the political system and other subsystems is a key element. This interrelationship is one in which *stress* in other subsystems generates *inputs* of *demands* on and *supports* of

Figure 2.3
A Simplified Model of a Political System

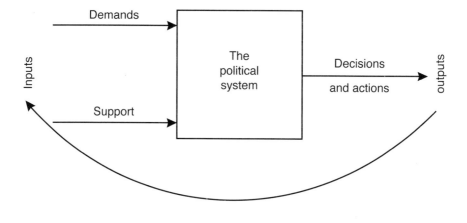

Source: Reprinted from *A Systems Analysis of Political Life* by David Easton by permission of the University of Chicago Press. © 1965 by the University of Chicago Press.

the *political system*. Actors in the political system then reduce or *convert* these inputs into public decisions or *outputs*. These in turn *feed back* allocated values and resources into the society where the process began. Figure 2.3 is a sketch of this set of interactions. These concepts seek to describe components of a dynamic, interactive, political system that may *persist* in the society.

The Model Illustrated for Schools

What does all this have to do with schools? The rest of this book will answer this question, but we can briefly illustrate our theme now. Schools allocate *resources*—revenues, programs, professionals—and they also allocate *values*—teaching Americanism. The interaction between schools and other subsystems can take two forms. The most obvious are *demands* whose characteristics increase today's political turbulence. For example, a group wants a special curriculum, more parental authority, or more teacher power, and these wants are directed as demands toward school authorities. A second form of interaction with the schools is *support*; that is, certain groups provide the school with taxes or with intangibles, such as a favorable attitude toward education.

The political system of the school that receives such demands must deal with them carefully because it lacks resources to meet them all. In short, a gap exists between what all groups want and the resources to meet those demands. In all times and places this gap is a powerful generator of social and political conflict. *So school systems must act politically because they must choose which demands to favor and which to reject.* The result of this decision is an *output*, for example, a state or federal law, a school board resolution, or a superintendent's program. Whatever form an output takes, all are alike in that they authoritatively allocate values and resources.

After this policy decision, as the arrow at the bottom of Figure 2.3 implies, the output must be implemented in order to cope with the inputs that originally gave rise to it. For example, a demand for driver education generates a district program, which is implemented by the resources of personnel and material that organize the program. In short, schools can be viewed as miniature political systems because they share certain qualities with large-scale political systems. And, as discussed later, the school professional must operate within this system in a way that shares much with the classical position of the politician. That is, he or she mediates among competing demands from school constituencies that have been organized to seek their share of valued resources from the school system. All that occurs because allocations are always limited so that not all get what they demand.

The Concepts Defined

A fuller statement of elements of systems analysis is appropriate here, beginning with the inputs, whether *demands* or *supports*.

Demands are pressures on the government for justice or help, for reward or recognition. Behind these demands lies the human condition of longing for something that is in short supply. Resources are never plentiful enough to satisfy all claims—a condition of tremendous importance to all aspects of our society, particularly for the political system. *Supports*, on the other hand, are a willingness of citizens to accept the decisions of the system or the system itself. A steady flow of supports is necessary if any political system is to sustain its *legitimacy* (i. e., the psychological sense that the system has the right to do what it is doing). So vital is this input that all societies indoctrinate their young to support their particular system, a task that is part of the school's work but is also shared with family and peers. One point about today's school turbulence is that some parents withdraw support from the public school system in seeking many types of reform.

The whole process of demands and supports can be illustrated in the issue of Southern school desegregation. Demands for desegregation arose from a racially based stress, long endured—but later unendurable—by blacks. Moving from private rancor across the political boundary to create a public challenge, blacks mobilized their resources, first in demands upon courts and later upon Congress but continually upon local school boards. The segregationists' counterdemands mobilized other resources to block and delay this challenge. The move to "deseg" private academies also withdrew support from the public school system.

The political system *converts* such inputs: sometimes combining or reducing them, sometimes absorbing them without any reaction. However, at other times demands convert them into public policies or outputs. Clearly not all demands are converted into policy, for the political system is more responsive to certain values, those that are dominant in the larger society. What inputs get through depends upon which values the conversion process reinforces and which it frustrates. They are also influenced by the values of the political authorities operating within this flow of inputs. For example, some educators insist that maintaining discipline is a prime value of classwork, while others prefer to achieve intellectual excitement that often looks undisciplined.

The authorities responsible for running the political system constantly interact in the conversion process with those either outside or inside the political system. Their interactions often stem in part from role definitions imposed by the political system itself. Such interactions generate certain pressures inside the political system—or *withinputs*—which in turn shape the conversion process and products. The result is the actors' commitment to a standard way of acting and believing that constitute a systematic way of life. That is a force contributing to its stability. It is also a force that generates challenge by those not benefiting from the outputs, as this book shows.

The outputs of the political subsystem once achieved require policy implementation that enhances the safety, income, and status of some while it also detracts from those of others. A resulting profile of public policy will mirror the structure of power and privilege and tells us much about what values currently dominate the political system. Moreover, the authorized purpose of the output will find meaning in reality only through the process of *feedback*. This is the interaction of an output with its environment, which becomes in time an established behavior—an *outcome*. Clearly, the gap between output and outcome becomes a major stimulus to future policymaking. That is, the action of the political system may not result in desired outcomes. Rather, because outputs can influence society, they generate a subsequent set of inputs to the political system through a *feedback loop*. That is, dealing with challenge causes a response in the system that is communicated to the political authorities, and so a new round of challenge and response begins.

The contemporary political turbulence clearly reflects this model of system and challenge about schooling. These concepts are incorporated in Figure 2.4's educational example of Easton's system analysis. Stresses affect the schools from events as far away as Saudi Arabia or Japan, or as close as meetings of local ministers or teachers. These events emerge in the school's political system as group challenges, for example, to cut school costs or institute school prayers. Whatever their content, these challenges are seeking to reallocate school values or resources. Officials in the school political system can reject some of these demands or convert others into formal outputs, such as an act of Congress or a local referendum. The resulting educational policy is then implemented as an administrative decision. In time that process has outcomes

Figure 2.4

The Flow of Influences and Policy Consequences in the School's Political System

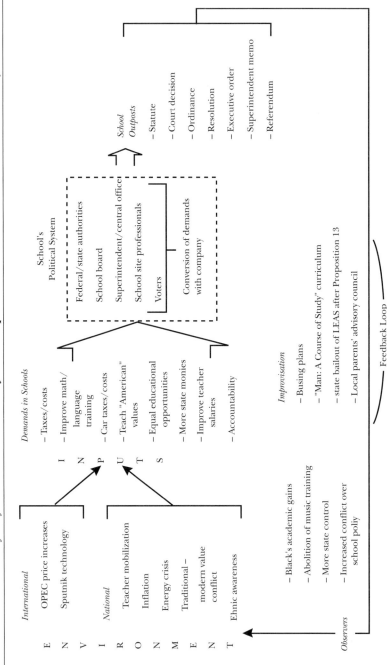

for particular groups who generated the challenge in the first place.

Note that this framework presents the political system as something other than just an allocative process. The belief that schools are embedded in society and responsive to its demands is a truism, perhaps the oldest in the study of education. We believe systems analysis can help illuminate this relationship more clearly through such specific concepts as *wants, demands,* and *supports.* Further, it seems to us that schools act out conversion processes like those in other subsystems that are more clearly recognized as political. That political authorities in schools do seek to maximize support through use of appropriate outputs also seems clear. Certainly a central question to be explored in this book is the degree to which the feedback loop operates between schools and society. In particular, the challenges to the qualities of schools in recent decades are of special interest.

In this book we seek something more. We want to know how valid such a general concept is in explaining the structure and increased challenge to the school system. As the first chapter noted, old forms and ideas in education are everywhere challenged, and not only by new interest groups seeking a reallocation of resources. Widespread resistance to school tax referenda, as well as the waves of reform, suggest disappointment, frustration, or malaise about our schools. Stress, then, is not an abstract academic concern. Rather, it is a characteristic of contemporary education that affects school boards, classrooms, administrators' offices, and professionals' conventions, as well as the decision-making forums at state and national levels. And, as polls show, the public's disenchantment with schools creates a nationwide condition of challenge to support the entire system.

This framework of analysis thus offers a contour map to stimulate thinking and research. Nor do we stand mute on the value questions that lie at the heart of turbulent issues. To do this, however, we will use this framework of analysis to make sense out of new actors, issues, and resources that are swirling among the contemporary challenges.

NOTES

1. M-E. Phelps Deily "Boards, Parents Seen as Powerful," *Education Week* (June 5, 2002): 5.

2. Deborah Land, *Local School Boards Under Review: Their Role and Effectiveness in Relation to Students' Academic Achievement* (Baltimore, Mary.: Center for Research on the Education of Students Placed at Risk, January 2002).

3. Lowell C. Rose and Alec M. Gallup, "The 32nd Annual Phi Delta Kappa/Gallup Poll of the Public's Attitudes Toward the Public Schools," *Phil Delta Kappan* (September 2000): 42.

4. Lowell C. Rose and Alec M. Gallup, "The 32nd Annual Phi Delta Kappa/Gallup Poll of the Public's Attitudes Toward the Public Schools," *Phil Delta Kappan* (September 2002): 42.

5. M. Newman, "American Public Ready for National Curriculum, Achievement Standards, Annual Gallup Poll Finds," *Education Week* (September 6, 1989).

6. David Tyack, *The One Best System* (Cambridge, Mass.: Harvard University Press, 1974).

7. Ibid.

8. David Tyack and Elizabeth Hansot, *Managers of Virtue* (New York: Basic Books, 1974).

9. David Tyack, *Seeking Common Ground* (Cambridge, Mass.: Harvard University Press, 2003).

10. L. Cremin, *The Transformation of the School* (New York: Vintage Books, 1964).

11. David B. Tyack, "Needed: The Reform of a Reform," in *New Dimensions of School Board Leadership* (Evanston, Ill.: National School Boards Association, 1969), p. 61.

12. Ibid.

13. Ibid.

14. Frederick Wirt and Michael Kirst, *The Political Dynamics of American Education,* second edition (Richmond, Calif.: McCutchan, 2001), pp. 31-33.

15. Diane Ravitch, *Left Back* (New York: Simon and Schuster, 2001).

16. David B. Tyack and Elizabeth Hansot, *Public Schools in Hard Times: The Great Depression and Recent Years* (Cambridge, Mass.: Harvard University Press, 1984).

17. Diane Ravitch, *The Troubled Crusade: American Education 1945-1980* (New York: Basic Books, 1983).

18. Frederick Wirt and Michael Kirst, *The Political Web of American Schools* (Boston: Little Brown, 1972).

19. Frederick Wirt and Michael Kirst, *Schools in Conflict* (Richmond, Calif.: McCutchan, 1982).

20. Anthony Cresswell and Michael J. Murphy, *Teachers, Unions, and Collective Bargaining in Public Education* (Berkeley, Calif.: McCutchan, 1980).

21. S.M. Johnson, *Teacher Unions in Schools* (Philadelphia: Temple University Press, 1984).

22. Lorraine McDonnell and Anthony Pascal, *Teacher Unions and Education Reform* (Santa Monica, Calif.: The Rand Corporation, 1987).

23. James W. Guthrie, Walter Garms, Lawrence Pierce, *School Finance and Education Policy* (Englewood Cliffs, N.J.: Prentice Hall, 1988).

24. Education Commission of the States (ECS), *Models of State Education Governance* (Denver: ECS, 2002).

25. Wirt and Kirst, *Political Dynamics,* pp. 209-254.

26. Michael W. Kirst and Robin L. Bird, "The Politics of Developing and Sustaining Mathematics and Science Curriculum Content Standards," in P.H. Thurston and J.G. Ward, eds., *Advances in Educational Administration,* volume 5 (Greenwich, Conn.: JAI Press, 1997): 107-132.

27. Diane Ravitch, ed., *Brookings Papers on Education Policy* (Washington, D.C.: Brookings, 2000).

28. Education Commission of the States (ECS), *No State Left Behind: The Challenges and Opportunities of ESEA 2001* (Denver: ECS, 2002).

29. Paul Hill, "The Federal Role in Education," in Ravitch, *Brookings Papers,* p. 19.

30. James G. Cibulka and William L. Boyd, eds., *A Race Against Time: The Crisis in Urban Schooling* (Westport, Conn.: Praeger, 2003), pp. 63-166.

31. Theodore Lowi, *The End of Liberalism* (New York: Norton, 1979), p. 145.

32. John Chubb and Terry Moe, *Politics, Markets, and America's Schools* (Washington, D.C.: Brookings, 1990).

33. Margaret E. Goertz, *Assessment and Accountability Systems: 50 State Profiles* (Philadelphia: Consortium for Policy Research in Education, 2001).

34. Susan Fuhrman, *Less Than Meets the Eye: Standards, Testing, and Fear of Federal Control* (Denver: Education Commission of the States, 2003).

35. A. Venezia, A. Antonio, Michael Kirst, *Betraying the College Dream* (Stanford, Calif.: Stanford Institute for Higher Education Research, 2003).

36. B.P. Gill, P.M. Timpane, K.E. Ross, and D.J. Brewer, *Rhetoric Versus Reality: What We Know and What We Need to Know About Vouchers and Charter Schools* (Santa Monica, Calif.: RAND Corp., 2001).

37. Michael Kirst, *Mayoral Influence, New Regimes and Public School Governance* (Philadelphia: Consortium for Policy Research in Education, 2002).

38. Neal Peirce in Lila N. Carol and colleagues, *School Boards* (Washington, D.C.: Institute for Educational Leadership, 1986), p. iv.

39. For a recent overview of political science theories, see James March and Johann Olsen, *Democratic Governance* (New York: Free Press, 1995).

40. David Easton, *A Systems Analysis of Political Life* (New York: Wiley, 1965), p. 490.

Part II:

POLITICS AT THE
LOCAL LEVEL

3

The Origins and Agents
of School Demands

The political system is subject to the demands that provide the more contentious essence of governance. We turn in this section to exchanges, across school boundaries, of wants arising from unsatisfied values. Exchanges promote stress in the school system. This chapter investigates how stress arises through value conflicts, and what agents transfer the resulting demands to the decisions of policymakers.

BASIC VALUES IN EDUCATION POLICY

Key Variables Defined

We have noted that groups use political power to satisfy their values and that politics is, in Easton's terms, "the authoritative allocation of values and resources." Now we wish to specify these values as they appear in educational policy. A study of such policy in six states focuses on four values that are pursued in school policy.[1]

1. *Quality:* "a substantial net improvement in the well-being of those affected by policy," best seen in states mandating standards of school performance and then providing resources and regulations to ensure their use. Typical are requirements for staff training, use of instructional resources, or performance by staff and students. This value is instrumental, a means to another value goal, namely, the fulfillment of diverse human purposes, thereby making life worth living and individuals worthwhile.

2. *Efficiency:* takes two forms, economic (minimizing costs while maximizing gains) and accountability (oversight and control of the local exercise of power). The first form is regularly seen in such state mandates as pupil-teacher ratios or the minimum needed for kindergarten schools. The second form is familiar in the details of procedures that local school authorities must follow (e.g., the budgetary process). This value is also instrumental, serving the goal of responsibility for the exercise of public authority—the central operating premise of a democratic nation.

3. *Equity:* "the use of political authority to redistribute critical resources required for the satisfaction of human needs." Two steps in policymaking are required in equity matters— the perception of a gap between human needs and the availability of resources and allocation of resources to close that gap. This value is seen most often in federal compensatory, handicapped, or bilingual programs over the last three decades; but much earlier policy was moved by equity concerns to redress the imbalance in local school finances (e.g., the foundation programs of the 1920s). This value is underlain by another and more basic value—fairness in the receipt of benefits needed for a better life.

4. *Choice:* "the opportunity to make policy decisions or reject them" by local school authorities. Such policies are often mandated but can exist even when no state law does (i.e., what is not prohibited may be done). Law can mandate selecting among alternative allocations of resources (textbook selection), can permit local authorities to use authority or not (program choice by parental advisory boards), and can leave it to special groups to exercise authority (voting

for or against bond issues). This value is also instrumental, serving the sovereignty of citizens in a democracy—the most fundamental of all American political views.

Attributes of Values in Operation

Manifest in statutes, these four values generate political conflict because they are not a nicely integrated schema or ideology. Rather, they may oppose, as well as reinforce, one another. These values often emerge in a particular sequence during policy conflict.

Choice can inherently oppose all values because nothing in the other values compels one to select them. The exercise of choice can—and has—rejected quality programs and equity programs in education; the South's de jure segregation is a classic example. *Efficiency*, on the other hand, reinforces all values except choice because efficiency is designed to realize quality and equity goals. Clear illustrations are the "state regs"—heavily oriented to efficiency—that seek compliance with state policy goals. Finally, the *quality* value opposes all but efficiency; the latter usually reinforces quality, as noted, but quality is unrelated to questions of what should be equitable and what should be chosen.

This brief argument makes a larger point, namely, each value is always pursued in policy that is linked to other values. Also, a tension arises among them because different policy actors back different values. Broadly expressed, professionals have historically left their mark on quality and efficiency values in education. They usually defined quality goals as well as the efficient means to achieve them. The participatory thrust of democracy can get in the way of this activity at times—but not always. This conflict depends on how the force of choice and the search for equity emerges either directly from citizens or from professionals who share these values.

Another attribute of these policy values is the way they are sequenced into law. The history of American education shows that the first efforts to build this service were based on a belief in quality. The movement stems from Horace Mann and other reformers' moral objection to an illiterate population. Decades later it was stimulated further by public reaction against big-city party machine control that had resulted in poor education. Efficiency values in policy would come second in this historical sequence because quality goals are not self-executing. Like all other good aims, they must be worked at to be realized. That necessity prompted considerations of what it would take to administer quality goals and how to ensure compliance.

Later, due to the maldistribution of educational services, equity values would be stimulated. The classic example is how the local property tax—a robust means of raising funds—had made the quality of a child's education a function of a district's wealth; equity-driven funding reforms in the 1920s and 1970s testify to that maldistribution. It is in the effort to redress these imbalances in the distribution of rewards that equity policy arises. Finally, choice values in policy do not follow this sequence; instead they pervade it at every step. Voters support elected school boards or tax levies to hold power accountable, and today, professionals must work within a "zone of tolerance," those constraints implicitly imposed by local citizens' preferences.[2]

The Infusion of Values in State Education Law

We see the reality of these values when we search state laws. One study subjected state codes to content analysis within the framework of these four values. Table 3.1 summarizes their findings in seven areas of state policy mechanisms, or policy domains, and in two states of differing political cultures, Illinois and Wisconsin. Across the first row, we can see the proportion of each value in the finance laws of each state. The table reports that finance and governance policies are dominated by the efficiency value, although Wisconsin offers more equity-based law. Personnel policy is dominated by different values in the two states, and other policies show more diffuse values. The results challenge any simple notion that a given policy domain is dominated by a single value.

Social Context and Educational Policy

Let us put the preceding discussion of values within the analytical framework of the preceding chapter. How do values and a political system interact to produce educational policy?

Table 3.1
Distribution of Values by State Policy Mechanisms in Illinois and Wisconsin

SPM	Quality		Equity		Efficiency		Choice	
	Ill.	Wis.	Ill.	Wis.	Ill.	Wis.	Ill.	Wis.
Finance	6	10	9	36	68	36	16	19 = 100%
Personnel	47	29	22	29	25	39	7	3
Testing and assessment	45	–	45	50	–	50	10	–
Program definition	34	27	28	30	17	23	21	20
Organization and governance	10	9	17	18	64	53	9	20
Curriculum materials	23	33	39	–	23	–	16	67
Buildings and facilities	26	27	21	27	29	31	24	15

Source: Frederick Wirt, Douglas Mitchell, and Catherine Marshall, "Analyzing Values in State Policy Systems," *Educational Evaluation and Policy Analysis* 10, no. 3 (1988). Copyright 1988 by the American Educational Research Association. Reprinted by permission of the publisher.

Filtered through the pluralist prism of our society, general values take on specific definitions. At times the private pursuit of these definitions produces cooperation and accommodation among groups. Yet other groups come into conflict because insufficient resources for satisfying all their values exist in private subsystems. As a result, some groups are rewarded and others are not. The resulting stress can mobilize the group that went unrewarded to drive for additional resources. This drive can transfer the resource struggle from the private to the political system. That system, in turn, seeks to maintain support for its political objectives by finding different ways of adjusting to such demands for value satisfaction.

Each school district reflects locally prevailing values to some degree. The guardians of community values, for whom schools are important instruments for keeping the faith, operate here. When insulated from outside forces, local guardians of orthodoxy can exist without challenge. But in this last century, as mentioned, obstacles to local autonomy abound. Local control over school policy has been weakened by those groups increasingly unwilling to accept the dominance of localism. A centralization to the state and federal levels of demands for quality and equity has resulted from this.

This centralization, though, is far from the bland uniformity of the French school system. Certain American schools still hold the theory of evolution to be suspect, while others teach evolution, calculus, or Asian history. The decentralization impulse of pluralism conflicts with centralizing national forces, such as professionalism and state and federal laws. In this process, education is not unique but merely reflects the tensions that emerge as well in many other policy areas of a federal system. But whatever the balance that once existed among these conflicting values before, it has been tipped by new nationalizing forces, such as the No Child Left Behind act, in recent decades.

Within this general framework of values and demands pursuing policy, we need to know more specifics about this exchange and conversion process. Who are the agents that transfer demand inputs into the political system from their position on its boundaries? We need some flesh-and-blood referents for these abstract "transfer agents." For our purposes, we focus on the transfer roles of interest groups, social movements, policy issue networks, and the media.

Some definitions of these various transfer agents are useful. *Interest groups* have a well-defined membership, regular funding, a long-term staff, and knowledge of how to operate within the political system. *Social movements* are based on a specific ideology (civil rights, women's rights), and include several core organizations and individuals. Their concerns are much broader than interest groups or policy issue networks. *Policy issue networks* have a narrower agenda than do social movements (for example, including creation science in textbooks), and may include interest groups, research organizations, government employees, individual opinion shapers, academies, think tanks, lawyers, and elected politicians. Education politics in the last forty years has experienced growth in the influence of social movements and policy issue networks.[3] Our final chapter describes this trend for school choice politics, and Chapter 8 includes the role of policy issue networks in state policy. Here we focus on individual interest groups.

INTEREST GROUPS AS TRANSFER AGENTS

Interest groups, working between citizens and educational authorities, are involved in the full spectrum of private demands on school systems. Claims for justice, help, reward, or recognition—all are sought in the pursuit of quality, efficiency, equity, and choice. Competing claims for scarce educational budget resources often mobilize them. They do more, however, than just transmit political desires from citizens to officials. As transfer agents for the political system, interest groups often reformulate demands so that they differ somewhat from citizens' desires. Also, interest groups do not confine their activities to just the input and conversion phases of the political system; they provide feedback on the implementation of school policy as well. Despite such political activities, the tradition that overt politics and schools should be separate has shaped these interest groups.

Individuals join interest groups and engage in collective action mostly because they get something for it. Others do not join because they can, without cost, benefit from gains the group may make. Leaders mobilize groups for the diverse benefits that group activity provides. Not surprisingly, past decades have witnessed an impressive growth in the numbers and types of educational interest groups. This complex array is part of the greater political turbulence with which educational policymakers must contend. The emergence of a wide spectrum of narrow-based interest groups reflects a weakening national consensus about schooling goals over the last three decades, as well as the diminishing influence of broad-based groups. Moreover, reforms such as compensatory, bilingual, and special education have created their own separate constituencies to preserve these policies and their funds. Such programs spawn cohorts whose prime allegiance is to the program rather than to the broad concept of a common school. Categorical programs from Washington and the state have generated a jumble of interest groups that includes local project directors, parent groups, and federal and state categorical administrators. In the past forty years education interest groups have become more specialized and focused on particular causes. Broad-based organizations like PTA have lost members and influence.

Educational interest groups also grow as spin-offs of broader social movements, including women's liberation in the 1960s and the Christian Coalition in the 1990s. These movements form political action groups with sections devoted to educational policies. For example, the National Organization of Women may urge a state board of education to include a broader variety of female occupations in textbooks, or the Christian Coalition will appear before local boards advocating that the account of creation be taught alongside that of evolution.

Another type of group includes networks of interstate experts and advocates who advocate particular policies, such as school finance reform or creationism in the textbooks. These policy issue networks, not so broadly based as social movements, emphasize technical expertise and assistance in their lobbying strategy. All of these newer groups are added to the collective action groups that have been around for years, including the PTA and the school administrators association. We will turn to these shortly.

There is a political wisdom that any political contest changes in nature when the number of participants changes. Two tenth-graders engaged in a schoolyard fight, one black and one white, are most likely working out their budding masculinity in a fashion characteristic of that age. But if a hundred students of each color are involved, it is not merely a melee; there are likely to be racial overtones to the fighting. Increasing the number of participants facing the administrator means that he or she is in a different kind of contest than before.

One of the major changes is that administrators must work with new interest groups. Sometimes the NEA will join forces with a local PTA, but at other times it will oppose local preferences and align with a state organization of big business. Because education has lost some general support, appeals for loyalty to the concept of public education will be insufficient to mobilize interest group support for many specific changes. Splintered interest groups want a specific "payoff," such as access ramps for handicapped children.

The next section categorizes the interest groups that confront policymakers at all levels. We explain their formation and growth, and underline the necessity for coalition formulation to enact and implement public school policy.

The Role of Interest Group Entrepreneurs

If forces at work in our society create interest groups, why do so many individuals join and contribute to them? The initial simple answer was that people join a group because they agree with the group's goals. Mancur Olson, in his *The Logic of Collective Action*, changed this straightforward emphasis on motivations.[4] As an economist, he stressed that individuals will *not* contribute to interest groups if they receive the same benefits through non-participation—as a "free rider." Why join the local teachers' organization if everyone receives wage increases through the efforts of those who give time and money? Olson answered this puzzle by focusing on the other benefits an organization can extend to or withhold from individuals. Anything of tangible value—group insurance programs, newsletters, tire discounts—can be contingent upon individual contributions. Interest groups thus attract members and resources by supplying benefits only partly related to politics or policies. Yet interest group political activities are possible because the people who join want private benefits, not because they share common values or goals. Olson's work helps explain why some interest groups grow and prosper, while others languish. Interest group formation is not spontaneous, but rather requires individuals to recognize their mutual interest, and possess sufficient incentives to do something about them.

Olson's thesis has gone through several adaptations, which help explain the broad array of motives for individual contributions to groups. Others have demonstrated that ideology, moral principles, and social pressures can also generate collective action.[5] In an analogy to the marketplace, lobbyists form groups because, like entrepreneurs, the benefits they can obtain exceed the costs they must invest in mobilizing others. Members of a group also join because the cost-benefit ratio is favorable. Benefits are not merely material, such as good teacher contracts. They can also achieve "solidarity," the intangible psychological reward that comes from belonging—the pleasure of sharing the company of like-minded others—as in a group of mothers protecting the neighborhood school against dangerous drugs. Benefits can also be "expressive," so that one's personal goals are incorporated into and expressed by group action. An example would be a belief in the value of education manifested by work in the PTA. The Sierra Club is one group that is a classic example of all these motivations. Other analysts have emphasized the motive of "imperfect information," as when individuals underestimate their ability to become a free rider or overestimate the importance of proposed education legislation for their job performance. Individuals' motives for collective action in interest groups may arise because they like to go to meetings or have feelings of responsibility.[6]

What inducements will make people join a group? Politics need not be a by-product of membership gained through discounts for auto rentals or tax shelter annuities. Interest group entrepreneurs can attract members through ideological appeal, emphasis on fairness, social pressure, and the structuring of meetings. However, we lack empirical studies on the perceptual and value characteristics that motivate membership in education lobby groups. We do know that numerous motivations exist and that the interest group leader is well advised to develop diverse appeals. At the core of this exchange, though, one trades off group dues for individual benefits.

A recent key change in education politics has been the decline of loyalty as a motivation for supporting education interest groups. The PTA and American Association of University Women have lost ground in membership to such groups as parents of handicapped children (Council of Exceptional Children), the Christian Coalition, and parents of limited-English-speaking children. Selective benefits are increasingly organized around categorical programs or professional specialties. Also, loyalty to the harmony of the education profession no longer inspires the membership as it did in 1970 when National Education Association (NEA) headquarters included administrators, professors, and schoolteachers under one roof.

Reflecting all this activity is the fact that expenditures for group action have grown dramatically since 2000. A state-local "arms race" results in creating Washington or state capital lobby offices for cities, categorical groups, low-wealth school districts, and women's organizations. Two examples illustrate this point. Table 3.2 is a listing of groups on one side of a school issue; they are opposed to vouchers or federal tax credits for private school tuition, a theme pursued in a later chapter. This staggering variety illustrates two qualities of current school politics. Education policy touches on a mosaic of American values—religious, ethnic, professional, social, economic—that often clash in politics. Table 3.2 also illustrates the shifting quality of coalitional policymaking; this amalgam will rearrange itself for other school issues. Some groups will drop out, for example, if the issue does not involve federal aid to private schools.

Another perspective on the proliferation of interest groups is seen in Table 3.3 showing a California statewide interest group coalition that supports increased unrestricted state aid for local schools. Note how many separate school employee and support groups are represented in Sacramento. Although rarely studied, much the same situation probably exists in most if not all the states.[7]

Table 3.2
Groups in Washington, D.C., Officially Opposing School Vouchers

American Association of Cooleges for Teacher Education

American Association for Health, Physical Education, and Recreation

American Association of School Administrators

American Civil Liberties Union

American Ethical Union

American Federation of State, County, and Municipal Employees

American Federation of Teachers, AFL-CIO

American Humanist Association

American Jewish Congress

Americans for Democratic Action

Americans United for Separation of Church and State

A. Philip Randolph Institute

Association for International Childhood Education

Baptist Joint Committee Public Affairs

Coalition of Labor Union Women

Council for Education Development and Research

Council for Exceptional Children

Council of Chief State School Officers

Federation Education Project of the Lawyers Committee for Civil Rights under the Law

Horace Mann League

Labor Council for Latin American Advancement

League of Women Voters

National Association for the Advancement of Colored People

National Association of Elementary School Principals

National Association for Hearing and Speech Action

National Association of Secondary School Principals

National Association of State Boards of Education

National Coalition for Public Education and Religious Liberty

National Committee for Citizens in Education

National Congress of Parents and Teachers

National Council of Churches

National Council of Jewish Women

National Council of Senior Citizens

National Education Association

National School Boards Association

National Student Association

National Student Lobby

National Urban Coalition

National Urban League

Student National Education Association

Union of American Hebrew Congregation

Unitarian Universalist Association

United Auto Workers

United Methodist Church

United States Student Association

Table 3.3
A California Collective Education Interest Group

American Association of University of Women—California Division
Association of California School Administrators
Association of California School Districts
Association of Low Wealth Schools
Association of Mexican-American Educators, Inc.
California Association of School Business Officials
California Congress of Parents and Teachers, Inc.
California Federation of Teachers, AFL-CIO
California Personnel and Guidance Association
California School Boards Association
California School Employees Association
California School Nurses Organization
California Teachers Association—NEA
The Delta Kappa Gamma Society—Chi State—California
Education Congress of California
League of Women Voters of California
Los Angeles Unified School District
Schools for Sound Finance
United Teachers of Los Angeles

A CLASSIFICATION OF SCHOOL INTEREST GROUPS

Differences among these educational groups parallel those found in interest groups of other areas, for example, in temporary versus permanent organization, special versus broad interests, and larger versus limited resources. The NEA illustrates the qualities of permanent organization, broad interests, and large resources; however, taxpayer-revolt groups exemplify the temporary, narrow, and limited-resource type of group.

A major distinction of all such groups centers on how broad their interest is in the many facets of education. Thus, there are those for whom education is an end in itself and those for whom it is a means to other ends. The first consists of professional educators or other school employees, and the second of those wishing to use the school to serve other values, such as reducing taxes, protecting moral or patriotic values, and so on. Policy issue networks are in some ways an interest group but do not fit any of the conventional definitions. Policy issue networks can encompass several interest groups, but will focus on a single issue such as teaching creation or creating a national standards board for teacher certification. In contrast, interest groups are concerned with numerous interrelated issues. The 1990s' movement to create statewide academic standards and tests had mobilized both interest groups and policy issue networks to support the cause. The issue networks included academics, think tanks, lawyers, and foundations, as well as interest groups like the American Federal of Teachers (AFT).

Professional Interest Groups

For many years the most numerous interest group—teachers— exerted only minimal political influence. Schoolteachers had traditionally hesitated in using collective action for transmitting demands to political authorities either within or outside school systems. The doctrine of the school administrator also played down the usefulness of teachers' collective organizations, stressing instead negotiations by individual professionals.[8] This doctrine also emphasized the authority of the superintendent and played down democracy and participation, as those terms are used in the current popular sense. Later, an altered conception of administration favored teacher participation, but only for its effects on morale building and consequent improved performance. Not surprisingly, until 1970 the views of teacher representatives differed only slightly from the administrators' tenets.[9]

The NEA's resources are very large. In 2002, it had over 2.7 million members, representing about 60 percent of our public schoolteachers. It has an extensive bureaucracy and hierarchy, although the executive staff usually makes policy with the concurrence of a board of ninety-two directors and an executive committee of eleven.[10] Every state has its own teacher's association, which is frequently a powerful interest group at the state level. Over fourteen thousand dues-paying local school affiliates filter their money through the state affiliates, and even more money is raised for high-priority elections.[11]

At the national level, the NEA functions as an umbrella for major segments of the teaching profession. Within the national organization are over seventy-five departments, divisions, commissions, and committees. Separate professional organizations within the NEA exist even for audio-visual specialists, as well as for home economics and speech teachers. The Political Action Council of the NEA spent $4.2 million in 1994 supporting Democratic political candidates at the national level. In one Washington building the NEA houses groups with specialized orientation and values that increasingly compete with each other in the political system. Principals and counselors feel that they are not well represented by either teachers or administrators, and so they get lost in an intermediary position. These divisions over priorities for money and values have spawned professional competitors who argue their cases before school boards and legislatures.

The most noticeable NEA competition comes from within the teaching profession itself. The American Federation of Teachers (AFT) restricts membership to teachers and administrators who have no direct authority over teachers. It has affiliates in one-half of the states and a membership of 1.2 million concentrated in or near large cities or nearby. However, it has not been able to take significant numbers of members away from the NEA in the last decade. While the two teacher groups take common positions on some policy issues, for example, increased state aid for teacher salaries, they still differ on others. NEA is much more opposed than is AFT to No Child Left Behind, contending that the law is massively underfunded, and is turning the schools into testing factories.

The AFT grew rapidly between 1960 and 1975 by contending that professional unity is a myth because value conflicts are inevitable between teachers and their managers who administer the school.[12] AFT rhetoric was replete with *we* and *they*, terms that reflect an adversarial relationship between an aggressive labor union and its employer. The AFT willingness to resort to a strike proved attractive to urban teachers but shattered the professional ethic of low-profile teacher activity. However, the organizing success of the AFT in the 1960s led to the NEA taking a more militant stance in stressing local collective bargaining.

The differences between the two unions are clear in their organization of political efforts, but they are the only education groups to give big money to political candidates. The two teacher unions gave $2,023,000 to federal candidates in 2001-2002, and 90 percent went to Democrats. Only 40 percent of teachers, however, say they are Democrats.[13] If the AFT has succeeded more in big cities, the NEA has been more effective at the state level, where its affiliates—one of the largest organized interest groups in the states—spend much time dealing with state politicians. The AFT, on the other hand, has few effective state federations, concentrating its efforts at the local urban level. Both have Washington offices, but under Republican administrations neither has been very successful in getting political demands approved by the president and Congress.[14] NEA support of Jimmy Carter led to his support for a cabinet-level Department of Education, and the Clinton administration worked closely with both unions. But Republican governors and legislators in Michigan and Illinois reduced the bargaining rights of teachers in 1995. The Bush administration is not close to teachers unions, and its support of vouchers and religion in public schools opposes the views of teachers groups. About 75 percent of teachers belong to the NEA or the AFT.

Major administrative groups of superintendents and principals (shown later) frequently make their own distinctive demands on the political system and maintain their own offices at the state and federal levels. The National School Boards Association (NSBA) has traditionally joined forces with the administrator-teacher groups at the state and federal levels. The NSBA is the most aggressive of the lay groups in the capitol.

Divisions among professional educators should not be overestimated, because powerful forces work toward their unity. The tradition of a unified profession and the common training and experience of professional educators have led them to agree on many fundamental values, a factor that tends to restrict the range of interest group activity. For example, most administrators move up through the teaching ranks, and accrediting associations are usually staffed by professional educators. Indeed, the faith that the public has in accreditation makes regional accrediting agencies a professional interest group of considerable importance, often bringing irresistible pressure to achieve their standards of faculty, budget, facilities, and curriculum.

Professionally Oriented Interest Groups

Other nonprofessional groups are also interested in educational policy as an end in itself. Like educators, they provide schools with diffuse support, but they also differ as educators do on some aspects of school governance and so present their own demand inputs.

The National Congress of Parents and Teachers not only is the largest group in this category, but also is the largest volunteer organization in the nation, with 6.5 million members. The PTA is a loose confederation of about twenty-six thousand local units concerned primarily with specific problems facing *specific* schools.[15] Similar to the decline in membership in many traditional civic organizations, PTA participation declined by 5.7 million members between 1968 and 2004. It is most influential and active at the local or district level, because its heterogeneous state membership precludes agreement on many controversial issues. The organization is still dominated by women,[16] and analysts of PTA history stress the generally dependent and close relationship it has to school administrators. However, such participation can have important positive social and psychological benefits for individuals.[17] Moreover, in the last two decades, the PTA has become more aggressive, asserting that it is a consumer advocate. Major PTA issues include reading improvement and opposition to vouchers and TV violence. The PTA is broadening its membership to include more minorities and becoming more active at the state level.

The PTA's local role is amplified at the national and state levels. However, it does not provide an independent source of demands into school policy; rather it proceeds as an instrument of educators who use it to reinforce or implement *their* policy. Indeed, the national PTA is a resolute member of the "Big Six"— a coalition of three professional groups and three lay groups in education: American Association of School Administrators, NEA, Council of Chief State School Officers, National School Boards Association, National Association of State School Boards, and National Congress of Parents and Teachers. Most studies show that legislators view the PTA as a useful friend but not a very bothersome enemy. In effect, the values of the PTA leadership and the school professionals are similar; as a consequence, the PTA does not sponsor many high conflict-oriented demands facing school policymakers. However, it can produce many letters to legislators on major education issues.

Professionally oriented interest groups also exist among numerous organizations that embrace education as a secondary concern, for example, the League of Women Voters and the American Association of University Women. These groups promote general social improvements, some of which touch on school programs and processes. They usually try to influence the legislature conversion process for education only when the members are deeply and widely concerned about a particular aspect of school policy. This condition occurs rarely, however, such as when the state constitution for education is revised or vouchers are on the ballot. Like the PTA, these are non-issue-specific groups that provide support for the ongoing system and so inject little conflict into it. They also constitute a resource for decision makers in times of crisis. They are losing active members as more women are working full or part time, leaving less time for community activity.

Transcendental Groups

Several kinds of interest groups see the schools as a means to ends that transcend the schools, such as reducing the tax burden, eradicating Communism, and so on. Around the turn of the last century, taxpayer organizations began to mold support for the elimination of "wasteful" public spending. Of particular interest is the finding that taxpayer organizations have been *supporters*, as well as opponents, of increased tax support—depending on the tax source. They are strongly opposed to local property taxes, but on occasion will support increases in sales or income taxes.

The recent involvement of the prestigious Business Roundtable, representing the chief executive officers of the nation's 201 largest corporations, is potentially of great importance. The Roundtable has committed itself to supporting the continuance of the federal law No Child Left Behind. Moreover, a group of major corporations will each adopt a state and work to reform its schools.

The corporations in each of these states plan to work closely with the governors and other political leaders in achieving common goals concerning school improvement and reform. Seven major business groups created the Business Coalition for Education Reform with the purpose of working "to elevate the dialogue on the need for changes in education policies at the national, state and local levels. . . ." The Coalition includes the Committee for Economic Development, Business Roundtable, U.S. Chamber of Commerce, National Association of Manufacturers, Conference Board, American Business Conference, and U.S. Hispanic Chamber of Commerce.

Relationships between these business players and the traditional leaders of education are not yet well formed. There is understandable tension, ambiguity, and uncertainty among all parties. It is much too early to assess such long-range business interventions, but the mere initiation of national efforts reflects a seriousness of purpose that should not be underestimated.

Conservative Christian Groups: Structure and Organization

Distinct from those whose main interest is material are those whose concern is the moral instruction in schools, which may include banning "immoral" course content.[18] The educational function of moral indoctrination dates from our schools' colonial origins. Concern for religious instruction has not disappeared either, as seen in the continuing outcry against, and disobedience of, Supreme Court decisions banning Bible reading and school prayers. The main focus of these groups is to guard orthodox values. Their support of the schools is secondary to their concern for maintaining certain community norms. The school is only one of many institutions whose moral sanctity must be protected against subversion or direct challenge.

The Christian Right began as a social movement, but now is a set of interlocking interest groups.[19] Political influence varies from group to group. Focus on the Family is the largest group, with a mailing list of approximately 4 million and an annual budget of $90 million.[20] In the mid-1990s the Christian Coalition had between 400,000 and 450,000 members in 872 chapters across all fifty states and an annual budget of approximately $12 million.[21] Christian Coalition membership and revenues have declined in the last few years. Citizens for Excellence in Education (CEE) has a somewhat smaller membership of 210,000, although it has 1,685 local chapters and church-based Public School Awareness Committees throughout the country.[22] Concerned Women for America claims an annual budget of $10 million, with 600,000 members in 800 chapters.[23]

The organizational structure of these groups is national, with extensive state and local chapters. Observed Reverend Pat Robertson, founder of the Christian Coalition, "We're grassroots all the way, with tremendous autonomy in the states. . . . We're training people to be leaders on their own."[24] This grassroots activity has been focused largely in rural areas or in small towns and cities, but the national leadership plays a very active role in local activities, providing literature, training manuals, legal advice, and speakers.[25] A more critical observer of the conservative Christian groups draws a tighter connection between the national and local chapters, noting "the soldiers in these battles are the local residents, but the generals are from national organizations."[26]

While all of the major Christian groups have chapters throughout the country, there seems to be some informal geographic division between them. The Christian Coalition has a strong national presence, while the Eagle Forum is concentrated in the Midwest, and CEE and Focus on the Family are more heavily represented in the West. The Christian Right encompasses mass media networks, think tanks, Bible colleges, and graduate schools.

In addition to geographic division, there has also been some suggestion that an "unspoken division of labor or . . . specialization" exists among the major Christian organizations.[27] While these groups often speak on the same issues, particularly educational issues, each does appear to specialize to some degree. Focus on the Family, for example, concentrates particularly on family solidarity and child rearing. Concerned Women for America emphasizes the traditional role of women. The Eagle Forum frequently focuses on sex education, while CEE is concerned with all aspects of public education.

Over the last several years, there have been changes in the targets and strategies used by conservative Christian groups to promote their agendas. Challenges to the public schools used to come from parents, who targeted specific books to which they objected. In the 1990s the movement shifted toward nationally orchestrated challenges of instructional programs and methods, textbook series, and restructuring efforts.[28] Christian organizations employ strategies that combine "up-to-the-minute technology with pinpoint targeting of school districts, church congregations, and specific local issues."[29] These strategies can be grouped into three categories: targeting school boards; direct contact through radio programs, pamphlets, and mailings; and legislation and litigation.

The most aggressive strategy employed by the conservative Christian groups has been influencing school boards throughout the country. This has been a strategy for the Christian Coalition and CEE. School board elections traditionally have low voter participation and limited media coverage, making it easier for groups to organize an effective campaign.[30] As one observer noted, the leaders of the national Christian organizations "know that a few hundred votes can decide almost any school board contest, and they mean to empty their churches to get them."[31] In addition to low voter turnout, election to a seat on the school board is often seen as a good way to enter the formal political system. Finally, Christian groups have turned to school boards because of limited success with other strategies, especially litigation. In most instances, the courts have upheld school board decisions and policies, whether in defending or restricting instructional programs. Because of this "judicial deference" to school boards, the conservative Christian groups have focused their efforts on influencing school board elections and policies.[32]

National organizations provide candidates with extensive "how-to" materials. CEE has published a guidebook entitled "How to Elect Christians to Public Office," which has been described as the "war manual" for the CEE movement.[33] Other groups have also distributed information about how to hide one's agenda, and how to talk to reporters. After gaining control of local school boards, Christian conservatives aggressively push their agendas, challenging programs and curricula that they find objectionable.[34] For example, in Vista, California, the fundamentalist Christian-controlled school board pushed to have creation science included in district science curricula. Because of extreme teacher opposition, though, the board settled for including this topic in the humanities program. The same board dismantled the district's sex education programs. In Round Rock, Texas, the conservative Christian-controlled school board lifted a ban on prayer during graduation ceremonies. And in Lake County, Florida, the conservative Christian-controlled school board canceled plans to open a Head Start program because it felt that "the government should not be offering services that families should . . . provid[e] to their young . . . [and] that young children should stay home with their mothers."[35]

In addition to attempting to influence policies and gain control of school boards, the national conservative Christian groups have employed the more traditional strategies of direct contact through media to further their agenda. These groups use radio extensively to communicate with members and others sympathetic to their causes. Focus on the Family, for example, produces ten radio shows broadcast on thousands of radio stations around the world.[36] Each of the other major organizations have at least one radio program.

All of the major organizations publish newsletters and pamphlets, which include "warning signs" of objectionable curricula as well as courses of action that can be taken to oppose specific programs or texts.[37] Focus on the Family publishes eleven magazines, targeted at specific groups such as doctors, teachers, and single parents.[38] Other organizations publish brochures and curriculum guides designed to convince parents of the "dangers" of particular instructional materials. Additionally, conservative Christian groups distribute books and fax weekly church bulletin fillers and suggested sermon topics to thousands of pastors.[39] These groups carefully manage their requests for information in order to build up their mailing lists, which are their main avenues for dissemination of much of this material.

Another strategy employed by conservative Christian organizations to advance their agendas is the use of legislation and litigation.[40] These groups have supported legislative efforts including choice and voucher plans, and pupil protection acts that would require parental approval of all textbooks, materials, and instructional methods. Conservative Christian groups have also supported home-schooling bills, which would require public schools to provide services and materials to educate children at home. The political influence of the Christian Right will wax and wane depending on their ability to coalesce. Individual groups will fade in or out, but the Christian Right is an enduring interest group. [41]

George Bush made the Christian Right a key part of his 2004 electoral coalition. In his first term, President Bush threw his support to several issues supported by the Christian Right. By creating a special office for private school concerns and supporting state choice programs in the Supreme Court, Bush backed voucher and charter school reforms. In using his office to provide federal aid to church programs for the poor, Bush endorsed a closer affinity of state and church than had been the norm in the last half-century.

Crisis Interest Groups

Despite the broad variety of interest groups in public education, not all interests or values show up in organized groups. Existing groups may choose not to carry their demands to school officials. Feeling the urge to impress their values on school policies, they create ad hoc and temporary organizations. Attempts by schools to change high school tracking patterns, particularly for advanced placements, can galvanize a new opposition group.[42] In a northeastern suburb two interest groups developed in one year and then dissolved after the school board elections.[43] One was a "taxpayers association," formed to defeat three board members and cut back school expenditures. The superintendent countered with a group called Save Our Schools in order to reelect the incumbent board members and pass the budget. Both groups conveyed their special values and demands in a political system where organized groups had not been important. Quickly formed, they just as quickly faded.

Testing Agencies, Foundations, and Think Tanks

Several groups that do not fit the usual idea of an interest group nevertheless do influence local schooling based on national and professional norms. Although this country does not have a system of national exams, we do have several private national testing agencies. The most important are ACT in Iowa and Educational Testing Service in Princeton, New Jersey. Most American schools do not have a choice in whether to provide their best students with courses in most of the subjects covered by college admissions exams. Because high school administrators want their students to score well on these exams, they do not have absolute flexibility to teach what they want. Such external constraints reflect value judgments on school quality urged in the interest of professionalism. This force of professionalism we earlier argued may be a more powerful external constraint on local school policy than are local demands or federal laws.

Further, while private philanthropic foundations are not thought of as interest groups, they do, however, exercise a major influence on curriculum reform, teacher training, testing, finance, facility design, educational television, and so on. Foundations have also used their grants to generate stress over value concerns. For example, foundations financed the development of instruments to assess national achievement in education, now called the National Assessment of Education Progress. This effort helped create a political issue that pitted those who opposed national testing against those wanting increased accountability by professional educators.[44] As a result, local school boards, state departments of education, and the United States Congress had to make a decision on whether to permit national assessment. The questions and approaches in the approved assessment represented many compromises, including a decision *not* to include local test comparisons.

A foundation does not act like a conventional interest group by seeking access to public policymakers and then advocating its case for public support. But, by using grants to fund policy studies or to start experiments and demonstration projects (often reflecting certain value orientations), foundations make value conflicts more visible. The Gates Foundation is providing hundreds of millions of dollars to create small secondary schools. Then this foundation effort can create a new demand that provides interest groups with an issue. Groups may modify the content of the demand as they transmit it to the school board or state legislator, but the foundations need interest groups in order to reach the political authorities through collective pressure.

Foundations have played a major role in debates about the

quality of education, in part through the funding of education policy research.[45] Currently, right-of-center foundations have helped create state-based think tanks that advocate choice, for example, Independence Institute in Colorado, Mackinac Institute in Michigan, and Pioneer Institute in Massachusetts. The Carnegie Corporation funded a major report calling for a national standards board to certify outstanding teachers. Carnegie then provided money to many interest groups and academies to promote this concept. Indeed, most major education reform reports from outside of government involve foundation subsidies.

National and state think tanks provide a larger marketplace of ideas about school reform. These ideas take root when sympathetic politicians are elected. The American Enterprise Institute, Cato, and Heritage Foundation have more influence when Republicans control Washington. The Economic Policy Institute, Progressive Policy Institute, and Brookings do better during Democratic eras. Think tanks house policy entrepreneurs who market novel reform approaches.

THE MEDIA AND SCHOOL POLITICS

Until recently, the political impact of media communication was little studied in political science. Primarily, media have been seen as something that politicians manipulated for their own ends. In recent decades, however, political scientists believe that the media themselves alter the democratic process, particularly in elections and policymaking, by affecting the information from which citizens make political decisions. What is striking is the absence of research within the study of politics of education concerning media impact on school politics, even though school administrators know the political problems that the media cause.

Political studies of the media have centered around the classic research questions of political scientist Harold Lassell that focus on, *"Who says what to whom with what effect?"* That is, focus is on the institution of the media, on media content, on audiences, and on their consequences for citizens. Journalists—electronic or print—summarize, refine, and alter what they learn in order to make it suitable for their audiences to hear or read—

and do so for a profit. However, the content of these choices
has consequences for shaping values and interests of audiences
who listen to the messages. What they hear or see shapes their
grasp of the world outside, including schools.

Some studies have demonstrated that there is a concentrated
ownership and control of the media, print or electronic.[46] Others have focused on the political orientation of media employees (often criticized as "liberal"), or on how they translate news
in a general way (often viewing politics as a "horse race" or essentially conflict-based).[47] Government operations, while the source
of great attention, are often seen as grounds for a battle rather
than for cooperation. That relationship of media and government is becoming increasingly close and increasingly less neutral. In effect, media sources, such as talk radio, take on a political
orientation in which their previous norm of neutrality or "objec-
tivity" is not always followed. And this focus on conflict and cynicism
increasingly dominates media reports on education.

The influence of the media on the political system has been
given much attention in political science—but very little of this
looks at local issues. Research on the media's effects on politics
is most often found in studies of voting. Television coverage is a
main source of information on choices for the presidency, but
much media trivialize policy discussions and view government as
arenas of conflicting interests. Increasingly "negative" campaigning via television dominates electoral campaigns at all levels, so
contact between voter and candidate is filtered through media.[48]

Also, the media have an impact on school government—an
audience itself. Research suggests that the media influence is
most often employed in generating clues about the policy environment, which makes the media one of those helping to set
the policy agenda of government. Governments also affect the
media by "managing" the news in order to shape media coverage and hence public views of school policy, but the linkage is
complex and often confused.[49] The First Amendment protects
the media against government censorship, of course, but Federal Communications Commission regulation also affects the use
of wave lengths and sometimes media content.

Surrounding all this has been the increasing concern for the
media's responsibility in a democracy. Maybe of more impor-

tance is the problem that triviality and conflict that overwhelm media coverage can distort citizens' perceptions of events.

SUMMARY

This chapter has set out the institutions having large interests in school policy and governance. At each level of American government, these institutions proclaim and pressure their views about schools' organization, finances, curricula, and instruction. Each group's actions illustrate one part of the dynamics of making and overseeing school policies. However, in combination, these institutions reflect the theoretical framework of this book with their focus on policy initiation and implementation that we term political inputs. Yet there is another major source of inputs, namely, the citizens, to whom we turn next.

NOTES

1. See writings by Catherine Marshall, Douglas Mitchell, and Frederick Wirt in *Culture and Education Policy in the American States* (New York: Falmer, 1989); a symposium on "State Politics of Education," in *Peabody Journal of Education* 62–64 (1985): 7–1154; and *Alternative State Policy Mechanisms for Pursuing Educational Quality, Equity, Efficiency, and Choice Goals* (Washington, D.C.: Office of Instructional Research and Improvement, U.S. Department of Education, 1986), chap. V; following quotations are from this source.

2. William Boyd, "The Public, the Professionals, and Education Policy Making: Who Governs?" *Teachers College Record* 77 (1976): 539–77. For a view on the influence of conservatives, see Michael W. Apple, *Official Knowledge* (New York: Routlege, 1999).

3. James Cibulka, "The Changing Role of Interest Groups in Education," *Educational Policy* 15 (March 2001): 15.

4. Mancur Olson, *The Logic of Collective Action* (New York: Schocken, 1965). See also Michael Mintrom, *Policy Entrepreneurs and School Choice* (Washington, D.C.: Georgetown University, 1999).

5. Robert Salisbury, "An Exchange Theory of Interest Groups," *Midwest Journal of Political Science* 13 (1969): 1–32. For a revision, see Theda Skocpol, "Associations Without Members," *American Prospect* 5 (August 1999): 66–73.

6. Terry Moe, *The Organization of Interests* (Chicago: University of Chicago Press, 1980). For a market theory analysis, see Michael Hayes, *Lobbyists and Legislators* (New Brunswick, N.J.: Rutgers, 1981).

7. See Marshall et al., *Culture and Education Policy.*

8. See Charles Kerchner, Julia Koppich, and Joseph Weeres, *United Mind Workers: Unions and Teaching in the Knowledge Society* (San Francisco: Jossey-Bass, 1997).

9. See Myron Lieberman, *The Teacher Unions* (New York: Free Press, 1997).

10. Ibid.

11. See Kerchner, Koppich, and Weeres, *United Mind Workers.*

12. AFT publishes a monthly journal, *American Teacher,* that provides current information on AFT policy directions.

13. Campaign contributions tallied by Common Cause. See also National Education Association, *Status of American Public School Teachers* (Washington, D.C.: National Education Association, 1997).

14. For a thorough review in schools, see articles in Hanne Mawhinney, ed., "Interest Groups in United States Education," *Educational* Policy 15: 1 (January and March 2001). William P. Browne, *Groups, Interests, and U.S. Public Policy* (Washington, D.C.: Georgetown University Press, 1998); Kevin W. Hula, *Lobbying Together* (Washington, D.C.: Georgetown University Press, 1998).

15. Robert Putnam, *Bowling Alone: The Collapse and Revival of American Community* (New York: Simon and Schuster, 2000).

16. Ibid.

17. Ibid.

18. The distinction offered here borders on that of the "sacred and secular communities" analyzed in Laurence Iannaccone and Frank W. Lutz, *Politics, Powers and Policy: The Governing of Local School Districts* (Columbus, Ohio: Charles E. Merrill, 1970).

19. F. Clarkson and S. Porteous, *Challenging the Christian Right: The Activists' Handbook* (Great Barrington, Mass.: Institute for First American Studies, 1993).

20. S. Roberts, D. Friedman, and T. Gest, "The Heavy Hitter," *U.S. News and World Report* 118 (1995): 34, 39; U.S. Newswire, "Religious Right Campaign Assaults Religious Freedom in America; New ADL Book Details Strategy, Tactics, Personalities," June 9, 1994.

21. M. M. Deckman, *School Board Battles: The Christian Right in Local Politics* (Washington, D.C.: Georgetown University, 2004). Martha McCarthy, "Challenges to the Public School Curriculum: New Targets and Strategies," *Phi Delta Kappan* 75 (1993): 55–60; George Kaplan, "Shotgun Wedding: Notes on Public Education's Encounter with the New Christian Right," *Phi Delta Kappan* 75 (1994): 11–12; L. Pappano and A. Sessler, "New Right Joins Fight Over Schools Across State," *The Boston Globe,* October 10, 1993; Carolyn D. Herrington, "Religion, Public Schools, and Hyperpluralism," *Journal of Education Policy,* 2001.

22. J. Impoco, "Separating Church and School," *U.S. News and World Report* 118 (1995): 30; Kaplan, "Shotgun Wedding."

23. Clarkson and Porteous, *Challenging the Christian Right.*

24. ABC Nightline, "God and the Grassroots," November 4, 1993.

25. Pappano and Sessler, "New Right Joins Fight."

26. E. Shogren and D. Frantz, "Schools Boards Become the Religious Right's New Pulpit," *Los Angeles Times*, December 10, 1993, A1. See also Kaplan, "Shotgun Wedding."

27. Kaplan, "Shotgun Wedding," 4.

28. For a synthesis of these concerns see Herrington, "Religion, Public Schools, and Hyperpluralism."

29. Kaplan, "Shotgun Wedding," 9.

30. Z. Arocha, "The Religious Right's March into Public Governance," *School Administrator* 50 (1993): 8–15.

31. Kaplan, "Shotgun Wedding," 10.

32. Diane Ravitch, *The Language Police* (New York: Knopf, 2003).

33. Shogren and Frantz, "School Boards Become Religious Right's Pulpit."

34. Tom Toch and K. Glastris, "Who's Minding the Schools?" *U.S. News and World Report* 116 (1994): 78.

35. Shogren and Frantz, "School Boards Become Religious Right's Pulpit," 1.

36. Roberts, Friedman, and Gest, "The Heavy Hitter."

37. J. Jones, "Targets of the Right," *American School Board Journal* 180 (1993): 22–29.

38. Roberts, Friedman, and Gest, "The Heavy Hitter."

39. Ibid.

40. G. Zahorchak, *The Politics of Outcome-Based Education in Pennsylvania*, unpublished dissertation, Pennsylvania State University, 1994. For a philosophical overview of these issues see James Fraser, *Between Church and State* (New York: St. Martins Press, 1999).

41. See Catherine A. Lugg, "The Christian Right," *Educational Policy* 15: 1(March 2001): 41-57. An overview of these groups is in John C. Green, Mark J. Rozell, and Clyde Wilcox, eds., *Prayers in the Precincts* (Washington, D.C.: Georgetown University Press, 2000).

42. Tom Loveless, *The Tracking Wars* (Washington, D.C.: Brookings, 1999).

43. Lesley Browder, "A Suburban School Superintendent Plays Politics," in Michael Kirst, ed., *The Politics of Education at the Local, State, and Federal Level* (Richmond, Calif.: McCutchan, 1970).

44. Robert Rothman, *Measuring Up* (San Francisco: Jossey-Bass, 1995).

45. See Ellen Lagemann, *The Politics of Knowledge* (Chicago: University of Chicago Press, 1989). For the political use of education research see E. Vance Randall, Bruce Cooper, and Steven Hite, "Understanding the Politics of Research in Education," in *Educational Policy* 13: 1 (January 1999): 7–22. A muckracking view of foundation activities is in Mark Dowie, *American Foundations: An Investigative History* (Cambridge, Mass.: MIT Press, 2001).

46. Ben Bagdikian, *The Media Monopoly* (Boston: Beacon, 2000).

47. Shanto Jyengar and Richard Reeves, eds., *Do the Media Govern?* (Thousand Oaks, Calif.: Sage, 1997).

48. W. Lance Bennett, *The Politics of Illusion* (White Plains, N.Y.: Longman, 1998).

49. James Fallows, *Breaking the News: How the Media Undermine American Democracy* (New York: Random House, 1997); Joel S. Spring, *Political Agendas for Education* (Mahwah, N.J.: Erlbaum, 2002).

4

School Policy Access:
Elections and Referenda

MODES OF CITIZEN POLITICAL CONTROL

Today's school turbulence finds many groups getting into policymaking, as the preceding chapter described. However, more direct access occurs when citizens participate through elections. Although many demands originate outside the political system, some enter it, as Easton notes, when they "are voiced as proposals for decision and action on the part of the authorities."[1] Some demands do not enter the political system, however, for at least two reasons. They may not be valued highly by society (e.g., deregulation of marijuana), or they lack sufficient resources to move the system to act adequately (e.g., the poor).

Public preferences have concerned school professionals long before recent turbulent times. Given that citizens vote on school officials and finances, unprecedented in democratic nations, it is not surprising that school officials have long sought to influence the public.[2] At the turn of the last century, reformers tried to depoliticize education by substituting nonpartisan for partisan elections, and election at large for election by ward.

Popular participation in school policymaking has traditionally taken two forms—election of officials and referenda on issues. Both operate independently of political parties. Contrary to popular impression, political parties at the *national* level have sought successfully to serve as a link between citizens and school policy.[3]

Consequently, direct and indirect popular control still exist. Directly, there is the widespread practice of electing school boards at the local level and boards and superintendents at the state level. Indirectly, control exists in the election of state legislators, executives, and judges, whose broad responsibilities include authority over many aspects of public education. In those elections, then, policymakers must operate within popularly derived limits that are vague, but elected officials know they do exist.

THE ARROYOS OF SCHOOL BOARD ELECTIONS

Although 93 percent of local school boards in this country are elective, the politics of these elections was a great unknown until the 1970s.[4] We know that these officials, five to seven on a board, almost always seek their three- or four-year terms on a nonpartisan ballot. We also know that the board appoints a superintendent, usually professionally trained, who operates under its general policy guides and who may also be removed by it. In the usual community, the theory of democratic control makes the board member a pivot between community demands and school operations. First we must see whether the election of board members provides popular inputs to the school political system. Some widespread general impressions about this interaction existed, but recent studies have provided a more highly complex picture of school board representation.

The Unknown Qualities of Board Elections

What was once known about boards raised more questions than it settled. One clear point remains, that most *school board elections have little voter turnout* (from about 10 to 20 percent), even less than that for other government offices. Since most board members do not live in big cities, three-fourths of school board members spent less than $1,000 to win. The reasons for low turnout are not clear. Is it because of the nonpartisan myth of school politics or because school board elections are held in off years, and at primary dates when turnout is low for all contests? Eighty-nine percent of board members are elected on nonpartisan ballots. Less than half of the elections do not coincide with other national or state elections. If there is variation in the degree of citizen participation in different states or cities, what accounts for it? Does the mere requirement of nonpartisanship preclude political parties from playing a direct role, as they actually do in Detroit, or do voters' party identifications influence their choices, as they do in some city council races? Does low turnout benefit some groups but not others? That is, might board elections more often represent the weight of Republicans—who go to the polls more often than Democrats—and consequently more often represent the viewpoint of groups attracted to the GOP?

It is clear, though, that campaigning in school contests is limited, candidate visibility low, and the contest rarely based on specific policies. (See Table 4.1.) Is this again attributable to the nonpartisan myth, which requires participants to act as if they were not engaging in political acts? Or is it due to the lack of highly visible issues that might stimulate popular interest? Under what conditions do election contests become visible and the public highly participant? For example, in 2003 a school board candidate in San Diego spent over $250,000 to unseat her opponent; one business group raised over $540,000 for all their San Diego endorsed board candidates. But just 15.5 percent of board members describe elections as "very competitive." Further, although most boards are elected, a minority in significant American cities are appointed. What difference does this make in representative roles? Is there any difference in policy orientation under the two methods; if so, can we trace such differences directly to the methods? A clue that this difference has policy consequences is suggested by the earlier finding that boards immune from elections were somewhat more able to move toward school desegregation than elected boards.[5]

Recruitment: Few Are Called, Fewer Chosen

In any political system, leaders must be recruited to fill the constitutional positions, but this process is not random. Rather, selection is in harmony with the dominant values of the larger

Table 4.1

Elections, Structure, and Issues Reported by Board Members, 2003

ELECTIONS

One-half above and below 50,000 students
Ninety-six percent respondents elected
Over one-half elected in large districts (others appointed)
Elected on nonpartisan ballot (89 percent)
Greater voter turnout if election is "high stakes" in candidates' judgments
Spent about $1,000 to win, but $10,000 in big districts
Source of funds? Two-thirds used personal wealth and friends' donations;
less from teacher unions or business
No incumbent defeated in one-half board elections since 1997
Judged district to be only "occasionally competitive"
Many groups involved in elections, but varies with district size

BOARD STRUCTURE

Board size from five to eight in 80 percent of districts; most with four-year
term
Two-thirds report no salary for service
Board member serves on about five subcommittees

BOARD ISSUES

Spends about twenty-five hours per month on board service
Ninety-four percent of boards provide training for members
Biggest issue before board is funding
Charter school issue appears in 16 percent of small versus 48 percent of
biggest districts

Source: Abstracted from Frederick Hess and David Leal, "School House
Politics: Expenditures, Interests, and Competition in School Board Elec-
tions," paper prepared for the conference on School Board Politics,
Harvard University, October 15–17, 2003.

system, just as the selection of kings and presidents tells us much
about the values of their respective societies.[6] Also, the process
by which a mass of citizens selects a few decision makers involves
winnowing away those who do not meet the dominant values.
Successful recruitment must be followed by effective role learning in the new board position of authority.

Recruitment in North American school elections is a process
of many being excluded, few being called to office, and even
fewer becoming leaders.[7] Being recruited comes from possessing

political opportunities, some formal, some practical. There is always an unequal distribution of these opportunities, a fact that provides a first screening of the total population. Formally, the legal code may set down minimum requirements—being a qualified voter, a district representative—but clearly these screen out from the enormous numbers only those who do not qualify to vote. Practically, eligibility is screened by social status, political resources (the more eligible have more of these), age, and gender (men get elected more, but less so today). The fact that such opportunities are structured in society, some having many and many having few, means that most citizens are filtered out of the recruitment process.

Note the results of this process found in the social composition of school boards. When the Progressive reforms of nonpartisanship in school matters began across the nation after 1900, the large working-class membership by the 1920s had almost disappeared from school boards, and white middle-class members dominated everywhere. Moreover, most of these members were male, married with children in the public schools, and active in the community. From the landmark study by Counts in 1927 to a replication by the National School Boards Association decades later, all the research substantiates this finding, but the percentage of female members has increased substantially in the last fifty years.[8] A test of the link between representation and the possession of resources appears in the case of African Americans.[9] Black representation on the 168 big-city boards was smaller than their resources (i.e., numbers, money, organization); at-large election systems effectively widened the gap between resources and board seats.[9]

A 2002 poll of boards by the National School Boards Association (see Table 4.2) found that members' first priority was not student achievement—despite the national furor over that topic—but rather ways to evaluate the superintendent's performance; in between the two were concerns with teachers, safety, and management. In short, despite all the call for strengthening boards, today most boards are doing pretty much what they had done in the past. Twenty-five percent of school board members say they live in a small town and 16 percent live in a rural area. Consequently, the use of district size in Table 4.2 is useful for interpretation.

Table 4.2
Leading School Board Concerns

Percentage Terming Issue One of "Significant" or "Moderate" Concern

	Large Districts (25,000+)	Medium Districts (5,000–24,999)	Small Districts (less than 5,000)	All Districts
Budget/funding	100.0	98.7	96.0	97.6
Student achievement	98.9	98.0	96.4	97.2
Special education	93.3	93.4	85.2	88.1
Improving educational technology	84.3	90.7	85.9	87.5
Teacher quality	91.2	88.2	84.9	86.8
Parental support/interest	88.9	81.0	77.3	79.8
Regulation	79.3	76.6	75.6	76.7
Drug/alcohol use	82.2	81.3	69.4	75.4
Discipline	81.3	78.4	68.8	73.7
Teacher shortages	95.6	76.9	65.3	73.2
Overcrowded schools	76.9	71.0	46.3	59.5
Total Districts	*	*	*	*

Source: Frederick Hess and David Leal, "School House Politics: Expenditures, Interests, and Competition in School Board Elections," paper prepared for the conference on School Board Politics, Harvard University, October 15–17, 2003.

Table 4.3
Political Views of Board Members

	Large Districts (25,000+)	Medium Districts (5,000–24,999)	Small (less than 5,000)	All Districts
Liberal	18.7%	18.7%	12.9%	15.9%
Moderate	51.6%	46.2%	41.4%	44.5%
Conservative	24.2%	32.8%	40.9%	35.7%
None of the above	5.5%	2.3%	4.7%	3.9%
Total Districts	91	305	379	775

Source: Frederick Hess and David Leal, "School House Politics: Expenditures, Interests, and Competition in School Board Elections," paper prepared for the conference on School Board Politics, Harvard University, October 15–17, 2003.

Table 4.4
Length of Board Service

	Large Districts (25,000+)	Medium Districts (5,000–24,999)	Small Districts (less than 5,000)	All Districts
Less than two years	9.6%	8.7%	12.4%	10.6%
Two to five years	39.8%	42.3%	40.2%	41.0%
Six to ten years	32.5%	30.7%	29.4%	30.2%
More than ten years	18.1%	18.3%	18.0%	18.1%
Total Districts	83	300	378	761

Source: Frederick Hess and David Leal, "School House Politics: Expenditures, Interests, and Competition in School Board Elections," paper prepared for the conference on School Board Politics, Harvard University, October 15–17, 2003.

A 2003 sample of winning candidates by the National School Boards Association provides a fuller picture of political philosophy and context of service, seen in Tables 4.3 and 4.4.

There are other interesting findings from this survey. A substantial majority (more than 56 percent) are elected at large, while 41 percent (mostly from large urban districts) are elected by subdistrict. If campaigns are "high stakes," then funding comes less from business and teachers, and more from personal or friends' wealth. Finally, the charter school issue, discussed more fully in Chapter 14, looms large in some big districts, but much less in small ones. In the board candidate recruitment stages the eligibility processes of our democratic system leave out a vast majority of Americans who cannot or will not seek school board office—or who simply don't care for the game.

But in the waves of reforms in the 1990s, advocates of these new ideas emerged in local board elections. They advocated choice, charters, curricular changes, and family values. What has emerged in the recent turbulence over school board elections has been another force of instability affecting the role of the superintendent. That change may account for the reduced tenure of this office in some cities, or for the increased superintendent effort at public relations in the community. Quite common have been superintendents elected by one board found shortly thereafter that a new board emerges—often with different agendas. Often too, such board changes precede changes in superintendents. That increased turbulence from the board also contributes to the new superintendent's role, not the "benevolent autocrat" of many years ago, but working in a "political" context with others who are also empowered.

Time and again, what emerges from board elections is that they are little-used channels for political change. Like arroyos in the Southwest, only rarely does intense turmoil surge through these channels. Certain occasions can, however, have the effect of flash floods through desert courses—enormous conflict followed by altered features in the immediate environment. Much more often, however, these election campaigns offer only slight variations in ideology or policy orientation, and voting for this office, if nonpartisan, depresses turnout. These conditions make the democratic model of informed citizen choice between significant policy options more a pleasant fiction than a hard fact. A national study of school boards summarized the issue:

> I found it compelling to read how much the public believes in the need for school boards, how much it remains attached to the concept of grass-roots educational self-governance. But it was equally disturbing to note, from this report, that the same public evidences essential illiteracy about the actual role and activities of school boards. Moreover, the public turns out in appallingly thin numbers to vote for the school boards it otherwise believes to be so essential. We are left with the disturbing question: If the school boards' popular constituency misperceives their role and doesn't care enough to exercise its franchise in their selection, how fully or forcefully will the boards *ever* be able to function?[10]

Teacher Unions and Election Outcomes

While the school board has recently generated more interest, there has been less scholarly attention to the role of teacher unions in local elections and school policymaking. A conventional view is that different groups interact to produce education policy; a concept called pluralism. That concept would apply if one thought of local board elections and policymaking as the result of interactions of a number of stakeholders, and no one group dominated. However, what would be the case if one group did? If business, farmers, ethnic constituents, or teacher and other employee unions dominated, then something other than democracy would exist. We are a long way from substantiating such a dominant employee mode model, partly due to the lack of scholarly research about the operations of local school politics.

However, quite recently that subject has come to the attention of scholars who ask questions about "schoolhouse politics." Does money shape election outcomes in local school contests? Does one group dominate local school decisions? Does the form of election shape the kind of persons elected who later have consequences for different policies? To answer such questions, there is a need for large voting and campaign data sets to explore theories.

Unions and Electoral Success. A study by Terry Moe of the perceptions of teacher unions by 504 school board candidates in 250 school districts in California is illuminating.[11] The author's concern is with the potential power of teacher unions that other scholars think has "emerged as the single most powerful interest group in the nation, outdistancing bankers, insurance companies, trial lawyers, farm groups, and all others."[12]

The California research supports that judgment of enhanced teacher power, but it also notes that such power varies across local contexts; it is not omnipresent in thousands of local school elections. Briefly, some of the findings about candidate perceptions of local power are useful:

1. The importance of the unions grows with the size of the district.
2. School board electoral competitiveness is low in small- and middle-size districts, but very high in the largest districts.
3. Candidates, rating the power of other local groups, find unions to be the largest; Moe concludes that "pluralism here is clearly entitled in favor of one special interest group—the teacher union."
4. However, that power is constrained by party and ideology (termed "political culture"). Thus, union interests are more easily achieved when the district is Democratic and liberal. The reverse is true in Republican and conservative districts. Even in the latter, though, unions can win some school board contests.

5. However, 76 percent of union-endorsed candidates win, regardless of the partisanship of a district.
6. Moreover, a vast majority of candidates (60 percent) are positive about collective bargaining, even within Republican districts, but then differ on specific aspects of its use.
7. Besides partisanship, there is another constraint on union power, the incumbency of candidates.

In short, the reputation of unions is reported as substantial in California, but even then its power is conditioned by several factors. Finally, Moe's view is that any notion of a pluralist democracy in school politics is unreal, because there is dominant power resting with the teacher unions.

Policy Consequences of Differing Elections. As we will see shortly, political scientists have learned that differing electoral arrangements have different consequences for policy and constituents. However, does that apply to little-studied aspects of school board elections? That is, do representatives from at-large or district (ward) systems have different effects on policies and students? A recent study by two political scientists of over one thousand Texas districts focused on Hispanic board members and the consequences for their students.[13]

The authors used those two systems of representation against two types of constituencies: (1) minority students whose group is a minority in the district and (2) minority students whose group is a majority in the district. Their findings are useful:

1. When the Hispanics are a minority in the whole district, at-large school board elections led to fewer Hispanic members on the boards. Fewer Hispanic board members is also associated with subsequent board policies, such as less hiring of Hispanic administrators and teachers. Other research shows that with at-large electoral structures, Hispanic students are placed mostly in low-status classes and less in gifted classes. They are most likely disciplined, fail standardized tests, drop out or do not graduate, and score lower on College Board examinations.

2. However, when Hispanics are a majority in the district, even with the at-large system, the Hispanics elected use the power to reverse these hiring policies and student results. The use of the district (ward) system, however, favored Hispanic employment even more. As the analysts conclude, "The biases of election structure, therefore, reverberate throughout the entire educational system and create additional biases."

Money and Board Elections. New interest in school board elections arose from local presence of choice reforms, "civic capacity," and special groups like unions, new businesses, minorities, and the Christian Right. Little studied, however, is the role of money in board elections. That is a curious omission given the historic linkage of money and elections reported in political science studies. However, recently a mail poll by political scientists, using a national sample of over eight hundred boards elections, matched to district-level census data, was carried out with assistance from the National School Boards Association. The questions addressed were: how much was spent, what interests supplied money, what interests were active in the campaigns, and how competitive were these elections.[14] Regression analyses of the findings supported these conclusions:

1. Most board elections involve minimal campaign spending: few receive even one-quarter of their funds from teacher unions or business.
2. Candidates saw neither religious nor race-based groups as very active in board elections.
3. Candidates, comparing the power of local groups, find unions the largest. If size is equated with power in democracies, it favors unions in school politics.
4. Growth in the size of districts was associated with more teacher union activity and electoral competitiveness.

In summary of the recent reports, as one analyst noted, then, "It is a mistake to imagine that unions are unilateral actors in board elections or that their influence is unfettered by context. . . . [However, they] are clearly the most significant interest in school district elections." Also, the analysts find that the larger the district, the greater union influence is in such elections.[15]

For some, that conclusion weakens any notion of a pluralist context to local school decision making. However, some other evidence from school board members is that this judgment is *not* a major matter in their understanding of local politics. They note the limiting conditions of partisanship and incumbency. Union dominance in big cities, however, looms large in these recent studies. However, in suburbs and farmland, little of this union effort was noticeable or important. The multiple interests of big cities generate much conflict in schools and elsewhere; the city and national media focus on this urban conflict, of course. Outlying the big city, though, where more homogeneity prevails and most districts operate, there are other considerations. There may well be opinions held in common among unions, boards, and citizens, and so a different pattern emerges than in the cities. As with board elections and other school matters, then, local context matters greatly.

Competition and Responsiveness

This pervasive condition is greatly affected by our history that is traced to the nonpartisan reforms begun over a century ago and now commonplace in American local government. Many scholars report that such reforms as nonpartisan ballots and at-large elections actually *lower* electoral school conflict, particularly in metropolitan areas.[16] Research demonstrates that changing elections from at large to subdistrict also changes the behavior of board members. They become oriented more to concerns and allocations for their own subdistrict, rather than to districtwide policy. But subdistrict elections do create more minority winners.

Nonpartisanship has a more qualitative effect on the nature of school elections in both city and rural districts. The nonpartisan approach and at-large elections affect the degree of competition, however one measures it. Is competition measured by whether candidates are fighting over a major change in school policy, by the degree of differences among candidates over a range of policy issues, or by whether they differ about the board's role? None of these attributes of competition increases if there are nonpartisan ballots or at-large elections involved. Partisanship, on the other hand, can increase turnout and competition.

In short, political scientists have found that what applies to nonpartisanship in other aspects of the local political scene holds true for school politics. Such reforms increase the cost of citizen participation, make the bridge between representative and citizen more tenuous, and consequently muffle expression of the full range of political interests within a community. Those constrained citizens who are affected tend to be of lower socioeconomic status, so that governing structures are clearly not value free. Rather, these reforms actually encourage the access and satisfaction of another group, middle-class and higher-status people. The rhetoric of Progressivism a century ago proclaimed the expansion of democracy—"the cure for the evils of democracy is more democracy" was their standard. The reality has been otherwise. Such reforms ensure that—until recently at any rate—the game of school politics was played by a few and mostly by those whom fortune favored. It is not yet clear in the new millennium that the recent criticism of public schooling has changed that judgment.

The citizen-board linkage in elections is not simple; it must be differentiated for different issues, times, and communities.[17] Moreover, expansion of statewide referenda on school issues is an important trend in twenty states that authorize it. A record number of statewide and local initiatives has emerged.[18] In just 2002, twenty of seventy state initiatives focused on change in schools, including eighteen in Oregon; one attempted to ban teaching about homosexuality and another changed teacher compensation. In Michigan and California initiatives tried and failed to create vouchers, in Washington, initiatives increased teacher pay and created smaller classes, and in Arizona and Massachusetts initiatives banned bilingual education. To fight some of these initiatives, the NEA gave its state affiliates $7 million. At the local level in 2003, tax increases for schools were defeated in record numbers as the national economic recession hit hard.

One of the matters that make a difference is status. The exact nature of the status alignments in voting may depend on the particular issue, that is, different policies generate different kinds of politics. Education in American society, however, seems to generate fierce status conflicts between ideologues, who also come into conflict over sex education or science; for example, the current evolution-creationism dispute.[19] A theoretical analysis of various policy politics has yet to be done, but a rich diversity is available in the recent challenges to school systems.

Policy Dissatisfactions and Community Conflict

A theoretical framework is needed to understand that the citizen role in local school policymaking must turn away from a static view of community context. The "dissatisfaction theory," on the other hand, provides a dynamic model of both quiescence and turbulence as sequences in community life.[20] At one point in a community's life, rough agreement will exist among citizens, board, and superintendent on the course of school policy. Citizens are satisfied with what they have, and their participation in such access channels as elections is quite limited because they support the whole school system.

This satisfaction can suddenly break down with growth in the local population that brings newcomers whose policy demands differ from what prevails, but at first these are rejected by the oldtimers. The result is dissatisfaction with existing school policy. A new protest then ensues before the school board, which is now less a reflective council than an arena where advocates for old and new policy views clash with great rancor. Another outlet for dissatisfaction is the channel of elections. Its use by newcomers in time will produce new board members. A new majority then fires the superintendent, and finally the new policymakers act in congruence with newcomers' policy preferences. At that time, citizen participation falls off due to satisfaction with the new system.

The advantage of this theoretical approach is that it captures shifts or sequences that researchers can explore further. The theory is dynamic, as the time quality is central to explaining what occurs. The traditional cross-sectional approach, on the other hand, as in Table 4.1, permits analysis at only one point in time.

Dissatisfaction theory has generated qualitative research in a few communities. A study of Santa Barbara from 1930 to 1980 found that the theory did explain what happened, but it needed to be specified more clearly. That is, all the old board members had to be replaced, the new superintendent had to understand the new mandate, and he or she must be able to express and implement it. Those conditions flow from a realigning election that ends with the voting public's influence evident on new school programs.[21] Similarly, a three-district study over two years, using records and interviews, found that dissatisfaction varied with the object or focus of the feelings. Dissatisfaction with board, superintendent, or both created different outcomes of challenge, as Table 4.6 summarizes. For example, if board and superintendent are a common focus of dissatisfaction, a high chance exists of arena-like council behavior and subsequent board and superintendent turnover. Table 4.6 predicts that the superintendent will be thrown to the wolves if the focus of dissatisfaction is on that person. That theory underlies the reality of an increase in that office's turnover in recent years, as noted later in Chapter 6.

Table 4.5

Policy Dissatisfaction and Political Challenge in Three Districts

| | | Focus of Dissatisfaction | |
Challenge Consequences	School Board	Board and Superintendent	Superintendent
Increased rate of school board member turnover	High	High	Low
Shift to arena-like council behavior	High	High	Moderate
Involuntary superintendent turnover	Low	High	High

Source: Modified from Roger Rada, "Community Dissatisfaction and School Governance," *Planning and Changing* 15 (1984): 246.

Why Citizen Participation?

During the period after the mid-1960s, many people called for more participation in school decision making. This call ran beyond seeking greater voter turnout in board and referenda elections. Rather, this movement sought a qualitative change in the process of policymaking by expanding the number who sit on the boards. This could be done directly, as in the New York City decentralization movement of the 1970s, which created thirty-three neighborhood school boards in place of one. Or it could be arranged by attaching "citizen advisory councils" to existing boards or local school sites. This change created great scope when an Illinois law in 1988 created local councils to select principals and allocate funds for over five hundred different school constituencies in the city of Chicago. This school-site control movement was not restricted to the United States, as it surfaced in France, Australia, Canada, Italy, England, Sweden, West Germany, and China.[22]

Several purposes motivated these changes. Some wanted increased participation for *instrumental* reasons, for example, to achieve specific policy changes. Thus, if more black or Hispanic parents were put on site councils, they could influence the system to be less racist by securing more-sensitive teachers and administrators, a multicultural curriculum, and so on. A second purpose for greater participation was *psychological*, that is, the process itself would improve the participant's sense of value as a person. There might not be much policy change, but participation would stimulate others to act and so permit the emergence of a "community will." A third reason was *political*, to avoid the bureaucracy of the central office that critics claimed had interfered with learning and was wasteful of dollars.

Social context is everywhere important in defining who participates and what participation means.[23] *Who participates?* Mothers with children deeply rooted in the community, and in the upper social strata, are more predisposed to participate than not. *How much?* The amount of participation does not seem to be highly influenced by family background and socialization. Having children in school is important, however, and some participation itself leads to more intensive participation. Participation has traceable but highly complex effects on one's personal development, level of information, social interaction, and subsequent civic involvement.[24]

What do they do? Participants in school politics of suburbia are more distinguished by *what* they do rather than by *how much* they do. Some only go to meetings, some specialize in contacting public officials, others talk to fellow citizens about school matters, and still others work primarily in school elections. These types work through different institutions—family and neighbors, political parties, voluntary organizations, the elections system, and school officials. Some who participate support public education, with trust in the honesty and effectiveness of its administrators; they are also sanguine about their own ability to influence local school policy. As an analyst concluded from a study of St. Louis suburbanites:

> There is broad support in these findings for the ancient view that the active citizen would also be the confident and effective citizen.... The central finding is that ... the more people participate, the greater will be the impact on them, and the greater the impact, the more likely it will take the form of enhanced personal growth and development.[25]

All this participation unfolds in a school politics that is dynamic—constantly changing actors, participants, issues, and conflicts. The changes that accrue from such participation are not dramatically large or abrupt; rather they are small and incremental. However, over time these subtle shifts add up to massive changes in the amount and quality of a policy service like education.[26] For example, the average number of school years attended in 1900 was 6.0; in 1990 it was 12.2 years. The change arose from no single decade, but from the incrementalism of small changes each year.

Those entering the policy world expecting fast, big changes are doomed to disappointment. No system, by definition, changes in this way short of violent revolution—and not even then, as the Soviet system illustrates. However, those entering the school policy world with a sense of developing their capabilities and generating challenge are much more likely to have small effects. Persistence with small effects can achieve major change if, as the poet Graham Greene noted, there is "patience, patience everywhere like a fog." Over time, as the American experience has shown, these people can transform an institution and thus benefit their children immensely.

NONLOCAL PARTICIPATION

To this point, we have focused only on the local channel of
the school board's authority. Yet partisan elections for state and
federal office can certainly impact local schools because of the
resources those levels transmit to schools. Increasingly, the budget
fight in every state in the legislature over funds for local schools
becomes an annual drama. The widespread budget crisis of all
states in the early 2000s cut funds for local districts everywhere.
Governors and legislators thus have a direct bearing on school
quality, equity, efficiency, and choice. As we will see in a later
chapter, this state role and its mandates make "local control"
more imaginary than real. Further, what the legislature says about
the taxing authority of local units is vital to local schools and
citizen pocketbooks. For example, in 1983 public opinion polls
showed dramatic increases in concern about education quality,
so that state governments were galvanized to enact numerous
reforms. The same but much more limited response occurred
later for "choice" plans. On the reverse side, though, budget
cuts in 2003 slowed state funds for schools, and new reforms
declined dramatically.

One other nonlocal channel for popular participation exists,
namely, the elections of Congressional members and the president. When the range of issues facing political authorities is
extensive at the state level, the reach becomes enormous nationally. This should mean that the importance of school issues goes
down when most persons vote for higher governmental offices.
That is, their concern over school taxes or curriculum is less
than for issues of war and peace or the national economy. However, citizens follow national affairs more closely than local affairs, but state affairs the least, when they pay any attention to
public affairs at all. As yet we have little research on citizen efforts to affect national authorities on school policy. Citizens may
have *opinions* on Washington's policies, as we shall see, but the
gap between popular opinion and action on many issues rivals
the Grand Canyon. Not many voters select their presidential
candidate based solely on education issues.

Some input is provided, however, through party channels in
the form of issue stands. Rather consistently in the past, those

identifying with the Democratic Party have been stronger supporters of federal aid to education than have Republican identi-
fiers. After 1965, as federal funds became increasingly available
to local school budgets already straining under an overloaded
property tax, this partisan difference began to disappear. It
reemerged in the Carter administration over creation of the
Department of Education. In 1980 Ronald Reagan campaigned
for its abolition and sought to do just that after his election,
including cutting federal funds for schooling. Forceful opposition frustrated both efforts, however; by 2004 the department
still stood, but federal school funds had been cut from a high of
9 percent down to only 7 percent.

Diffuse attitudes on federal school policy can crystallize, however, under certain circumstances. For example, there was intense support for the GI Bill of Rights after World War II; to
oppose this was to oppose our soldiers' efforts in that war. Similarly, as we will see later, during the late 1960s national attitudes
coalesced in profound opposition to school busing during the
desegregation controversy. On the other hand, citizen input into
national arenas deals rarely with educational policy, and little
evidence shows that it flavors the decisions of voters in federal
elections. Yet, if a perceived threat to a closely held value exists,
opinions can have electoral impact. After all, some of the support for Ronald Reagan, and later George W. Bush, was from
supporters of prayer in school.

In summary, then, although elections in the United States serve
as potential channels for citizens to have school inputs in a way
that is rare among nations, they seem little used. Board elections are barometers, normally reflecting little dissatisfaction with
the environment, but subject to sudden change. Additional examination of changes that produce dissatisfaction or "rancorous
conflict" would be immensely valuable.[27]

Such analyses would have several uses. Practically, they would
describe the conditions under which school administration can
trigger public concerns. Theoretically, they would help develop
an understanding of the links between private wants and public
outputs under stress conditions that yield to equilibrium. These
practical and theoretical concerns generate interesting questions.
Practically, how much can the superintendent support external

demands for quality or equity from the profession and state government when local community standards reject or resist them?
Does the frequency of superintendent turnover—chronic in the
profession and especially so in larger cities—inhibit or enhance
this executive's efforts at financing, curriculum and staff improvement, or desegregation? We will return to the superintendent's
situation in Chapter 6.

Any theoretical questions we posed are in contrast to the available evidence that American schools receive a minimum of significant input through the direct channel of elections. Yet from
this, one must *not* conclude that the political authorities of school
or state ignore the wants of citizens. The possibility always remains that a school issue that agitates the community or the
nation deeply enough could suddenly focus on the channel of
elections, suddenly displacing the old with the new. For example, state referenda in California have cut property taxes in half,
earmarked 40 percent of the state budget for schools, and curtailed bilingual education. Dissatisfaction theory research explains
such events.

Even in the satisfied stage, school officials are confined by a
"zone of tolerance" that is based on community expectations.
Thus in the dissatisfied stage, voters use elections to focus their
demands and restructure the local policy system. In either case,
school officials must keep tuned for public signals, no matter
how muted they are. While nearly 60 percent of Americans thought
parents and other members of the community should have more
say in allocating funds and deciding curriculum, less than 15
percent of administrators and 26 percent of teachers shared this
view.[28] This difference clearly reflects the participatory-citizen
conflict noted throughout this book. That is, the profession is
not tuned in unless a particular issue generates such rancor that
it mobilizes the community.

REFERENDA AND POLICY CONVERSION

A second input channel is the referendum by which citizens
vote directly on such school policy as budgets, bonds, or levies.
The referendum is thereby a device for registering the extent of

public support for specific school policies. Unhappiness with excessive spending, insensitive teachers, lack of student discipline, objectionable curriculum, or even the losing football team can all generate lack of support. Simply voting "no" is a convenient and low cost way of expressing this dissatisfaction, so school boards and administrators have to pay attention to this potential support. In short, they must become "political" by seeking to mobilize group support within the community for what they see as necessary funding. In recent decades, however, some school authorities have found that this support is drying up. This development is yet another part of the current political turbulence that fills American schools today.

Background and Significance

By the end of the nineteenth century, many Americans were disgusted with the greed and corruption of local government. Reformers in the Progressive movement at that time altered many forms and practices in local policymaking.[29] More significantly, they altered the dominance of the political party in the "nonpartisan" movement noted earlier.

However, the use of referenda to pass budgets, levies, and bonds in education did not arise from progressives. School referenda were the handiwork of *conservatives* seeking to *prevent* passage of bond issues and to keep property tax rates down by state law. These laws made school referenda to be voted on only by property owners, and these required extraordinary majorities to pass. Conservatives thought that few such efforts would succeed, given these barriers, but that is not what happened. The unintended consequences of this reform were that local revenue sources, particularly the property tax, declined, and pressures escalated on the state to bail out the locals. After 1900, this process generated pressures for new state taxes and later led to the widespread adoption of the sales tax and new taxing arrangements for using income for local schools. Consequently, "the local tax limitation schemes begat state fiscal policy centralization, and a web of state-local fiscal relationships and interdependence."[30]

In two respects the referendum is more significant for education than for other areas of public policy. It is the necessary device for securing financial support of schools in almost all states. Also, this device may be viewed as a process that bypasses the school board and authoritatively allocates values, *a direct policymaking process*, while it also allocates school resources in levies and bond issues. The act of voting thus links the individual citizen to the school in a direct and intimate way that is unparalleled for other major public policies, here and abroad.

LINKAGES AMONG VOTING AND REFERENDA SUCCESS

These conceptual distinctions are well illustrated by voting patterns for bond issues. Figure 4.1 traces these dynamics over the turbulent recent decades featured throughout this book. What it shows is that popular satisfaction with the steady-state school system of the 1950s and 1960s is seen in the high degree of support for referenda; about four in five supported these across the nation. However, the dissatisfaction with schools we have noted earlier was followed by a sharp decline in referenda support; in 1986 only about one in three showed support. Results over the later years in the twentieth century show the same lack of support. In one sense, indeed, the curve on elections is a mirror of the politics of education in these decades—the emphasis is on dissatisfaction.

A citizen's vote on a secret ballot does not tell us much about his or her motivation. However, that knowledge is important for officials who must cater to the diverse feelings of citizens. Policy events in schools move voters—at least some—to turn out to pass or reject referenda. How a citizen votes may be affected by his or her own characteristics, by the school district or site, or by school events. Personal influences may lean heavily on the voter as the "rational actor," that is, one who evaluates what is gained or lost by a vote. Or, voters may lean heavily on the reinforcing nature of the district, so that, as research shows regularly, a wealthy district reinforces support while less wealthy districts may not. These independent variables explaining voter turnout are displayed by this model seen in Figure 4.2.

Figure 4.1
Three Decades of School Bond Approval, 1957–1986

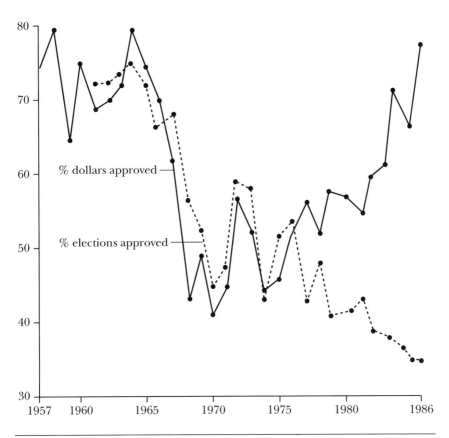

Source: Annual Reports, National Center for Educational Statistics, 1957–1976; combined report 1977–1986 (August, 1987).

Who Votes and Why?

Research *historically* pictures voters who are school supporters, those who do turn out and support these referenda. However, many do not, mostly those disadvantaged by income, education, or ethnicity. So accepted is this judgment that a survey of late 1990s' literature continued to confirm this finding.[31] The largest explainer of voter turnout is *status*—voters are mostly the middle- and higher-status members of the community. Measures of

Figure 4.2
Model of Research into Financial Referenda

Vote Characteristics:	Individual-Level Explanations	Turnout	Voting Outcome	Subsequent Policy Events
Variable – status – ethnicity – ideology – school attitudes	Economic—optimization Ethos—other-regarding Psychological—alienation	Percent of eligibles Social composition	Size of support Social composition of yeas and nays	Future frequency of referenda Results of future referenda Amount of funds in future referenda Board turnover Superintendent turnover Board policy (program changes)
District Characteristics: Demand levels: resources school age cohort Structural requirements: – voting – majority submission Amount of politization	System-Level Explanations Environmental—macroanalysis Political access—legitimation Community conflict			

income, education, occupation—all show much the same thing, a descending cascade of turnout and support running down from upper to lower status. This research topic was widely explored prior to 1970, but since the growing defeat of referenda (noted in Figure 4.1), there has been little research interest in this matter.

Other factors confound, however, the influence of status, for example, *ethnicity*.[32] In the absence of political parties' providing cues for voters on how to vote, ethnicity may be a cue to voting. Earlier research showed differences among racial and ethnic voters (Irish and Polish give less support, blacks more).[33] But a large research agenda remains untouched after the turbulence of the last several decades. Does the ethnicity of those who have newly come to power in big cities (blacks, Hispanics, Asians) vary with status—particularly among supporters and opponents? Or does status within these groups differ, so that middle-class ethnics support referenda and poorer members do not? Does support vary with the school issue at hand, such as curriculum, teachers' salaries, and so on?

A largely abandoned reason for voting on referenda was that citizens vote in response to an *ideology* or ethos that is centered around the school in the community. Those who hold a "public-regarding ethos" (primarily Protestant, middle-class) were thought to support the community's general interest in school support. However, those who held a "private-regarding ethos" (primarily immigrants, lower-class, or working-class) centered on supporting their own special interests in their family or group.

These private versus public orientations are suggested in Figure 4.3. The types of voters implied there suggest that self-interest looms large when community interest fades. What accounts for such fading? Fewer children in public schools is a cause when child-bearing is postponed, especially in the middle-class localities. Also, constant criticism of the "failure" of schools would weaken the public-interest motivation for referenda support. Or, a decline in disposable income would cause private interest to loom even larger over that of a public interest in school support. Much of that research in the new era of the challenge to schools has not yet been undertaken. But the wide availability of computer-based voting data suggests a relatively easy analysis.

Figure 4.3

Personal and Community Orientations to Voting in School Referenda

Direction of vote	Voter Motives	
	With Children in Public Schools	Without Children in Public Schools
For	Mixed	Community
Against	Personal	Personal

Community	=	Has first commitment to community, second consideration for economic costs of referendum, and consequently reasons in voting: Community benefits > personal costs
Personal	=	Has first commitment to self-family-ethnic group, second consideration to community, and consequently reasons in voting: Personal costs > community/personal benefits
Mixed	=	Motives may be either personal or community benefit as primary consideration, but not both, and consequently reasons in voting: Indeterminate

These attitudes about schools involve the citizen's perceptions and sense of worth about schools. What the school system communicates to its public can generate support or opposition. Even direct involvement by parents in schools generates much more support and greater credibility to schoolpeople.[34] Or, citizens' sense that expenditures for schools is "a good thing" or that government taxes are a "bad thing"—vague as these feelings seem— may move citizens at their deepest level to affect turnout and support. As polls of the last decades show, when citizens come to increasingly distrust government in general, they may accept the concept that any governmental expenditures is bad. Indeed, as elections are channels for funneling many kinds of attitudes, one attitude—personal alienation—may be salient for thinking about schools. The sense of being ignored by a society that is seen as controlled by a conspiracy of a few (who are quite different from one's self) would weaken any support for school referenda. We should not overestimate the number of citizens so alienated, but neither should we underestimate their role in defeating referenda.

These are new possibilities about voters' attitudes, quite different from the traditional analysis of district qualities affecting the vote. While we are far from knowing the origins of these attitudes and perceptions, future work on these cognitive maps of voters may well provide information to school officials and boards with funding needed for school programs and facilities.

On the other hand, though, there is an underlying support of goodwill for public schools. By the late 1990s polls showed that Americans liked their schools somewhat more, especially those they knew close to home. As one scholar of polls noted, "Despite all the outcry about school 'failures,' public confidence in those responsible for education ran ahead of all other institutional leaders except doctors."[35]

However, that underlying support may mean less in the face of a changing demography of voters. Fewer public school parents today means fewer motivated to vote for referenda due to personal or community interests. The minority drawn into private or voucher schools seem an unlikely support for public schools, although there is little research on the linkage. Nevertheless, the striking factor is the growing number of citizens without children in public schools. Both the young and oldest voters and those with children in private schools are unlikely to support referenda. Many California districts have overcome demographic restraints by focusing campaigns solely upon likely supporters, and by not trying to persuade fence-sitters or opponents. The strategy uses volunteers to deliver a surgical strike and is crafted to likely "yes" voters.

THE LOCAL CONVERSION PROCESS IN TRANSITION

This chapter has pointed to the dual interest by officials and professionals who must rely on referenda for continued sustenance, and by scholars of democratic politics. School officials do not like referenda. Although they express little of that feeling publicly, no evidence suggests that many elections will be abolished any time soon.[36] Low-key community relations used to be the norm in affecting school decisions.[37] The professionals' decisions withdrew somewhere into the crevices of their policy world; supporters inside and outside the system were maintained and reinforced; and a closed world of policymaking existed for a select few. There was only a limited citizen control over schools, except occasionally from episodic events.

Yet the recent turbulence has affected traditional systems. Political forces at the local level require adaptation, and often new training, in administrative roles as well, as shown in Chapter 6.[38] Training administrators has shifted somewhat from an emphasis on organizational theory as explaining their decisional environment to an emphasis on political context, as this book emphasizes.[39] Certainly the superintendent today needs to understand much more than just the old notion of keeping the referenda campaign low key in order to win. Partial theories of explaining what goes on in voters' minds in these elections abound, as we have shown. Indeed, the professional needs to know much more about the politics of decision making in a democracy, and for this, one must grasp other political theories—rational, incremental, implementation, and so on.

Finally, whatever new role the professional adopts within this current turbulence, he and she will have participated in the most recent skirmish of our historic clash between participatory and meritocratic values. James Madison, Alexis de Tocqueville, or Lord Bryce, brought back to life and observing the events discussed in these last two chapters, would understand quite well what they meant. These observers and many others have grasped the basic underlying dynamic of American politics and policymaking. That is the tension generated by a nation of diverse groups seeking to realize their values—often conflicting—through the subsystems of society, including the political.

NOTES

1. David Easton, *A Framework for Political Analysis* (Englewood Cliffs, N.J.: Prentice-Hall, 1965), p. 122.

2. A thorough review of this linkage is found in the articles in V. Darleen Opfer and Kenneth Wong, eds., "The Politics of Elections and Education," *Educational Policy* 164: 1 (January and March 2002). Kathryn McDermont, *Controlling Public Education* (Lawrence: University Press of Kansas, 1999).

3. Richard J. Brown, "Party Platforms and Public Education," *Social Studies* (1961): 206–10.

4. All statistics on board elections in this chapter are from Frederick M. Hess, *The Nation's School Boards at the Turn of the Century* (Alexandria, Va.: National School Boards Association, 2002).

5. Jennifer Hochschild, *The New American Dilemma: Liberal Democracy and School Desegregation* (New Haven: Yale University Press, 1984.)

6. Lester G. Seligman, *Political Recruitment* (Boston: Little, Brown & Co., 1972).

7. Peter J. Cistone, "The Recruitment and Socialization of School Board Members," in Cistone, ed., *Understanding School Boards: Problems and Prospects* (Lexington, Mass: Lexington Books, 1976), chap. 3, and Cistone, "The Ecological Basis of School Board Member Recruitment," *Education and Urban Society* 4 (1974): 428–50.

8. George S. Counts, *The Social Composition of Boards of Education* (Chicago: University of Chicago, 1927).

9. Ted Robinson, Robert England, and Kenneth Meier, "Black Resources and Black School Board Representation: Does Political Structure Matter?" *Social Science Quarterly* 66(1990): 976–82.

10. Neal Peirce, Preface in *School Boards: A Strengthening Grass Roots Leadership*, by Lila N. Carol and colleagues (Washington, D.C.: Institute for Educational Leadership, 1986). See also Jacqueline P. Danzberger, Michael W. Kirst, and Michael Usdan, *Governing Public Schools* (Washington, D.C.: Institute for Educational Leadership, 1992).

11. Terry Moe, "Teachers Unions and School Board Elections," in William Howe, ed., *Besieged: School Boards and the Future of Education Politics* (Washington, D.C.: Brookings Institution, forthcoming).

12. Clive Thomas and Ronald Hrebnar, "Interest Groups in the American States," in Virginia Gray and Herbert Jacobs, eds., *Politics in the American States*, 7th ed. (Washington, D.C.: CQ Press, 2003).

13. Kenneth Meier and Eric Juenke, "Electoral Structure and the Quality of Representation: The Policy Consequences of School Board Elections," in Howe, *Besieged*.

14. Frederick Hess and David Leal, "School House Politics: Expenditures, Interests, and Competition in School Board Elections," in Howe, *Besieged*.

15. Moe, "Teachers Unions and School Board Election."

16. Sande Milton, "Participation in Local School Board Elections: A Reappraisal," *Social Science Quarterly* 64 (1983): 646-54; Sande Milton and Robert Bickel, "Competition in Local School Board Elections: Findings in a Partisan Political Environment," *Planning and Changing* 13 (1982): 148–57. For a recent overview of national voting see Warren E. Miller and J. Merrill Shanks, *The New American Voter* (Cambridge, Mass.: Harvard, University Press, 1996).

17. The earliest studies (before 1960) included Richard Carter, *Voters and Their Schools* (Stanford: Institute for Communications Research, 1952). Analysis after 1960 included L. Harmon Zeigler, M. Kent Jennings, and G. Wayne

Peak, *Governing American Schools.* (North Scituate, Mass.: Duxbury, 1974), pp. 60–62; David Minar, "The Community Basis of Conflict in School System Politics," *American Sociological Review* 31 (1966): 822–34; William Boyd, *Community Status and Conflict in Suburban Schools* (Beverly Hills, Calif.: Sage, 1975); and Christine Rossell, "School Desegregation and Electoral Conflict," in Frederick Wirt, ed., *The Polity of the School* (Lexington, Mass.: Lexington Books, 1975), chap. 4.

18. V. Darleen Opfer, "Introduction: Elections and Education—A Question of Influence," in Opfer and Wong, "Politics of Elections."

19. James Hottois and Neal A. Milner, *The Sex Education Controversy* (Lexington, Mass.: Lexington Books, 1974).

20. Frank Lutz and Laurence Iannaccone, eds., *Public Participation in School Decision Making* (Lexington, Mass.: Lexington Books, 1978).

21. Ruth Danis, "Policy Changes in Local School," *Urban Education* 19 (1984–85): 125–44.

22. Fred S. Coombs and Richard I. Merritt, "The Public's Role in Educational Policy Making: An International View," *Education and Urban Society* 9 (1977): 169–96.

23. The following relies upon Robert H. Salisbury, *Citizen Participation in the Public Schools* (Lexington, Mass.: Lexington Books, 1980).

24. For an overview of participation see Steven Rosenstone and J. Hansen, *Mobilization, Participation, and American Democracy* (New York: Macmillan, 1993).

25. Salisbury, *Citizen Participation*, pp. 177, 199.

26. In education, see Diane Ravitch, *Left Back* (New York: Simon and Shuster, 2000).

27. William Gamson, *Power and Discontent* (Homewood, Ill.: Dorsey Press, 1968), although the focus here is not upon school issues.

28. William Boyd, "The Public, the Professionals, and Educational Policy Making: Who Governs? *Teachers College Record* 77 (1976): 556–58.

29. Steve Faskar, *Educational Reform: The Players and Politics* (New York: Public Agenda Foundation, 1992).

30. Howard D. Hamilton and Sylvan H. Cohen, *Policy Making by Plebiscite: School Referenda* (Lexington, Mass.: Lexington Books, 1974), p. 3.

31. Philip K. Piele and John S. Hall, *Budgets, Bonds, and Ballots* (Lexington, Mass.: Lexington Books, 1973). Carliss Lente, "Predicting School Referenda Outcomes: Answers from Illinois," *Journal of Education Finance* 24 (1999): 459–82. For evidence, see Pauline Schneider, "Social Barriers to Voting," *Update on Law-Related Education* 20–3 (1996): 31–33.

32. On ethnic attitudes, see Nathan Glazer and Daniel Moynihan, *Beyond the Melting Pot* (Cambridge, Mass.: MIT Press, 1980); Emmett Buell, Jr., *School Desegregation and Defended Neighborhoods: The Boston Story* (Lexington, Mass.: Lexington Books, 1981); Dianne Pinderhughes, *Race and Ethnicity in Chicago Politics* (Champaign: University of Illinois Press, 1987).

33. See Samuel Popkin, *The Reasoning Voter* (Chicago: University of Chicago Press, 1991). For a less encouraging view see Roy A. Teixeira, *The Disappearing American Voter* (Washington, D.C.: Brookings, 1992).

34. For example, Thomas A. McCain and Victor D. Wall, Jr., "A Communication Perspective of a School-Bond Failure," *Education Administration Quarterly* 12, no. 2 (1974); 1–17; for a review of this aspect, see Piele and Hall, *Budgets, Bonds, and Ballots*, pp. 83–91, 130–34.

35. Philip K. Piele, "Public Support for Public Schools: The Past, the Future, and the Federal Role," *Teachers College Record* 84 (1983): 690–707.

36. Hamilton and Cohen, *Policy Making*, pp. 271–73.

37. Minar, "Community Basis of Conflict," p. 285

38. Larry Cuban, *Urban School Chiefs Under Fire* (Chicago: University of Chicago Press, 1976), App. 2.

39. See McDermont, "Controlling Public Education;" see also Lorraine McDonnell, Michael Timpane, and Roger Benjamin, eds., *Rediscovering the Democratic Purposes of Education* (Lawrence: University Press of Kansas, 2000).

5

Local School Boards, Politics, and the Community

Elected school boards and appointed professionals alike are criticized, removed from office, and, in general, as distrusted as all political institutions have been in the last three decades. To understand this challenge with Easton's theory about the political system, we need to know more about how the school system operated when stress arose in the environment and focused on school governance. In the next two chapters, we will explain the behavior of boards, superintendents, and teachers to see how they have adapted to challenges to their authority.

We can understand these events within the analytical framework set out in Chapter 2. Our focus here will be on the formal school system—board, superintendent, and principals—where most policymaking and implementation takes place on a day-to-day basis. Their work is to routinize activity in order to rationalize objectives and economize resources. The consequence of such behavior is to maximize system persistence. Such decision making, however, also has varied consequences for different groups. A second major local force—voter influence—provides episodic inputs to the school system, as described in the preceding chapter.

THE SCHOOL BOARD'S COMPOSITION AND HISTORY

The school board and professional educators, in Easton's terms, authoritatively allocate values in creating and administering public policy for the schools. Service on the board was once an extremely low-profile, low-conflict position, but in the last two decades, board members have been thrust into the middle of politically turbulent issues. In the process their roles changed; some became champions of lay groups, but others supported professional groups. A board member now needs to know and judge issues in finance, discrimination, textbooks, teacher demands, and so on—a lengthy list of crucial and excruciating demands on school resources. Board membership has become challenging in terms of the ancient Chinese *curse*, "May you live in exciting times."

Whether meeting or blocking a citizen demand, however, the board is not static nor are its members value free. They modify, regulate, innovate, or refuse political demands in response to a variety of value preferences. On the one hand, they are somewhat controlled in this conversion function; the board may have conflict within itself, higher system levels can constrain it, and voters may disrupt it. In short, board members and administrators are not "passive transmitters of things taken into the system, digesting them in some sluggish way, and sending them along as output."[1] Rather they reflect a highly personal element in the interplay of school politics. Policy output, then, partly depends on the feelings and values, failures and successes of human beings. Consequently, it is important to know something about what school board members are like.

As noted in the previous chapter, their social characteristics have changed little since the famous Counts survey of 1927.[2] A 2002 national survey found board members are predominately upper-middle class, a pattern that holds for all districts regardless of size.[3] Forty-five percent are professionals or businessmen, but more than 25 percent are homemakers or retired.

We cannot understand the meaning of the social qualities of this governing agency without some sense of its political function. A historical sketch will help set the framework for understanding the school board's current role.[4] When public schools began, no administrators intervened between teachers and board;

the board itself was an administrative body. Each member undertook responsibility for a special school task. Growing enrollments and new professionals transformed the board into a legislative body. Its major function altered to set broad policy guidelines and act as watchdogs over their implementation. Yet even that function was transformed in the last century with the increased control over local schools through state and national laws, along with the increased power of professional administrators and teachers unions.

Prior to the mid-1960s a description of the board's function would be something like this: School boards most often mediated major policy conflicts, leaving determination of important policy issues to the professional staff or to higher external levels; if no evidence of community concern showed up, they might do nothing. In the process, they legitimated the proposals of the professional staff, making only marginal changes rather than representing citizens. Board members spent the bulk of their time on details but established a policy "zone of tolerance" within which the administration could act. A pivot between community notions of schooling and professional standards of service, the board must be seen in some larger perspective. By 2005, most of these historical roles had changed.

BOARD SUPPORT FROM THE COMMUNITY

Boards are small political systems, reflecting the ever-present tension in a democracy from the demands of school values of quality, equity, efficiency, and choice. We expect education to be decided by and be responsive to the people in general but also, and simultaneously, to be technically advanced and determined by standards of quality. Despite fervent wishes to the contrary, the two expectations do not always coincide. So the board is caught up in an ideology of an informed citizenry participating in democratic decision making.

In fact, citizens are poorly informed on such matters and seemingly disinterested in acquiring such information; hence they participate little. However, even if this does describe citizen inattention and inactivity, it does not mean that citizens do not affect schools. For, some argue, this lack of citizen information and participation has generated a massive public loss of support for schools that is potentially devastating. Actually, the evidence can support both the pessimist and the optimist on this matter.[5] Pessimists can point to

- Gallup polls that show low rating of schools, especially in big cities, and
- in 2000 education was rated the number one public problem in national and state polls.

Optimists can point to

- the failure to evaluate confidence in schools or achievement records over long enough periods of time;
- growing funding for most schools;
- education's relative vote of confidence compared to other American institutions (much better than for big business, news media, Congress, and organized labor, and a bit better than for the Supreme Court);
- high support for maintaining or increasing current service levels by those also voting to limit taxes and expenditures; and
- movement of African Americans into college and of more people into adult education.

One must understand the school board's role partly in terms of this systemic support for education as a whole. Media fastened on evidence of urban "failure" or "crisis" and accentuated—maybe even stimulated—this perception of breakdown. This signal did not jibe with many boards' perceptions of their problems, though.[6] Consequently, serious problems of support exist for some aspects of schools, particularly in an era when the public is far more critical about everything in public life, and uninterested in looking for school successes.

Some evidence suggests that our schools today may have done a better job with more people, compared to earlier eras and other nations.[7] But in politics what is important is what citizens *think* is reality—not reality itself. The past two decades were a period of skeptical challenge to boards and professional educators for the job they were doing. Teacher union activity in board elections keeps growing, and can swing local elections to union-endorsed candidates. What occurred was that the usually dry arroyos of community-board linkage became flooded by challenges over a disparity between expectations and reality in school quality.

What are the consequences of this gap for the school board, the system's authoritative local agency? There is evidence of what we noted earlier as "the dissatisfaction theory of democracy."[8] It asserts that voters' dissatisfaction rises as the gap between their values and demands and those of board members and superintendent increases. In districts characterized by rapid population shifts—either expanding or contracting in size—dissatisfaction is particularly strong. Newcomers' values, expectations, and demands differ sharply from those of older residents. At some point, the dissidents become strong enough to defeat board incumbents, and a new board replaces the superintendent.

Rare in its use of longitudinal research, this theory presents convincing evidence from over fifteen years of testing, leading to a strong affirmation that school boards are indeed democratic. It depends on the question put to the system: Who governs? Do administrator actions coincide with citizen preferences? Who has access to modify the governance, under what conditions, and how?[9] If those are the critical questions, it seems likely that once the public knows, it can redefine the needs that they want the school system to meet. Continued dissatisfaction with board efforts to meet these new needs produces not simply changes in board membership, but also new agendas, new constituents, new resources, and in time even new structures of governance.

THE BOARD AND STATUS POLITICS

Another view of the community and board linkage stems from status differences between the two. If a community were homogeneous in status, board members' tasks would be simple—just consult one's own preferences, which would largely reflect the community's. Studies of small-town school politics show that such congruence does exist between citizens and their boards. This research also shows up in the pervasive role of the high school

within the rural black community where the school embodies
the latter; among whites, the school is only one aspect of institutional community life.[10]

However, American community life is becoming much more
varied, as boards face competing demands of a diverse community. The historical record of such a process is clear, although
there is debate about which groups were favored or not as a
result. We already noted in Chapter 2 the 1900 to 1920 shift
from working-class to middle-class and business domination in
board composition. For some scholars this was evidence of in-
dustrialists controlling schools in order to provide a trained labor
pool; for others, this was evidence of capitalists foisting education on a proletariate in order to control them. But historical
analysis of this shift in board role demonstrates something else.
The spread of professionalization in the schools was actually
encouraged by trade unions. It attracted the middle class to the
schools; and at least in the case of three major regional cities, it
was welcomed, not resisted, by the middle class.[11] In the past
this status context underlay the control of schools in our cities.
Reformers focused on changing the structures of power, which
are never value-free but rather they dispense varying rewards to
different groups. Certainly this was what the business groups who
supported such reform believed.[12] Large districts have fewer professionals or businessmen on their boards, and more educators,
retirees, and homemakers.[13]

Today, this status orientation to understanding school conflict
is backed by some research.[14] The role behaviors of superintendents
differ in urban working-class, as opposed to middle-class, suburbs far from the city center. Before the 1970s, higher-status
districts had fewer political conflicts (that is, votes for losing
candidates), lower electoral participation in board elections, and
less challenge to superintendents' administrative decisions than
did lower-status districts. Associated with these differences were
dissimilar cultural norms about citizen involvement with schools
and school professionals.

These findings were qualified by later events. Thus, when an
issue becomes significant to the traditionally low-conflict, higher-
status community, its members can actively challenge boards and
school professionals. This had been the case in Northern cities

in the 1970s in the matter of desegregation, where higher-status elements became just as vocal as South Boston working-class citizens. Both status groups were protecting their social neighborhoods, on racial grounds in this case, although it was also done for other matters such as freeways, low-income housing, or heavy-industry location.[15]

Further, some evidence suggests that the status of the district affects the "board culture" of that school.[16] Homogeneous districts develop a board style of "elite" councils—small in size, seeing themselves as guardians of the public but separate from it, making decisions privately, consensually, and in limited range, and exhibiting administrative, judicial, and legislative functions. On the other hand, "area" councils exhibit the opposite qualities within a heterogeneous community. However, the elite cultural system has usually prevailed, modifying inputs from different ethnic, religious, and status groups so as to subordinate them.

A special case arises in school consolidation. It is a factor that has increased not only the volume but also the conflict of status demands on boards enormously. What was once an archipelago of districts in America, each island homogeneous with board and community in harmony, has been fused into larger, more varied districts. The 89,000 districts of 1948 became 55,000 five years later, 31,000 by 1961, and 14,000 by 2005. During the 1970s, on any given day, three districts disappeared forever between breakfast and dinner. Even earlier in the 1960s, however, that many had evaporated between breakfast and the morning coffee break, with another seven gone by dinner. As a result, not only are there now more diverse values and broader status bases confronting board members, but there are also fewer board members to handle this increased input. As one scholar calculated, "Where a school board member once represented about 200 people, today each . . . must speak for approximately 3,000 constituents."[17]

Accommodating increasingly diverse views underlies the dissatisfaction theory of democracy noted earlier. Evidence of this mixing of districts is suggested by the finding that more interest groups came to board attention in metropolitan areas but fewer in nonmetropolitan districts.[18] Teachers and other employee unions can dominate elections in some urban areas despite a number of other interest groups.

The Mosaic of Status Politics

No consensus about the board's link to the community exists in the literature mainly because it spans different periods and issues. However, the view that a board's openness to its community is a variable does emerge. That is, the linkage should be different under conditions of low versus high community dissent over school policies. We could expect that when little conflict exists, boards are less receptive to community input. When more intense community conflict exists, however, the board becomes more receptive to challenging established policies.[19] This linkage appeared in four possible styles of board politics, illustrated in Table 5.1.

Like all typologies, this is a still life of a reality that nevertheless covers many communities, but it hints at a dynamic process. That is, the four board styles shown in Table 5.1 represent different stages of the dissatisfaction theory of school conflict. Both typology and theory have their respective uses, but the more dynamic theory is capable of generating more powerful hypotheses. That is, boards do not merely transmit what the community says, for often it says very little; nor do boards dictatorially block off any signals not on their wave lengths. Rather, when issues heat up the local environment, considerable evidence shows that boards become much more receptive to citizen inputs, and more willing to oppose the traditional direction of school policy. There is a particularly political quality to this response of school boards, best caught in the aphorism of V. O. Key: "Public opinion is that opinion which politicians find it prudent to pay attention to." In this and other respects, board members are true politicians.

THE BOARD AS A DECISION-MAKING AGENCY

A question that is analytically separate from the role of community inputs is how boards make decisions, although the two merge in reality. Several older models of this process were characterized by their naivete. One was that the school board necessarily reflected the social composition of its members. As we have

Table 5.1
Styles of School Board Politics

	Numbers in Conflict	
Skills of Opposition	High	Low
High	I. Reform ideal of citizen democracy	II. Challenge by takeover group
Low	III. All-out battle	IV. Continuity under traditional ruling group

Source: Reprinted with permission from Leigh Steizer, "Institutionalizing Conflict Response: The Case of Schoolboards," *Social Science Quarterly* 55 (1974), in Frederick Wirt, *The Polity of the School*, table on p. 81. Copyright 1975 by Jossey-Bass Inc., Publishers. First published by Lexington Books. All rights reserved.

just seen, that does not work as an explanation of who governs and, as we will soon see, it does not answer the further question, How does it govern? Another naive model was found for a long time in education administration literature. This described the board as the *maker* of school policy and the superintendent as the *administrator* of that policy, with a clear separation of function. Empirically, that has not been the case, for the two stimulate and affect each other. Thus, a national sample of superintendents showed in the early 1980s that their policy involvement had become greater by two-thirds, and one-half reported that their professional judgments were increasingly accepted by their boards. Similar results were found for city managers and planning directors.[20]

Multiple Currents of Decision Making

Another, more sophisticated way of viewing board decision making is to see it as different processes for different kinds of issues. In Figure 5.1 we see that any naive model of decision making is confounded by a more varied reality. In the *null response model* we are looking at what happens to most demands made upon a political agency—the agency does not respond. The blocked arrow symbolizes this process, and extensive evidence validates this model. Thus only a small fraction of proposed bills ever become laws in legislatures at any level of American

Figure 5.1

Models of Decision Making in a Political System

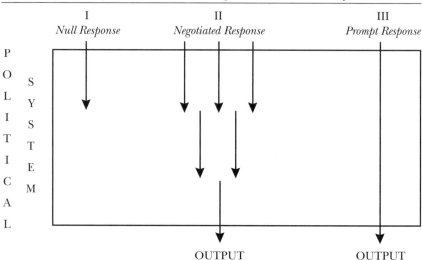

government, and only a fraction of appellate court appeals are ever accepted for hearing and decision. As for the school board, its time is primarily spent elsewhere, as noted below.

Under special conditions, the *negotiated model* of Figure 5.1 describes other board decision making. The several arrows here indicate the flow of competing demands into the political system over an emerging issue; in time these demands become narrowed as alternatives are formulated and a decision is authorized in the form of board policy (output). Here, the board member's role is that of negotiator among competing community groups, "working out things" over time, seeking compromises that create a coalition majority. Such action, though, is episodic, an occasional decision rather than a regular agenda.

The third model, *prompt response,* moves us to two quite different occasions when the political system responds quickly to community demands. One of these occasions occurs during a *crisis,* a sudden combination of threats either to the school system or its constituents. The crisis might arise from physical causes— buildings burned, flooded, or blown away—or from social causes that generate conflict over values the schools serve and the resources they distribute. A crisis has a curious quality in that most political actors must agree that a crisis exists or it does not. The danger must be clear to those helped or those helping, and the remedy must be relatively simple, understood, and accepted by all. If not, then some group or board member will question the necessity of taking fast action. Much of the conflict in local school politics arises from some claims that a "crisis" exists while opponents deny it and then redefine the situation to agree with their own interests.

There is a second and quite different aspect to the prompt response model that involves *routines.* These include filling in the details of major policy decisions. They are found in reports received and acted on, procedures for implementing a given policy, budgetary support for accepted programs, and so on. The unusual aspect of this context is that there are so many outputs of this kind. Indeed, much political decision making, including board actions, consists of routines as measured by the volume of personnel, funds, paperwork, and so forth issuing from a political agency.[21]

As noted earlier, in every typology a longitudinal model is crying to get out, and so it is with Figure 5.1. If these three models are seen as a sequence, they form a rough chronology of policy evolution. That is, many demands begin as the unthinkable found in the first model, supported by only a few "crackpots" and ignored by the political system. An illustration would be blacks seeking equal resources for their segregated schools decades ago in the South. Then, later, the second model starts to work. New combinations of societal events generate more support for the now "reasonable" idea so that its opponents must exert larger energies to block it; over time, however, opposing sides move toward resolutions that yield a new output. For example, under Supreme Court threat, the Southern school systems first moved to deny discrimination, then to equalize resources for black education without desegregating, then reluctantly and under pressure to accommodate external pressures by desegregating, and recently back to resegregation after new rulings from the Supreme Court. Another example is the pattern of invasion of city folk into rural areas where they succeeded in developing new suburban school systems after World War II. Given enough time, resolution of conflict results in opinion closure. What was unthinkable is now conventional, so that schools in the South and suburbia show few signs of formerly raging conflicts. At this stage, the third model dominates decision making in the form of routines.

Rational and Other Decision Making

Another conceptual framework exists for analyzing the decision making of school boards. This concept focuses on the degree to which officials use "rational" versus other methods of arriving at decisions.

An analysis of three major decisions by the Chicago school board over several decades uses alternative perspectives, set out in Table 5.2. Depending on the issue, decision making could take the form of bargaining among members. This could be of two kinds, (1) protecting or promoting relatively narrow organizational or electoral interests ("pluralist bargaining") or (2) involving broader interests rooted in protection of race, class, or a regime ("ideological bargaining"). Alternatively, decision making could take different forms, that is, a "unitary" model found in organizational theory, assuming rationality in decision making. The author made a highly useful adaptation to an intense debate over the possibility of "rational" policy that was more realistic. That is, it meant that "board members agreed on certain objectives, that reference to these objectives was made during the course of policymaking, and that policy outcomes were consistent with these objectives."[22] Prior to this analysis in Chicago, any discussion of rationality was so bounded by unrealistic empirical requirements that no decision could be termed rational; yet thousands of board members thought they were, in fact, acting rationally.

JUSTIFICATIONS FOR A STRONG LOCAL POLICY ROLE

The school board is the public's main vehicle for continuing local control of education. Consequently, strengthening the school board is vital to the public interest. Why should the local role in education policy be maintained and even strengthened in certain states where it has declined precipitously? As one scholar notes:

Table 5.2
Models of School Board Decision Making

Pluralist

Theme: Decisions are the result of a contest among groups lacking much common interests.

1. *Pluralist:* decision the result of a contest among board members representing narrow-purpose groups and designed to defend and enhance as many group interests as possible, for example, budgetary contests among curriculum interests.
2. *Ideological:* decision the result of a contest among board members representing broad-purpose groups designed to defend and enhance interests of a class or a race, for example, affirmative action policy on teacher promotions or principal appointments.

Unitary

Theme: Decisions are the result of interactions among groups that share some qualities which presume an overreaching unity among them.

1. *Organizational:* decision the result of board members motivated by desires to promote objectives of the school organization, for example, maintenance of professional standards against challenges by laypersons.
2. *Rational:* decision the result of board members agreed on a set of educational objectives, which are referred to in decisional debate and which are consistent with the decision itself.

Source: Abstracted from Paul E. Peterson, *School Politics Chicago Style* (Chicago: University of Chicago Press, 1976).

1. Public opinion supports more local influence and less influence for higher governments.
2. Local school politics tend to be more democratic in several important ways than are decisions made at higher levels.
3. While there will be tension between state and local policymakers, the result is policy that is better adapted to diverse local contexts.
4. Further erosion of the local role risks diminishing public support for the schools.[23]

Evidence of these beliefs is found in surveys of the public. Figure 5.2 shows the results of a recent survey that the public believes local government is the most cost-efficient level. On the

Figure 5.2
*The Public's Perception of Which Level of Government
Spends Tax Money More Wisely*

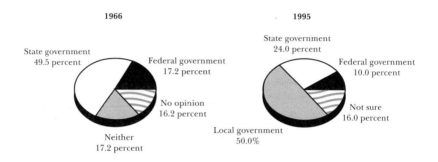

Source: 1966 Survey by the Gallup Organization, December 8–13, 1996; 1995 survey by the Hart and Teeter Research Companies for the Council for Excellence in Government, March 16–18, 1995.

other hand, it is concerned about state and federal governments' ability to spend tax money wisely.

Advantages of Local School Policymaking

Another criterion of local school policymaking is its compatibility to democratic ideals. Numerous and conflicting positions exist on this matter. The issue here is whether school politics is more democratic with local control than by federal or state authorities. Most citizens have a greater opportunity and chance of policy influence in their local district than with policymakers or administrators at the federal or state level. Local school policymakers serve fewer constituents than state officials and are much closer both geographically and psychologically.

Local board elections also provide a much more direct means to influence local policymakers than through a state legislator representing many areas. In the nation's thousands of small school districts, a significant proportion of the community knows at least one board member. Local media provide better information on education and can capture the citizen attention more effectively than reports from a distant capital. All of this is not meant to claim that all local school politics approaches the democratic ideal. However, local school officials can better anticipate the zone of tolerance that local people permit than can outsiders. But school system employee groups with large contributions of money and election worker can override the local context.

Most states are too large and diverse for uniform policies to be effective in all areas. In area after area, there exists a "nested policy in which the states provide the general contours and the local districts fill in with more specified policies."[24] Local school boards, however, hear local demands for much more than basic academic achievement. Local citizens want sports, bands, art classes, high school electives, vocational education, and many more functions from their schools. This condition creates a tension that tends to provide more appropriate and adaptable policies than statewide specification. In effect, the state can hardly micromanage affairs in the many districts in its border—but it can macromanage some broad goals for all. There are large areas, however, like civil rights and equal opportunity, where local flexibility has been restricted. Yet most states, for example, prescribe teacher certification requirements, but leave hiring and compensation issues to local districts.

The final argument for enhancing local discretion is based on the linkage between political efficacy and public support of schools—citizens will participate in politics more if they believe that they can have an impact on policies. The local level offers the best opportunity for efficacy; therefore, a lessening in local efficacy will lead to less participation in education policy. The reasoning here is that people's satisfaction with the results of collective decisions will be greater if they have taken part in making those decisions. Consequently, less local control leads to more citizen dissatisfaction. In California, for example, local parents are told that the school board is too constrained to remedy their grievances. The citizen is referred to a state office or in some cases to a court order. This kind of inaction could lead to alienation from the local public school.

Increasing Local Influence by Institutional Choice

How can one evaluate the arguments favoring redistributing power from higher levels to lower levels? One useful concept called "institutional choice" focuses on the crucial policy decision of which institution should be the decision maker. For example, courts have been reluctant to delegate civil rights protection to the institution of local schools. Another type of institutional choice is whether to place various functions in the hands of markets (e.g., vouchers) or politics (e.g., school board elections). The recent state reform movement has included an institutional choice to enhance the curricular and testing role of state government.

There are two general characteristics of institutions that are important: agreement on substantive goals and the capacity to achieve them. Substantive goals are crucial because of the need to insure support for a policy. Courts may be more supportive of civil rights than school boards, but its support must be buttressed by capacity. Courts cannot run school districts. So which institution should be chosen? A method for choosing can be called "comparative institutional advantage," that is, "the distrust directed at one decision maker must be carefully weighed against the advantages of that decision maker and both the advantages and disadvantages of alternative decision makers. . . . The logic of comparative institutional advantage also implies the futility of seeking perfect or ideal implementation of a policy. . . . The real world offers a 'least worst choice' of imperfect institutions."[25]

The preceding sections point up the complexity of the seemingly simple proposition of local control of schooling. Values and actions on the local scene reflect the influence of diversity that affects all aspects of the political system and its policy outputs. As system and policy grow ever more complex, local control becomes less and less a real description. In this change, however, much may have been lost for the citizen's role in democracy.

SCHOOL BOARDS AND EDUCATION REFORM

In the 1990s criticism began to intensify about the weakness of school boards. Why is there so much concern about the effectiveness of boards at this time in our history? One major reason is the lack of attention to school boards in most recent national and state education reforms. For example, rather than not discussing school boards, the reformers could have said that the school board is the crucial agent for school improvement and that state reforms should be directed at strengthening the local school board's capacity to bring about and monitor change. Instead, the unstated implication of many reforms is that school boards are part of the problem, and have not exercised leadership and authority to improve education.[26] This message further implies that boards need to be circumvented, if not through direct state regulation, then certainly through vastly increased state prescriptions and monitoring. Many state reformers felt that the school board agenda, as they understood it, did not match state policy priorities. That is, mismatched priorities exist in such matters as curriculum content, years required in academic subjects in high school, review of student academic standards, teacher evaluation, and rigorous testing of students' advancement through elementary and secondary schooling.

This suspicion about the inability of school boards to provide academic leadership was exacerbated by the predominant emphasis of research on effective schools.[27] It was the school site that was the crucial focus for improvement, and the principal was the key catalyst. Where did school board stimulus and assistance fit into this view? The answer was unclear and vague compared to the checklists and criteria for effective schools. This relative lack of emphasis in the reports on school district policies is surprising, given the research on successful school improvement.

Thus, an apparent paradox characterizes the education reform movement. On the one hand, reformers have felt free or obliged to circumvent local boards; on the other hand, reformers focus on improvement at the school site that is governed by a school board. To this point, local school boards have seemed to be either ignored or cast in a passive role as weak reactors or even deterrents, rather than as partners, in shaping educational improvement. Many school boards contend, however, that they initiated and enacted most of the reforms in local districts prior to state action.

RETHINKING THE SCHOOL BOARD ROLE

One major problem plagues all attempts to understand and prescribe policy for school boards. There are too many school boards (about fourteen thousand) and too many board members (some ninety-seven thousand) to be able to generalize about the behavior of all boards. Earlier in this chapter we did so but only for large-scale decisions. Consequently, the research base is confined to the study of a single case, a few comparative cases, or some nonrepresentative sample chosen for a particular purpose. Moreover, the research techniques employed range from surveys to self-assessments to full-scale case studies. Most research focuses on metropolitan areas or big cities. Horror stories dominate the media, and special attention is paid to conflict and operational failures. We know the least about the most common type of school board—the board of small districts. For example, much study of minority problems in schools deal with no more than one hundred of the big-city districts.

Evaluating the Role of School Boards

The last major change in the roles and operations of urban school boards took place between 1900 and 1920. That the basic structure and role were established so long ago suggests strongly the need for a review in the twenty-first century. By 1910 the conventional wisdom had evolved among schoolpeople and the leading business and professional men who spearheaded the reforms. The governance structure needed to be revised so that school boards would be small, elected at large, and purged of all connections with political parties and officials of general government, such as mayors and councilmen.

While the turn-of-the-century reformers tried to model the revamped school board on the big corporations, they left the board with a mandate to oversee and become involved in all areas of local school operation. The American school board combines the legislative, executive, and judicial functions of government. This role is too expansive and often leads boards to try to do everything by not doing much of anything in depth.

School boards play a *legislative* role when they adopt budgets, pass regulations, and set policies. Moreover, they provide the constituent-services component of a legislator's district office. Parents will phone board members about fixing showers in locker rooms, relocating school crossing guards, and reclassifying children placed in special education. Many board members believe that an essential part of their role is to "fix" these individual complaints, because failure to respond may mean defeat at the polls.

School boards play an *executive* role when they implement policy. Many school boards approve not only the budget, but also almost every expenditure and contract for services. For example, a half-day consulting fee for a university professor must be approved by the school board. The board performs the same role as the U.S. Department of Education's contracting office and the General Accounting Office. Many boards approve the appointments of principals, vice principals, categorical program administrators, and even teachers.

Judicial hearings concerning student suspensions, expulsions, interdistrict transfers, and pupil placements can consume an enormous amount of time. After all administrative remedies are exhausted, the board is the final body for appeal, though citizens may still turn to the courts in some cases.

Can School Boards Do It All?

Can any school board composed primarily of part-time laypeople perform all these functions well? Often, board meetings are dominated by administration progress reports and parental complaints about very specific needs. Moreover, state "sunshine laws" require boards to conduct all business, including many personnel matters, in public sessions. Does the essential policymaking role of the board suffer as other roles and functions become more important? Again, we simply do not know about all school boards, but surveys by the Institute for Education Leadership (IEL) suggest that, in many districts, it is difficult to perform all these roles well. [28] The turn-of-the-century reformers attenuated the board's role in providing connections between city and county governments for the delivery of integrated services for children. In trying to insulate school boards from city politics and politi-

cal parties, the reformers severed the board's connections with
other city and county government service providers. Today, wors-
ening conditions for children and the interrelated nature of their
family problems require some to consider undoing the work of
the early reformers. If boards are to play a larger role in such
areas as children's services, their existing role must be cut back.
Playing a smaller role in some of these functions would give boards
more time to influence children's policy.

Another policy area requiring more board time has to do with
the growing movement for adopting new curriculum standards
as part of comprehensive reform. School boards will need to
spend more time on systemic policies that help implement curriculum frameworks based on state standards. Boards will need
to ensure that their assessment, instructional materials, staff development, categorical programs, and fiscal policies are aligned
with the curriculum content standards that embody what students need to learn and be able to do. No Child Left Behind
(NCLB) emphasizes that the school board must play a crucial
and unique role as the vital link in making sure that high test
scores actually happen. The school board is the only entity that
can ensure that various components of NCLB are linked coher-
ently, and do not become merely disjointed projects.

To do this, the school board's consistent message to the entire school system must be that educational reform is its main
mission and not just an experiment. The board has a major role
in orchestrating numerous policies and looking for gaps in policies and conflicts between them. The state assessment requirements, for example, might conflict with local categorical programs,
or board curriculum requirements might conflict, for example,
with local categorical programs.

Can a school district in a large city lead systemic reform and
continue to perform the entire range of legislative, executive,
and judicial roles? The increased role of mayors in Chicago, Boston,
Cleveland, Philadelphia, and New York, suggests that the big-city
board is endangered. The overall task for the board becomes
even more complex in large districts if decentralization to the
school site is under way.

Change in Electoral Districts

From 1900 to 1950, reformers were adamant in their belief that school board members needed to be elected at-large and not by subdistricts. They contended that board members should represent the entire community and that policy should *not* be based on the particular needs of subcommunities or ethnic groups. Boards were urged to view the district as a *unitary entity* and not differentiate the curriculum for particular neighborhoods. All of this was part of the notion that centralization was desirable and that schools should not be influenced by the particularistic concerns of politics. Both of these positions are now being questioned, but the current all-encompassing school board role evolved from this era over one hundred years ago.

Dramatic changes have taken place in school board elections since the last era of reform. In 1996 more than fifty-three thousand board members were elected at large and thirty thousand were elected by district. Many communities use a combination of district and at-large elections to choose board members.[29]

The civil rights movement has increased its pressure to improve minority representation through district/ward elections— at least one hundred school systems have switched to district elections since 1994. This dramatic transformation of the electoral base suggests the need to rethink the roles of the school board. Perhaps the turn-of-the-century reformers were partially correct. A board that appoints personnel at the school level or second echelons of the central administration and approves contracts for supplies will be more prone to base its decisions on politics if that board is elected by ward or district rather than elected at large. For example, the IEL studies found board members elected by subdistricts became concerned with how school policy could improve the economic development of their own districts.

Another major change in board selection since 1920 has been the active participation of employee unions in board elections. As a later chapter shows, unions were not major players in school board elections until the 1970s. Today, unions can be the most influential participants in school board campaigns, in terms of both money spent and campaign workers supplied. With the turnout for board elections often falling below 15 percent, it is possible for unions in some localities to elect both sides of the collective-bargaining table. This raises again the question of whether we should re-evaluate the appropriate role of the school board in personnel decisions and other administrative areas.

Suggesting that changes may be needed in the structure and roles of school governance cannot be equated with a conspiracy to remove the schools from citizen control. Whether one agrees with specific ideas for structural changes or not—ideas that range from municipal authorities appointing school boards to state licensing of individual schools—the debate does not exclude citizens from exercising some type of political control of the schools. School boards are deeply embedded in the U.S. political culture and proposals for radical change in their roles will encounter well-organized grass-roots resistance.

THE LOCAL CAPACITY TO REFORM

Given this mix of stakeholders and of conflicting values in local education, there have been many—and varied—efforts at reform in recent decades. Some have been from the top down from the states in the form of curriculum additions and testing of students and teachers. Others have been from the bottom up from the school site in the form of school choice or site-based management. Yet others have been focused on the school board.

A basic question, however, underlies the effort to reform at the local level: Is this system capable of reform? That question was one of several that motivated scholars in the 1990s to study big cities undergoing school reform.[30] A "civic capacity" concept, based on experiences in big cities, suggests that the prospect for meaningful and sustainable reform depends on lines of conflict and cooperation among a wide array of actors, both inside and outside the educational system. Businesses, local foundations, labor unions, and community nonprofits must coalesce with city educators to create a long-term force for school improvement. Given state reform efforts, how did these urban civic capacities operate? The summary of a considerable body of sophisticated research found some degree of success and some barriers.

Why these barriers to reform? The local culture may cause a policy context that can weaken school reform capacity (e.g., in Pittsburgh, Newark, and St. Louis). Race, for example, may complicate reform when reform threatens those who have dominated local policymaking institutions (e.g., in Atlanta, Baltimore, Detroit, and Washington). Further, there are deep historical reasons for the presence of racial barriers to reform, as seen in Baltimore. Indeed, as the population of cities becomes more multiethnic, there may be a volatility to policymaking both in the schools (e.g., in Denver, Los Angeles, San Francisco, and Boston) and in municipal government.[31] There is little volatility in local politics when one group dominates urban policy and jobs; Irish dominance of big cities for a century reveals this pattern. However, as minority groups grow in numbers—and in voting—they seek more control over policy and jobs, and thus volatility grows. The recent rise of Hispanics in Los Angeles, Chicago, and New York shows this pattern.

This reluctance of local government to respond to state law fully is matched by the reluctance of local authorities to go along. Examples are the "school choice" and "accountability" reform efforts; by 2000 forty-eight states increased their state testing.[32] Reform takes different forms, of course, but it is seen as "the struggle for the soul of American education."[33] Such measures extend the idea of using market concepts to alter the weak qualities of public schooling.[34]

Did market reforms "work," given the different definitions of that term? Many supporters of these reforms used strong rhetoric in support of the policies, but there was also some early evaluation by researchers of the effects of these reforms on democratic theory and student learning. Distinguished scholars such as Paul Peterson and John Witte debated the effect of vouchers on quantitative measures of Milwaukee students' learning. Critics cite a lack of empirical support for improvement, point to the unsubstantiated assumptions of such changes, and even note the "failure" of market reforms.[35] In reality, however, the evidence thus far is not conclusive concerning either the success or the failure of state reforms on student learning, as we elaborate in Chapter 14.

This effort to break up the former bureaucratic/professional governance of local schools permeated reform currents. However, its presence is not very great among the 14,000 school districts or in the many more thousands of school sites across America. It is important to note that this reform occurs not simply here, for England, Australia, and New Zealand have taken a lead in governance reform, and comparisons have some uses.[36]

MAYORS AND PUBLIC SCHOOL GOVERNANCE*

Another type of major governance reform is mayoral takeover of schools. In recent years, a spate of cities—including New York, Boston, Chicago, and Cleveland—have shifted governance structures to give more control to mayors in the hope that such changes would ultimately lead to improved school quality and student achievement, as well as to diminished scandal and turmoil in the school systems. A closer look at these instances, however, shows that these governance changes have to be understood within the broader context of a particular city, and the particular frustration and challenges that led to the willingness to alter the top levels of educational control. The ways in which mayors have become more engaged with schooling have varied—from low involvement (for example, trying to influence traditional school board elections) to high involvement (gaining formal control over the schools or appointment of school board members). Just as each city is different, so are the impacts (such as can be determined) of governance changes. Most important, it is difficult to link these governance shifts to improved instructional practices or outcomes.

Background

Changes in American big-city school governance frequently focus on reform of an older prior reform.[37] Los Angeles, for example, decentralized central office control somewhat by creating regional superintendents in the 1970s, abolishing them in the 1980s, and then reinstating them in 2000. Reformers at the turn of the twen-

---

*This section is adapted from Michael Kirst, "Mayoral Influence, New Regime, and Public School Governance," CPRE Research Report Series, May 2002, the Consortium for Policy Research in Education, University of Pennsylvania.

tieth century wanted to overcome both the excessive decentralization of ward-based school boards with fifty to one hundred members each, and the corruption of mayoral and city council influence in teacher hiring. Tammany Hall was the symbol of city government in 1900. Consequently, reformers wanted school boards independent of city government, and touted the school board as the best vehicle for hiring a superintendent who would hire the teachers. One of the prime functions of the executive centralization of a small board and certified administrators was to create a uniform citywide curriculum. Mayors were seen as part of a discredited, inefficient, corrupt regime that did not fit with the industrial model of governance that envisioned the school's superintendent as a chief executive officer.[38]

From 1960 to 1996, some large cities like Chicago and Philadelphia preserved a role for the mayor in appointing school board members. In Baltimore, however, the mayor continued to exert policy control over the schools. As the performance of Baltimore's schools stagnated, various governance prescriptions, including subarea decentralization and weakly implemented school-based management, failed to improve performance. City school board members increasingly saw their role as redistributing school jobs and contracts to benefit residents in the geographic slice of the city that they represented.[39]

In the late 1960s and early 1970s, mayors like John Lindsey of New York City and Jerome Cavanaugh of Detroit stressed that city economies could not be substantially improved without good schools and middle-class students. But these mayors hesitated to seek operational control of the schools because they feared that the school improvement would not be enough to justify their reelection. During the 1980s, new African American mayors such as Harold Washington in Chicago and Coleman Young in Detroit focused in part on redistributing school jobs and services to minority communities.[40]

The 1990s produced a 180-degree reversal in the negative Tammany Hall mayoral image of the early 1900s. Some mayors projected an image of efficient public managers less interested in redistributing jobs to minorities and more interested in improved services. Mayors argued that City Hall needed to provide more integrated and coherent public services, including services for children. Better schools were essential to attracting the middle class and business to the central city. Anti-union Republican state legislatures in Illinois, Michigan, and Ohio were ready to cut the influence of teacher unions and the splintered school boards that faced repeated financial crises. Education reformers stressed that the churn of new policies of each new superintendent created lots of wheel-spinning, but little educational attainment.[41]

It is too soon to assess whether mayoral control in such cities as New York, Chicago, Cleveland, Harrisburg, and Boston will provide more coherent governance and improved pupil performance. But there are some positive signs. According to polls, citizens in Boston and Chicago are more pleased with mayoral control than the school boards that they replaced. Politicians from all over the United States have visited Chicago to see the new governance model where former city employees have taken over key bureaucratic operations such as personnel and facilities. But in Baltimore, after years of dismal pupil attainment and public dissatisfaction, the mayor (who never lost formal power over the schools) had to surrender control to the state.

Each new form of governance depends on a specific city context, and the willingness to make significant changes in governance emerges from an intense and long-gestating desire for a major shake-up in school policy and performance. Looming in the background in several of these cities is the fear of targeted or massive voucher schemes if mayoral action fails to improve the schools. Vouchers and mayoral control co-exist in Cleveland, Ohio, for example, where the ultimately dominant governance pattern is in doubt.

The arguments for mayoral control have strong appeal for some. Proponents justify giving the mayor control of, or an increased role in, the schools because it provides a single point of electoral accountability, greater integration of children's services with schools, and better pupil attainment. Such improvements will spur city economic development, stimulate more middle-class people to live in the city, and forge a closer alliance between city government and businesses. Mayors stress that they are in a better position to integrate citywide services (such as land use, transportation, after-school programs, and children's social services) with the schools. Political losers in this governance shift are district central-office professionals and, most important, the school board.

Opponents to mayoral control assert that a school board appointed by the mayor will result in less democracy because voters have fewer electoral choices and cannot vote for a board member from their section of the city. An Institute for Educational Leadership study found that electing school boards by subdistricts changed the role and behavior of school board members.[42] Boards became more attentive to the particular needs of certain geographical sections of their cities. The citywide education policy perspective lessened, and board concern with geographic redistribution of jobs, contacts, and constituent services grew. Minority representation on school boards, however, increased when citywide selection was changed to geographic districts. Hispanic groups in the West, for example, strongly support subdistrict board elections in order to increase representation of minority groups on school boards. Whether the alleged policy benefits of mayoral control are worth the loss of better geographic representation cannot be decided by general theories, but should be submitted to the local electorate.

The 1900-1920 movement to centralize school governance was justified in part by a perception that a citywide curriculum was needed to offset multilingual approaches.[43] This perceived need for centralization reoccurred in 1990 when city reading scores fell extremely low. Proponents hoped that increasing centralization through mayoral appointment would lead to a more intense and coordinated focus on reading in big cities. Again, we see the reform of an earlier reform. It was the alleged excessive centralization of curriculum in city schools that during the 1960s led in part to the call for urban decentralization to better meet the needs of diverse pupils.[44]

Every City Is Different

The striking thing about the growth of mayoral influence over schools is the distinctiveness of each city. There are no established patterns; form, function, and operation of mayoral influence are all over the map. These differences reflect diverse city contexts, local political cultures, interest group structures, state/

local relations, legal basis of city government, historical school governance structures, and other specific city characteristics. The personalities and ambitions of individual mayors are also important. Mayor Tom Menino of Boston, for example, featured his school role in his successful re-election campaign.

The array of mayoral interventions, described next with some specific examples, range from low to high influence. In addition, we will examine in greater depth some interesting impacts of mayoral intervention on cities.

Low Mayoral Influence. Mayors have threatened to take over schools, but pulled back when school policy changed in Akron, Ohio, and in West Sacramento, California. Mayors in St Louis, Los Angeles, and Sacramento endorsed slates of school board candidates and provided substantial campaign money and workers for their board choices, but they did not seek to overthrow the school boards' powers or to appoint board members.

Low-Moderate Mayoral Influence. Mayors appoint some school board members, but not a majority of the board. Voters in Oakland, California, approved a city charter amendment enlarging the school board from seven to ten members, and allowing Mayor Jerry Brown to appoint three members. The mayor's appointees formed a minority voting bloc that opposed the superintendent more often than the elected members. The Oakland mayor wanted to appoint the entire school board, but could not obtain city council approval for more than three of the ten members. Of the three candidates endorsed by the mayor, only two were successful.

Until recently, the mayor of Baltimore, Maryland, appointed all school board members because Baltimore never had an elected school board. However, in 1997, Baltimore received $230 million in state aid and, in return, the mayor lost his prerogative to appoint all members of the board of education. In its place, the mayor and governor jointly appointed a new nine-member board of commissioners, based on a nominating slate provided by the State Board of Education.[45]

After Anthony Williams was elected mayor of Washington, D.C., in 1998, he sought more control over school policy by proposing that he would appoint all eleven school board members. As in Oakland, the city council resisted this, arguing in favor of more electoral representation. The parties compromised by creating a hybrid nine-member board—four selected by the mayor, four elected from new geographic districts, and the president elected in a citywide referendum.[46] No one seems satisfied with this D.C. governance structure.

Moderate Mayoral Influence. The Detroit mayor appoints six members and the governor appoints one member to the city's school board. In some decisions, however, the governor's choice has veto power over the mayor's six appointees.[47]

The Cleveland mayor, under state legislation, appoints the school board and the district's chief executive officer (CEO). After thirty months, however, the mayor can fire the CEO, but only with concurrence of the board he appointed. Mayors Michael White and Susan Campbell have chosen not to get visibly involved in school policy or operations. Mayor White's relationship with CEO Barbara Byrd-Bennett was similar to the relationship between a nonexecutive chairman and a CEO in private business.[48] Mayor White was most active in improving facilities, but he met infrequently with the school board. He kept informed, but chose to let CEO Byrd-Bennett be the public leader. In 2002 Cleveland voters decided whether or not to reauthorize mayoral control.

> Philadelphia moved to the high-influence category after the voters approved a 2000 charter initiative enabling the mayor to appoint all school board members at one time. Philadelphia's previous mayor, Ed Rendell, could appoint board members in staggered terms, and he chose to defer to his choice for superintendent on matters of education policy and operational decisions. A district deficit in 2001 forced Mayor Street to negotiate with the state to provide more aid to Philadelphia schools in exchange for greater state policy control. The governor hired the for-profit Edison Schools to rethink governance and school improvement.[49]

In response to Mayor Street's objections, the governor agreed to drop Edison's central management of the system, but insisted on district governance by a five-member School Reform Commission, with three members appointed by the governor and two appointed by the mayor. A super majority of four is needed for many key decisions, including selection of the district CEO, adoption of the Commission's by-laws, selection of an independent evaluator, borrowing of money, and appointment of a general counsel. In effect, the mayor's two appointees have veto power over these important matters. Philadelphia hired former Chicago superintendent Paul Vallas in 2002.

High Mayoral Influence. The 1995 Chicago governance changes granting an enhanced role to the mayor were layered over reforms instituted in 1988. The earlier reforms, which were supported by state Democrats and civic activists, shifted power from the district to Local School Councils that appointed principals and allocated significant discretionary money at each school. The mayor's ability to appoint the city's school board was decreased under the 1988 legislation. The impetus for decentralization was not a desire to increase the influence of educators. One analyst noted, "Educators were blamed for the problems and their discretion curtailed."[50] Rather, the legislation was designed to enhance the influence of parents and community members.

The 1995 changes gave the Chicago mayor more authority than any mayor since the Progressive Era, effectively turning the public education system into a department of city government.[51] The 1995 legislation eliminated the school board nominating committee, which had effectively minimized the mayor's ability to select school board members, and replaced the traditional board with a corporate-style board. Under the new structure, only one of the five board members was to focus on education (the chief education officer), and there was a CEO, rather than a superintendent. The legislation limited the rights of unions to strike, and redefined a large number of issues as nonbargainable. The 1995 legislation enabled Chicago to contract for many building repairs, services, and purchases instead of employing numerous union personnel as under the old system.

Mayoral appointment of the school board in Boston began in 1991. In 1996 Mayor Menino made his choice for superintendent, former San Diego Superintendent Tom Payzant, a member of his cabinet. The school board had been reduced to an advisory role, and the mayor urged voters to hold him accountable for school performance. A 1996 referendum to retain the mayoral-appointed board was supported by 70 percent of Boston's voters, with only African American communities opposed. Board meetings were generally brief and poorly attended, while the real decisions were made by the superintendent and mayor. Mayor Menino acknowledged that the appointed board had not been accessible to public concerns, but said he and the superintendent would attend more to this function.[52]

In 2002 Mayor Bloomberg of New York guided state legislative approval to take control of the New York City Schools. The school board is advisory to the mayor, and Bloomberg removed members in 2004 who did not agree with his student promotion policy.

Impact of Mayoral Control

It is not possible to link some changes to school policy and practice to changes in governance. Some major trends can be attributed in part to mayoral intervention, although there is no apparent relationship between level (low, moderate, or high) of mayoral influence and the impact on schools. For example, Mayor Joe Serna of Sacramento (*low influence*) recruited, financed, and supported a slate of school board candidates, but left them alone to do their jobs. *Education Week* reported the following results:

> Many in California's capital city of 369,000 credit Mr. Serna, who died of cancer November 7, 2001, for pushing changes that now have more children reading at earlier ages, more school buildings scheduled for repair, and more politicians and parents backing an urban school system that was once considered a total loss.
>
> In the past year, the 52,000-student district's test scores in elementary-age reading and math have shown dramatic increases that would be the envy of any school system. A focused, determined school board, with a majority of members who were backed and supported by Mayor Serna, has ended the bickering and deadlock that plagued the district's governance for years. The public has shown renewed confidence and interest in the schools by passing, in October, the district's first bond measure for school repairs in more than twenty years.
>
> And despite some criticism of how the changes are being carried out, Sacramento is being looked at nationwide as a model of urban school success.[53]

Los Angeles Mayor Richard Riordan (*low influence*) used a school board electoral strategy that raised $2 million for a successful election. The mayor's reform board recruited former Colorado

Governor Roy Romer to be superintendent. Romer recentralized some instructional policy and, like Sacramento, installed Open Court as the standard reading program. The Los Angeles results on the state test (Stanford 9) have been as impressive as Sacramento's to date. Mayor Riordan also used the influence of his office to speed approval of new school construction in this rapidly growing district.

Among the *moderately influential* mayors, Cleveland's Mayor White actively promoted the successful $1.4 billion 2001 referendum to replace aging roofs, faulty wiring, rotting windows, and other chronic school building problems. Cleveland political observers contend that the voter support needed to upgrade the schools (average age of fifty-one years) was generated in part by increased public confidence in the new CEO, Barbara Byrd-Bennett. In 1999, Byrd-Bennett announced instructional reforms and accountability changes that centralized the system and de-emphasized past policies to provide parents with greater school site influence.[56] The impact of her reforms is unclear, but Byrd-Bennett is so popular that mayoral candidates hoping to replace Mayor White in 2001 sought her endorsement.

Mayors perhaps have the least impact where the mayor's powers are least clear, as in Oakland and Detroit. In Oakland (*low-moderate influence*), Mayor Jerry Brown has focused more on charter schools; his three mayoral appointees did not coalesce with the seven elected board members and their appointed superintendent. The new superintendent in Detroit has a lot of formal power, but has not sought a close relationship with city government. The Washington, D.C., school system has made little progress in restoring public confidence under the leadership of experienced superintendent Paul Vance, who once headed the large nearby suburban system in Montgomery County, Maryland.[55]

The state-ordered demise of the Detroit school board was viewed by city voters as usurpation without any local legitimacy.[56] Despite media support for the new regime (*low-moderate influence*), public opinion polls have indicated that voters, under the referendum allowed by the state law, want to return to an elected board in 2004. The last president of the Detroit school board was indicted on corruption charges. The new superintendent has managed to build more schools and make badly needed repairs.[57]

The cases of Boston and Chicago (*high influence*) have received the most academic scrutiny. In both cities, the primary movers behind the governance changes granting more power to the mayors were the business community, the mayor (especially in Boston), and state legislators. Local groups, such as community activists and minority group representatives, were not directly involved; educator organizations including the teacher unions were either peripheral to the debate or opposed to the change.

The proponents of the governance changes in Boston and Chicago had certain similar goals, but also some important differences. There was a strong emphasis in Chicago on improving the efficiency of the public schools, particularly the fiscal efficiency of the district. One analyst notes that the 1995 governance changes were a continuation of longstanding efforts to improve efficiency and restructure accountability. This emphasis reflected the interests of the Chicago business community. Improved efficiency was a factor in Boston, but not as central as the issues of standards and curriculum.[58]

The governance changes that shifted power toward the Chicago and Boston mayors set the stage for substantial alterations within these two school systems. The mayors and their chosen leaders took advantage of the new structural changes to implement substantive reforms. Paul Vallas, former Chicago budget director, assumed the new position of CEO of the Chicago Public Schools. The selection of Vallas reflected the business community's interest in a leader from outside traditional public education. Vallas believed that clear accountability, in combination with running the district more like a business, would lead to an improved organization. In this top-down change model, management creates the vision and defines clear sanctions for individuals and schools that fail to progress toward that vision.[59]

The selection of Tom Payzant as superintendent of the Boston schools was a far more traditional choice for district leader. His selection reflected Mayor Menino's interest in a professional educator who would avoid, to some extent, the political issues that consumed much of the time of previous superintendents. Payzant's approach was within the framework of traditional education reform; his primary focus reflected a professional education model involving higher standards and capacity-building.[60]

Scholars have compared the effects of mayoral takeover in Boston and Chicago with state takeover in Lawrence, Massachusetts, and in Compton, California. They concluded that mayoral takeover had a positive impact on pupil achievement:

> First, mayoral takeover is linked to increases in student achievement at the elementary grades. Second, gains in achievement are especially large for the lowest-performing schools, suggesting that mayoral takeovers involve a special focus on these failing schools. Third, mayoral takeover seems less effective for the upper grades, where the cumulative effects of many years of poor schooling are not easily reversible. Fourth, when state takeovers produce administrative and political turmoil, student achievement suffers. After a period of adjustment, however, state takeovers may also be able to produce positive achievement gains.[61]

Mayoral control had other attributes:

> Our analysis of city and state takeovers suggests the following conclusions. First, there are significant differences between mayoral takeover and state takeovers, and mayoral takeovers appear to be more productive in terms of academic improvement. Mayoral takeovers may make a significant impact on the lowest-performing schools. Second, takeovers may also produce more efficient financial and administrative management, and in the case of mayoral takeover, lead to a broadening of management expertise. Third, both city and state takeovers bring with them a heavy emphasis on academic accountability, and mayoral takeovers are more likely to utilize additional tests beyond state-mandated exams.[62]

The Six-City Study. Research scholars have conducted case studies of six cities (Chicago, Boston, San Diego, Seattle, Philadelphia, and Baltimore) that used mayoral control or school boards that appointed unconventional superintendents who had no prior experience in education administration.[63] In general, under mayoral control they found improvement over the previous regime of school boards, but little evidence of reaching higher goals such as widespread instructional improvement in classrooms. The researchers did find "partial evidence of increased city and school coordination," but not at the level that mayoral-control advocates hoped would take place. An overview of the findings for the three mayoral-control cities is presented in Table 5.4.

Table 5.4
Outcomes in Mayor-Controlled School Districts

Outcome	Boston	Chicago	Philadelphia
Aligned curriculum, tests, professional development, and rewards/penalties	Moderate	Low	Low
Political support of district reforms	High	High	Low
Improved coordination of city and school services	Slight	Slight	None
Increased turnover among:			
Teachers	Moderate	Moderate	High
Principals	High	High	High
Improved test scores:			
Elementary	Slight	Moderate	Moderate
Secondary	No	No	No
Reduced gap between white and minority scores	No	No	No

Source: L. Cuban and M. Usdan, *Powerful Reforms with Shallow Roots: Getting Good Schools in Six Cities.* New York: Teachers College Press, 2002.

The six-city study found that Boston was making progress in aligning the various elements of its systemic strategy to support principals and teachers in helping students to improve academic performance, but Chicago and Philadelphia were not. Support from business, media, and elites were strongly favorable of mayoral actions in Boston and Chicago. But researchers noted:

> Although the Chicago and Philadelphia cases offer instances of CEOs decisively acting in determining budgets, waiving rules, and slicing through bureaucratic layers the accumulated evidence for the two cities counter civic and business leaders' deep wish to connect governance changes and better management to improved student outcomes.[64]

These analysts applaud Boston for its leadership stability in extending Superintendent Payzant's contract from 1996 to 2005. They contend that a school without broader linkages to city, community, and private out-of-school services has little chance of success.

Conclusion

There is no political majority urging return to school board-dominated regimes in any of the cities that moved toward greater mayoral influence over the schools. Boston voters have reauthorized mayoral control in Boston, and the Illinois legislature extended the Chicago mayor's regime for another three years. Sacramento does not regret former Mayor Serna's campaign for a new board. Detroit has seen the president of its prior school board indicted for corruption. Still, the impact of enhanced mayoral influence on instruction remains tenuous and unclear.[65] Mayors are able to help balance the budget, improve buildings, and increase school supplies, but intervention in the classroom is more difficult. The most notable trend in these cities, however, is the diversity of the governance arrangements and how local context and civic culture determine whatever outcomes ensue.[66] While some mayors got involved in the details of school management, others provided their appointed superintendents wide discretion in running the schools. Increased centralized control of education policy was a consistent trend among these districts; there was no district where mayoral influence was primarily oriented to decentralizing policymaking to the schools.

Mayor Menino of Boston and Mayor Daley of Chicago sought to become the central symbol of school accountability, while Detroit Mayor Archer and Cleveland Mayor White preferred to stay behind the scenes and have the superintendent the focus of accountability. Several mayoral regimes need to be reauthorized by the voters in the next five years. These elections will determine in large part whether 1995-2001 was just another quick cycle of mayoral influence, or a more lasting governance change.[67] Even if these new regimes are extended, there are limits to mayoral influence and control:

> In other words, mayoral control of urban schools is merely one reform strategy. Changing governance arrangements clearly can make a difference in the way urban public school systems function, but such a strategy requires the right combination of ingredients—committed and skilled leadership by the mayor, willingness to use scarce resources, a stable coalition of supporters, appropriate education policies, and a cadre of competent, committed professionals to implement the reforms.[68]

State domination of governance, where mayors play a secondary role to the state as in Philadelphia and Baltimore, is one possibility for more urban districts. Mayors may have to demonstrate increases in pupil attainment and financial stability in order to ward off state intervention. The mayors of Baltimore and Philadelphia traded increased state aid for increased state control, so city economic growth may be a crucial factor. Slow-growing city economies will reduce local tax revenues and lead to calls for financial bail-outs by the states. States, however, seem less inclined to provide more money without a greater governance role, including state appointment of board members.

Some research suggests that efforts to change institutions often lead only to permutations of the institutions that had previously existed.[69] Thus schools controlled by mayors may well end up operating in a similar manner to the institutional structures they replaced.

A key issue is whether mayoral control can improve classroom instruction and the everyday lives of teachers and students. Historically, changes in school governance have not had much impact on classrooms, but the recent experiences in Chicago and Boston demonstrate the differential impact of local context on school improvement strategies. In the short run at least Mayor Daley had a significant impact on schools and students scoring below the fifteenth percentile on the Iowa Tests of Basic Skills. Mayor Menino has opted for a strategy that includes staff development and a new curriculum.

Whatever its impact, there are political and geographic limits to the spread of mayoral control. Many cities are not contiguous with school districts. For example, San Jose, California, has twenty school districts within its boundary, and southern cities are part of county school districts. The decline in the number of teacher strikes has also removed a crucial trigger for mayoral takeover. But test scores in many cities have not risen sufficiently to offset state and local dissatisfaction. More efforts at mayoral takeovers seem likely. And, if the mayors do not succeed in cities like Chicago, Boston, and Cleveland, voucher advocates will have a stronger case—at least for the worst-performing big-city schools. In sum, reformers will continue to use governance and organizational changes in an effort to improve the performance of education, even though these mechanisms may offer an indirect and uncertain strategy for improving classroom instruction.

NOTES

1. David Easton, *A Framework for Political Analysis* (Englewood Cliffs, N.J.: Prentice-Hall, 1965), pp. 132–33.

2. George S. Counts, *School and Society in Chicago* (New York: Harcourt, Brace, 1928).

3. Frederick M. Hess, *The Nation's School Boards at the Dawn of the Twenty-First Century* (Alexandria, Va.: National School Boards Association, 2002), pp. 14–18.

4. Patricia First and Herbert J. Walberg, *School Boards: Changing Local Control* (Richmond, Calif.: McCutchan, 1992).

5. Michael W. Kirst, "Loss of Support for Public Secondary Schools: Some Causes and Solutions," *Daedalus* (September 1981), assembles the contrary evidence noted below.

6. For the poll data from both sources see ibid.

7. See the evidence in David C. Berliner and Bruce J. Biddle, *The Manufactured Crisis* (Reading, Mass.: Addison-Wesley, 1995).

8. Frank W. Lutz and Laurence Iannaccone, eds., *Public Participation in Local School Districts* (Lexington, Mass.: Lexington Books, 1978).

9. Frank W. Lutz, "Methods and Conceptualizations of Political Power in Education," in *The Politics of Education*, 76th Yearbook of the National Society for the Study of Education (Chicago: University of Chicago Press, 1977), p. 32.

10. Frederick A. Rodgers, *The Black High School and Its Community* (Lexington, Mass.: Lexington Books, 1975). See also Catherine Marshall, ed., *The New Politics of Race and Gender* (London: Falmer, 1992).

11. Paul Peterson, *The Politics of School Reform* (Chicago: University of Chicago Press, 1985). See also Frederick Hess, *Spinning Wheels: the Politics of Urban School Reform* (Washington, D.C.: Brookings, 1999).

12. Raymond E. Callahan, *Education and the Cult of Efficiency* (Chicago: University of Chicago Press, 1962). See also Jane Hannaway and Robert Crowson, eds., *The Politics of Reforming School Administration* (London: Falmer, 1989).

13. Hess, *The Nation's School Boards*, p. 14.

14. William L. Boyd, *Community Status and Conflict in Suburban School Politics* (Beverly Hills, Calif.: Sage, 1975); and Hannaway and Crowson, *The Politics of Reforming*.

15. Christine Rossell, "School Desegregation and Community Social Change," *Law and Contemporary Problems* 42 (1978): 133–83; and Emmett H. Buell, Jr., *School Desegregation and Defended Neighborhoods: The Boston Controversy* (Lexington, Mass.: Lexington Books, 1981).

16. Boyd, *Community Status*; and Marshall, *The New Politics*.

17. Carol Mullins, "School District Consolidation: Odds Are 2–1 It'll Get

You," *American School Board Journal* 11 (1973): 160; James W. Guthrie, "Public Control of Public Schools," *Public Affairs Report* (Berkeley: University of California, Institute of Governmental Studies, 1974), p. 2.

18. Rossell, "School Desegregation," and James Cibulka, ed., *The Politics of Urban Education in the U.S.* (London: Falmer, 1992).

19. Leigh Stelzer, "Institutionalizing Conflict Response: The Case of School Boards," *Social Science Quarterly* 55, no. 2 (1974).

20. Frederick M. Wirt and Leslie Christovich, "Administrators' Perceptions of Changing Power Contexts: Superintendents and City Managers," *Education Administration Quarterly* (1989). See also Hess, *Spinning Wheels.*

21. Lila N. Carol et al., *School Boards* (Washington, D.C.: Institute for Educational Leadership, 1986).

22. Paul E. Peterson, *School Politics Chicago Style* (Chicago: University of Chicago Press, 1976), pp. 134–35.

23. Fred S. Coombs, "The Effects of Increased State Control on Local School District Governance" (paper presented to the annual meeting of the American Educational Research Association, 1987). See also Deborah Land, "Local School Boards Under Review: Their Role and Effectiveness in Relation to Students' Academic Achievement," *Review of Educational Research* 72: 2 (Summer 2002): 229-278.

24. Coombs, ibid.

25. William H. Clune, *Institutional Choice as a Theoretical Framework for Research on Education Policy* (New Brunswick, N.J.: Center for Policy Research in Education, Rutgers University, 1987), p. 4.

26. See Lila Carol et al., *Improving Grass Roots Leadership* (Washington, D.C.: Institute for Educational Leadership, 1986). A major data base is contained in Jacquelin Danzberger, Michael W. Kirst, and Michael Usdan, *Governing Public Schools* (Washington, D.C.: Institute for Educational Leadership, 1992). See also First and Walberg, *School Boards*, pp. 177–95.

27. Michael W. Kirst, "The State Role in School Restructuring," in Chester E. Finn, Jr., and Theodor Rebarber, eds., *Education Reform in the 90s* (New York: Macmillan, 1992), pp. 23–35.

28. Danzberger, Kirst, and Usdan, *Governing Public Schools.* The following observations and quotations are drawn from this source. See also, Paul T. Hill, *School Boards: Focus on Performance, Not Money and Patronage* (Washington, D.C.: Progressive Policy Institute, 2003).

29. Del Stover, "More School Boards Switch to Electing Members by District," *School Board News* 16, no. 22 (December 10, 1996): 1. See also, Kenneth Meier and Joseph Stewart, *The Politics of Hispanic Education* (Albany: State University of New York Press, 1991).

30. Summarized in Clarence Stone, ed., *Changing Urban Education* (Lawrence, Kansas: University Press of America, 1998). Jeffrey Henig, Richard Hula, Marion Orr, and Desiree Pedesleaux, *The Color of School Reform* (Princeton, N.J.: Princeton University Press, 1999).

31. The sources for each sentence in this paragraph are, in order, Lana Portz and Robin Jones, *City Schools and City Politics* (Lawrence: University Press

of Kansas, 1999); Henig, Hula, Orr, and Pedescleaux, *The Color of School Reform*; Marion Orr, *Black Social Capital* (Lawrence: University Press of Kansas, 1999).

32. Michael Kirst, *Accountability: Implications for State and Local Policymakers* (Washington, D.C.: OERI, U.S. Department of Education, 1990).

33. Peter Cookson, Jr., *School Choice* (New Haven, Conn.: Yale University Press, 1994).

34. John Chubb and Terry Moe, *Politics, Markets, and America's Schools* (Washington, D.C.: Brookings, 1990).

35. In order, Bruce Fuller and Richard Elmore, with Gary Orfield, eds., *Who Chooses? Who Loses?* (New York: Teachers College Press, 1996); Terry Astuto, David Clark, et al., *Roots of Reform* (Bloomington, Ind.: Phi Delta Kappan, Foundation, 1994); Seymour Sarason, *The Predictable Failure of Educational Reform* (San Francisco: Jossey-Bass, 1990). See also, Jeffrey Henig, *Rethinking School Choice* (Princeton, N.J.: Princeton University Press, 1994).

36. Ami Volansky and Isaac A. Friedman, *School-Based Management: An International Perspective* (Jerusalem, Israel: Ministry of Education, 2003).

37. David Tyack and Larry Cuban, *Tinkering Toward Utopia: A Century of Public School Reform* (Cambridge, Mass.: Harvard University Press, 1995).

38. David Tyack, *The One Best System* (Cambridge, Mass.: Harvard University Press, 1974).

39. Danzberger, Kirst, and Usdan, *Governing Public Schools.*

40. Peter Beinart, "The Pride of the Cities," *New Republic* (June 30, 1977): 16–24.

41. Frederick Hess, *Spinning Wheels.*

42. Danzberger, Kirst, and Usdan, *Governing Public Schools.*

43. Tyack, *The One Best System.*

44. Jane Hannaway and M. Carnoy, eds., *Decentralization and School Improvement* (San Francisco: Jossey-Bass, 1993).

45. James Cibulka, "Old Wine, New Bottles," *Education Next* 1:4 (2001): 28-35.

46. Ibid.

47. Community Renewal Society, *Catalyst: For Cleveland Schools* 2:5 (2001): 6, 12.

48. Ibid.

49. *The Philadelphia Inquirer*, "Lessons from School Takeovers: Big Change at Districts, Less So in Classrooms" (November 4, 2001): 1.

50. D. Shipps, *Regime Change: Mayoral Takeover of Chicago Public Schools* (Consortium for Policy Research in Education, University of Pennsylvania, unpublished manuscript, 2000).

51. Ibid.

52. G. Yee, *From Court Street to City Hall: Governance Change in Boston Public Schools* (Consortium for Policy Research in Education, University of Pennsylvania, unpublished manuscript, 2000).

53. www. Edweek.org., "Sacramento Mayor's Legacy: Improved Schools" (February 2, 2000).

54. P. Ryan, "Can't Let Go," *Education Next* 1: 4 (2001): 36-41.

55. Cibulka, "Old Wine, New Bottles."

56. C. Gewertz, "Detroit Board Splits Over Superintendent Choice," *Education Week* (January 26, 2000), p. 5.

57. D. Plank, interview, November 2001.

58. Yee, *From Court Street to City Hall.*

59. Shipps, *Regime Change.*

60. Yee, *From Court Street to City Hall.*

61. Kenneth Wong and F. Shen, "Does School District Takeover Work? Assessing the Effectiveness of City and State Takeover as a School Reform Strategy," paper presented at the annual meeting of the American Political Science Association, San Francisco, California.

62. Ibid.

63. Larry Cuban and Michael Usdan, *Powerful Reforms with Shallow Roots: Getting Good Schools in Six Cities* (New York: Teachers College Press, 2002).

64. Ibid.

65. Wilbur Rich, *Black Mayors and Schools* (New York: Garland, 1996).

66. C. Stone, *Changing Urban Education* (Lawrence: University of Kansas, 1998).

67. William Boyd and James Cibulka, *Reforming Urban School Governance* (Westport, Conn.: Ablex/Greenwood, 2002).

68. Cibulka, "Old Wine, New Bottles."

69. Paul DiMaggio and Walter Powell, "The Iron Cage Revisited: Institutional Isomorphism and Collective Rationality in Organizational Fields," *American Sociological Review* (April 1983): 147–60; and James G. March and Johan P. Olsen, *Rediscovering Institutions* (New York: New York Free Press, 1989).

6

The Chief Administrator as Professional and Politician

THE SUPERINTENDENT PROFESSION

Before exploring the current political role of the superintendent, it would help to explain the background of this profession. Table 6.1 pinpoints several key social aspects of the superintendency as the twentieth century ended. Common to both private and public institutions, the profession is heavily male and white, although the number of women and people of color increased through the 1990s. Studies report, however, a crisis growing from the fact that fewer men or women, whether minority or white, are willing to undertake this job; there are more job openings than qualified applicants. The reasons lie in the preceding chapters. Some cities turned to nontraditional sources in the 1990s. Seattle selected a retired Army general as its superintendent; Los Angeles, a former Colorado governor; Milwaukee, a former social service director; and San Diego, a former prosecuting attorney. New York and Philadelphia have hired CEOs from private business. It is also clear that boards of education do poorly in recruiting women and minorities for these positions; minorities are more often offered jobs in districts of their own ethnicity.

175

Table 6.1

Demographic Aspects of Superintendents, 2000

Race	95 percent white
Gender	87 percent male
	—82 percent women believe school boards fail to see their gender as strong managers; 41 percent men agree
Age	52–55 years (up since 1992)
Tenure	5–6 years in current position
Role	More women than men share power with school board
Party	One-third each—GOP, Democrat, independent
Profession in crisis	88 percent agree
Number of new jobs	1,000
Untapped candidates	Women, 13.2 percent (up from 6.6 percent in 1992) minorities, 5.1 percent (up from 3.9 percent in 1992) —found mostly in districts composed of one's own ethnicity
Board approves suggestions	89 percent (for 90 percent of time)

Source: Abstracted from two reports by the American Association of School Administrators in 2000: *The 2000 Study of American School Superintendents*; and Bruce Cooper, Lance Fusarelli, and Vincent Carella, *Career Crisis in the School Superintendency?*

The data in Table 6.1 show that women believe strongly that boards do not see them as strong managers, and over 40 percent of the men agreed that boards hold this view.

For such reasons, the superintendent's role is being rethought as urban applicant pools are smaller. Some of this is caused by political turbulence. While superintendents overwhelmingly believe their boards accept their recommendations (hardly a sign of constraint), often these recommendations were made with an eye on board or other constraints. We need to study constraints that arise in a shared decision-making context.

Whatever independence superintendents once knew, the environment around them today is quite complex, as this chapter will set out. As an introduction to that theme, note the conclusions of the Danforth Foundation from case studies of a wide range of fifty-five superintendents in the 1990s who defined the administrative environment they now face.[1] This environment is summarized by the following chapter titles in its report on the "challenges and dilemmas" of that group:

- Negotiating City Politics and Controversy
- Responding to Reform Goals and Mandates
- Doing More with Less: The Financial Crunch
- Resolving Conflict with Boards
- Coping with Daily Crises
- The Personal and Professional Toll

The title of this last chapter on tolls should be no surprise. Only two of these fifty-five superintendents were in office one year after the study; also, there were six superintendents in seven years at Dallas. Details of their complaints provide a very personal sense of the work, including

- long work days (about which the spouse complained),
- weakening of spirit (losing the "fire in the belly"),
- hassles from a greater number of citizen groups and teachers, and
- a growth in violence within schools.

These are the personal costs for superintendents that result from the broader concept of political "turbulence" used in this book. "Pressure cooker" might be a better term to describe the environment in which the superintendent must work. The main reason superintendents leave the job (81 percent) is politics and federal, state, and local bureaucracy. Low pay and higher standards issues are a distant second; indeed, salaries are high even in smaller districts. Half of the superintendents say legal issues require too much of their time. Ninety percent want more autonomy to run schools while holding them accountable for getting results.[2]

THE PROFESSIONAL AS DECISION MAKER

If the community is only occasionally active and the board feels limited, school professionals should retain a greater influence on policy issues. After all, professional educators have their resources, too. They define choices, produce research, provide specific recommendations, and shape the formal agenda. Using these resources, professionals generate their own pressures and information that can affect, if not determine, the board's deliberations and decisions. In Easton's framework, the school superintendent and staff provide "withinputs" to the school board and the bureaucracy. Many specific policy issues, however, may never reach the school board if the superintendent and staff act under broad discretion set by the school board. Consequently, both board and superintendent are authorities seeking to gain support from the community through using appropriate resources like budget, curriculum, teacher selection, and so on.

The administrative staff does operate under certain constraints, however. They must anticipate reactions of board members to their actions because the board does have the basic power to constrain or even fire them. They also know that the ultimate power of a provoked electorate is to remove them by changing the board, as noted earlier. It is also likely that the superintendent would act in keeping with the school board's wishes on many issues even *without* the threat of job loss. It is natural to assume that board members would hire a person whose values were similar to their own. An example of this is the low rate of turnover in smaller districts, which tend to be more homogeneous in their values. In effect, the board's impact on specific decisions may be more indirect than direct, but it is nevertheless real. The superintendent operates with considerable latitude as long as he or she stays within the board's ideological "zone of tolerance." But big cities are a more complex context, and it is harder to find or sustain governing coalitions. The completed tenures of the twenty-five largest urban superintendencies shrunk from an average of fourteen years in 1900 to just under six in 1990. However, some cities perpetuate very short tenures, while others create longer ones.[3]

Do superintendents mold school boards by control of policymaking by means of the board's socialization to professional values? Research in the past seemed to support that claim, as our first edition pointed out in detail. The limited knowledge of board members who work part time created little pressure on the superintendent and the central-office staff. Moreover, the board accepted their expertise on a range of school policies, rooted in the profession's standing. However that past research failed to tap what political scientists term the "law of antici- pated reaction," which is the capacity of the administrator to estimate the limits within which to act without board concern for the "zone of tolerance" in organizational theory. That is, su- perintendents inhibit their own behavior by knowing the con- trols these boards *might* exert. Subtle and hard to measure, this influence is still a reality that superintendents will detail in end- less anecdotes.

NEW ROLES FOR THE SUPERINTENDENT

Much current school politics has put the professional at odds with the community, the antihero of school democracy. Many of the challenging trends set out in this book have affected other professions besides education, often termed a "revolt of the cli- ent." It appears not only in education but also in law, in medi- cine, among clergy, and in other areas. This is happening not only here but in other English-speaking nations as well. The consequence of this tension between the professional and a mis- trustful client is that training schools have begun to redefine the professional role so that graduates are more sensitive to citi- zen needs. One aspect in schools of education is the growing attention to defining the "political" role that the educator must play. This book carries that theme. Nevertheless, the traditional apolitical myth still holds for many educators. However, future administrators are often being taught that they operate in a web of external demands to which they must respond and balance in some fashion.[4]

An obvious outcome is that old role concepts become out- moded. Given political turbulence, by adopting the role of "ne- gotiator-statesman" one is more effective than any notion of be- ing a neutral technician. The new role sees conflict as inevitable in human affairs and regards interest group demands as legiti- mate, to be dealt with and reconciled as part of the job. The superintendent is not just a leaf floating helplessly on the flood of turbulent politics. Yet note how far this role brings us from that of the earlier school administrator who was then seen as an omnipotent, insensitive figure—the benevolent autocrat.

Superintendents today face a conflict in theories of their leadership. Facing "top down" to "bottom up" reforms, leadership is confused by the decisional context. Unintended consequences have wrecked many in the last quarter-century. Many and more complex tools of management and leadership are needed to do the job. One analysis of how superintendents spend their time stresses the large amounts of verbal interactions with so many people for a short period of time. Little time exists for reflection, while much time is spent on the persuasion and discussion that are the essence of building internal coalitions—that is, a political role.[5]

SUPERINTENDENTS, POLICY PRESSURES, AND CONFLICT MANAGEMENT

In this section we wish to explore the kinds of pressure on superintendents. All the issue demands from new core constituencies were shown to have an impact first on the school board, which then focused them on the superintendent. How does this person act when political shot and shell explode around the school? A clearer picture is that many decisions are standard, unchallenged—even almost ritual. Many others are different, though. First we need to review superintendents' own perceptions of their high-pressure milieu and their judgment of its effect. Then we conceptualize the new roles and skills needed to manage this conflict.

Evidence of Pressure

What specifically was creating job stress?[6] A 2001 survey of hundreds of school administrators found the prime pressure was adapting to new politics, unfunded mandates, inability to remove bad teachers, school board interference, and special education.[7] Note that each source is from outside his or her office. The second largest stress came from trying to get public backing for school programs, and the third from involvement in collective

Table 6.2

Superintendents' Perceptions of Group Pressures

1. From how many groups have you perceived increasing demands?

8	7	6	5	4	3	2	1	0	N
5.8[1]	3.3	20.8	12.5	20.0	15.8	11.7	7.5	2.5	131

[1]That is, 5.8 percent perceived that all eight groups had increased demands on them; 3.3 percent perceived seven groups, and so on.

2. Which groups in particular have increased demands?

Group	Percent Replying "More" and "Much More" Demands Perceived*
Traditional:	
Business	48
Labor	62
Citizen:	
Clientele	52
Minorities	50
Lay opinion	61
Officials:	
Elected local	34
State	50
Federal	54

*More than one choice was possible.

Source: Frederick Wirt and Leslie Christovich, "Administrators' Perceptions of Policy Influence: Conflict Management Styles and Roles." *Educational Administration Quarterly* 25 (1989): 5–35. Reprinted with permission of Sage Publications.

bargaining. The ranking may shift among superintendents, but they remain heavyweight pressures. Note that all these stress sources are also aspects of the job becoming ever more political; that is, all three sources affect the emerging political tasks of the position.

What were these groups creating such pressure about? And was this different from other local officials? A national sample of superintendents in 2001 identified many specific groups with pressures that were significantly greater than that known earlier in their careers.[8] Table 6.2 summarizes the situation even earlier. Almost 60 percent found four or more groups had increased their demands (more than that reported for city managers and planning directors in the same study). Was this greater pressure simply from citizens? Using three different ways of defining citizens, Table 6.2 reports that this pressure is not much different from traditional and official groups; one suspects the high percentage for "lay opinion" might have been professional deference to the democratic image. The point is that, aside from elected local officials (e.g., school boards), all groups were increasing their demands, especially from teachers. In an open-ended question about what aspect had most changed since starting their career, the answer was overwhelmingly "politics," often written with exclamations.

Does this mean that increased group pressures had weakened acceptance of the superintendent's policy judgments? Quite the contrary, as superintendents noted in Table 6.1. One-half also reported in Table 6.2 an *increased* acceptance of those judgments by board and citizens; only 12 and 7 percent, respectively, reported that their acceptance had declined. One might think the answer to such influence would vary with the kind of community. However, regression analysis reported no significant relationship among measures of communities. One might infer from the two data sets of these tables that as group pressure on this office expanded so, too, did the need for conflict management techniques in order to get one's recommendations approved.

However, because not all superintendents can win all the time, one cost of the job is undoubtedly professional stress, reflected in the shortened job tenure and the pervasive illnesses the literature reported. Yet the findings support two ideas usually seen as contradictory, namely that the superintendent is "beleaguered" but also dominates school decision making. The reality may well be that this professional fits both descriptions, but pays considerable costs for both activities.

These results agree with the dissatisfaction theory of democracy discussed earlier. That is, administrators can operate with minimum public concern until an issue arises reflecting popular dissatisfaction with some professional decisions. Whether it is the big-city milieu—where single-issue or district-oriented board members insist on power sharing[9]—or smaller districts that face school closing, a new policymaking environment for superintendents emerges. Or it may arise from "culture wars" over ideological views, such as book censorship, use of prayers, and so on. Clearly, this new context requires the professional to act in a representative, coalition-building way—actions well known to "politicians" in government. Caught as they are between old role definitions and new demands, no wonder that superintendents have suffered more turnover, illness, and early retirement.

Whatever the reason for reduced tenure, by the year 2000 many districts were facing a new problem—the retirement of a large minority of administrators and the difficulty of replacing them.[10] For example, administrator groups in Illinois reported in 2000 that

- superintendents in 41 percent of 892 districts would retire in the next five years,
- one-third of 4,000 principals would retire in the next five years, and
- in Chicago in Fall 2000 one-half of all principals were eligible to retire in Spring 2001.

Elsewhere the difficulty in finding leadership has been equally stark. In 2000 in New York City 163 of 1,145 schools opened with only a temporary principal. In Iowa one-third of all administrators opted to retire in four years. In Washington 300 principals left in 1999–2000.

What is happening? Aside from the tensions noted earlier, one major impetus is that many states have provided early retirement that administrators are taking in large numbers. Legislators thought this would reduce school costs (by getting rid of high-salary administrators), but it has led to a fierce competition among districts to offer even higher salaries to get candidates. In Illinois, for example, salary *averages* for superintendents in 2001 increased to $100,000 (the U.S. average is over $112,000). Some superintendents found they could retire and be rehired by a nearby district to almost double their income. Some superintendent candidates, in noting the openings for principalships, found that their salaries were no better than those for head teachers—a job with less stress.

Backing away from the particulars of this new stress on the

system, we witness in these figures the fading of one portion of the "baby boomer" generation. The larger picture, though, is that the educational system faces a major problem at the turn of the millennium—adequate leadership in the numbers needed. The old practice of ignoring women or minorities for these positions may well have to give way, especially when boards are faced with a list of white male candidates who have no experience and with women and minorities who do. It is remarkable that, knowing the turbulence that faces these jobs, a newer generation keeps coming to take it on.

ROLE, STYLE, AND CONFLICT MANAGEMENT

As professionals are not simply reflexive responders to their communities, we need to describe the varieties of superintendent behavior today amidst so much educational change.

A Dynamic Model of Superintendent Response to Change

Much of what any executive does involves managing routines to implement decisions about allocated resources. Each profession provides training in such routine management (budgeting, personnel, planning, dissemination), and its practitioners fill their early careers with these tasks. However, even routine management is not without its potential for conflict. The fight each year to get more personnel is a typical example. This routine conflict looks like a standard dramatic play in which "actors" play their roles in pursuit of more resources. However, such interplay still operates within bounds set by authority (e.g., deadlines), by reality (e.g., revenue limitations), and by the compromise principle (nobody gets everything, nobody gets nothing, everybody gets something.)

How do superintendents manage the conflict that comes from such groups? In theoretical terms, our concerns are with two questions: What variation exists in the styles of conflict management, and how does one explain that variation? For the practitioner, the question is, Can managing conflict advance one's survival and career enhancement? This is important as evident from reports of superintendent dissatisfaction and turnover.[11]

Encompassing these major questions is the basic paradigm of forces working on administrators:

Change generates *demands* in *policymaking* arenas to which *superintendents respond* with *differing roles and styles* of conflict management.

We will provide some ideas about each of these emphasized terms.

THE INFLUENCE OF CHANGE

As changes in the decision-making environment generate new demands, there is conflict with which the superintendent must deal. What forces of changes are there?

Population Alteration: Changing the Players

Change in the social composition of the population has been a constant in urban history, everywhere transforming political, economic, and social institutions and programs.[12] Thus, recent transformations stemming from the growth of minority and poor populations in the biggest cities have had a major impact on city resources needed to cover the high-cost problems of welfare, crime, and education. Or the suburban exodus after World War II transformed politics on the city's rim from rural quiescence to conflict over better services brought on by the upwardly mobile.[13] In short, changing the players in the community means changing the policy games and the rewards.

The grand transformations in school politics lie partly with population growth or decline. Growth has curious effects on social structures and their performance. For example, an *arithmetical* growth of population inevitably brings on a *geometrical* increase in demands for services, both in quantitative and qualitative terms. A familiar example for the city manager is that as population grows, the ratio of police to citizens increases. Another example is suburbanites flooding the urban fringe who want better, not simply more traditional, services. On the other hand, population decline also has different effects on urban services and their administrators. That effect is seen in rural consolidation; fewer students mean less need for teachers. Most voters (65 percent) do not have children in public schools, and turnouts are lower for Hispanic than white parents. The major point is that change in the social mix of the population has consequences for the administrative environment of superintendents in facing new demands and pressures, and hence more conflict.

Fiscal Context: Living with Boom or Bust

Recent decades have witnessed a "riches to rags to riches" story for schools and superintendents. Prosperity makes for easy leadership, whether as president or superintendent. Recessions, though, make all leaders look bad. But in either case, local conflict is generated.

However, even when prosperity grows and superintendents hit it rich, conflict can still develop. As property values inflate, paying the property tax (the main source of school revenue) becomes ever more burdensome. Also, while addressing problems of equity, the appearance of federal riches in the form of categorical and bloc grants over the last thirty years has also created conflict. Bigger cities fell into greater fiscal dependency on federal grants that often carried requirements that altered the local policymaking context. Under the stimuli of such programs, public participation was enlarged,[14] minority and poor groups gained influence in the urban power structure,[15] and consequently public demands on policy needs altered. More significantly, these grants brought state and federal officials into local systems.[16]

In short, prosperity introduces conflict to superintendents in the form of new calls for distributive and regulatory policies. Conversely, when recession tightens local budgets, superintendents face another conflict over redistributive policies that involves taxing one group for the benefit of another, always a hotly contested issue unless it aids business. Consequently, changes in the national economy send waves into the local economy and political system that generate conflict for the superintendents.[17]

THE ARENAS OF POLICYMAKING

The way that local governance is organized affects which groups will get access and services. Accordingly, variations in policymaking arenas affect the forces of external change and the superintendent's environment.

Regular Players of the Game: Different Lineups and Scores

In urban politics, interest groups, legislatures, bureaucracies, and executives constitute *regular players* in the local policy game.[18] How these actors manage conflict can exert an independent influence on decision making, a point we expand on later. Superintendents face conflict within their own organizations, either downward with their staff or outward with community groups. Amid this array of actors in conflict management, the central question is how change systematically affects them and superintendents.

The reaction to change moves superintendents in decisional stages from

- *reflexive resistance* (i.e., if change were needed, we would have already done it);
- to *damage control* (i.e., let's reduce the effects of external change);
- to *intense conflict* (i.e., they can't do that!);
- to a final *conflict resolution* (let's compromise);
- to *acceptance of changes* within the educational system (i.e., we can live with this).

Also, it is not clear how large a part of the superintendents' actions involve both episodic and routine conflict. If conflict is extensive (i.e., being pecked to death by ducks), superintendents' time for professional matters, such as planning and oversight, is reduced. In short, the superintendent exists in a political web of pressures with the local actors, all coping with external influences, that create conflict locally.

The Structure of Policy Arenas: Different Fields and Games

The organizing of the field on which such conflict is played out can influence the process. An axiom of social science is that organization is not value free, i.e., different forms of organization reflect different values. Early in this century education reformers understood this axiom when their middle-class zeal overthrew the party-dominated forms of nominations and elections. The proposition was put precisely decades ago by political scientist E. E. Schattschneider:

> All forms of political organization have a bias in favor of the exploitation of some kinds of conflict and the suppression of others because organization is the mobilization of bias. Some issues are organized into politics while others are organized out.[19]

Consequently, reformed governments featuring nonpartisan election on a city-wide basis show striking policy differences from partisan governments. For example, the reformed governments spend less for many services and give civil rights groups less favorable policies than do the second type. The unreformed types facilitate access to voting and representation by working and lower classes—and racial minorities—while the reformed types do the same for the middle class.[20] This is the meaning of the "mobilization of bias."

Outside big cities, superintendents usually preside over a policy arena of reformed governments, which are more open to middle-class interests—just as Progressive reformers early in this century had in mind. Against this middle-class context, in the 1960s new challenges appeared to that class from new federal policies that supported the interests of poor, working-class, and some middle-class groups. *Thus the bias of local structure confronted the bias of external policies.* In the process, superintendents' conflict management was influenced by different structures of governance.

SUPERINTENDENT ROLES AND CONFLICT MANAGEMENT

Differences in roles and styles among superintendents provide another way of understanding conflict management. One review of the research expressed some of the dilemmas:

A job that self-report surveys discover to be increasingly tension-filled and declining in attractiveness nevertheless finds its role incumbents express- ing confidence in their abilities, with a sense that they are very much "up" to their job challenges. A role that is growing in reputation as a high- conflict part of public officialdom is simultaneously described as much less burdened by conflict than the comparable job of city manager. A position known for its visibility and beck and call responsiveness to school board and community is nevertheless described as a position that at its core is more heavily focused *inward* toward management of the school district and its professionals.[21]

The Significance of Role

At the center of any social structure is the individual perform- ing functions, or roles, learned through socialization. *Role* refers to expectations of one's behavior by significant others within the social structure. Professional schools socialize newcomers to the roles expected of instructional leaders by the community. Of course, roles have changed throughout this century from neu- tral technician, or manager, the benevolent autocrat, to a power- sharing, active advocate of programs, the politician.

Role also implies behavior in the pursuit of significant values. One problem in much writing about superintendents is the unstated assumption that they pursue all values with equal strength. Can they strive equally for quality, equity, efficiency, or citizen choice? That seems unlikely in practice because personal resources are finite. However, certain values are so vital to the administra- tor that she or he would expend more resources on these than on others. In those important values, the administrator will fight harder, even when faced with adverse community pressure. Moreo- ver, not all superintendent ties with the community are conflictual, so the degree of conflict provides another variable in studying the superintendent in community conflict. In short, superintend- ents will pursue their values differently given different degrees of community conflict.

We can structure this micropolitics of superintendent values and community conflict into potential role models. Table 6.3 ranges degrees of community conflict against degrees of super- intendent value intensity; from this we can infer different role behaviors. We estimate from the research literature that there

Table 6.3
Community Conflict and Superintendent Values

Superintendent Value Intensity	Community Conflict High	Community Conflict Low
High:	BESIEGED PROFESSIONAL	DOMINANT PROFESSIONAL
Outcome	Win or lose	Win
Frequency	Limited	Unknown
Low:	COMPLIANT IMPLEMENTER	OVERSEER OF ROUTINES
Outcome	Win	Win
Frequency	Unknown	Extensive

are many occasions where the Besieged role behavior takes place, and there are many occasions for the Overseer of Routines role; in the other two cases the frequency is indeterminant. Included in the Overseer of Routines role are the tasks of routine management and intraorganizational conflict noted earlier. Much professional training takes place in this area, but much less training is provided for conflict management.[22]

What role behavior is likely when community conflict is high? When the superintendent's values are intensely engaged—the Besieged case—he or she will have at least one of four orientations to conflict management: competing, accommodating, collaborating, or compromising.[23]

Again in Table 6.3, when community conflict is low and superintendent value intensity is high, the model of the Dominant Professional arises. Here, the superintendent dominates policymaking out of a professional orientation of "managing" the service provided to citizens. This role type characterizes the long period before recent challenge and conflict.[24] However, when the community is highly conflictual and superintendent values are not intense, the latter can play another role. Assisting the community to devise and administer a program, this Compliant Implementer role behavior implies that no major challenge to professional standards or no fear of job security exists.

Viewing the professional in this micropolitical fashion provides a fuller understanding of role behavior. The typology also makes the point that no role is dominant; rather a number of roles exist that the superintendent may select as conditions warrant. Further, this view prompts us to look at different policy contexts where conflict may or may not exist. The point is that these roles are like a collection of hats; the superintendent may choose one to fit the situation. Of course, the typology does not provide a precise measure of these two qualities of superintendent value and community conflict. But it encourages thinking in patterned terms about the administrative environment when conflict exists.

SUPERINTENDENT STYLES AND CONFLICT MANAGEMENT

Another personal aspect of the superintendent is *style*, or the quality of one's individuality expressed in action. Style is distinguished from role because style is a matter of choice rooted in individual emotions and judgments. Role is more narrowly confined to actions to which one was socialized in professional training and experience. Style is little studied in the scholarship of professionals of any kind, although significant anecdotes imply how different styles do operate. All of us have experiences with doctors who grate us; in medical schools they seem to have flunked Bedside Manners 101. Yet studying style is important because the different roles noted in Table 6.3 permit individualization within each.

A Typology of Conflict Styles

Conflict styles are few because individuals in conflict tend to fit into a few patterns of behavior. However, different styles are all versions of the classic "fight-flight" or "exit-voice-apathy" characterization of how individuals act when confronted by threatening situations. That is, when confronted one may actively oppose others, leave the scene, or loyally stay but not act. In Table 6.4 we label these three styles in facing conflict as Avoid, Mediate,

Table 6.4
Community Conflict and Superintendent Styles

| | Community Conflict | |
Superintendent Style	High	Low
Avoid	Presider	Delegator
Mediate	Compromiser	Facilitator
Fight	Assertive	Professional

and Fight. Mediation style can involve such strategies as accommodation, collaboration, and compromise.

How does this range of styles interact with a range of intensity in community conflict? If the characteristic style of conflict management is Avoid, then when high community conflict occurs, the superintendent will seek only to preside over, but not to direct or oppose, the conflict. This includes not taking stands, assuring that rules of procedure are followed, and, in effect, deflecting the decision to the authoritative action of the school board. But when conflict is low, the Avoid style will delegate authority to other professionals within the organization and later approve their decisions.

If the superintendent's style is more inclined to Mediate, conflict produces two different roles. One may seek conflict resolution through compromise; note that this style enables one's own policy values to be incorporated into the final result to some degree. When conflict is low, however, the Mediate style may act as facilitator, a "first among equals" style of assisting other professionals to do their job while assuring that the general direction of the organization is maintained.

The Fight style of conflict management is the most dramatic, the subject of "war stories" about "beleagured" professionals whose norms have been challenged. This is most evident when community conflict is high, and the superintendent style becomes assertive, mobilizing group support and building coalitions to deal with problems of change.[25] By competing with other groups, but accommodating where politically feasible, assertive styles differ dramatically from the presider style. When conflict is low, though, the Fight style involves the kind of administrative leadership that training schools and textbooks urge, the style that has created the modern service bureaucracies. This includes thinking in terms of the once dominant benevolent autocrat.

REFLECTIONS ON CONFLICT BEHAVIOR IN URBAN PROFESSIONS

Research into these diverse superintendent styles and roles operating amid a shifting world of conflict has enriched our conceptualizations. Which role or style the person selects may well involve cost-benefit calculations about getting the job done, advancing professional goals, and enhancing one's career.

The growing fragmentation of the managerial, political, and educational tasks that superintendents perform is implied in these styles and roles. The distinction between administrator and leader that runs through them has been reinforced by superintendents' training and experience. A leading text in educational administration draws the distinction that typically applies to all superintendents:

> In sum, the professional administrator is likely to view his or her role as that of one who finds out what consumers want from the schools and who delivers educational services accordingly. The educational leader, by contrast, is very much concerned with the issues of purpose and direction.[26]

The administrative function exists in all but the Beseiged role of Table 6.3 and the presider and delegator styles of Table 6.4. However, all other roles and styles in these tables describe the leader. The leader is usually characterized by strong professional values and proactive behavior; the administrator is portrayed as having uncertain attachment to professional values and a reactive stance amid conflict. The implications for this style within schools will be reviewed later in research studying principals who are leaders when their superintendents are.

Research Prospects

Though we can apply broad questions to these role and style concepts that need empirical evaluation, we can only raise general questions here. What are the conditions under which shift will occur in role and style? What does "turning around the district" or "success" or "failure" mean in these contexts? Between 1992 and 1995, the typical urban district launched at least twelve large-scale reforms, or a new reform every three months.[27] What are the skills most useful in both behaviors? Do these skills include articulating professional goals, brokering them amid group pressures including those from political masters, strategizing plans drawn from valid concepts of the political territory, using professional knowledge, and so on? Finally, does the professionals' training in the universities provide relevant skills and styles of micropolitics as they do for other professional roles?

We leave such research questions with the understanding noted earlier that the superintendent is not a pure type because individuals vary and the context of conflict is not static. We see these administrators driven by professional values amid a turbulent environment that is roiled by currents of change arising from outside the organization's boundaries.[28] Often he or she is struggling to do more than simply manage routines—that is, to lead within a context of increasing power-sharing.[29]

NOTES

1. Gene Carter and William Cunningham, *The American School Superintendent* (San Francisco: Jossey-Bass, 1997).

2. Steve Farkas and colleagues, *Trying to Stay Ahead of the Game: Superintendents and Principals Talk About School Principalship* (New York: Public Agenda, 2001).

3. Gary Yee and Larry Cuban, "When Is Tenure Long Enough?" *Educational Administration Quarterly* 32 (1996, supplemental issue).

4. The school of education role in recent decades is seen in Geraldine Clifford and James Guthrie, *Ed School* (Chicago: University of Chicago Press, 1988), Part 3.

5. Larry Cuban, "Transforming the Frog into a Prince: Effective Schools Research, Policy, and Practice at the District Level." *Harvard Education Review* 54 (1984): 129–51. See also Tom Loveless, *The Tracking Wars* (Washington, D.C.: Brookings, 1999).

6. Larry Cuban, "Conflict and Leadership in the Superintendency," *Phi Delta Kappan* 67, no. 1 (1985): 28–30.

7. Farkas and colleagues, *Trying to Stay Ahead.*

8. The study by Farkas and colleagues, *Trying to Stay Ahead,* was a random survey in 2001.

9. Clarence Stone and colleagues, *Building Civic Capacity* (Lawrence: University of Kansas, 2001).

10. The following data are from a survey in the *Chicago Tribune* (November 28, 2000): pp. 1, 14, based on reports of state associations of superintendents.

11. Frederick Wirt and Samuel Krug, "From Leadership Behavior to Cognitions: A Constructivist Theory of U.S. Principals," *Journal of Educational Administration* 36 (1998).

12. Lewis Mumford, *The City in History* (New York: MJF Books, 1961).

13. James Guthrie, "The United States of America: The Educational Policy Consequences of an Economically Uncertain Future," in Frederick Wirt and Grant Harman, eds., *Education, Recession and the World Village* (Philadelphia: Falmer, 1986).

14. Stuart Langton, ed., *Citizen Participation in America* (Lexington, Mass.: Lexington, 1978).

15. Rufus Browning, Dale Marshall, and David Tabb, *Protest Is Not Enough* (Berkeley: University of California Press, 1984).

16. Harmon Zeigler, Ellen Kehoe, and Jane Reisman, *City Managers and School Superintendents* (New York: Praeger, 1985).

17. Clarence Stone, ed., *Changing Urban Education* (Lawrence: University of Kansas, 1998).

18. Dennis Judd and Paul Kantor, *Enduring Tensions in Urban Politics* (New York: Macmillan, 1992), Part II.

19. E. E. Schattschneider, *The Semisovereign People* (New York: Holt, Rinehart and Winston, 1960), p. 71.

20. This rich literature is reviewed in Charles Jones, *Governing Urban America* (Boston: Little, Brown, 1983), pp. 256–60.

21. Robert Crowson and Van Cleave Morris, "Administrative Control in Large City School Systems," *Educational Administrative Quarterly* 21, no. 4 (Fall 1985): 51–70.

22. James Cibulka and William Boyd, eds., *A Race Against Time: The Crisis in Urban Schooling* (Westport, Conn.: Prager, 2003).

23. Ibid., pp. 205-224.

24. The stages of profession-laity conflict are explored in Frederick Wirt, "Professionalism and Political Conflict: A Developmental Model," *Journal of Public Policy* 1 (1981): 83-112.

25. Cibulka and Boyd, *A Race Against Time*, pp. 23-44.

26. Thomas Sergiovanni, Martin Burlingame, Fred Coombs, and Paul Thurston, *Educational Governance and Administration* (Englewood Cliffs, N.J.: Prentice-Hall, 1980), p. 170.

27. Frederick Hess, *Spinning Wheels: The Politics of Urban School Reform* (Washington, D.C.: Brookings, 1999).

28. In an overview see Susan Moore Johnson, *Leading to Change* (San Francisco: Jossey-Bass, 1996).

29. Edwin M. Bridges and Barry R. Groves, "The Macro and Micro Politics of Personnel Evaluation," *Journal of Personnel Evaluation in Education* 13: 4 (1999): 321–37.

7

The Micropolitics within Schools

A recent focus in the politics of education has been on politics *within* the local schools rather than between them and governments. Clearly, the boundary between the local and the external is not that sharp in reality. However, the focus of this "micropolitics" is on "the overt and covert processes through which actors (individuals and groups) in an organization's immediate environment acquire and exercise power to promote and protect their interests."[1] More specifically, micropolitics directs attention to the informal public and private transactions that shape policy implementation. Here the local education "authorities" and "partisans" manage conflict and meld consensus regarding the distribution of scarce but prized material and symbolic resources.[2] Since schools are a democratic political system, they are open to conflicting demands of both authorities and partisans who debate the use of resources and values. We begin with an exploration of micropolitical conflicts between professionals and citizens concerning schooling decisions. However, note also that professionals and citizens also agree in many areas on what schooling should be.

THE TYPES OF MICROPOLITICAL CONFLICT

The micropolitics of education features *local actors with their resources seeking to accomplish distinctive goals within a context where conflict regularly prevails.* Understanding who these actors are is the key to understanding local politics and agendas. Table 7.1 shows how the professional, citizen, principal, teacher, and other actors relate to one another. Different politics exist for the

Table 7.1
Interactions Between School Actors and Research Agendas

	Professional–Citizen		Principal–Teacher	
	Formal	*Informal*	*Formal*	*Informal*
Research Agendas				
Stakes	A	B	C	D
Dominant patterns	G	H	I	J

Source: Abstracted from Betty Malen, "The Micropolitics of Education: Mapping the Multiple Dimensions of Power Relations in School Polities," in *The Study of Educational Politics,* Jay Scribner and Donald Layton, eds. (Washington: Falmer, *Politics of Education Yearbook, 1995*).

- different stakes involved,
- dominant patterns of interaction among actors,
- strategies and styles that each actor employs, and
- policy outcomes.

Table 7.1's cells (see alphabet) are the intersection of these actors and their agendas. All these interactions shape "micropolitics." Of these interactions we focus on only two to exemplify such behavior, those in the first column of Table 7.1—the professional and the citizens.[3]

Their *formal* relationship includes how professionals interact with citizen groups like advisory councils or school boards. Formally, the *stakes* (A in Table 7.1) differ over school activities. The *dominant pattern* (G in Table 7.1), however, is professional domination, with limited parent influence at the school-site level.

However, in the informal linkage, these interactions shift. New groups seek and obtain new policies (B), and professionals are constrained by citizen groups (H).[4]

The abstractions of Table 7.1 become real in the Chicago experience in citizen site-based management noted in an earlier chapter. Two patterns of local governance emerged over time with this reform, labeled "adversarial" and "democratic." However, the prevailing pattern that was found in hundreds of local Chicago councils is the familiar outcome—principals maintain or consolidate power.[5] Chicago parents still like the reform, and professionals welcome parental support for their efforts. It is clear that organizational history creates inertial forces that support an ongoing steady state.[6]

MICROPOLITICS AND ORGANIZATIONAL POLITICS

While standard management theories often stress formal structures of authority, micropolitics emphasizes informal aspects of self-interest and bargaining among actors. In other words, a micropolitical analysis of bargaining among actors must take into account various informal agendas. A micropolitical approach also allows us to consider individual and group interests, whether these are professional (e.g., the preparation of curriculum) or personal (e.g., improving one's own status or work conditions). Micropolitics differentiates between visible or formal interests and their parallel informal interests that are often hidden in the process of bargaining. For example, such interests may reflect diverse values held by members of different generations within a school, such as "newcomers" challenging the authority of an "old guard." Interests may also be based on attitudes toward policy change (e.g., traditionalist vs. reform), on gender concerns (e.g., approaches to administration), or on networks of friendship.

Finally, and most important, micropolitics focuses on the concept of power and its uses. In formal organizational analysis, authority and hierarchy are the bases for power. However, in the arena of micropolitics, power rests on the personal ability to mobilize influence and to affect decision making. It is important to understand that the contrasting concepts of organizational

Table 7.2
Conceptual Contrasts of
Organizational and Micropolitical Theories

Micropolitical Theory	Organizational Theory
Power	Authority
Goal diversity	Goal adherence
Ideological disputation	Ideological neutrality
Conflict	Consensus
Interests	Motivation
Political activity	Decision making
Control	Consent

Source: Stephen Ball, The Micro-Politics of the School (London: Methuen, 1987), p. 8.

science and micropolitics, displayed in Table 7.2, are "ideal types," representing a range of possibilities.

Different theories can be used to interpret micropolitical interactions.[7] For example, exchange theory assumes that actors engage in activities by trading benefits and rewards. Thus, bargaining theories involve a "bargaining zone" of individuals or groups that attempts to establish collective agreements through influence and negotiation. Other ways of interpreting micropolitics include formal theories of organizational politics, game theories, and even interactionist analysis.[8] In "loosely coupled" schools, for example, principals have authority but may not regularly use it. Teachers in such schools have much autonomy in instructional matters, and this may lead them to challenge the principals' authority. So in order to exercise control, principals must rely on using concepts like exchanges and bargaining.

The interaction between principals and teachers over decision making becomes particularly important in efforts to create reforms like site-based management. Here, much of the authority previously held by districts and state agencies is devolved to the school site, which then has greater authority to formulate and manage local policy. Principals and teachers, often with diverse goals, enter into a new set of negotiations about how this increased site authority should be shared.

As can be seen in Table 7.3, both sides have resources or "goods" that can be traded in order to reach understandings on policies

Table 7.3
Resources of Principal and Teachers in Local Influence Patterns

Principal vis-à-vis Teachers	*Teachers vis-à-vis Principal*
Material resources	Esteem
Promotion	Support
Esteem	Opinion leadership
Autonomy	Conformity
Lax rule enforcement	Reputation

Source: Eric Hoyle, *The Politics of School Management* (London: Hodder and Stoughton, 1986), pp. 336–37.

and regulations. Each item in the one column can be linked to those in the other columns, forming complex diagrams of a personal search for influence over the allocation of resources. Such influence constitutes a system of exchanges that are not necessarily reflected in the formal organizational system of authority. It is often this informal interweaving of strategies, goals, and influence that many professionals deride as "political." Yet such informal politics is to be expected in any organization where people pursue limited resources to realize a variety of goals.

THE PRINCIPAL AS MANAGER OR LEADER

The subordinate administrator—the principal—is often in a bind. A principal must follow requirements of the system, but also he or she may wish to lead. Thus, a principal can be either a supporter of the status quo or an agent of change. Much of the research on educational administration has found that the primary role of the principal is that of a maintainer of the system, a role suggested by the designation of a principal as "manager." However, when principals do want to lead, other research suggests that real change can result. How do these roles operate?

The Principal as Focus of Pressures

From a micropolitical perspective, the principal is the focus of a set of consistent pressures at the local site:

- The central office and the superintendent impose major policy directives, rules, procedures and money that limit the autonomy of the principal.
- Community neighborhoods impose an often vague—but sometimes vocal—sense of goals. These can include, for example, demands to improve sports programs or to increase discipline for students.
- The faculty have private interests (about salaries or work conditions) and professional concerns (about improvement of their teaching or the curriculum) that focus on the principal.
- The profession of school administration itself holds standards related to goal setting, and a principal's own views about what constitutes good education motivate him or her to take action.

All of these pressures create problems for school administrators. For example, groups generating these pressures may have divergent views, such as how to enforce student discipline. Principals have certain responsibilities that cannot be escaped (e.g., attendance reports), even though they may believe that their time might be more productive attending to other matters like instruction.

Coping Strategies Employed by Principals

Whether promoting reform or defending the existing system, how does the principal influence others to achieve his or her objectives? To put it another way, how does the principal seek to manipulate the micropolitical environment?[9] Following an ancient political tradition, the principal can divide the opposition in order to rule. Rivals can also be co-opted in order to weaken opposition. New issues can be advanced in order to deflect teacher and parental concerns about other matters. One may create a focus on "red herrings"—relatively innocuous issues that can distract attention from real problem areas. Further, control information by deciding who gets it or how it is presented. This strategy changes the ancient Greek concept of knowledge as "virtue" into a more modern formulation. Knowledge is "power"—a good that can be employed to influence outcomes.

By incorporating some or all of these strategies, principals can manipulate the outcomes of meetings and conferences to meet their goals. These tactics can involve such matters as the arrangement of agenda items; "losing" or diverting opposing recommendations; recruiting neutral or indifferent staff to one's side; reinterpreting arguments in such a way that a false consensus is created; and even "massaging" the minutes of meetings. As an example of the last strategy, an apocryphal exchange has one school board member gloating, "You didn't get your own way today," while the administrator replies, "You haven't read the minutes yet!"

Faced with a variety of current challenges to decision making, what are the responses of principals, and how important is the principal in either rejecting or accommodating challenges?

Differing Responses to Change

Principals respond to challenges in just a few ways: remain within the existing channels of the organization; exercise leadership in instruction; or react to challenge with "burnout." A review of these three strategies will be useful.

The Principal as Organizational Man or Woman. This type of principal focuses on following all rules and regulations, commonly referred to as "operating by the book." By adopting the familiar role of system maintenance—not "rocking the boat"—such principals follow all requirements handed down from the central office or outside government agencies. On the other hand, this type of principal will do little to respond flexibly to current challenges or to promote change at the school site. To do so entails stepping out of the organization's channels and upsetting routines.

Underlying this maintenance response may be an invisible contract by the principal with teachers that is based on relations of mutual exchange. The principal combines her authority with "influence strategies." An example of the use of such influence is getting teachers to do their basic job in the classroom, but without causing an uproar among parents or community that could create problems for the principal (or extend beyond the school). This strategy generates support among teachers for the principal's policies. By way of an exchange for the teachers, such a principal may help in furthering his private and professional goals. In this scenario, a principal may respond to new challenges by first fulfilling some of the externally imposed duties; but he may not adapt these requirements to his own school's needs by not exerting internal leadership.

In short, this is the *model of the organizational man or woman,* whose primary purpose is to defend the *existing* allocation of values and resources. By using her influence to exchange "goods" with teachers and by not exerting the leadership needed to adopt new goals, the principal may shelter herself from criticism from other actors at the local site. Of course the disadvantage of reform when facing such a strategy is also clear—the principal deflects or blocks changes to the existing system imposed from outside. But internal politics may also stymie the principal's initiatives such as eliminating high school tracking.[10] Teachers do not want to change very much the way they teach. Parents fear high-achieving pupils will be assigned to low-performing teachers and disruptive students. Professional development to implement detracking may, it is argued, cost too much.

The Principal as Leader. Some principals shape their environment, work within the pressures, but still define a new mission for their schools. The role described here is "leader," defined classically as one who moves others to adopt his or her values and thereby change the organization's goals.

While writings on principals describe both manager and leader types, the latter is the source of much mystery. The observer can see a principal and know from others' behaviors that this is indeed a leader. However, it is impossible to predict who will be a leader or to train persons to have these motivations and skills. How do these two types of principals—manager and leader—approach their main tasks?

Recent research has sought to distinguish between these two roles, noting that both relate to five dimensions of action about which principals hold mental pictures termed "constructs."[11] These five dimensions are

- defining the school's mission,
- promoting the instructional climate,

- managing the curriculum and instruction,
- supervising teaching, and
- monitoring student progress.

A national poll of principals sought to determine whether leaders more likely favored some dimensions (e.g., defining mission) while managers favored others (e.g., supervising teaching). Many attitudinal questions about these missions were used to determine principals' personal attitudes on the dimensions.

However, the principals' attitudes might well be a mask for more basic factors in their lives that shape them, termed "contexts of operations." Five of these contexts, composed of sets of variables, were devised to explain attitudinal differences about leadership. These were: attitudes about teacher bargaining units, system qualities of schools, and community consensus. Each of these contexts suggests that it might explain principals' attitudes— for example, differences in types of schools (i.e., elementary versus high school) or in kinds of students (i.e., wealthy or poor, ethnic or Caucasian). These contexts and construct variables are noted in more detail in Figure 7.1, which describes the logic of analysis that involved regressions to sort out differences.

To summarize the findings,[12] many of these context variables had *little* explanatory power except for three. *Leaders, as distinct from managers, spent many hours at work* or with parents, they *had faculty support,* and—most significantly—they *worked with superintendents* who held professional expectations, supervised their enforcement, and supported principals in pursuing them. Surprisingly, there was little significance in differences in principals' personal qualities or in local school politics. *Rather, it was this professional network of goal setting by superintendent, hard work by principals, and support by faculty that helped make the principal a leader rather than a manager.* It is not the place of work but the personal element that shapes leadership.

The Burned-Out Principal. Another way that principals respond to challenges is by making all the required reforms at the site. However, when only limited results occur over time, these principals may become increasingly frustrated. In this case the principal tries to do everything but is vitiated by the effort. Even in the absence of school-based pressures, this principal soon be-

Figure 7.1
Model of Context-Cognitive Interaction

Model of Context-Cognitive Interaction

Context Components   Cognitive Components

Personal
Status—gender, age, ethnicity
Experience—years in administration,
  as principal in current job, goal of
  superintendent schooling
Activity—with superintendent hours
  of work, hours with parents

Teacher Bargaining
  contract exists, type of union,
  importance of contract, qualities
  of union, cooperation of union
  and school

School Qualities
Type—elementary, junior high,
  senior high
Composition—school size, district
  size, urban locale, student income,
  and ethnicity
Inputs—student interest in school
  and college, parental pressure,
  teacher attitudes
Outputs—student achievement,
  absenteeism, vandalism

Principals' Constructs
  Defining mission
  Promoting instructional climate
  Managing curriculum and
    instruction
  Supervising teaching
  Monitoring student progress

Community Consensus
Board elections—degree of
  competition, turnout in contested
  and uncontested elections, issues
  in elections
**Group Ranking on Influence on
  School Policy**
Central Administration—interest of
  central office, superintendent time
  spent in supervision, support,
  expectations, superintendent
  tenure

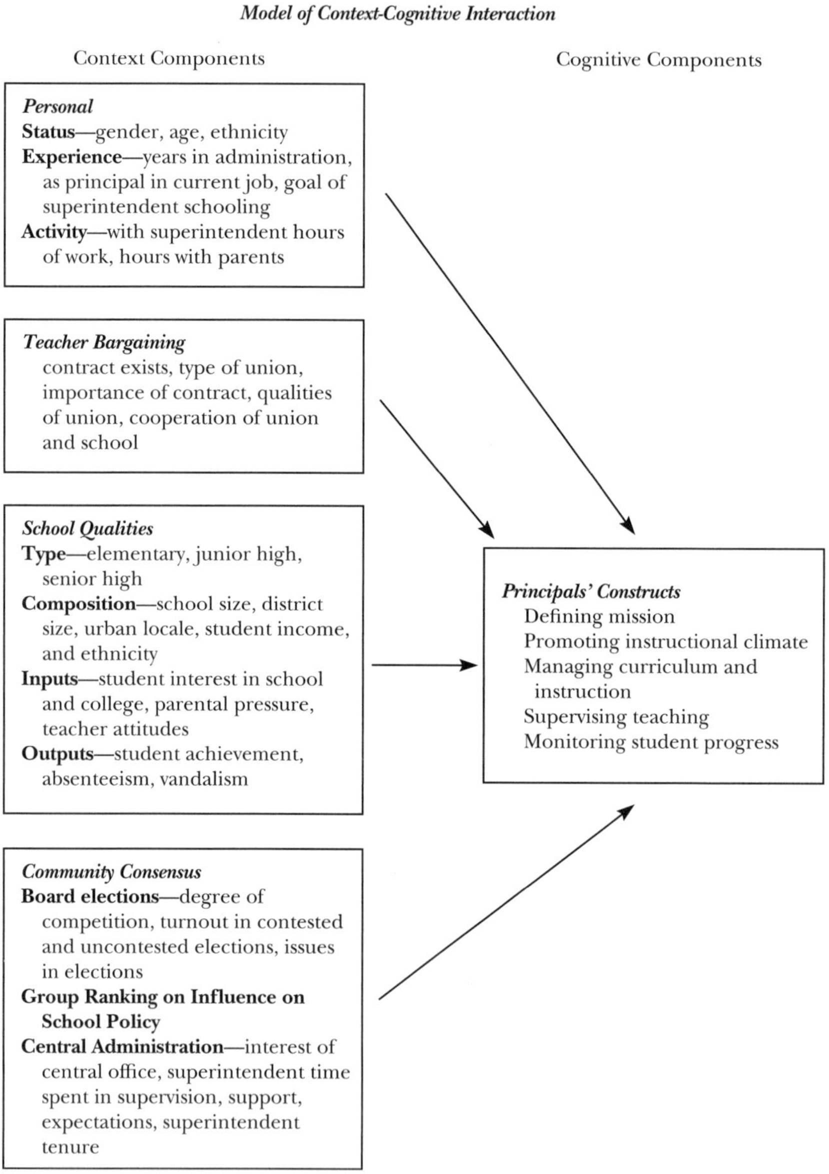

comes overwhelmed by the district- or state-level mandates. The principal finds herself obliged to engage in extensive micropolitics such as exchanges with teachers or dealing with newly "empowered" parents. However, student outcomes may not improve despite all the changes and new involvement of adults.

Some principals lack the training or experience in micropolitics to deal effectively with recent challenges, so they often face criticism that grows larger and more intense. These principals soon feel crushed when faced with community indifference or opposition, and they sense a lack of control over schooling. Returning home from a long day at work, they feel as if they have been "pecked to death by ducks." Eventually, these principals may become "burned out," even to the extent of withdrawing from school life and, indeed, from the profession. This response by principals—characterized by reform, frustration, and eventual burnout—also represents a failure of educational leadership.

THE TEACHER AS A POLITICAL ACTOR

No group has increased its influence on education policy in recent decades as much as have teachers. The timid rabbits of forty years ago are today's tigers in the jungle of school systems. Unionism has produced this change and consequently has made teachers into major political actors. One study of city schools made a strong argument that as a result of teacher unions a total system transformation in who rules local schools had occurred. Those schools were earlier governed after the Civil War by political machine rule, later by an administrative rule (which meant a professional educational bureaucracy); and they are now governed by union rule. These three models differ in structure, process, and actors. However, contemporary union rule is characterized by a crucial political quality—lack of control by elected officials. Thus, a continuing question of the democratic polity is whether union rule can be considered an enduring form of urban government.[13]

Certainly their size alone (2,740,000 belonging to a teachers' union in the mid-1990s) enables organized teachers to be a local pressure group that regularly confronts the district board and

superintendent. Every autumn, threats of teacher strikes in major cities become a staple news item along with the closing days
of the baseball season. Nor are these features found only in big
cities. As collective bargaining became ever more authorized by
state laws, medium and small communities experienced the unprecedented—a teachers' strike. The results can dramatically
rearrange traditional power within the school system. This mili-
tancy was not always the case, because as recently as the mid-
1960s a majority of teachers opposed collective bargaining or
the endorsement of political candidates. Note that 80 percent of
our teachers are women who at one time were successfully discouraged from union or political activities by male administrators. Also, some teachers believed that collective bargaining and
political campaign activities were "unprofessional."

By 2004, however, thirty-seven states had collective-bargaining
statutes covering teachers. Even states without such laws have
some locals with long-standing collective-bargaining agreements
(e.g., Texas and Mississippi). As a result, 90 percent of all full-
time professionals belonged either to the American Federation
of Teachers (AFT) or the National Education Association (NEA).
In short, collective bargaining is now an accepted part of school
governance.

We can attribute much of the rapid increase in collective bargaining beginning in the mid-1960s to the rivalry for members
between the NEA and the AFT (discussed in Chapter 4). Initially, neither group would endorse strikes; however, it took until 1973 for the strike to become official NEA policy. Recently,
the incidence of strikes has been declining from a high of 218
strikes in 1975 to less than 20 in 2003.[14] The recent decline in
strikes is in part caused by the large increases in teacher salaries, the post-1983 education reforms, and a 1990s' booming
economy until the early 2000 recession. When teacher salaries
are rising, then there is less need or incentive to strike. Not
surprisingly, then, teachers are overwhelmingly supportive of unions
as seen in a 2003 poll.[14] Teachers believe the unions are their
main bulwark against capricious actions by federal, state, and
local policymakers.

However, recent elections produced more Republicans in legislatures and governorships who proceeded to introduce legisla-

tion to curtail strikes, limit tenure, and restrict the scope of collective bargaining in Michigan, California, Illinois, Indiana, Pennsylvania, and Wisconsin. Michigan passed a law that challenged all these teacher prerogatives as well as to approve charter schools that are not covered by prior teacher contracts. GOP candidates for governor and the presidency urged choice or vouchers by the 2000 election year. When the No Child Left Behind (NCLB) law came under discussion in 2001, union leaders were heard, but none of their ideas were accepted. In 2003 the NEA approved a lawsuit that would undercut some key provisions of NCLB.

The Impact of Teacher Contracts

The outcome of collective bargaining is a written and time-bound agreement covering wages, conditions of employment, and many other topics. Large-district contracts are over three hundred pages. As well as involving the specifics of the contract, major disputes can occur over the scope of bargaining and grievance procedures.[15] The negotiated contract, however, does not affect teachers until it is implemented in the work setting at the school site. The board's contract language necessarily must be interpreted to apply to specific circumstances. This means that the site principal, teachers, and union building representatives must become very familiar with the contract's terms. Yet even such familiarity does not forestall many disputes about a specific teaching arrangement. These disputes can lead to teacher grievances whose settlement can clarify the contract.

Thus teacher influence varies by district *and* site. Teachers at school sites sometimes permit exceptions to the district contract if they believe specific school conditions warrant them.[16] Teacher unions have had the most difficulty enforcing such contract provisions as pupil discipline, building maintenance, and security because teacher grievance procedures are less effective. On the other hand, seniority and teacher transfer clauses were the most highly implemented because of grievance use. Information on contracts is available in a national sample of teachers from 1987 to 2000 (the School and Staffing Survey of the U.S. Department of Education). Teachers consistently had major levels of control over selecting the particular teaching techniques they used in classrooms. In contrast to high teacher influence over academic instruction,

> in none of the important school and resource allocations did teachers on average have even moderate influence. Teachers had little input over decisions about their schedule, their class sizes, the office and classroom space they used, and the use of school funds for classroom materials. Teachers usually had little input into hiring, firing, and budgetary decisions. On average, teachers had very limited input over which courses they teach [or textbooks]. In other words, teachers had little input in the day-to-day management of their work and workplace.[17]

Unions' influence, however, may come rather more from influencing decisions at state and federal levels that can then percolate down to the local school system in the form of mandates. There is a major potential for rearranging traditional school governance by teachers lobbying in state capitals to specify local operations. For example, California's state education code is over four thousand pages, many of which arose from teacher groups; these state education codes affect what happens in even the smallest school districts. Of the two national groups, the NEA has a much stronger presence at the state level, while the AFT has fewer members, primarily those from big cities.

What happens to administrative authority, particularly among principals, when contracts filter down through the loosely coupled school system? While some provisions tightly limit administrative freedom of action, as noted, others get redefined to fit the requirements at the site level. The principal has to balance such factors as teacher interests, educational consequences, administrative leadership, and staff allegiance. How he or she works with the contract also affects teachers' respect for this official. Teachers want the contract respected, but the contract also allows for the principal's interpretation if she or he is seen as seeking a good school. In short, having standards and expecting much of teachers earns principals a tolerance and even respect from teachers in interpreting the contract. For teachers, a good school is more important than union membership, close observance of a contract, or running the schools. This is because, as one administrator observed, "Teachers like to be part of a winning team." But union contracts specify teacher salary structures, and determine tenure criteria as well as dismissal procedures.

Yet the ultimate effects of collective bargaining may not be as great as was once thought. Contract effects are deep and pervasive, but not so extreme or uniform as critics often suggest:

> Collective bargaining has not been shown to have increased teachers' commitment to their work or enhanced their standing as professionals, but neither has it destroyed the schools. Caricatures of strait-jacketed principals, Kafkaesque school bureaucracies, or schools under siege by militant teachers scarcely represent the experiences of these sample districts. Overall, the organizational effects of collective bargaining appear to be both moderate and manageable. This is not to suggest, though, that labor relations practices look the same in all districts or all schools. In fact, negotiations, contract language, and administrative practices are remarkably diverse.[18]

Understanding these consequences is confused by the diverse practices that have emerged in local systems. No single factor accounts for this diversity in local labor practices, but certain important variables include the history of local labor practices, the local political culture, and—most important—the people at the center of negotiations and contract management. In California, the same districts regularly have strikes or acrimonious labor disputes near the expiration of every contract. Some of this is caused by personalities, styles, and relationships, and some is caused by a long and bitter history of labor-management relations. However, in other districts, both sides prefer cooperation over a long period of time. No simple predictive model can account for these factors, and the diverse outcomes are similar to the range in outcomes from federal grant programs.

It is clear that collective bargaining has increased the complexity of the principal's job because he or she cannot apply the contract in a routine and standard manner. Moreover, there are some overall impacts of bargaining, as scholars have concluded:

1. The breakdown of the unitary command structure and its replacement by a multilateral bargaining system, or, in some cases, by a bilateral system.
2. The introduction of new participants into school decision making, including labor professionals (both advocates and

neutral third parties), organized and unorganized citizens, and elected officials outside of education.
3. The movement of the locus of decision making to central offices within school systems and to locations outside of school systems, including legislatures, courts, and public administrative agencies.
4. The broadening scope of issues that fall into the labor relations arena—both issues raised during formal negotiations and those joined to the collective-bargaining process during the administration of contracts.
5. The changing nature of managerial work, since there is evidence that school administrators face different types of issues, new constituents, different managerial roles, and new criteria for success in their jobs.[19]

These constraints on the principal's role, in light of what happens to the contract at the site level reviewed earlier, suggest a complex concept of this professional's tasks. The constraints also point to a centralization of decision making within the total school system. On the other hand, local development of contract implementation points to a decentralization of interpretation by the principal. Both developments mean that the professional at this level, as well as at higher levels, must increasingly work within a power-sharing context. Educational leadership is still possible here, but it is much more complex.

Issues in Collective Bargaining

That complexity is seen in reviewing several issues in bargaining. Educators have adopted the private industry model for bargaining, but several groups assert that this is inappropriate. In private industry only two parties, labor and management, are at the bargaining table. However, parent advocates had pushed for bargaining in open meetings with public observers or even a place for parents at the bargaining table. Nine states have enacted public participation with the hope that it would dampen expenditure increases for salaries and personnel. Whatever the practical merits of these arguments, however, the public has not shown much interest.

Despite the significant effect of collective bargaining on school costs and tax rates, the general public shows little sustained interest in teacher bargaining except during times of crisis. Citizens may simply assume that their elected representatives on school boards take an active part in negotiations, but we have seen that this rarely happens. In any case, community participation advocates appear to lead a phantom army. However, general public attitudes toward organized labor and collective bargaining do affect the very broad parameters of contracts, probably through election of sympathetic board members who then appoint like-minded school executives.[20]

Another improvement in collective bargaining might be accomplished through the issue of a merger of two rival unions. It is alleged that their rivalry leads to increased and unnecessary union truculence. Despite frequent attempts by top union leadership to merge, however, no visible progress has occurred by 2005 except in a handful of large cities. The NEA still has a huge numerical majority over the AFT (2.2 million to 875,000, which include teachers at all levels of education), and it sees little need to compromise, particularly when its tactics are virtually indistinguishable from the AFT's. The NEA claims that it provides militant collective bargaining while being untainted from affiliation with "unprofessional" unions in the AFL-CIO.

A major new bargaining issue fueled by advocacy to circumvent university teacher training is the control of teacher certification. New teachers are licensed by the states, but there also are national certificates from a national professional standards board for experienced teachers.[21] Originally the concept was to have the national board recognize experienced teachers who could meet unusually high standards. Unions have sought control of state certification boards for years and have succeeded in several states. They have also cut back the influence of the universities and administrators by achieving more teacher members on these state licensing boards. The unions believe a true profession must control the entry of its own members and not cede this prerogative to others, such as universities. Moreover, union contributions to state legislators have given them influence that universities cannot match. A Carnegie task force also proposed "lead teachers" who would share some of the principal's responsibilities in the instructional and teacher evaluation areas. This enlarged role in administration for teachers has engendered resistance from some administrator and school board groups.

A crucial bargaining issue has been whether the private bargaining model should be modified and adapted to the particular circumstances of public education. The authors have reviewed briefly a range of proposals seeking to alter this model. None of the alternative concepts, however, has engendered much support, and consequently, private sector labor-management bargaining techniques seem embedded in the American public school culture.

By the late 1990s, however, teacher shortages had appeared in several parts of the nation, as noted, due to greater enrollments and large-scale retirements. This change helped trigger a rethinking of the professional basis for a teaching career. Maybe more teacher control could be exercised; professionals like lawyers and doctors have more control over all aspects of their careers than teachers. However, older models of control continue in education. The early reformers used the industrial model with male administrators presiding over a largely transient female labor force. More recently, however, a model involving collective bargaining was a first step in changing this power relationship. It is uncertain whether any more major shifts in teacher power will take place soon. However, more recent efforts at teacher empowerment at the site level (e.g., site-based management, restructuring) do suggest a newer model of control over curriculum and other matters.

This shifting pattern in the power of teachers, and the new reforms faced after 2000, fits a cyclical pattern of institutional change in education.[22] First, the old ideas and practices come under challenge for failing to meet social needs. Second, many reform suggestions create a turbulence of ideas about change in which reformers and defenders contend. Third, resolution of this conflict leads to policy change, which in the final stage brings new ideas accepted that later became institutional norms. Then later, somehow the cycle begins again, seen in periods both early in and at the end of the twentieth century that show such a pattern.

These stages are common to social change in education and in other institutions. The cycle parallels the theory of dissatisfaction in school democratic practices noted earlier, for this attitude may well drive these stages of change. Note further that the conflict of this cycle provides a basic tension to a society.[23]

Teachers as Political Brokers with Students

There is a different way to view the teachers' micropolitical role, namely, in their relationship with their students. One aspect is the teachers' role in political learning by students. As in all nations, teachers help transmit the national civic culture and shape children's values about it. Even in such a seemingly value-free subject as elementary arithmetic, however, the teacher is not simply an implementer of educational policy. As a report by scholars presenting a political perspective concluded:

> In this semi-autonomous role, teachers are better understood as political brokers than as implementers. They enjoy considerable discretion, being influenced by their own notions of what schooling ought to be as well as persuaded by external pressures. . . . This view represents a middle ground in the classic sociological contrast between professional autonomy and bureaucratic subordination. It pictures teachers as more or less rational decision-makers who take higher-level policies and other pressures into consideration in their calculation of benefits and costs.[24]

In a real sense—by allocating public resources in such matters as choosing which students get what kind of curriculum content—the teacher takes on a political role. Earlier, Southern teachers could ignore the role of African Americans in history; today they do not.[25] In each case teachers played a political role. Similarly, decisions in elementary math about what will be taught, to whom, and for how long are matters that teachers usually decide. For example, Americans' learning about the concept of "percent" rests on cases of earning interest by investment; in the former U.S.S.R., learning rested on production goal improvements. Some pressures, however, also come from the influence of students (e.g., what has worked with them in the past predisposes its re-use by teachers) and from external sources. Teachers receive different messages about what to teach from state, professional, and local sources. Externally, a varied urban environment with its ambiguous messages about instruction is much more likely to free the teacher to make such decisions compared

to those found in a small, homogeneous rural setting. Centralized versus decentralized state requirements—for example,
statewide text adoption by the state board—are another kind of
external factor affecting teacher discretion. Even within the school
organization, however, there are factors of organizational rigid-
ity or receptivity that create expectations in teachers about how
they use this power. A 2003 national survey of teachers showed
state testing programs resulted in major changes in teachers'
instructional practices. Teachers reported state testing changed
what and how they teach, particularly in states with high-stakes
testing.[26]

Much of the preceding suggests an organizational structure
for schooling that is characterized by "loose coupling." This quality
is the tendency of educational organizations to disconnect policies from outcomes, means from ends, and structure or rules
from actual activity.[27] Such a non-structure puts the teacher's
behavior beyond the control of the central office and principal,
who themselves have no chain of command with straight lines
and precise directions for teaching policy. Within such disjointed
relationships, one would not expect program innovations origi-
nating outside the local unit to have much impact. Yet research
suggests this looseness is not that firm. A survey of the history of
classroom reforms found there are lasting results only if the
changes are structural, create a new clientele, and are easily
monitored. Vocational education and driver training are good
examples of this. However, attempts to change classroom pedagogy have largely been unsuccessful because they lack these essential characteristics.[28]

Many policymakers have been adamant about linking additional
benefits to teachers by the creation of a more performance-based
profession. Several state governors, for example, propose new
methods, like testing new teachers and using student tests in
evaluating teachers, uniform accountability reporting systems, and
performance-based compensation. However, most teachers would
be uncomfortable with a system that does not allocate benefits
uniformly on the basis of seniority and educational attainment.
Consequently, if teacher unions embrace the reform movement,
they may lose the support of rank-and-file members. On the other
hand, if the teacher unions oppose "reform" and "professional-

ism," they will lose public support and alienate many top policymakers.[29] Gradually, the NEA unions have moved from opposing certain key reform proposals to accommodating and modifying them. The AFT has been quicker to lead in shaping the initial version of the reforms. However, both teacher unions oppose most forms of charter school legislation that remove schools from collective-bargaining contracts and state education code restrictions. These charter schools thereby become independent from local central offices for most functions. Teacher unions envisage that charter schools may lead to vouchers. A later chapter also reevaluates this development.

Ironically, a national study of local teacher organizations concluded that reform policies were quite peripheral to their local mission and interests.[30] Consequently, opposition to reform was typical, and there was little need to depart from the traditional collective-bargaining model. The rank-and-file teachers expect unions to obtain material benefits such as higher salaries and better working conditions. However, they are not particularly interested in such "professional" strategies as teacher participation in school-site decision making or performance-based compensation. This rank-and-file viewpoint is particularly troublesome for union leaders who endorse reforms such as site-based management. Given the budget cuts from 2001 to 2003, for the next few years there are few major improvements likely in teachers' working conditions. Given this lack of progress on "bread-and-butter" items, the grass-roots endorsement of teacher reforms at the building level is highly problematic.[31]

Thus the role of teachers in local governance is much more than just trade-union politics. We need more knowledge of the classroom as a significant screen between external influences and the student. The teacher as a political agent, allocating subject matter time within the classroom, is confronting external efforts by states and central offices to shape curriculum to meet the public's wishes. In the micropolitics of the local site, principal and teacher interact continuously as they contend with other stakeholders for limited resources to meet different goals.

NOTES

1. Laurence Iannaconne, "Micropolitics of Education: What and Why," *Education and Urban Society* 23 (1991): 465. For a recent case study of micropolitics see Kathryn A, McDermott, *Controlling Public Education* (Lawrence: University of Kansas, 1999).

2. Betty Malen, "The Micropolitics of Education," *Education and Urban Society* 23, no. 4 (1991). See related articles in same colloquium, edited by Catherine Marshall and Jay Scribner.

3. This review follows the judgments of the literature found in Malen, "The Micropolitics of Education."

4. On the administrator-community interaction experience, see Daniel Brown, *Decentralization and School-Based Management* (New York: Falmer, 1990); Joseph Murphy, *Restructuring Schools* (New York: Teachers College, 1990); Joseph Murphy and Philip Hallinger, eds., *Restructuring Schooling* (Newbury Park, Calif.: Corwin, 1993).

5. Sharon Rollow and Anthony Bryk, *Grounding a Theory of School Micropolitics: Lessons from Chicago School Reform* (Chicago: Center for School Improvement, University of Chicago, 1993). See also John Meyer and Brian Rowan, "Institutionalizing Organization: Formal Structure as Myth and Ceremony," in Walter Powell and Paul DiMaggio, eds., *The New Institutionalism in Organizational Analysis* (Chicago: University of Chicago, 1991), pp. 41–62.

6. An early survey of student effects elsewhere in the nation was equally discouraging; see Betty Malen, B. Ogawa, and J. Kranz, "What Do We Know about Site-Based Management? A Case Study of the Literature—A Call For Research," in W. Clone and J. Witten, eds., *Choice and Control in American Education*, Vol. 2 (New York: Falmer, 1990). For a theoretical perspective, see Paul DiMaggio and Walter Powell, "The Iron Cage Revisited," in Powell and Dimaggio, *The New Institutionalism*, 63–82.

7. These concepts are further elaborated in Stephen Ball, *The Micro Politics of the School Management* (London: Methuen, 1987), and Joseph Blasé and Gary Anderson, *The Micropolitics of Educational Leadership* (New York: Teachers College Press, 1995).

8. For a more detailed explanation of these theories see Eric Hoyle, *The Politics of School Management* (London: Hodder and Stoughton, 1986). For an application see Tom Loveless, *The Tracking Wars* (Washington, D.C.: Brookings, 1999).

9. From Hoyle, *Politics*, pp. 140–48.

10. See Bob Johnson and Janice Fauske, "Principals and the Political Economy of Environmental Enactment," *Educational Administration Quarterly* 36: 2 (April 2000): 159–185.

11. The following is based on preliminary testing by Martin Maehr, University of Michigan, and Samuel Krug, MetriTech, Inc., and a national poll conducted of 1,200 principals in the late 1980s by Krug and Frederick Wirt, under auspices of the National Center for Educational Leadership, University of Illinois, under a federal grant.

12. Frederick Wirt and Samuel Krug, "From Leadership Behavior to Cognitions: A Constructivist Theory of U.S. Principals," *Journal of Educational Administration* 36 (1998). See also James P. Spillane et al., "Investigating School Leadership Practice," *Educational Researcher* (April 2001): 23–28.

13. For a recent overview see Gerald Grant and Christine Murray, *Teaching in America* (Cambridge, Mass.: Harvard University Press, 1999).

14. For information on strike incidence, see *Education Week* (September 14, 2003): 4; for the poll of teachers, see *Education Week* (June 4, 2003): 3.

15. See Edwin M. Bridges and Barry R. Groves, "The Macro and Micro Politics of Personnel Evaluation," *Journal of Personnel Evaluation in Education* 13: 4 (1999): 321–337.

16. Susan Johnson, *Teacher Unions in Schools* (Philadelphia: Temple University Press), pp. 162–63. For a different view see Tom Loveless, ed., *Conflicting Missions? Teacher Unions and Education Reform* (Washington, D.C.: Brookings, 2000).

17. Richard M. Ingersoll, *Who Controls Teachers' Work?* (Cambridge, Mass.: Harvard, 2003), pp. 75-76.

18. Johnson, *Teacher Unions*, pp. 164–65. For teachers' views of parents' role, see Public Agenda Foundation, *Playing Their Parts* (New York: Public Agenda, 1999).

19 Anthony Cresswell and Michael Murphy, *Teachers, Unions, and Collective Bargaining in Public Education* (Richmond, Calif.: McCutchan, 1980), pp. 386–87.

20. Lorraine McDonnell and Anthony Pascal, *Organized Teachers in American Schools* (Santa Monica, Calif.: The Rand Corp., 1979), pp. 87–88

21. Carnegie Corporation, *A Nation Prepared: Teachers for the 21st Century* (New York: Carnegie, 1986). For an overview of teacher preparation politics see *Educational Policy* 19: 1 (January 2005).

22. Charles Kerchner and Douglas Mitchell, *The Changing Ideas of Teachers' Union* (Bristol, Penn.: Falmer, 1988). For the teachers' view of their unions see Steve Farkas, Jean Johnson, and Ann Duffett, *Stand By Me* (New York: Public Agenda, 2003).

23. Charles Kerchner, Julia Koppich, and Joseph Weeres, *United Mind Workers* (San Francisco: Jossey-Bass, 1997).

24. John Schwille, Andrew Porter, and Michael Gant, "Content Decision-Making and the Politics of Education," *Educational Administrative Quarterly* 16 (1980): 21–40; Michael Apple, *Education and Power*, second edition (New York: Routledge, 1995).

25. For a detailed review, see Frederick Wirt, *We Ain't What We Was: Civil Rights and the New South* (Durham N.C.: Duke University Press, 1997).

26. Joseph Pedulla, *Perceived Effects of State Mandated Testing Programs on Teaching and Learning* (Chestnut Hill, Mass.: Boston College Center for Study of Testing, 2003). Robert Crowson, William Boyd, and Hanne Mawhinney, *The Politics of Education and the New Institutionalism* (New York: Falmer, 1996).

27. Karl Weick, "Educational Organizations as Loosely Coupled Systems," *Administrative Science Quarterly* 21 (1976): 1–19. Also Susan Johnson and Jonathan Landman, "Sometimes Bureaucracy Has Its Charms," *Teachers College Record* 102 (2000): 181–91.

28. Michael Kirst and Gail Meister, "Turbulence in American Secondary Schools: What Reforms Last?" *Curriculum Inquiry* 15: 1 (Spring 1985): 1969–86.

29. Lorraine McDonnell and Anthony Pascal, *Teacher Unions and Education Reform* (Santa Monica, Calif.: The Rand Corp., 1987), p. 3. See also Kerchner, Koppich, and Weeres, *United Mind Workers.*

30. McDonnell and Pascal, *Teacher Unions,* p. 5.

31. Ibid., pp. 6–8.

Part III:

STATE, FEDERAL, AND JUDICIAL POLITICS

8

The History and Evolution of the State Role in Education Policy

Who controls education is not easily answered. Under the United States Constitution, education is a power reserved to the states. In turn, state constitutions charge the state legislatures with responsibility for establishing and maintaining a system of free public schools that are locally operated. Control by the school district has been a hallmark of American education, distinguishing the U.S.A. from most other Western nations. However, as we have noted, an unprecedented growth of state influence over local education has taken place since the 1960s, and accelerated in the 1990s' state standards movement. In the 2000s, President George Bush introduced unusual federal control through oversight of state standards on accountability.

States show different historical patterns of control over local policies, but all states establish minimum standards for local school operations. The state's requirement to provide for the general welfare came to mean a basic educational opportunity for all children. For example, states require a minimum number of days at school, certain courses of study, and standards for teacher certification. Most states also require localities to levy a minimum property tax and to guarantee a base level of expenditures.

However, there has been an urban-rural distinction to this state role. Earlier in the twentieth century, states began upgrading the standards of the rural schools, while the cities received less attention because their expenditures and property wealth were already the highest in the states. Indeed, Chicago, New York, and Philadelphia had special statutes that exempted them from major areas of state control. Decades later, in the 1990s, state reforms created special provisions to take over poorly performing big-city districts; in No Child Left Behind (NCLB) the federal government can force changes in the state role to include reconstituting failing schools.

A principal reason for state intervention is that only it can ensure equality and standardization of instruction and resources. This rationale is contested by local-control advocates, who contend that flexibility is needed to adjust to diverse circumstances and local preferences. Local-control advocates stress that no proven educational technology is optimal for all conditions. This dispute over state versus local control really centers on two values—centralized equity and local choice. The traditional compromise has been to provide state minimums but with local options to exceed the minimums. However, this historic compromise was challenged by state reformers because state minimums are either inadequate or localities' test scores are too low.

SOME CAUSES FOR THE GROWTH OF STATE INFLUENCE

Some of the major policy areas that show the dramatic increase of state influence in the last two decades are found in: administration of federal categorical grants, education finance, educational accountability, specifications and programs for children with special needs, and efforts to increase academic standards. Substantive changes have become possible in large part due to an increase in the institutional capacity of states to intervene in local affairs.[1] Thus most state legislatures have added staff and research capacity, and they also now meet annually or for more extended sessions than in earlier years. Over the decades, the states also diversified their tax sources and expanded their fiscal capacities.

The capacity of state education agencies (SEAs) to intercede in local school policy has also mushroomed in the last forty years. Ironically, the federal government created the impetus for this expansion. The Elementary and Secondary Education Act (ESEA) of 1965 and its subsequent amendments required state agencies to approve local projects for federal funds. This move was both a redesign of federalism and a search for supportive implementers. Such arrangements covered education for disadvantaged, handicapped, bilingual, migrant children, and educational innovation. In each of these federal programs, 1 percent of the funds were earmarked for state administration. Moreover, Title V of ESEA provided general support for state administrative resources, with some priority given to state planning and evaluation. New staff capacity from such federal laws was available for SEA administrators or state boards that wanted to take a more activist role in local education.[2] Recent academic reform has galvanized a significant increase in state testing and use of curricular experts. State staff has increased to implement new standards policies, including assessment based on state curriculum.[3] The 2004 California Education Department has 1,600 employees, but only 400 are paid from state funds; the rest are federally funded.

Another factor for state growth is the increased confusion among, and decreased respect for, traditional supporters of local control. Thus local-control advocates—such as teachers' unions, school boards, and school administrator associations—feud among themselves and thereby provide a vacuum that state control activists can exploit. These local education groups cannot agree on common policies with their old allies such as parent organizations. The loss of public confidence in professional educators and the decline of achievement scores also cause many legislators to feel that local school employees should no longer be given much discretion. However, a local-control reaction occurred in the 1990s. Some state legislatures acted to forbid mandates without funding for local districts, which was a local concern against "big government." The movement to vouchers and charters also reflect this lack of regard for local school governance.

VARIETY AND INDIVIDUALISM

If variety is the spice of life, educational decision making in the fifty American states is a veritable spice cabinet. The situation is reminiscent of Kipling's aphorism that there are a thousand ways to worship God, and they are all correct. This variety reflects much about the basic value of individualism in the American system. We need not rely merely on assertions about this variety. Figure 8.1 sets forth the patterns of selecting and staffing administrative positions for education in the fifty states. Not only are there differences between the state board and chief administrator, but also within either office. Moreover, the ranges are impressive in board members' terms, size, and employees. The trend in the last thirty years has been to decrease the number of elected chief state school officers (CSSOs) to fifteen states. The most common method of appointing CSSOs is through the board of education—twenty-six states use this method.

Such variety reflects a pluralism of views on how to express the taproot value of individualism. That value has been reflected through a prism of diverse historical experiences (the impact of losing versus winning the Civil War), different natural resources (the poverty of the South versus the richness of the North), demographic mixes (rural homogeneity versus urban heterogeneity), and so on. Through this tangle of past and present, the creation of institutions had to take various forms. The very basis of democratic life—the political institutions of party, pressure group, and voting—took different forms from region to region as a result of these combinations of events, resources, and population.[4] We should not be surprised, then, that the evolution of educational institutions took different forms as well. For one thing, ideas about how to organize and provide schooling were affected by varied historical experiences. The New England states' violent opposition to George III instilled in them a fear of state-centralized services, including schools, which remains today. On the other hand, the states of the Confederacy were so devastated by the Union troops' destruction that financing by county institutions was wiped out. State control and moneys had to be provided in large amounts, then and ever since.

Even the precise meaning of something that all states agreed

Figure 8.1
Chief State School Officer (CSSO) and State Board of Education (SBE) Selection Patterns and Possibilities.

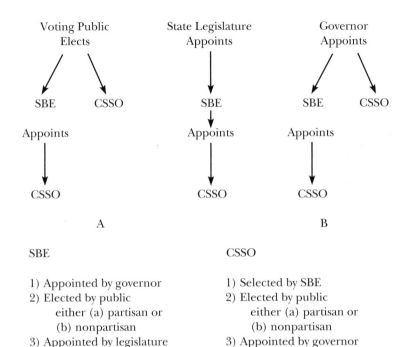

SBE

1) Appointed by governor
2) Elected by public
   either (a) partisan or
   (b) nonpartisan
3) Appointed by legislature

CSSO

1) Selected by SBE
2) Elected by public
   either (a) partisan or
   (b) nonpartisan
3) Appointed by governor

The only combination which presently does not exist is A3/B3. In 1996 state boards of education were elected in thirteen states and appointed in thirty-six states. The CSSO was elected in fifteen states.

Source: From James W. Guthrie and Rodney Reed, *Educational Administration and Policy* (Englewood Cliffs, N.J.: Prentice-Hall, 1986), p. 36. Copyright © 1986. Reprinted/adapted by permission of Allyn & Bacon.

to in principle—compulsory schooling—was affected by an intervening individualism. Massachusetts was the first state requiring school attendance in 1852. By 1900 thirty-five states had done so, but the last state, Mississippi, did not adopt such legislation until 1918.[5] In short, it took two-thirds of a century to institutionalize acceptance of even an idea that had wide popular support. Today, though, it is not clear what the meaning of this requirement is; differing political, economic, sociological, and organizational explanations abound.[6]

K-16 POLITICS*

A profound organizational, political, and cultural chasm persists in most states between the governance systems of K-12 and higher education. The two sectors continue to operate in separate orbits and to live apart in separate professional worlds, associations, and networks. These issues also lack an immediate audience or constituency, and remain peripheral, ad hoc, and largely invisible because they fall between the cracks of separate governance systems. Within each state—and at the federal level as well—a division exists that is based on the historical and pervasive assumption that K-12 schools and colleges and universities should be guided by policies exclusive to each sector. As a result, the public policy "tools" that influence one sector—funding, accountability, and governance systems, for instance—have little in common with the policy tools that influence the other. Moreover, there are separate state boards of education for each level; separate legislative committees, and boards that coordinate one level (e.g., postsecondary education) without the other. In recent years, a number of policymakers and educators have questioned the premise that the policies guiding K-12 schools and higher education ought to be totally distinct. They consider this assumption to be anachronistic and an impediment to educational improvement at both levels.

The Changing Imperative for K-16 System Alignment

Education issues critical to the nation, the states, and students remain on the margin of the policy agenda—and are no one's direct or primary responsibility. These issues include inadequate preparation for college, high school redesign, career and tech-

*This section will be part of a forthcoming monograph by Michael Kirst et al. to be published in 2005 by the National Center for Higher Education and Public Policy.

nical education, and K-12 school reform itself, due to new expectations for college preparation for nearly all students.

First, there is growing disaffection with American high schools. Reports documenting the increasing dropout rate and the poor use of student time in the senior year have drawn attention to "early colleges." Early colleges blend the eleventh and twelfth grades with the thirteenth and fourteenth grades (the freshman and sophomore years in college) into a coherent, accelerated learning opportunity. While early colleges have the potential to serve bright students as well as at-risk students, separate governing boards affecting high schools and community colleges create different fiscal, accountability, and personnel systems that limit the potential for early colleges to be a widely available alternative to high schools that fail to challenge and retain youth.

Second, career and technical education needs more rational and coordinated policymaking structures and processes. Career pathways, so vital to a volatile information-based economy, suffer from a lack of direction and commitment to career and technical education. Control is frequently diffused between and among institutions in both K-12 and higher education. The latter generally is disinterested in an educational area with relatively little prestige. The secondary schools, for their part, are preoccupied with traditional academics and pressures to increase test scores in the current state K-12 assessment environment. Without coordinated governance, vocational-technical education will continue to float either uncontested or consumed by turf wars in states.

Ultimately, the success of the K-12 school reform movement hinges on aligning the standards movement with college admission and placement policies. Without rewards for student achievement that students' parents value—namely, postsecondary admission and placement—the impetus for increasing standards will break down. Today, more high school seniors aspire to attend college than ever before (90 percent as compared to only 55 percent in the 1950s). These students face inadequate college preparation, and high remediation and dropout rates because the standards, assessments, and accountability systems at both levels have evolved separately.

K-16 Governance Prior to the 1990s: Lessons from the Past

Despite the fact that more states are interested in K-16 issues (twenty-five states report some cooperative activity, particularly in the area of teacher education), there has been little progress in implementing governance and coordination entities that would ensure more focused and systematic long-range policy attention and action. A brief historical review shows the great majority of K-16 initiatives have not been sustained, and the issue remains largely rhetorical in many jurisdictions. Where progress is made, it has occurred at a glacial pace.

Consolidated Governance. The New York Regents, created in 1784, is the broadest educational governance body in the nation. The Regents' scope of authority includes public and private elementary, secondary, and higher education; the licensed professions, including medicine, nursing, law, and accounting; libraries, museums, and historical societies; and public television and radio stations.

The birth of the State of New York (SUNY) system in the 1960s led to a dramatic decline in the Regents' attention to, and impact on, higher education. All colleges and universities—public, nonprofit independent, and for-profit proprietary—are members of the SUNY system; SUNY has budget authority over the state's higher education appropriations. Every eight years, the Regents develop a Higher Education Plan that is subject to the governor's approval, but it is not viewed as a K-16 policy-determining document.

With a disproportionate focus on K-12 issues, the Regents have retained one mechanism that aligns secondary and postsecondary education: the Regents examinations. When first conceived, student performance on these end-of-course-based exams was a factor in university admission and financial aid eligibility. As the exams' purpose evolved to certify minimum standards for high school completion—and the SUNY system's clout increased—they have been used less frequently for admissions and financial aid decisions. The Regents exams do still, however, provide information to high school students about postsecondary academic content standards. Moreover, the City University of New York

(CUNY) uses the K-12 Regents exams as its own placement examination, a policy that can reduce remediation.

The lesson from New York's experience is that a consolidated governance structure—in and of itself—does not lead to the policy development that aligns K-12 and postsecondary education.

Gubernatorial-Appointed Secretaries of Education. In the 1970s, several states, including Idaho, Massachusetts, Pennsylvania, South Dakota, and Virginia, tried to bridge the K-16 gap through gubernatorial-appointed Secretaries of Education. The positions were created with the expectation that centralized, state-level leadership for K-12 and higher education could better coordinate and integrate education policy, including such areas as teacher education. After twenty-five years, however, the system goals and policies in none of these states are as aligned as they were originally intended:

- In *Idaho*, strong public concern for the quality of K-12 education has pulled the Secretary and Board's attention to K-12 issues, which has led to greater independence and less scrutiny of higher education.
- In *Virginia*, compulsory eleventh-grade end-of-course examinations contain relevant content to judge higher education readiness, but there has been no serious discussion of using Virginia's K-12 standards of learning for postsecondary admission or placement. Similarly in *Pennsylvania*, students' performance on the low-stakes high school exit examination does not link to any postsecondary standards.
- In *Massachusetts*, higher education leaders increased academic requirements and decreased remedial courses at public colleges. This policy, however, was initiated by the higher education system without significant involvement of the Secretary of Education or K-12.
- In *Oregon*, the state tried to improve K-14 educational pathways by placing the community colleges under the State Board of Education. But Oregon's State Board makes policy for K-12 schools and community colleges separately. Oregon's promising competency-based exit examination, the Certificate of Advanced Mastery (CAM) for eleventh- and twelfth-grade students, is not fully developed, and the community

colleges have not been enthusiastic about incorporating CAM. Once again, we find that alignment of governance does not necessarily occur with a more consolidated structure, unless that structure leads to an integration of goals, performance measures, and policy development.

Voluntary K-16 Collaboration. The disappointing results from the 1970s' attempts to integrate K-12 and postsecondary policymaking with structural governance changes was followed by the attempts in the 1990s to provide less formal and more voluntary K-16 linkages. These initiatives have made some incremental progress, but they will depend for longevity on a next generation of committed leaders from both levels.

The most ambitious of these efforts are the Georgia and Maryland P-16 councils. The goal of these councils is to profoundly change the ways in which school and colleges operate, not just to add new "early-intervention-style" programs. In order to bring separately governed and financed systems together on issues of mutual interest, a voluntary P-16 council must have access to key leaders—including policymakers, communities, business, and labor—and state policy levers (e.g., accountability provisions or shared student-level data). While still evolving, Maryland and Georgia's P-16 councils have put much more effort in teacher education than in improving student pathways from secondary to postsecondary education. Recently, the Georgia statewide P-16 council has been establishing academic standards for the first two years of college that are linked to the state's K-12 standards. It is too early to reach a final verdict on these voluntary K-16 educator alliances. A major question is whether they will survive the unusual leaders who instigated them. Will ad hoc, voluntary institutional policies lead to sustained governance changes?

SOCIOECONOMIC DIMENSIONS OF VARIETY

Multiple Responses to Systematic Problems

Understanding a state's politics of education requires a grasp of its distinctive societal background. In the case of the fifty

American states, such a demonstration quickly overloads even eager students because of the varied and many dimensions for categorizing units of government. The fifty states and their fourteen thousand LEAs vary along all the traditional dimensions of demography—age composition; size of school-age population; parents' education, occupation, and income; economic resources; and so on to form an almost endless list. Districts run from the behemoth, with over a million students in New York City, to a hamlet with a dozen in the graduating class. Economics range from extremely wealthy suburbs to poor farm villages. Their resources vary just as much, from a multiple-building high school in a California suburb to a one-room schoolhouse on the Nebraska prairie.

This variety means that the total school system will adjust differently to impinging nationwide events or even state law. No such thing as state education policy exists; what does exist are differential state responses to common external and internal events, all of which work on the local political system. For example, the state reaction to the 1983 reform movement varied enormously. Some states enacted omnibus bills with extensive state mandates. Other states did little and left what few programs they did enact to local discretion. Table 8.1 shows how many of the forty recommendations in the 1983 *A Nation at Risk* report were adopted in the first two years after its publication. The data reflect a heavy response in the South (and California as well), which suggests that those states used the reform publicity to push changes that would move them toward national standards. Three major forces that caused these state reforms were more activist governors (including the later President Clinton), heightened involvement of big business, and the influence of interstate reform networks.[7] A later variation is seen in state responses to Bush's No Child Left Behind. While all reported to Washington in the first three years, some federally mandated reforms were incomplete, and others like rural states found huge problems in finding highly qualified teachers.

Table 8.1

Number of Reforms Adopted by State Legislatures

Number Adopted	Number of States	States
0–4	17	Alaska, Ga., Md., Mass., Mont., Nev., N.H., N.M., N.Dak., Ohio, Oreg., Pa., R.I., S.Dak., Utah, Vt., Wyo.
5–9	16	Ala., Colo., Del., Hawaii, Ind., Ill., Iowa, Kans., Mich., Minn., Mo., N.J., N.Y., Va., W.Va., Wisc.
10–14	9	Ariz., Conn., Ky., La., Maine, Nebr., Okla., Tex., Wash.,
15–19	6	Ark., Calif., Ind., Miss., N.C., Tenn.
20 or more	2	Fla., S.C.

Source: Doh Shinn and Jack Van Der Slik, "Legislative Efforts to Improve the Quality of Public Education in The American States: A Comparative Analysis" (paper presented to the annual convention of the American Political Science Assn., New Orleans, 1985), p. 36.

The Dimension of School Finances

School financing is another useful illustration of variety in local implementation, for money plays such a large part in the American politics of education. Schools have traditionally been heavily financed by local taxes, with the states providing only a small share and the federal government the tiny remainder. That commonality aside, though, almost total diversity characterizes school financing. Each state's contribution has varied with its own resources, traditions, and values, as well as with the general economic effects of wars and recessions. While the overall state share has increased between 1900 and 2000 from about 20 to 50 percent, variations among the states are huge. Thus in 2001, Hawaii, rooted in a royal tradition of centralism, provided 92 percent, while New Hampshire provided about 21 percent.

Though greater disparities exist among the LEAs within each state, much stability still shows up in the ways that states react to local needs.[8] Relatively rich and poor states remain very much the same over long periods of time; thus, the amounts of state aid or the patterns of other policies demonstrate that little shift exists in these states' *relative* standings on such matters.[9] Thus, the pattern is one of both stability and variety among the American states. No conceivable socioeconomic dimension exists on which the states do not show such variation. Even the constitutional position of education in these states reveals pluralism.

However, some national events—war, depression—shape the state responses to education often across the board. Table 8.2 illustrates one of these effects of a national recession in the early 2000s on education budgets and shortfalls. Budget cuts were brought on by reduced revenue from sales taxes, capital gains, and reduced market sales. All these cuts feed into a state's total revenue picture. Moreover, the problem was also caused by increased demand from other state programs, such as Medicaid, but even "rainy day" reserves were gone by early 2003.[10]

Within this fifty-state range there is considerable variation in the size of a state's education budget, often linked to population size (thus California and Texas versus Idaho and Vermont). Most states, though, had a deficit, some severe, such as California and Texas). A few states had no change (six), and the natural resource-based economy in Wyoming created a surplus. Nor does the concept of political culture explain this variation; in the traditionalist and moralist Southern and Plains states the range of spending is low to moderate. The major point, though, is that the social context of a state shapes its response to external events, and there is great variety across the panoply of federalism.

EVOLUTION OF A NEW STATE ROLE

The shift in the state role has been drastic in recent decades, and the rate of involvement has increased dramatically. The original thirteen state constitutions made no mention of education. Today all states refer to education, sometimes briefly (Connecticut's schools rested on three paragraphs until well into the twentieth century), and sometimes at length (for example, California with a four-thousand-page code). As we have noted, state involvement started at the end of the last century with school reforms that introduced more professionalism. The authorization of districts and the limitation on their taxing appeared everywhere at that time. Consolidation also emerged pervasively around

Table 8.2
State-by-State Financial Shortfall, January 2003

State	Deficit (in million $)	Education Budget (in billion $)
Alabama	200	17.0
Alaska	859	2.4
Arizona	500	6.2
Arkansas	No change	No change
California	3 billion	78.0
Colorado	700	13.8
Connecticut	500	13.0
Delaware	91	2.3
Florida	1.7 billion*	30.0
Georgia	None	16.1
Hawaii	None	3.5
Idaho	160	0.9
Illinois	600	52.6
Indiana	860	10.8
Iowa	220	4.4
Kansas	310	2.7
Kentucky*	2.6 percent cut	
Louisiana	75	16.3
Maine*	10 cut	
Maryland	344	22.0
Massachusetts	297	22.0
Michigan	460	36.0
Minnesota	356	13.9
Mississippi	79	1.7
Missouri	152	18.9
Montana	5	1.2
Nebraska	673	2.6
Nevada	100	1.9
New Hampshire	80	4.0
New Jersey	77	23.4
New Mexico	No change	No change
New York	2,000	89.6
North Carolina	No change	14.4
North Dakota	43	5.0
Ohio*	30	7.8
Oklahoma	513	5.3
Oregon	600	12.0
Pennsylvania	433	4.1
Rhode Island	130	2.7
South Carolina	246	5.4

South Dakota	54	0
Tennessee	No change	No change
Texas	5,000 (2 years)	113.8
Utah	117	7.3
Vermont	38	0.9
Virginia	1,500	24.7
Washington	2,000 (2 years)	23.0
West Virginia	250	0
Wisconsin	185	11
Wyoming	202 surplus	0

*School budget figures only.

Source: Summarized from state totals in Education Week (January 8, 2003): 18–19.

World War I. By 1925 one-third of the states already had state supervision set out in detailed, minimum standards for some matters. These included local sites, buildings, lighting, heating, outdoor and indoor equipment (including even the size of a globe), academic and professional qualifications of teachers, length and kinds of courses, requirements for hygiene, and community relations programs.[11]

One significant example of this centralizing process is the number of states requiring a university degree to teach, from none in 1900 to all fifty in 1965. A 2001 survey shows growth of the state in their functions, including teachers' use of classroom practices consistent with state mathematics standards.[12] All states do certain things, such as keeping records on pupils, but only a few states do other things, such as guidance and counseling. These regular policies are part of the "system maintenance" capacities that professions use to control the functions they deem most vital.[13] In other words, the *potential* for state intervention in local schools, once remote but always possible, has today become a pervasive reality.

This constitutional position does not, however, exhaust the political aspects of schools. We may now turn to more evidence of schools' political nature.

Increasing State Control over the LEA

Just as no political action takes place without having different effects on different groups' values, educational policymaking is

contentious because some participants win and some lose. Recall that in Chapter 1 we noted that politics is not only conflict
over the distribution of resources, but also and more basically
over the distribution of group values. This concept leads us to
expect that the basic interactions among schools, political system, and society must deal with who and what is to be valued in
the educational process. So schools are caught up in a competition for resources, status, and value satisfaction like other institutions of our society.

Central to this situation is the value of local control discussed
in Chapter 5, a value that permits individualism to take the
manifold forms so characteristic of American education. State
control—constitutionally given—has worked in tension with this
passion for local control.[14] Controls take several forms: service
minimums that the LEA cannot fall below; encouragement of
LEAs to exceed minimums (for example, by cost-sharing a new
goal); testing and accountability; emphasis on efficiency methods, and so on. Such controls assume that the state can provide
equality better than the LEA through standardizing instruction
and resources. Advocates of local control assert, however, that
greater payoffs will flow from a more flexible, hence more decentralized, system of schooling. Indeed, the 1990s saw local
pressures causing some states to forbid any state mandates without full state funding.

Thus the state-local clash has been between two major values—the provision of state equity versus freedom of local choice.
More recently, states have emphasized a third value—efficiency—
by placing more controls over teaching, budgeting, testing, and
so on. Today equity and efficiency are more stressed by state
action, but local curriculum choice has been reduced despite
much contention over vouchers and charter schools. This cap-
sule account highlights the point generally accepted by students
of education, namely, that local control as a value and operational fact has declined.[15]

CONSENSUS AND DIVERSITY IN STATE POLICY SYSTEMS

The fifty states are not fifty unique laboratories of schooling policy. Rather, *distinct state clusters of behavior prevail* so that state policy is a matter of limited patterns. Indeed, many state policy areas share a common agreement among the states on policy for schooling. It is this mixture of consensus and divergence that characterizes other institutions and policies in American federalism.

Policy Values Among the States

We start with Easton's view that the function of the political system is to authoritatively allocate values and resources. Consequently, understanding what values are sought in education policy is a first task in grappling with the diversity of American federalism. The important values here are basic instrumental values, that is, those used to pursue an even more fundamental political value. These instrumental values are four—quality, efficiency, equity, and choice—according to an analysis of values in education policy in six states.[16] (Quality and equity are often also called excellence and equality.) Their explanation sets the background for understanding how policymakers use public resources to realize values. We use these value definitions here, set out briefly in Table 8.3.

Policy Preferences Among the States

These four values are evident among state education policymakers and interest groups in a study of six states from 1980 to 1988.[17] What were the common and diverse policy elements of such state policy elites?

First, despite differences among the states, much consensus existed about the relative importance of seven basic *domains,* or broad areas, of education policy. Finance policy was everywhere seen as most important; then, personnel, student testing, and school program policies followed in importance; the governance and curriculum materials policies were ranked next; and finally, buildings and facilities policies were of least interest. The im-

Table 8.3
Definitions of Basic Policy Values and School Policy Linkages

CHOICE

Legislated options for local constituencies in making decisions.
  Example: Choice of textbooks.
Instrumental to realize basic democratic value of popular sovereignty, that is citizens' legitimate authority over officials' policy actions.

EFFICIENCY

Either:
  Economic mode, minimizing costs while maximizing gains.
  Example: pupil-teacher ratio.
Or:
  Accountability mode, means by which superiors oversee and hence control subordinates' use of power.
  Example: Publicizing stages of budgetary process.
Instrumental to basic organizational value, namely, responsibility of power-wielders to those who authorize it.

EQUITY

Equalizing or redistributing public resources to meet morally and societally defined human needs.
  Example: Compensatory or handicapped education.
Instrumental to basic liberal value, namely, the worth of every individual and society's responsibility to realize that worth.

QUALITY

Use of public resources to match professionally determined standards of excellence proficiency, or ability.
  Example: Certification of teachers.
Instrumental to the basic social value that education is crucial for the future citizen's life chances.

Source: Abstracted from Catherine Marshall, Douglas Mitchell, and Frederick Wirt, *Culture and Education Policy in the American States* (New York: Falmer, 1989), Chap. 4.

portance of these priorities operated in parallel fashion among the states, with minor variations, as Table 8.4 shows. Second, state policymakers were pushing for greater state action in all domains but especially in personnel, finance, governance, and buildings. Third, much agreement also prevailed about specific *programs* within each policy domain in all but governance, as listed in Table 8.4. Policy elites reported that these programs were

Table 8.4

High Agreement on Education Policy Programs Among
Policy Elites of Six States, 1982–83

Domain	Specific Programs
Finance	Equalization
	Establishing overall funding level
Personnel	Preservice certification and training
Student testing	Specifying format or content of required tests
School program	Setting higher standards for graduation
Curricular materials	Specifying scope and sequence of instruction
Buildings and facilities	Remediation of identified architectural problems
Governance	None

Source: Abstracted from Catherine Marshall, Douglas Mitchell, and Frederick Wirt, *Culture and Education Policy in the American States* (New York: Falmer, 1989), Chap. 5.

receiving the most attention by their legislatures compared to other alternatives. However, beyond such commonalities, considerable variation still existed among them in both policy domain and program, especially governance, finance, and testing.

This snapshot of state policy structure in the mid-1980s may alter over time. The 1960s and 1970s had exhibited a greater policy emphasis among all fifty states on the value of equity, namely, redistributing state finances to close the spending gap between rich and poor districts. In the 1980s, though, as inflation and the Reagan administration's withdrawal from equity programs combined to drive the states to seek greater resources. So more policy emphasis shifted from equity to efficiency and quality as end values in education.[18] The emphasis shifted to constraining educational goals and to improving the services provided. By 2003, greater emphasis lay with accountability and improving student test scores. Pressures from above in Washington and from below in charter schools altered the policy scene. In a few cases, states took over failing schools and districts, forcing out local administrators and school boards. In the future, though, with a different economy and political leadership, a restructuring of these value priorities is certain.

In any period, however, a state's policy structure will result
from both national and state influences, one example of the
confluence of central and peripheral influences working within
any modern nation. In short, a current of ideas about policy
preferences, such as state standards and tests, will swirl through
America from time to time, generated by new political movements, emerging perceived needs, or changes in the economy.
Illustrative of such national reforms in education policy have been
the concern for educating the poor after 1965, the Reagan administration's devolution to the states, and the states' curriculum and testing reforms after 1990.

A second component of a state's policy structure stems from
influences that are special to that state that reflect a local culture. We already noted how past events had produced a political
cultural outlook on the issue of state versus local control of schooling. This cultural influence can affect specific education policies
as well. It takes only a little knowledge of American education
to realize that citizens in Connecticut and Mississippi provide
different resources, view their leaders' role differently, and expect different qualities of education. Does this cultural explanation affect what state policymakers see and do in their respective
worlds?

Political Culture and State Policy Choices

These differing peripheral influences will reflect *political culture*, that is, "the set of acts, beliefs, and sentiments which give
order and meaning to a political process and which provide
the underlying assumptions and rules that govern behavior in
the political system. It encompasses both the political issues
and the operating norms. . . ."[19] These "acts, beliefs . . . assumptions and rules" are not infinite in number among the fifty states,
rather they group into clusters. One scholar has developed three
distinctive state political cultures with consequent differences in
state political behavior.[20]

1. *Traditionalistic culture (TPC)*: Government's main function is
   maintaining traditional patterns, being responsive to a governing elite, with partisanship subordinated to personal ties.

2. *Individualistic culture (IPC)*: Government is a marketplace that responds to demands, favors economic development, and relies on the political party as the vehicle for satisfying individual needs.
3. *Moralistic culture (MPC)*: Government is the means for achieving the good community or commonwealth through positive government action, social and economic regulations are legitimate, parties are downplayed, and bureaucracy is viewed positively as an agent of the people.

State education policymakers believe that the citizens of their own states possess distinctive "beliefs and sentiments" about the political system.[21] Thus views about government's role, political parties, elections, bureaucracy, and policies—even corporal punishment for students—in one state will cluster differently from those held in another state; this occurs in ways that fit the historically based (but still relevant today) designation of the three cultures.[22] Figure 8.2 reveals data in the 1980s of the education policy elites' perceptions in six states of their citizens' political views. Their answers clustered in such a way that Wisconsin anchors one end of the moralistic-individualistic continuum, with Illinois at the other end. California and Pennsylvania also fall on the continuum in the direction that their cultural origins would place them. While this dimension accounted for most of the variation in answers (81 percent), another dimension (the vertical axis in Figure 8.2) helped distinguish the traditionalistic culture of Arizona and West Virginia. In short, these policy elites perceived their constituents' political culture in the same way that historical evidence suggests.

Yet what difference in education policy do these cultural differences make? Because democratic leaders reflect citizen values—no matter how roughly—these elite perceptions of constituencies should be linked to distinctive education policies. The policy domains and programs fit the cultural perceptions of these elites among states. Virginia's education policies are very different from Maryland's even though only the Potomac River separates them. Pennsylvania has different state policies than does California or North Carolina. Arizona has much less state control than does Georgia. Some of the even broader policy domains—

Figure 8.2
State Centroids of Political Culture on Two Functions

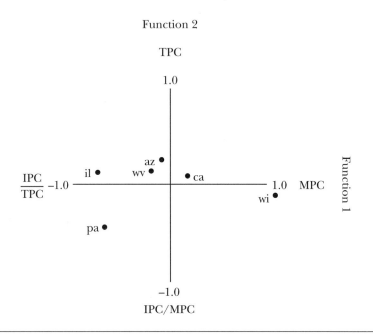

Source: Abstracted from Catherine Marshall, Douglas Mitchell, and Frederick Wirt, *Culture and Education Policy in the American States* (New York: Falmer, 1989), p. 117.

defining school programs and preparing curricular materials—demonstrated high, even significant, correlations in this six-state study. Such findings strengthen the belief that political cultures are influential in shaping state policies, even amid multiple, detailed program choices that are characteristic of the American states.

There are other ways to measure state political variation. Scholars created dynamic measures of the ideology of a state's citizens based on polls of voter attitudes. This is compared to the ideology of a state's political leaders using roll call voting scores of state congressional delegations, the outcomes of congressional elections, the partisan division of state legislatures, the party of the governor, and various assumptions regarding voters and state political leaders.[23] Some scholars have created an index that has the most liberal ideology at 100 and conservative at 0. They contrast the views of the electorate (citizen ideology) to the behavioral indications in elections and legislative voting patterns. Table 8.5 presents two summary measures for all these state characteristics. On "government" the scores range from traditional and conservative—a 4 in Wyoming—to liberal—a 94 in Maryland. That range is similar on "citizen role," from 26 (Alabama) to 82 (Iowa). Political cultures of the states, discussed earlier, do help distinguish such scores. On both measures, the scores of the moralist culture states are higher than those of the traditionalist states. However, even within a culture there is still variation. Within the traditionalist states, Virginia has the highest of both scores, while Arkansas has the lowest on one score and intermediate on the other. As a group, then, these measures enumerate much of the diversity in our society that generates much policy conflict, particularly on the role of state government in society.

None of this analysis tells us what the best state education programs are, though; that was not its purpose. However, we now know that state policies result from both national currents of reform as well as from local historical influences. The latter reflect variations in how policymakers and their constituents think of the political system and how they want the system to act. History thus shapes contemporary policy actions through socialization to "beliefs and sentiments" that differ among the states and regions, and thus with Walt Whitman, to create "a nation of nations."

STAGES OF POLICYMAKING AND EDUCATION

Studies of state policymaking usually employ a chronological sequence, even though these stages often mesh into others. Analytically, though, we can use this sequence to understand state policies.

Agenda Setting and State Policy

The early phases of public policy are directed toward stimulating government to consider a problem, that is, agenda set-

Table 8.5
Different States, Different Ideologies

State	Government Ideology	Citizen Ideology
Alabama	40	26
Alaska	75	44
Arizona	45	45
Arkansas	10	40
California	88	56
Colorado	16	49
Connecticut	59	67
Delaware	74	57
Florida	17	49
Georgia	87	48
Hawaii	94	82
Idaho	34	58
Illinois	64	48
Indiana	56	48
Iowa	9	26
Kansas	7	37
Kentucky	48	26
Louisiana	37	33
Maine	74	83
Maryland	94	70
Massachusetts	69	62
Michigan	12	51
Minnesota	53	52
Mississippi	72	47
Missouri	38	35
Montana	6	44
Nebraska	54	33
Nevada	86	51
New Hampshire	37	67
New Jersey	50	50
New Mexico	51	68
New York	21	62
North Carolina	17	35
North Dakota	46	57
Ohio	16	51
Oklahoma	29	23
Oregon	57	58
Pennsylvania	27	54
Rhode Island	63	71
South Carolina	72	53
South Dakota	10	47

Tennessee	45	47
Texas	24	41
Utah	13	38
Vermont	27	45
Virginia	92	71
Washington	68	46
West Virginia	28	52
Wisconsin	43	62
Wyoming	4	30

Source: Adapted from William Berry, et al., "Measuring Citizen and Government Ideology in the American States," *American Journal of Political Science* 42:1 (January 1998): 327–348.

ting. It is difficult, though, to isolate the subparts or stages of the agenda-setting process as discrete events.[24] We define agenda setting by state policymakers as active, serious consideration of a concrete and specific issue.

To get "on the agenda," an issue must pass through four stages: (1) issue recognition, where legislators notice an issue and believe it to be a topic for potential action; (2) issue adoption, when legislators acknowledge the legitimacy of government responsibility and the possibility that an appropriate response could be found; (3) issue prioritizing so that the existing agenda is reordered to include the new issue; and (4) issue maintenance so that the new issue remains on the agenda after initial consideration.

The stimulus for this process is often transmitted through interest groups, as an earlier chapter pointed out. However, the agenda spread of state testing and curricular standards during the 1990s was not caused by this traditional role. Consequently, we will explore a variety of other causes.

Influences on the Early Phases of Public Policymaking

Movements and the Media. Public opinion and the news media are often seen as playing important roles in political agenda setting. New ideas can gain ground rapidly if initial events and important influences surface in the mainstream and so become issues of public debate or conflict.[25] Social movements and groundswells of public opinion create a broader context within government for decision making; they also allow for greater discretion in the creation and design of new programs.

There is the impact of media and public opinion on traditional special interests in agenda setting.[26] The notions of pluralism or elite pluralism do not adequately explain broad social movements such as environmentalism and women's rights. In the cases of large-scale political or social movements, coalitions form with established interest groups and elements of political parties. Elected officials are then quick to follow the trend and so create the bandwagon phenomenon. From this initial coalition, "generations of lobbies" grow in response to the social movements. Television news, in particular, hastens their development or demise.

The news media directly influence members of state legislatures. At one time, party discipline, legislative apprenticeship, and deference to seniority were the most important factors in determining a legislative member's role in political agenda setting. Now the passage of legislation is more and more dependent on symbolic politics. Symbolic laws do not deal with the policy problem, but enact emotional symbols instead. Requiring each student to wear a uniform will not be sufficient to improve test scores. State policymakers rely heavily on printed and electronic sources "to gain insight into relevant social science findings."[27]

State Political Environment. A second strand of agenda-setting concepts emphasizes policy environment. Of particular value to agenda setting is the finding that many social and economic factors create a political milieu that seems to affect a state's receptivity to new ideas. Some states are more innovative, and some are not. One scholar finds that "innovative states are both wealthier and more competitive between political parties than their sister states at the time of adoption of a particular law."[28] The notion is that wealthier states will create more innovative policy agendas, because their citizens have high income, urbanization, industrialization, and education. However, these variables clearly differ in their significance depending on the policy issues being decided.[29] Linkages exist between interest groups and state socioeconomic complexity; for example, states with a few strong interest groups do not have complex economies. These major interest groups (e.g., agriculture in Kansas) have a very influential role in determining a state's agenda.[30]

In education a six-state study of influence found from a ranking of elites that teachers and other educators were ranked fourth behind the influence of formal state agencies. But traditionalistic state cultures placed teacher groups much lower in influence.[31]

Intragovernment Factions. Factions within federal and state government can determine the policy agenda, including the "professional-bureaucratic complex" and the "intergovernmental lobby" that form the centers of influence in policymaking. The professional-bureaucratic complex is a "core of officials with scientific training working in close cooperation with legislators and interest groups."[32] The formal organizational structures of bureaucracies allow members to communicate with policymakers with relative ease and promote the influential role of state bureaucrats as "policy shapers." The "career bureaucrats often 'know best'—in a technical sense how to deal with problems . . . or even to determine whether a particular situation requires a state response."[33]

Policy Issue Networks. One scholar defines the key concept in our agenda-setting analysis—a policy issue network—at the federal level and distinguishes it from the "iron triangle":

Issue networks . . . comprise a large number of participants with quite variable degrees of mutual commitment or of dependence on others in their environment; in fact it is almost impossible to say where a network leaves off and its environment begins. Iron triangles and sub-governments suggest a stable set of participants coalesced to control fairly narrow programs which are in the direct economic interest of each part to the alliance. Issue networks are almost the reverse image in each respect. Participants move in and out of the networks constantly. Rather than groups united in dominance over a program, no one, as far as one can tell, is in control of the policies and issues. Any direct or material interest is often secondary to intellectual or emotional commitment. Network members reinforce each other's sense of issues as their interests, rather than (as standard political or economic models would have it) interests defining positions on issues.[34]

A policy issue network differs from a political movement in that movements focus on many issues, and exhibit great uncertainty about who authentically speaks for the cause.

A policy network is part of the large policy system and is made up of both those from the larger community outside government and those within it with official decision-making power. Policy networks cut through various layers of government and extend outside government. The definition we employ views policy issue networks as linked to specific issues rather than attached to general policy areas (e.g., the environment) or to broad interests like teachers. The policy goals of an issue network are more specific than a political movement.

Interstate issue networks are led by policy entrepreneurs who play a critical role in translating technical and academic data into "plain English" for other bureaucrats and politicians. Policy entrepreneurs take up a cause like charter schools and reframe issues through policy issue networks. They shift the political debate.[35]

Our study of policy issue networks in education points to these conclusions:

1. Policy issue networks, such as charter school advocates, are an important concept for understanding the early phases of state policymaking. These networks may be characterized along such internal organization dimensions as membership, central guidance and promotion, conceptual agreement, and information flow. Variability in these dimensions can generate differences in state agenda-setting processes.
2. Networks may also be characterized by the kind of policy solution they advocate. Along this policy dimension, networks vary from a complete, inflexible statute (e.g., scientific creationism) to similarly motivated but highly variable programs and legislation (e.g., minimum competency testing).
3. The content or subject matter of a policy issue network, and the grounds on which the arguments are advanced, may add to how the networks develop, the kinds of policy solutions they advocate, and their designation into distinct types. Ranging from arguments primarily based on philosophy (e.g., creation science) to legal constitutionally based arguments (e.g., school finance) to advantages of markets (e.g., charter schools), the network message will help determine variation in the operation and success of policy issue net-

works. Moreover, centrally driven networks create similar state statutes, as seen in the difference between centrally led collective bargaining and minimum competency testing.

4. Interstate policy issue networks can frequently override political and socioeconomic constraints for state agenda setting. On the whole, network effectiveness—rather than fiscal capacity, legislative capacity, or state policy centralization—accounts for certain issues on a state policy agenda.[36] Thirty-three states have charter school laws that encompass 2,000 schools and 500,000 students. Issue networks are not the only means of agenda setting, but they have been overlooked. In some states (e.g., West Virginia), though, the political culture is so hostile to charter school network issues that they never reach the state legislative agenda.

Further research on issue networks within the American states is needed to test the dimensions, classifications, and assertions that have emerged from existing cases and to gain an understanding of how issue networks interact with interest groups to influence state policymaking and agenda setting.[37] Now that we have analyzed the broader concepts of state education policy, it is appropriate to examine next the institutions and actors as they make policy.

NOTES

1. Keith E. Hamm and Gary F. Moncrief, "Legislative Politics in the States," in Virginia Gray et al., eds., *Politics in the American States* (Washington, D.C.: CQ Press, 1999).

2. U.S. General Accounting Office, *Federal Share of State Education Expenditures* (Washington, D.C.: GAO, 1995).

3. Susan Lusi, *The Role of State Departments of Education* (New York: Teachers College Press, 1997).

4. An excellent review of this regional variety and its political consequences is found in Daniel Elazar, *American Federalism: A View from the States* (New York: Crowell, 1984). For a different view see David C. Nice, *Policy Innovation in State Government* (Ames: Iowa State University, 1994).

5. George Collins, "Constitutional and Legal Basis for State Action," in Edgar Fuller and Jim Pearson, eds., *Education in the States: Nationwide Development since 1900* (Wash., D.C.: National Education Association, 1969), pp. 29–30.

6. For a review of five interpretations, see David Tyack, "Ways of Seeing: An Essay on the History of Compulsory Schooling," *Harvard Educational Review* 46 (1976): 355–89. Also useful is Michael S. Katz, *A History of Compulsory Education Laws* (Bloomington, Ind.: Phi Delta Kappa Educational Foundation, 1976).

7. Tim Mazzoni, "State Policymaking and School Reform," in Jay B. Scribner and Donald H. Layton, eds., *The Study of Educational Politics* (London: Falmer, 1995), pp. 53–74.

8. Richard Winters, "The Politics of Taxing and Spending," in Gray, *Politics in the American States*.

9. The definitive review of these events, policies, and results is Walter Garms, James Guthrie, and Lawrence Pierce, *School Finance: The Economics and Politics of Federalism* (Englewood Cliffs, N.J.: Prentice-Hall, 1988).

10. *Education Week* (February 4, 2003): 47.

11. A useful set of essays on many of these historical developments since 1900 is found in Fuller and Pearson, *Education in the States*. For a more recent analysis, see Thomas B. Timar, "The Institutional Role of State Education Departments: A Historical Role," *American Journal of Education* 15: 3 (May 1997): 231–260.

12. Christopher B. Swanson and David Lee Stevenson, "Standards Based Reform in Practice," *Educational Evaluation and Policy Analysis* 24:1 (Spring 2002): 1–27. See also Betty Malen, "Tightening the Grip? The Impact of State Activism on Local School Systems," *Educational Policy* 17: 2 (May 2003): 195–216.

13. Frederick M. Wirt, "State Policy Culture and State Decentralization," in Jay Scribner, ed., *Politics of Education* (Chicago: Yearbook of the National Society for the Study of Education, 1977), pp. 164–87. A brief statement is in Frederick M. Wirt, "What State Laws Say about Local Control," *Phi Delta Kappan* 59 (1978): 517–20.

14. Neil D. Theobold and Betty Malen, *Balancing Local Control and State Responsibility for K-12 Education* (Larchmont, N.Y.: Eye on Education, 2000).

15. See William Chance, *The Best of Education* (Chicago: McArthur Foundation, 1987), and the annual "Quality Counts" surveys of *Education Week*.

16. Catherine Marshall, Douglas Mitchell, and Frederick Wirt, *Culture and Education Policy in the American States* (London: Falmer, 1989).

17. Douglas Mitchell et al., "Building a Taxonomy of State Education Policies," *Peabody Journal of Education* 62:4 (1985): 7–47.

18. David Clark and Terry Astuto, *The Significance and Permanence of Changes in Federal Educational Policy 1980–1988* (Bloomington, Ind.: Policy Studies Center of the University Council for Educational Administration, University of Indiana, 1988).

19. Lucius Pye, "Political Culture," in *International Encyclopedia of the Social Sciences*, Vol. 12 (New York: Crowell, Collier and Macmillan, 1968), p. 218.

20. Elazar, *American Federalism*.

21. For a review of that literature, see Frederick M. Wirt, "'Soft' Concepts and 'Hard' Data: A Research Review of Elazar's Political Culture," *Publius: The Journal of Federalism* 213 (1991): 1–14. One article in this symposium shows

culture affects even student discipline; Sue Vandenbosch, "Political Culture and Corporal Punishment in Public Schools," pp. 117–22.

22. Elazar, *American Federalism*; see also Marshall et al., *Culture and Education Policy*, chap. 5. For a recent study see Kerstin Le Floch, "Context is Key" (paper presented at the annual meeting of the American Educational Research Association, Seattle, Washington, 2001).

23. William Berry et al., "Measuring Citizen Ideology in the American States," *American Journal of Political Science* 42:1 (January 1998): 327-348.

24. F. R. Baumgartner and B. D. Jones, *Agendas and Instability in American Politics* (Chicago: University of Chicago Press, 1993). For a state comparison see Juekyung Lee, "State Activism in Education Reform," *Educational Evaluation and Policy Analysis*, 19:1 (Spring 1997): 29–43.

25. Michael Mintrom, *Policy Entrepreneur and School Choice* (Washington, D.C.: Georgetown, 2000).

26. See James Kingdon, *Agendas, Alternatives, and Public Policies*, 2nd ed. (New York: Harper Collins, 1995).

27. Douglas E. Mitchell, "State Legislatures and the Social Sciences" (Stanford, Calif.: Institute for Finance and Governance, Report 81-A10, September 1981).

28. Virginia Gray, "Competition, Emulation, and Policy Innovation," in Lang C. Dodd and C. Jillson, eds., *New Perspectives on American Politics* (Washington, D.C.: Congressional Quarterly Press, 1994). See also Mazzoni, "State Policymaking."

29. See Hamm and Moncrief, "Legislative Politics," pp. 183–185.

30. Ibid., p. 184.

31. Marshall et al., *Culture and Education Policy*, p. 23.

32. Samuel H. Beer, "Political Overload and Federalism," *Polity* 10 (Fall 1977): 12.

33. Richard Elling, "State Bureaucracies," in Gray et al., *Politics in the American States*, 1994.

34. Hugh Heclo, "Issue Networks and the Executive Establishment," in *The New American Political System*, Anthony King, ed. (Washington, D.C.: American Enterprise Institute, 1978), pp. 98–99. For charter school network analysis see Michael Mintrom, *Policy Entrepreneurs and School Choice* (Washington, D.C.: Georgetown, 2000).

35. Michael W. Kirst, Gail Meister, and Stephen R. Rawley, "Policy Issue Networks," *Policy Studies Journal* 13: 2 (December 1984): 247–264. See also Mintrom, *Policy Entreprenuers*. For a supplementary perspective see Frances Berry and William Berry, "State Lottery Adoptions as Policy Innovations," *American Political Science Review* 84 (June 1990): 395–415.

36. Hanne Mawhinney and Catherine Lugg, eds., "Interest Groups in United States Education," in *Education Policy* 15: 1 (January and March 2001): 3–216.

37. For an overview of network analysis see David Knoke, *Political Networks: The Standard Perspective* (Cambridge, England: Cambridge University Press, 1990).

9

The State Political Process

Policymaking involves representatives of formal government agencies, special interests, and the public in general. The process is mainly centered around the incremental changes to the vast body of decisions already in existence. However, this flow of incremental action is disrupted ever so often by the sudden call for nonincremental innovative policy change. These involve new uses of public resources to achieve old educational values of quality, efficiency, equity, and choice. Empirically, the last quarter-century has known much more innovation at all levels of government, arising from the political turbulence and challenge discussed throughout this book.

Amid such change, how have the state policymakers acted? Is it a case of fifty sets of policymakers doing fifty different things? We find that the process is more patterned, however, because some commonalities are evident in each state. For example, the same set of officials operate in each state; they have somewhat similar influence on policymaking; and all these actors must deal with limited policy options as they do their job. We turn to review the influence of these actors and their outlook on the policy process for education.

PATTERNS OF INFLUENCE AMONG POLICY ACTORS

Viewed across the states, how do policy actors think and act? A six-state study found that educational policy elites ranked one another's influence with surprising consistency.[1] (It is likely that a 2005 ranking would place the governors higher.) In Table 9.1 we see the composite ranking for eighteen types of policy influentials; the result is a picture of concentric circles of influence.

Table 9.1

*Ranking of Policy Influentials: All Six States**

Cluster	Six-State Rank	Policy Group
Insiders	1	Individual members of the legislature
	2	Legislators as a whole
	3	Chief state school officer
	4	All education interest groups combined
Near	5	Teacher organizations
Circle	6	Governor and executive staff
	7	Legislators staff
Far	8	State Board of Education**
Circle	9	Others***
Sometime	10	School Boards Association
Players	11	State Administrator Association
	12	Courts
	13	Federal policy mandates
Other	14	Noneducator interest groups
Forgotten	15	Lay groups
Players	16	Education researcher organizations
	17	Referenda
	18	Producers of educational materials

* The six states were Arizona, California, Illinois, West Virginia, Wisconsin, and Pennsylvania.
** Based on Arizona, Illinois, West Virginia, and California. Wisconsin has no state board of education.
*** "Others" includes, for example, Illinois' School Problems Commission and West Virginia's School Service Personnel Association.

Source: Catherine Marshall, Douglas Mitchell, and Frederick Wirt, *Culture and Education Policy in the American State* (Falmer, 1989), p. 23.

The Insiders have constitutional authority in making laws, namely, the powerful legislators or the legislature as a whole. This finding confirms other research on the central influence of legislators in state policymaking of all kinds. Next in influence are the Near Circle, namely, school professionals (especially teachers) and specialists in the executive branch (especially the chief state school officer or CSSO). Next are outer circles more removed from pervasive influence. The Far Circle is influential but not vital to policymaking; among these, the state board is most prominent. Yet other actors have little if any influence. For example, Sometime Players are the pressure groups for local boards and administrators who are sometimes heard on special issues. The Forgotten Players, like courts, may affect only one state; an example is the powerful impact that West Virginia's and Ohio's supreme courts had in altering local school financing However, in the policy worlds surveyed here, many of this last cluster did not even come into view. We suspect the biggest change in policy influence in recent decades is caused by the growing impact of the governors.

The ranking of each policy elite varies among the states. A state board can have no influence if it does not exist (Wisconsin), and the usually high influence of the CSSO was low in Illinois—just before he was replaced after this research. In Arizona the often low-ranking state board and local board associations rated well; Illinois and West Virginia had many differences from the six-state average ranking, although California matched the average ratings quite closely.

Most important in this analysis, however, is the rough agreement among state policy actors on the crucial importance of the legislative branch. This finding means that informal influence matches constitutional authority, a condition that adds to the legitimacy of the policy process. While similarities and differences showed among the rankings, "the regularity speaks to the impact of institutionalizing democratic practices across the nation. The differences speak to the distinctive impact on policy services and decisional systems made by state political cultures and the culture of each state capitol."[2] Recent years of governors giving education a high priority will change these rankings in future studies.

RULES OF THE GAME OF POLICYMAKING

Remarkable uniformity prevails also in the lawmaking procedure of the fifty states because they are rooted in the British
and colonial traditions. Nevertheless, just how that uniform procedure is perceived and conducted depends very much on the
different perceptual screens that different actors bring to lawmaking. In the words of those studying these six states, "These
perceptions related to the expected behaviors, rituals, and judgments about feasible policy options. This perceptual screen we
term the assumptive worlds of policymakers."[3] However, no printed
manual of these perceptions exists in each state. Rather, these
"assumptive" worlds emerge from the words and stories of
policymakers when they informally discuss the persons and processes of their world.

This instructive use of qualitative data to build a grounded
theory suggests that hidden within the operations of policymakers
is a set of questions about their work to which they give answers
in experience. How questions are answered often varies, but the
basic questions remain the same:

1. Who must, and who has the right to, *initiate policy action?*
   Experience reveals that actors' answers focus especially on
   the roles of the legislature (as noted above) and others in the
   policy elite. In each state the elite easily reveal who has this
   authority in their anecdotes and responses to influence scales.
2. What are the *unacceptable policy initiatives?* Again, experience
   shows that they are ideas that trample on group, regional,
   or big-city interests; lead to refusal of agencies or citizens
   to obey; clash with existing practices; challenge dominant
   economic interests; or promote unorthodox values. Even
   limited inquiry among the elite will provide agreed-on accounts of what policy ideas won't fly.
3. What are the *appropriate policy actions?* Experience again points
   to such rules as: to get along, go along; carry out informal
   rituals that will recognize and define the boundaries of power;
   mobilize everyone who can benefit from a proposed policy;
   don't let friendship block policy action; utilize policy issue
   networks within and across the states; and so on.[4]

As a concept, then, assumptive worlds are derived from answers to fundamental questions arising everywhere in policymaking; of course, a particular state culture will contribute a distinctive cast to these answers rooted in its own history. Moreover, these culturally shaped answers are imposed on new actors entering the state's educational policy world, a classic form of political socialization.

Behind these assumptive worlds lie attributes of political culture discussed in the previous chapter. West Virginia's elite-based and traditionalistic culture has consistently constrained the expansion of education, until its own supreme court compelled otherwise. Minnesota's open society and moralistic culture has spurred an expansion of school choice policies in the search for the best education. In either state, though, such attitudes about the acceptable policy ideas have a dual effect; they keep the policy environment predictable, and they help policymakers build group cohesion that can produce policy outputs.

Consequently, such aspects of influence and assumptions attending the making of education policy reveal patterns for understanding it, despite the profusion and ambiguity of fifty state arenas. Broad expectations are widespread about which people have policy authority and how they should act amid policy conflict. State variations in these expectations do exist, though, due to varying histories and emphases in education values. Yet the common patterns among states do provide clarity, not confusion, to the policy system of American federalism. And it is the patterns that enable the testing of theory building in social science to thrive.

STATE-LEVEL INTEREST GROUPS

Among the many factors that could influence a state's policy system, major ones are variations in party competition, party cohesion in the legislature, interest groups, and the socioeconomic context.[5]

Patterns of Interest Groups

Strong political parties co-exist with powerful interest groups, but this is not the only pattern, for what emerges is not one pressure pattern among the states but many.[6] One is an *alliance of dominant groups,* much like a strong-lobby syndrome; agriculture in Kansas is a good example. Second, a *single dominant interest* pattern emerges in states with undiversified economies, two-party competition, and some legislative cohesion; the role of gambling in Nevada is an example.

Third, a pattern of *conflict between dominant groups* is visible where a diversified economic base generates differences that the two-party system expresses, for example, manufacturers versus trade unions in Michigan. Fourth, a *triumph of many interests* appears where lobbies can freely interact in a legislature with flexible party control. Thus in California, a highly diversified economy generates multiple interest and shifting legislative coalitions. Clearly, though, state lobbying among all patterns overrepresents the business and professional strata of society.[7]

The chief lobby for education, though, has been the professional, particularly teachers. Chapter 3 sketched this lobby's evolution from 1900 to 1960 in the National Education Association (NEA) as an umbrella organization for teachers, principals, superintendents, school board members, and others.[8] We also noted that, beginning in the 1960s, events led to a more militant teacher movement, climaxing in successful collective bargaining drives in most states.

Changes in Lobby Types

What best describes the lobby type that exists in the fifty states? In research up to the mid-1960s, a scholar found that the statewide monolith of allied professional educators and school boards was most prevalent. However, another study a decade later of twelve states reported a major shift to the statewide fragmented type in nine of these states.[9] Coalitions of schoolpeople had once formerly composed education law in their private councils and then issued an agreed proposal to the legislature. The legislature accepted it because education was hard to be against, and it would reap the legislators little reward to oppose it.[10] Yet in a few decades this pattern had been broken by growing conflicts of interest within education, and by the increased interest and capacity of legislatures and governors to initiate their own policies. Added complexity came from those forces that were making the legislatures' policy systems everywhere more pluralistic and open.

When school lobbies sought success in the legislature, what were their resources and strategies? Clearly, they possessed numbers and money (teachers) and high status (administrators and school boards). They transformed these resources into power by different means. All used professional staffs, but teachers rely more on their campaign money and votes, while administrators and school boards rely more on information resources and local legislator contacts. Unlike the other two, teachers were much more likely to campaign in elections, transforming their prime resource of size directly into votes.

As a result of such uses of power, school lobbies were seen by their own leaders and legislators as the most powerful pressure groups in the state. As we saw in the last chapter, legislators gave highest marks to the teacher associations, while administrators received the lowest. They found: teacher associations generally the more effective of the school lobbies and administrators the more efficient (obtaining the most for their fewer numbers and less money); the smaller teacher federations inconsistent; labor-management relations the dominant issue of such politics; and former school coalitions increasingly crippled by splits over issues. So long as schooling issues were regarded as "educational," school boards and administrators were more influential because they could rely on their higher status to be heard. However, when teacher groups changed the criteria for deciding issues from the professional to the "political," the teachers benefited from their greater numbers and money. Nevertheless, as criticism of student learning grew, teachers' status underwent a decline in popular opinion.

Specific State Educational Interest Groups

An alternative tool for distinguishing state-level lobbies is to divide them into "general focus" and "special focus" groups.[11]

The former—typified by teacher, administrator, and school board organizations—are broad based and must, therefore, represent the full spectrum of educational interests and issues. Given their size and resources, they are often assumed "to have more political clout than they actually have." Their resources are scattered over a wide range of issues at the federal, state, and local levels. Despite formal procedures and often sophisticated state leadership, teacher power is essentially decentralized. They are "characterized by a strong 'bottom-up' flow of power wherein there is a continuous and taxing necessity of building coalitions among significantly autonomous local NEA unions." This is also true of the administrator associations, whose independent-minded membership is reluctant to cede authority to state executives. Consistent with Olson's interest group theory of collective action discussed in Chapter 3, the costs of organizing large-member groups are high, while group cohesion around specific policy goals is uncertain.

In contrast, the small-member group with a single "special focus" finds it easier to reach optimal effectiveness and to outmaneuver the larger associations. Special-focus groups fall into two kinds. One is functional, such as those representing special education, and the other is geographic, such as the big-city school district. Because of their narrow interests and concentrated power bases, these organizations are becoming increasingly influential in state politics.

The functional type generally pays attention to the source of its special funding, often the federal level and the state administrative unit that dispenses those funds. A typical arrangement involves only a few governmental officials, as most state policy actors never enter the narrow realm of the special interest. For example, in Michigan the directors of the respective special and compensatory education units within the state department were reported to be among the most powerful individuals in state educational politics. They were able to mobilize the highly motivated and frequently volatile constituents and practitioners who support the causes of handicapped and compensatory education.[12]

The highly effective, geographically based, special interests are even better embodiments of the institutional interest group. Here school districts in a given locale form natural alliances with other local and state government agencies, and they employ other groups to augment their gains in the allocation process. Their greatest resource is their direct link to legislative delegations, which in the case of a large city, such as New York, Chicago, or Los Angeles, can have enormous influence. In a reaction against teacher influence and response to reformers, Illinois in 1988 legislated for Chicago over five hundred school-based management systems with an elected parent presence on the council of each.

With these descriptive concepts in mind, we can now delineate individual groups, beginning with the broadly based interests.

NEA and AFT State Teachers Association. Teachers affiliated with the NEA remain a strong, if not the strongest, group in most states (see Table 9.1 earlier). Although weakened by the growth of the rival AFT and the expulsion of school administrators, local associations possess a powerful resource advantage over other groups. Due to sheer numbers, the money from dues used for political action, and their sophisticated staffing, they remain giants by comparison to other employee interest groups.[13]

This assessment of the associations' influence must be tempered by the fact that we cannot measure power by a simple aggregation of membership, money, and information. Rather, internal cohesion is crucial to effective mobilization of those resources. For example, the Michigan Education Association (MEA), although much larger than many others, is so internally divided over local political strategies that sometimes it cannot maximize its influence at the state level. MEA's power is thus more apparent than real; the key policy determining factor in the late 1990s was a Republican governor in Michigan. Although growing in some urban areas, the AFT affiliates have a tendency to downplay state-level lobbying in favor of local bargaining. This underdeveloped and inconsistent state influence does not apply in New York, though.

Classified School Employees Associations. The nonprofessionals who work in schools are usually ignored by commentators on state educational interest groups. Classified employees include custodians, secretaries, and food service personnel. That neglect stems from their relatively recent emergence in state politics. They are labor unions whose sole objective is the protection of their membership's financial interests. These classified employees have been able to rely on local collective bargaining strength where they negotiate contracts separate from teacher unions. Their sheer numbers and financial resources give them considerable potential clout at the state level.

The State School Boards Association.   Members of this group find themselves pitted against the teachers in an effort to hold the lid on salaries. Increasingly, local school boards—confronted with the politically, economically, and legally complex realities of increased state control—rely in varying degrees on the data and expertise that the state association could muster. At the state level, policymakers view school board groups as deserving respect and empathy because they represent locally elected officials who, in turn, unselfishly represent the interest of the public.[14] This status and prima facie credibility are augmented by small but generally efficient lobbying staffs funded by the highest membership dues of all the education groups.

The State School Administrators Association.   School administrators often try to be "a bridge over troubled waters" for school principals, business officials, superintendents, personnel managers, and other administrators. Administrator groups often find themselves allied with the school board groups in order to provide some semblance of balance vis-à-vis the teachers. Legislators accord administrator groups respect as representatives of educational leadership in their districts. In fact, engaging in face-to-face contact with legislators in their home districts is a prevalent political strategy. This generates a locally based, disparate, interest-group politics. However, this predilection for going it alone can hamper the group's lobbying efforts. The administrators pay high dues, second only to the school board's, and maintain an effective state lobbying staff.

Other Groups.   There are many categorical interests such as vocational education, and associations of geographically based groups, such as rural districts, too numerous to mention. They have their champions in the legislatures, either individuals with pet interests, constituency links, or the black and Hispanic caucuses. Their bureaucratic home bases have a vested interest in sustaining and adding to categorical programs, and they often have recourse to the threat of judicial intervention. In short, many special focus groups have influence disproportionate to their numbers.

The PTA. Associations representing nonprofessional or lay persons interested in education, while locally oriented, have both state and national organizations. The National Congress of Parents and Teachers is not only the largest of these groups but also the largest volunteer organization in the United States. Its strength is felt primarily at the local level where it actively pursues solutions to specific problems at specific schools. At the state level, its influence diminishes due to the heterogeneity of its membership and to the lack of any method for maintaining internal discipline.

Labeled "good government groups," the PTA and its allies, the League of Women Voters (LWV) and the American Association of University Women (AAUW), are granted formal representation on advisory committees in educational coalitions. They generally restrict themselves to monitoring policy developments and providing lay support for professionals' recommendations. The professionals who gain the most from PTA activism are the administrators. Others tend to regard them as useful friends when they agree but not a very bothersome enemy in the event of conflict. As we saw in Chapter 3, though, many PTA participants obtain psychological rewards from their involvement in school politics.

The LWV and AAUW exist to promote much broader social improvements. State branches may have a specialist in education, but they tend not to posit controversial views, preferring to provide general support for public education as an ongoing social good.

Business Groups. State business groups became major state players after the 1981–83 recession, and have continued their strong support for state academic and assessment standards. State business roundtables use their campaign contributions and access to governors in order to advocate reform such as a nine-point plan that includes professional development and technology. Most big business groups have not supported vouchers, but are favorable toward charter schools and supported Chicago's site-based management system in 1988. This positive role toward education is a shift from the tax limitation focus business had in the 1970s.

Business's impact on education policy varies across the states, with Ross Perot playing a major role during 1983–84 in Texas, and other big business success recently in Washington and Ohio. But business support of teaching mathematical problem solving and new science curricula is opposed by traditional Christians and others who want a more basic curriculum. Business-backed proposals for curricular standards were defeated in the early 1990s in Connecticut and Pennsylvania. Those who believe business always dominates policy should note that influence actually varied in a six-city study in 2002.[15] Governors and legislators reformulated proposals backed by business, so business is just one of several influential actors at the state level.

The larger businesses have not built coalitions with small business groups, like the Chamber of Commerce, in order to construct and implement state systemic reform. Such coalitions would be politically effective at the state level and may yet develop. State business roundtables of large companies have not retreated from their stand favoring statewide academic standards and more complex assessments, despite pressure from both left- and right-wing state lobbies. Consequently, state business roundtables are often allied with education groups such as the AFT and school administrators concerning standards issues. Currently, the business agenda is mostly defensive, that is, trying to hold on to standards reform in an era of fiscal decline.

Lobbying Strategies

Whatever their type, mass groups are more than just structures of interests. They appear most clearly as dynamic parts of the policy process, from the emergence of new issues. We can see this dynamic quality in case studies of single-issue conflicts, such as that over creationism in textbooks, but little systematic knowledge emerges from this kind of understanding. We can portray the interaction more fully by focusing on the lobbying strategies that education interest groups use.

Both personal experience and research suggest that lobbying strategies in the states parallel those at the national level. Partisanship is risky in competitive two-party states except where party identification of interests is a given. Thus many lobbies tend to support both the Republican and Democratic parties. Timely campaign contributions sprinkled across party lines are an effective means of obtaining access and occasionally influencing a vote. However, individual lawmakers do not want to become obligated or "owned" over the long haul. In general, campaign contributions are of much lower volume in state politics than at the national level, although a little money goes a longer way at the state level.[16] Volunteers and endorsements in association newsletters are also popular tactics, especially in large membership labor groups. In heavily unionized states, the labor organizations can take on the entire job of running a campaign. The mass public relations pressure, more prevalent in national politics, is usually too expensive and too complicated for state education interest groups.

Direct contact with state legislators is easier, cheaper, and still more effective. Consequently, most education lobbying strategies are fundamentally low key; they emphasize expertise and professionalism. Lobbyists prefer to work within the conventional mode; they are, after all, representatives of the dominant social interests and have a corresponding commitment to maintain the status quo. If the moderate approach fails in a particular instance, contributions of money and election workers to assist specific legislators may help. Another step often adopted before "all-out-war" takes place is cooperative lobbying and coalition building. Some of the lobbying has been effective because K-12 budgets were cut much less from the 2001 to 2004 recession than were higher education budgets.

State Coalition Concepts

In large part, politics involves fashioning coalitions of influence in an attempt to determine what values government will authoritatively implement. As we have just noted, different individuals and groups bring various interests and objectives to state educational policy forums. Amid this tangle, an essential quality of a state education leader is to build political coalitions.

The coalition view of state decision making is that any decision is possible if enough support for it exists among interest groups. In order to secure support, various "trade-offs" are undertaken. A trade-off is an exchange among parties of goods that each party wants in exchange for providing a vote. Accordingly, policy proposals are modified to include (or exclude) items of concern to key potential supporters; agreements are made to trade support on other or future state policies for backing on a current issue; and third parties are encouraged to intervene. In short, coalitions are formed by horse trading until an acceptable policy is reached.

Several theories on coalitions can be validated in reviewing state education lobbying.[17] Most coalitions take place within a specific institutional context that will contain rules, constraints, and historical events that will influence the coalition. The growth of coalitions depends on the ability of leaders to attract followers by offering "side payments." These include anything that has value for possible coalition members, including money or promises on policy. Sometimes coalition leaders have a stock of side payments in their hands as working capital when they begin negotiations. As they dispense promises, they use this capital, which presumably will be replenished from the future gains of a winning coalition. More typically, in our judgment, education leaders operate on credit; that is, they promise rewards with the understanding that they will honor their promises only if successful. There is a curious pattern of honesty in all this that contradicts the notion of "dirty" politics.

Leaders and followers are differentiated according to whether they offer or receive side payments. A leader rarely has enough resources to pay everybody. Also, excess members of a winning coalition cost something to acquire, and they lessen the gains. Thus at some point in the process of making side payments, the leader decides that all has been paid out that is worth winning. Yet as some factions are still left out, the attempts to form a coalition generate opposition that could result in an opposing coalition.

These kinds of side payments can be illustrated from education lobbying.

1. *The threat of reprisal.* This side payment consists of a promise not to carry out the threat, so the follower simply gains an escape from prospective misfortune. For example, a governor can threaten to campaign against an elected state superintendent of schools.
2. *Payment of objects that can be converted to money.* One example is appointing a major financial backer of a key legislator to a position in the state education department, or a university board of trustees.
3. *Promises on policy.* A leader accepts an amendment to her or his bill that brings the support of the state teachers' association, but modifies the policy thrust of the bill.
4. *Promises about subsequent decisions.* The speaker of the assembly can promise to support an agricultural bill if rural interests will vote for an income tax dedicated to education.
5. *Payments of emotional satisfaction.* Some legislators will follow the educational decisions of a charismatic governor.

These strategies involve lobbyists in subtle considerations, for the possibilities in any single policy conflict are numerous. The ways these considerations can be combined in practice are particularly complex. Such analysis requires making judgments and answering strategic questions.

Is there a winning coalition? Is the goal to be achieved by a winning coalition unique? Is anything (for example, a particular legislative provision) clearly excluded? Would the possibilities (for example, more school finance reform) be changed by expanding the coalition slightly? It follows that in some situations several potentially winning coalitions exist. Consequently, there is a role for leadership in constructing a particular coalition and thereby limiting the policy options and goals. It is this matrix of lobbies that the state legislatures face.

State Legislatures

With exceptions, the following qualities characterize American state legislatures as they have responded to the increased pressure from many sources to address many state and local problems.[18] This institution has:

1. Primarily political, not value-free, qualities.
2. Recently been subject to more demands.
3. Recently been taking on a more professional cast, for example, more and better staff.
4. Better apportionment as a result of Supreme Court actions that resulted in an increased voice for urban and suburban interests, and more responsiveness to new needs.
5. Often been recruited to office by political parties, but the turnover rate is high and the influence of the party on legislative votes varies widely with state tradition.
6. Electoral competition for seats is limited to a minority of legislative districts.
7. A general public evaluates legislatures negatively (mostly for wasting time).
8. Some policies that are innovative (usually controversial), but many that are incremental (for example, budgets), so that reforms are adopted in different degrees among states.
9. Influence from external and internal sources (committees, caucuses, governors, lobbies, experts, and so on), but the influence of the legislators themselves as noted earlier in this chapter, is high.
10. Pressure groups everywhere influential, but one group's influence varies from state to state (most often mentioned with high influence: bankers, trade unions, teachers, manufacturers, farmers, doctors, and utilities).

We have noted that the legislative role in school policymaking has recently increased. Education was once of limited interest to legislators, but since the 1980s they have taken a strong hand in education standards and school violence.[19] In particular, lawmakers are now more involved in the distribution of state revenue, both its proportion and uses. The reasons for this change reflect other changes.[20] That is, because legislatures now are better staffed, groups can turn to a body ready and willing to act; and as their sessions became longer, they were readier longer. Legislatures are also developing closer ties with other states and exchanging ideas about program possibilities.

Explanation of the legislature's role in state education policy-making is related to four categories of capacity:

The [states in the first category] are those that are "professionalized," a group that includes highly unionized states with large populations, such as California, New York, Pennsylvania, Massachusetts, Michigan, Ohio, Illinois, Wisconsin, and New Jersey. These legislatures tend to have higher compensation, unlimited time in session, large professional staffs, and members who define their occupation as legislator.

The second category comprises about half the states and is best described as transitional, having some characteristics of both the highly professionalized legislatures and the more traditional citizen legislatures.

The states in the third category (about fifteen) are termed traditional legislatures. They are generally limited in session length, have higher turnover rates, and members who do not see legislative service as a career. These legislatures are found primarily in New England and the less populous agricultural states of the Midwest and West.

The 1990s brought about what may become a fourth category of legislature—those with term limits. Eighteen states throughout the country now have limits on the time members can serve. As term limits become more widely implemented, the differences between legislatures with term limits and those without will be significant.[21]

American Governors

Head of state and of party, the American governor has had to weave these two roles together to be effective.[22] However, the recent increase in demands on all states has brought this office under greater cross pressures. The widespread budget deficits of all but a few states in the early 2000s typifies these pressures. Service demands continue to increase, but so do demands to stabilize taxes that would pay for services. The social welfare needs of the central cities are opposed by suburban and nonmetropolitan legislators who are less responsive to those needs. Most observers would agree that beneath the federal level the governor is the most important agent in American policymaking. This fact emerges in many individual studies of policymaking, even though it runs counter to earlier macrolevel analyses that stress the primacy of the state's environment (especially economic factors) rather than the political context.[23]

What is the significance of the governor for education policy? The limited research of this role prior to the 1970s generally found it minimal, "and when it did exist it appeared sporadically, reflecting the idiosyncratic character of particular governors and/or educational crises in specific states."[24] When the first truly comparative analysis of these figures appeared in the early 1970s, it found a much wider range of behavior across the states and the stages of policymaking.[25] As policymaking progresses, the governor's influence declines, that is, governors are most active in budget control and defining educational issues before their authorization, and least active in having a decisive effect on legislative enactment. Again however, the spread expresses the usual American style—a wide range of possibilities. But the academic and teacher quality reforms of the 1980s and 1990s produced a new activism and a greater influence on the part of governors (see Table 9.1 earlier).

Strong gubernatorial leadership has emerged in most states. Governors from the South were very active in initiating the 1983–93 reforms featuring higher academic standards. The governors of South Carolina, Tennessee, Florida, Virginia, Georgia, Arkansas, Texas, and North Carolina made national news with their comprehensive ideas. One prime leader in the South was Arkansas' governor and later president, William Clinton. President Bush featured his Texas education reforms in his successful 2000 presidential campaign.

The governor is also most likely to be involved and powerful where a traditional policy climate exists of supporting education by creating much more state than local revenue: North Carolina, Florida, and California. As recently as mid-2002, Southern governors announced new educational goals to improve this service. These were the same as set out in 1988. They include more and better preschool and higher graduation rates.[26] The weaker governors appear in locally oriented policy cultures: Nebraska, Colorado, and New Hampshire. In the 1990s governors in several states advocated improved testing of students to improve education, citing international competition. Obviously, this office is becoming more active in educational policy, as are other agencies of government.

As with interest groups and legislatures, the governor's office fails to provide regular leadership for the development of educational policy in the American states. Some do so, of course, but only on limited issues and episodically. Like Sherlock Holmes' nonbarking dog, the systematic importance of this office is that it does not consistently do the expected. For example, governors from 1992 to 1996 did not provide as much focus on education policy innovation as they did from 1983 to 1992. Some governors, however, maintain strong alliances with big business that are favorable to state education standards. One role of the governor in galvanizing new state accountability policies has increased dramatically when one compares 2000 to 1980.

THE IMPLEMENTERS OF STATE SCHOOL POLICY

The initiation and authorization of major school policy do not complete the policy process, for laws are not self-executing. The implementation stage in state school policy involves three agencies: the state board of education (SBE), the chief state school officer (CSSO), and the state education agency (SEA). The diversity of these authorities has already been suggested earlier in Tables 8.1 and 8.3, so again our focus is on patterns of behavior.[27]

The State Board of Education and Chief State School Officer

School policy implementation has been spread among these three agencies, with the SBE and CSSO responsible for oversight and innovation and the SEA for daily administration. The linkage between the SBE and CSSO is complex because their methods of appointment and authority are so diverse. They may be independent (elected, appointed, or a mix), or the SBE may choose the CSSO. Some SBEs only issue regulations, while others have operating responsibilities (e.g., vocational schools, state colleges, or universities). Rarely, however, are such broad responsibilities unified in a single office (except for the New York Board of Regents).[28]

SBEs are usually appointed by the governor and the CSSO by the SBE, but the linkage is not ministerial. The selection methods of the SBEs seem to have consequences for their policy behavior. That is, elective bodies are designed to be open to more conflict, while appointed bodies respond to their appointers. That is the case with the SBEs, where 69 percent of those appointed reported little internal disagreement compared with 42 percent of those elected.[29]

Whatever their origins, these actors have differing influences. One observer reported that SBEs are "only marginal policy actors in the legislative arena and are largely overshadowed by the CSSO in state education."[30] Elected SBEs appear to have more influence with the CSSO and legislature, for they can speak with independent power. Few SBEs are elected, and their elections are rarely competitive, visible, or draw many voters; such elections are "nonevents." In the main, then, the SBE is a weak policy actor, especially where the board is unable to hire or remove the CSSO who has major constitutional oversight of state education. The SBE is also usually poorly staffed or organized to operate effectively and often lacks political links to the legislature and governor. SBEs seem to wander about on the fringes while the battle is being fought on a plain somewhere else.

The CSSOs, however, know where the action is and are often in the thick of it. SBEs look to them for leadership and information in policy conflict and seldom oppose them. But the CSSO is not an influential office with the legislature unless one is elected, and has a big staff and formal powers. The same office can be used for quite different policy concerns by different occupants. Thus in California in the 1970s, categorical programs for the disadvantaged were a priority, but in 2004 accountability and testing was the priority. However, the impact of state political culture still limits the role and impact of all state administrators.

> The element of political culture that most affects state policymaking is the strength of local control norms. Both the role SEAs play in state education policy and their capacity to assist local districts largely depend on the support they receive from general government and whether the political culture sanctions an active presence in local jurisdictions. This finding suggests that state political culture, in effect, preordains SEA roles and that SEAs in states with a strong local control ethos will always play a less active role and have less capacity than their counterparts in states where a strong central government is seen as legitimate.[31]

The State Education Agency

The daily job of implementing state policy goals rests in the hands of anonymous bureaucrats in the SEA. When the century opened, these agencies were tiny, but then succeeding waves of school reform policies were left with the SEAs to administer, and so they expanded greatly.

Today, SEAs supervise a vast array of federal and state programs, either through direct administration (for example, state schools for the blind) or through overseeing state guidelines. Their compliance techniques include requiring and reviewing a torrent of reports from the LEAs; enforcing mandated levels of service (for example, curriculum); assisting LEAs in designing and staffing newly required programs; providing continuing career education for professionals; and so on.[32] In a larger perspective, they were given the task of institutionalizing the professional model of the schools that states adopted over the last century. Programs that fell to them sought in 1900 the "Americanization" of immigrants and vocational training for farm and city work. After World War II they upgraded language and math training, improved resources for educating disadvantaged and minority children, and on and on in an almost unending list.

Specialists in little niches of expertise, SEAs constitute a complex of daily spear carriers for curriculum, finance and accounting, administration, personnel, and many other matters. Their political influence may be the most subtle, that of inertia in defending the status quo. Their role in innovation and its implementation is one of the many unstudied aspects of the educational policy system, but it appears to be increasing because of state initiatives concerning testing, teacher quality, and local academic standards. A fundamental problem for SEAs is that they have been organized around categorical programs like federal Title I, but new standards require cross-cutting implementation that links curriculum and instruction. The role of state education departments continues to increase under No Child Left Behind and state reforms with a commensurate increase in state department of education staff. Consequently, the lack of staff depth may become a critical liability for enforcing No Child Left Behind, and helping improve failing schools. [33]

State Political Parties

In democracies numbers count, as do organizations of voters. The chief organization is the political party, so its role in shaping any public policy must be looked at. After all, the institutions reviewed above are products of electoral impulses diffracted through political parties in times past. And the epitome of individualism is not merely voting for officeholders but speaking directly on policy matters through the initiative and referendum.

A surprisingly little studied aspect of state school policymaking is the role of political party. Available reports show that parties differ on school policymaking, although no consistent pattern in this difference emerges. Yet schools worried voters, and so both parties featured education. Thus in all governor elections in 2002, every candidate had an education program on small classes, vouchers, and accountability. Once in office, regardless of party, they were entangled in budget cuts.[34]

Some studies of parties are of single states in which the party is seen as a significant agent affecting policymaking. State legislatures are frequently quite partisan, such as the 1995 California case where a Republican governor preserved his budget through straight party-line votes. An analysis of the link between parties and the adoption of school reforms from the 1983 study *A Nation at Risk* provides a rare chance to trace statistically the influence of parties. Findings show that adoption rates were little associated with the degree of party competition, but adoption had occurred much more often in states where parties had usually not taken policy stands (e.g., the South). In the main, though, party factors were not significant. Yet we still have no fifty-state comparison using such process-oriented studies.[35]

STATE POLITICS IN THE NEW MILLENNIUM

State governments are on the move everywhere through expanding education policies. Education remains the number one political issue throughout most states, and it is also featured in elections. The traditional value of local control is eroding, but it is still a powerful brake on state activism. The shifting balance of control seems to favor more state control in the near term.

NOTES

1. Catherine Marshall, Douglas Mitchell, and Frederick Wirt, *Culture and Education Policy in the American State* (New York: Falmer, 1989).

2. Ibid., "Influence, Power, and Policy Making," *Peabody Journal of Education* 62:1 (1985): 88 .

3. Ibid., "Assumptive Worlds of Education Policy Makers," *Peabody Journal of Education* 62:4 (1985): 90–115; citation is at p. 90.

4. Michael Kirst, Gail Meister, and Stephen R. Rowley, "Policy Issue Networks: Their Influence on State Policymaking," *Policy Studies Journal* 13: 2 (December 1984): 247–64.

5. The following is drawn from Olive S. Thomas and Ronald J. Hrebenar, "Interest Groups in the States," in Virginia Gray et al., eds., *Politics in the American States* (Washington, D.C.: CQ Press, 1999).

6. Ibid., pp. 119–131.

7. Ibid., pp. 134–135.

8. Lorraine McDonnell and Anthony Pascal, "National Trends in Teaching Collective Bargaining," *Education and Urban Society* 11 (1979): 129-51. See also Tom Loveless, *Conflicting Missions: Teacher Unions and Education Reform* (Washington, D.C.: Brookings, 2001).

9. J. Alan Aufderheide, "Educational Interest Groups and the State Legislature," in Roald Campbell and Tim Mazzoni, Jr., eds., *State Policy Making for the Public Schools: A Comparative Analysis* (Richmond, Calif.: McCutchan, 1976), p. 201.

10. See the review of Iannaccone's typology using twelve-state data in Raphael Nystrand, "State Education Policy Systems," in Campbell and Mazzoni, *State Policy Making*, chap. 7. Nystrand's analysis may not have fully tested this typology, according to some critics.

11. William Boyd, "Interest Groups and the Changing Environment" (paper presented to the American Education Research Association, Washington, D.C., 1987). The following quotations are from this source.

12. Susan Lusi, *The Role of the State Departments of Education in Complex School Reform* (New York: Teachers College, 1997).

13. Thomas and Hrebenar, "Interest Groups", pp. 133–135.

14. Ibid., p. 134.

15. Larry Cuban and Michael Usdan, eds., *Powerful Reforms with Shallow Roots: Improving America's Urban Schools* (New York: Teachers College Press, 2003).

16. Keith E. Hamm and Gary Moncreif, *Legislative Politics in the States*, in Gray et al., *Politics in the American States*, pp. 152–155.

17. William H. Riker, *The Theory of Political Coalitions* (New Haven, Conn.: Yale University Press, 1962); James G. March and Johan P. Olsen, *Democratic Governance* (New York: Free Press, 1995).

18. For a useful introduction to this literature, see Samuel Patterson, "State Legislatures and Public Policy," in Virginia Gray, Herbert Jacob, and Robert Albritton, eds., *Politics in the American States*, 5th ed. (Glenview, Ill.: Scott, Foresman/Little Brown, 1990), chap. 5.

19. Jerome T. Murphy, "The Paradox of State Government Reform," in Milbrey McLaughlin, ed., *Educational Policymaking*, 1978 Yearbook of the National Society for the Study of Education (Chicago: University of Chicago Press, 1978).

20. Hamm and Moncreif, pp. 179–181.

21. William T. Pound, "The Modern Legislature," *State Legislature* (August 1999): pp. 28–33. The best overview of state legislative capacity is Alan Rosenthal, *Heavy Lifting: The Job of the American Legislature* (Washington, D.C.: CQ Press, 2004).

22. The following draws on Thad L. Beyle, ed., *Governors and Hard Times* (Washington, D.C.: Congressional Quarterly Press, 1992).

23. The seminal work is Thomas Dye, *Politics, Economics, and the Public* (Chicago: Rand McNally, 1966).

24. Laurence Iannaccone, *Politics in Education* (New York: Center for applied Research in Education, 1967), p. 44.

25. See Thad Beyle, "The Governors" in Gray et al., *Politics in the American States*, 1999.

26. Beyle, "Governors," pp. 203–215. Recent Southern governors are reviewed in *Education Week* (June 19, 2002): 21.

27. A full catalogue of these traditional authorities is Sam Harris, *State Departments of Education, State Boards of Education, and Chief State School Officers* (Washington, D.C.: U.S. Government Printing Office, 1973).

28. For their history and variety, see Lerus Winget, Edgar Fuller, and Terrel Bell, "State Departments of Education," in Edgar Fuller and Jim Pearson, eds., *Education in the States: Nationwide Development since 1900* (Washington, D.C.: National Education Association), chap. 2.

29. Fuller and Pearson, "State Departments of Education," *Education in the States*, p. 83.

30. For suggestions on how to improve state boards, see Michael Cohen, "State Boards in an Era of Reform," *Phi Delta Kappan* 69:1 (September 1987): 60–64.

31. Lorraine M. McDonnell and Milbrey W. McLaughlin, *Education Policy and the Role of the States* (Santa Monica, Calif.: Rand, 1982), p. 79.

32. Susan Lusi, *The Role of State Departments of Education in Complex School Reform* (New York: Teachers College, 1997).

33. Marc Tucker and Thomas Toch, "The Secret to Making NCLB Work: More Bureaucrats," *Phi Delta Kappan* 86:1 (2004): 28-33.

34. John L. Bibby and Thomas Holbrook, "Parties and Elections," in Gray et al., *Politics in the American States*, 1999, pp. 66–112. The centrality of schools in governor races, and the resulting budget problems, are reviewed in *Education Week* (October 23, 2002): 16 and *Education Week* (February 4, 2003): 18

35. Doh Shinn and Jack Van Der Slik, "Legislative Efforts to Improve the Quality of Public Education in the American States: A Comparative Analysis" (paper presented to the annual conference of the American Political Science Association, New Orleans, 1985). For an overview of state policy innovation, see Frances Berry, "Sizing Up State Policy Innovation Research," *Policy Studies Journal* 22 (1994): 442–456.

10

Evolution and Implementation of Federal Aid

The 2000 presidential election catapulted education from a secondary issue to one of the most visible and contested in these close races. Public concern focuses on the quality of K-12 education, while postsecondary education is not viewed as a major problem. Ever since the recession in 1981–83, education has been rated near the top of public issues. Currently, the public is frustrated that so little progress is being made, and it is receptive to bold and expensive presidential initiatives. But despite President Clinton's visible leadership in education, federal expenditures never exceeded 7 percent of total K-12 spending during his administration. President Bush's new education program, No Child Left Behind, may not push this share much higher, because of the need to finance his tax cut. All the attention to education during national elections obscures the limited federal role from public view.

Despite the heated partisan rhetoric, what emerged from the 2000 federal election is a surprising bipartisan consensus about new policy directions, but with one exception, namely, federal vouchers (renamed "portability" to make the idea more palatable). Both parties want more federal testing, consolidation of

fragmented categorical programs, more money for reading improvement, enhanced accountability, and tuition aid for middle-
income college students. However, the political devil will be in
the details, where Democrats will resist some consolidations of
popular categorical programs and continue to champion politically popular Clinton initiatives like class-size reduction and school
construction. Bush made education his first public policy proposal after the 2001 inauguration. He created a bipartisan coalition to pass a significant education bill. The Democratic swing
votes for his coalition in his first term, however, may not last as
Democrats strive to construct their own education agenda. While
national high-stakes testing seems dead for now, both parties want
to use federal muscle to intensify state and local testing.

The current political debate is built on layers of bedrock laid
down from prior federal political activity. This bedrock will not
be blasted away but will most likely increase. Before we revisit
the current federal debate, it is necessary to look back at how
we have gotten to where we are. Briefly, the federal role grew
dramatically in the second half of the twentieth century, but it
has not begun to eclipse the education policy roles of state and
local governments.

Since the current base operating expenditures for all of K-12
education exceeds $400 billion, another $1 billion per year in
federal aid is not as big a factor as the newspaper headlines
suggest. So far, federal aid is big politics, but it does not have a
big local school impact except in some specific areas like special
education, Head Start, college aid, and after-school programs.
President Bush's nationwide voucher proposal had the most
potential to shake up education, but he realized early that vouchers
could not pass the evenly divided Congress. However, presidential visits to schools and reading to little children for the television news is only potent political fodder.

EVOLUTION OF THE FEDERAL ROLE

The federal government has always been a junior partner to
state and local agencies in financing and operating American
schools.[1] The impact of federal policies on the nation's class-

rooms, however, continues to fascinate researchers, policymakers, and the public. Interest and concern about this role intensified during the 1960s and 1970s, motivated in part by expanding expenditures as well as by the increasing oversight of most new federal policies.

Through the 1970s the federal role emphasized securing extra services for traditionally underserved students, promoting innovation, and supporting research. In 1950, when the U.S. Office of Education (USOE) was transferred from the Department of the Interior to the Department of Health, Education, and Welfare, it had a staff of three hundred to spend $40 million. By 1963 forty-two departments, agencies, and bureaus of the government were involved in education to some degree. In 1963 the Department of Defense and the Veterans Administration, however, spent more on educational programs than did the Office of Education and the National Science Foundation combined. The Office of Education appointed personnel who were specialists and consultants in such areas as mathematics, libraries, and school buses; these specialists identified primarily with the National Education Association (NEA). Federal grant programs operated through deference to local and state education agency priorities and judgments. State administrators were regarded by USOE as colleagues who should have the maximum decision-making discretion permitted by federal categorical laws.

The era of 1964–1972 brought dramatic increases in federal activity, but the essential mode of delivering federal services remained the same. This differential funding route sought bigger, bolder categorical and demonstration programs. The delivery system for these programs stressed the need for more precise federal regulations to guide local projects. Indeed, the current collection of overlapping and complex categorical aids evolved as a mode of federal action that a number of otherwise dissenting educational interests could agree on.[2] This collection of categorical programs was not the result of any rational plan for federal intervention, but rather an outcome of political bargaining and coalition formation of a type suggested in an earlier chapter. In 1967 former Department of Education head, Harold Howe, expressed its essence this way:

Whatever its limitations the categorical aid approach gives the states and local communities a great deal of leeway in designing educational programs to meet various needs. In essence, the federal government says to the states (and cities), "Here is some money to solve this particular program; you figure out how to do it. . . ." But whatever the criticisms, which can, in justice, be leveled against categorical aid to education, I believe that we must stick with it, rather than electing general aid as an alternative. The postwar period has radically altered the demands we place on our schools; a purely local and state viewpoint of education cannot produce an educational system that will serve national interest in addition to more localized concerns.[3]

An incremental shift in the style of the Department of Education administration also came with expanded policy categories. The traditional provision of specialized consultants and the employment of subject matter specialists were ended in favor of managers and generalists who had public administration, rather than professional education, backgrounds.

In the 1980s the federal government's spending for elementary and secondary education did not keep pace either with inflation or with state and local support of schools. Relative to state and local spending, the Department of Education's share of elementary or secondary school expenditures dipped to 6.1 percent by the 1984–1985 school year, its lowest share in almost twenty years.[4] Federal expenditures for education increased slightly during the 1988–1992 Bush administration to 7 percent of total spending, and held at 7 percent during Clinton's administration.

MODES OF FEDERAL INFLUENCE

There have been basically six alternative modes of federal action for public schools:

1. *General aid*: Provide no-strings aid to state and local education agencies or such minimal earmarks as teacher salaries. Clinton began moving toward general aid with his programs for class-size reduction and school construction. However, no large-scale general-aid bill has ever been approved by the Congress.

2. *Stimulate through differential funding:* Earmark categories of aid, provide financial incentives, use demonstration projects, and purchase specific services. This is the approach of No Child Left Behind and newer programs for safe and drug-free schools.

3. *Regulate:* Legally specify behavior, impose standards, certify and license, and enforce accountability procedures. Title IX women's equity regulations are a good example.

4. *Discover knowledge and make it available:* Have research performed; gather and make other statistical data available. The National Science Foundation has performed the first function, and the National Center for Education Statistics the second.

5. *Provide services:* Furnish technical assistance and consultants in specialized areas or subjects. For example, the Office of Civil Rights was once used to advise school districts that were designing voluntary desegregation plans. That service faded after the weakened national effort to desegregate, noted in an earlier chapter.

6. *Exert moral suasion:* Develop vision and question assumptions through publications and speeches by top officials. After recent school shootings, the first President Bush advocated character education in numerous speeches in the popular media. This mode of federal influence is termed the "bully pulpit" by the press. For example, the second President Bush castigates critics of No Child Left Behind as giving in to the soft bigotry of low expectations for pupil achievement.

The use by presidents and secretaries of education of the "bully pulpit" as a major, independent policy strategy has been inadequately examined. There is broad recognition of the widespread public and professional reactions to presidential speeches about education, but most commentary on these speeches has little if any empirical base, and has been more public-relations filler than systematic assessment. A challenge for researchers of the federal role in elementary and secondary education will be to design and conduct systematic assessments of the origins and impacts of the modern use of the bully-pulpit strategy. Nevertheless, modern presidents regularly speak as if they believe talk has a positive function, either convincing someone (voters, legislators, media) or oneself.

THE EVOLUTION OF FEDERAL POLITICS

The major political breakthrough in education policy was in 1965 after President Lyndon Johnson's landslide 1964 election. Both Houses had huge Democratic majorities poised to enlarge the federal role. President John Kennedy tried unsuccessfully to get general aid for local districts that would be used for anything that they wanted. Later Johnson linked federal funds to special-needs categories (e.g., low-income/low-achieving pupils) that existed in every Congressional district. Johnson began the federal role of stimulating innovation and experiments with new schools and teaching methods. This type of categorical federal role dominated politics from 1964 to the election of President Reagan in 1980. Nixon, Ford, and Carter all embellished and refined the categorical approach, while federal regulations increased. Periodic attempts to de-categorize large amounts of funds by creating bloc grants to states and districts for their disposition were resisted by Democrats who held the majorities in both houses. Note that such categories create and intensify interest groups, including special education parents, bilingual educators, and computer companies. Such groups become highly effective in sustaining federal funding. A major Nixon innovation was to allocate a large amount of funds to help desegregate the schools. Also, Nixon was able to increase federal audits of local schools, and thereby better target federal aid to its specific purposes.

From 1970 to 1980 there was bipartisan support in Congress for a more aggressive federal enforcement of its restrictions on local spending.[5] For example, local schools had to make sure that Title I for the disadvantaged supplemented, but did not supplant, local resources for these children. Supporters of various federal categories formed a coalition for full funding that agreed on increases for all categories, rather than lobbying against each other for larger shares. The more powerful lobby groups such as special education got the largest increases, while the smaller lobbies like libraries received lower increases. The more evenly divided Congress from 1976 to 1980 prevented President Carter from expanding the federal role greatly, but he fought off Republican attempts to loosen the federal strings and categories.

This incremental federal politics from 1965 to 1980 was disrupted by the election of President Reagan. The administration endorsed a tuition tax credit to reimburse parents who send their children to private schools. This proposal helped solidify Christian conservatives behind the Republican Party. Although various members of Congress pushed this idea for decades, this was the first time a president had endorsed it. While Reagan's tax credits were defeated by a Democratic Congress, federal aid to private schools continued to be a major issue in federal aid during the 1990s. Funding private schools is vociferously and unanimously opposed by public education interest groups and by some Protestant and Jewish church groups. President Bush supported tax-free savings accounts that can be used for private school tuition, and this proposal was included in the huge tax cut passed in 2001 under his son's new law.

Overall, the Reagan administration promoted six other basic changes in federal educational policy in addition to assisting private schools, moving[6]

1. from a prime concern with equity to more concern with quality, efficiency, and state and local freedom to choose;
2. from a larger and more influential federal role to a mitigated federal role;
3. from mistrust of the motives and capacity of state and local educators to a renewed faith in governing units outside of Washington;
4. from categorical grants to more unrestricted types of financial aid;
5. from detailed and prescriptive regulations to deregulation; and
6. from stressing desegregation to weakening its federal support.

However, the Reagan administration made no progress on financial support for private education, but was able to implement a policy shift by diminishing the federal role as the initiator of education change. The 1994–1998 Congressional Republican agenda was very similar to Reagan's, so his call for change from 1981 to 1984 was a harbinger of future Republican policy in 2000.

For two decades (1960–1980) the equity value, that of promoting equal educational opportunity, had been the most pervasive theme of federal education policy. The Reagan administration tried but could not substitute choice or efficiency priorities as the major orientation of federal policy, because the Democrats controlled Congress. The most enduring expression of federal equity is through numerous categorical grants targeted to students who were not adequately served by state and local programs (e.g., the disadvantaged or handicapped). The Reagan administration attempted to scale back aggressive federal activity in such areas, and hoped to overcome hardening of the categories with flexible bloc grants to states.

Federal Policy and the Clinton Administration

The Goals 2000 legislative debate was the most high-profile initiative of the early Clinton administration but faded from the limelight as the administration and the Republican Congress pursued other issues.[7] Goals 2000 focused on improving curricular standards and tests, but Clinton changed his priorities to class-size reduction and school construction by his second term. Goals 2000 moved in the same direction as the recent intensive state reform activity on academic standards. It used federal funds to reinforce three key reforms that spread throughout the nation from 1995 to 2004:

1. Challenging academic standards for what all students should know and do in each subject matter area. Forty-nine states by 2004 had done this in most academic subjects—a remarkable change in the historic state role.
2. Aligning policies—such as testing, teacher certification, and professional development—and accountability programs to state curricular standards. All states but Iowa and Nebraska had statewide student achievement tests in 2001, and most were addressing the other systemic components by 2001.
3. Restructuring the governance system to delegate overtly to

schools and districts the responsibility for developing specific instructional approaches that meet the broadly worded academic standards for which the state will hold them accountable.

Known as "standards-based systemic reform," the overarching objectives of this policy approach are to foster student mastery of more rigorous, challenging academic content and to increase the emphasis on its application. But Goals 2000 appropriations never exceeded $400 million compared to over $8 billion for Title I.

It is impossible to isolate the distinctive contribution of Goals 2000 legislation to the rapid spread of standards-based state and local policies. It has helped, but how much is uncertain. Goals 2000 state-level funding added flexible state money for test and standards development as well as systemic initiatives that state categoricals rarely permit. But 90 percent of the money was allocated to local school districts, and its effectiveness is problematic. For example, the California local grants were often add-on projects that did not focus on broad Goals 2000 activities or systemic reform. Small amounts of Goals 2000 money could easily get lost within a school district in a blizzard of state standards initiatives in California and other states.

Goals 2000 legislation was eclipsed in 1995 by Clinton support for a voluntary national test (VNT). This proposed fourth-grade reading and eighth-grade math test, however, has never been authorized, because of bipartisan opposition. Clinton tried to use the VNT as another installment in the attempt to enhance the federal role in standards setting. A logical successor to Goals 2000, it ended up stymied by a rare congressional coalition of conservative Republicans, blacks, and Hispanics. The Republicans were wary of excessive federal control from the VNT, and the minority Democrats were concerned about lack of opportunity in low-income schools to learn the content of the federal test.

FUNDING, POLITICS, AND INTEREST GROUPS

The federal government provides support to education through numerous agencies including the Departments of Labor, Health and Human Services, and Agriculture, and the National Science Foundation. The creation of a Department of Education in 1980 was justified partly because it would consolidate more education programs in a single accountable department. But many interest groups resisted this change, preferring to stay in separate agencies. Several of the lobby groups with programs outside of the U.S. Department of Education did not want their programs controlled by a department that they presumed would be dominated by professional educators. Consequently, school lunch aid is still provided by the Department of Agriculture, and the National Science Foundation provides research and demonstration grants for secondary school science. Head Start is part of the Department of Health and Human Services, even though it is designed to help preschool children in their transition to public school kindergarten.

The past decade has produced a consensus on ways to improve the probability that federal categorical programs will be implemented at the state and local levels. This consensus includes (a) having a precise and feasible objective, (b) securing broad-based state and local political support for the intervention, (c) generating a sense of urgency for achieving the objectives, and (d) concealing the federal government's weaknesses in forcing the state and local units to comply.[8] The federal threat to recover funds by audits is used sparingly because it is difficult to enforce through the courts. Federal administrators succeed better when they build vertical networks of like-minded administrators in the state and local bureaucracies, such as Title I, vocational education, or special education administrators. A skilled observer of this level stated,

> Federal programs have deliberately put schools under new political pressures. On the assumption that past neglect of disadvantaged students was caused by local politics, in which their parents had few allies and little influence, federal programs tried to change the balance of local political forces. All large federal programs were expressly organized around constituency groups, helped parent groups organize, and gave parents official roles in school decision-making. Some gave parents new access to judicial remedies, on the assumption that the ability to threaten litigation would increase their influence on schools. Most tried to colonize state and local education agencies with individuals paid to advocate for compliance with

federal program rules. As a result teachers are sometimes forced to treat students differently, depending on their links to organized external groups that have been set up and empowered by government actions.[9]

Interest Groups and Federal Aid

Almost every major and minor education interest group has an office in Washington, D.C. So many state and local groups are there that they find it very convenient to meet on state and local issues, and it is possible to attend hundreds of meetings on education policy where the federal role is not a major topic. Nonetheless, each interest group has a federal liaison person who lobbies the federal agencies and Congress for its cause. Alliances and coalitions are constructed on some issues (e.g., more money), but collapse on others (e.g., targeted aid to big cities). Interest groups roll in and out of coalitions depending on their self-interest. Many want more federal money, but not much more testing. Fear of federal control is still salient among school boards, administrators, and teacher groups.

AFT and NEA in an alliance with AFL-CIO provide the most campaign money and workers, but over 90 percent of their money goes to Democrats. However, since the education issue has become so prominent in the media, other groups can help or hurt politicians significantly. For example, the existing Head Start workers, including many teacher aides, have mobilized to keep Head Start in the Department of Health and Human Services. They resist President George W. Bush's proposal to move Head Start to the Department of Education, and focus it more on formal instruction. Special education parents battle school administrators over pupil discipline policies, and many federal legislators support the parent groups. Interest groups want access to key decision makers, and one way to gain access is to place trusted friends in key positions within the Department of Education. But some key education positions are filled by referrals from party leaders in the White House, and reflect different political priorities than that of the education interest groups.

One of the main federal issues concerns funding priorities. The federal share of K-12 funding grew to 10 percent in 2003 from a much lower 7 percent in 1990. Title I funds for disadvantaged students increased by 41 percent between 2001 and 2004 to a total of \$12.2 billion. States and localities are also spending much more on K-12 education, so the federal share cannot increase much more. Bush's largest percentage increase is for a new phonics-based reading program. Figure 10.1 shows the total discretionary spending from 1980 to 2003 by the Department of Education. Federal categories that are growing include special education, afterschool centers, and charter school start-up funds. The increases they show are independent of political party control. What differs is not money but how it is spent. Note the presidency of George W. Bush

POLITICS AND THE BUSH ADMINISTRATION

President George W. Bush featured federal education policy in his 2000 election campaign and made education his first priority after election. He has faced a very complex task of constructing a bipartisan coalition in a slightly majority Republican Congress.[10] He relied on Democratic swing votes to pass a compromise version of his proposed budget. One of Bush's prime targets for his coalition is the "Blue Dog" Democratic group who come from Congressional districts in states like Nebraska, Montana, and North Dakota that voted for Bush. Other key potential Democratic coalition members for Bush are conservative southern Democrats (called "Boll Weevils"), and "new Democrats" who support bloc grants. The president has found scant support from traditional "liberal" Democrats from big cities and minority representatives, who are wary of Bush's key law, No Child Left Behind. He proposed testing all children in grades three through eight, so he had to convince Republicans that this was a wise policy to override state and local testing prerogatives. Bush has led the Republicans to favor strict federal accountability control through testing, annual yearly progress, and to takeover low-performing schools.

Bush has adopted a much more visible and aggressive federal education role than Reagan did. Reagan's and 1996 Republican candidate Robert Dole's proposals to abolish the U.S. Department of Education are gone, and in 2005 Bush appointed Margaret Spellings, his White House Domestic Policy Coordinator as his Secretary of Education.

The key Bush compromise to build a coalition with Democrats in Spring 2001 was to drop his voucher or "portability" proposal. Bush advocated that parents in failing schools get a $1,500 voucher to use at a public or private school, or for tutoring. "New Democrats," like Senator Lieberman (D-Conn.), were willing to approve a few bloc grants, but not vouchers. Consequently, the build up of categoricals during the Clinton administration has slowed down, and Bush has obtained some consolidation of past earmarked federal money. Categorical aid seems to proceed in cycles of expansion and consolidation, but the big ones like special education and Title I persist.

The Republican Party has traditionally opposed many federal controls of state-local operations. Indeed, presidents Reagan and the elder Bush had sought more state-driven programs in education through providing bloc grants. However, the new law of the younger Bush, No Child Left Behind, which passed with bipartisan support as noted, did something different. The law, with a set of 378 pages of regulations, involved:

- annual tests in reading and mathematics in grades three through eight.
- scores broken down by demographic subgroups.
- results that must show "adequate yearly progress" for schools and districts.
- requiring all teachers to be "highly qualified."
- federal tests to generate a database on states' progress toward meeting NCLB requirements.

Bush has been criticized for refusing to amend NCLB, and ignoring state and local pleas for more administrative flexibility.

What was meant by "accountability" in this law? There are at least five types. *Political* accountability links leaders to local constituents, as reflected in school boards and other groups seen earlier in this book. *Bureaucratic* accountability links leaders to procedures from state and federal agencies that seek justification for actions and oversee any variation in such rules. *Profes-

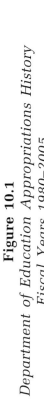

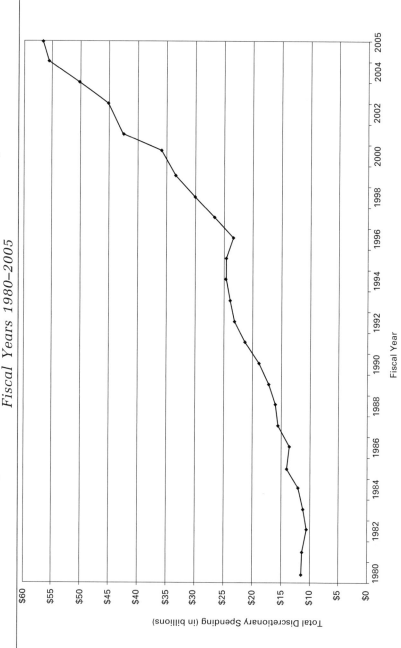

Figure 10.1
*Department of Education Appropriations History
Fiscal Years 1980–2005*

Source: Compiled by CFF authors from various editions of *Education Week*. see *Education Week*, Dec. 1, 2004, p. 30 for latest

sional accountability links leaders to decisions based on intellectual and education standards set by the profession, such as acting as social change agents in instructional tasks. *Market* accountability links leaders' needs to secure more funds by seeking students, government aid, foundation grants, and bonuses, that is, leaders seek to satisfy their "customers" such as parents or corporations. Finally, *moral* accountability links teachers' behavior to deep values in the society, for example, enhancing children's life chances through instruction.

The average leader must face all these forms of accountability, often simultaneously. The problem lies in trying to make sense out of mixed signals on behavior that these types impose, especially if they conflict. Pick any two of these and think about real events that oppose meeting them fully. A current example lies in the twenty-seven state agencies that imposed sanctions in the fall of 2003 on low-performing schools for low student scores on state tests, but left local leaders to secure local funding that may not be there to improve scores.

The outcome of increasing accountability may well lead in time to confusion, litigation, and—in the end—some kind of Congressional compromise on the high standards imposed by law. States differ on defining student proficiency, some by lowering requirements to pass tests. Arkansas called students "proficient" even when they miss minimal performance goals. Eventually, the current focus may be just one of those directives from above that one filters into the realities of educational life, a nostrum that many reformers sought but which faded on the fire of reality. There is another more important matter here. Much of the new requirements in No Child Left Behind or similar laws are a form of *external* control. Yet there is some evidence that it is *internal* accountability—with the school among teachers, administrators, and families—that enhances student learning. To achieve that accountability is much harder to realize. One visible sign is the fact that early in 2005 some forty state legislatures were calling for resistance to NCLB.[11]

FEDERALISM AND INTERGOVERNMENTAL POLITICS*

Federal politics operates within an intergovernmental context whereby higher levels of government try to get lower levels to change policies and practices. The history of federal aid has been dominated by regulations, categorical programs, and technical assistance by higher levels of.[12] There have been many metaphors to depict education policy within intergovernmental relations, including "marble cake" or a "picket fence." The marble cake recognizes that the federal, state, and local levels are not distinct, and policy spills over from one level to another. The picket-fence metaphor is based on categorical programs like Title I or special education, whereby the federal and state levels interact to mandate or stimulate specific local programs. Each picket in the fence includes administrators (e.g., of vocational education) at all levels of government, and auditors to ensure that federal/state funds are spent within a separate picket (or policy sphere).

Intergovernmental policies have more to do with legitimating change or with structure than with the nature of teaching or classroom practice. A useful metaphor is that of an "ecology of games" that are largely separate, but do interact and provide inputs to each intergovernmental unit. For example, there is a state legislative game, a state administrative game, a district and school administration game, and a teaching game.[13] Each game has separate players, rewards, and inputs to other games, and each provides outcomes to other games. Programs from higher levels are just one of many influences on the local school district and classroom game. State programs interact with local demands, local taxes, and needs of local board members, local employees, and community groups.

For some players, winning the local game focuses on obtaining federal or state categorical and general aid to create more local programs. But many local administrators are not particularly rewarded in the intergovernmental game, so they tend to

---

* This section adapted by permission of the publisher from Michael Kirst, "Recent Research on Intergovernmental Relations in Education Policy," *Educational Researcher* 24, no. 9 (August 1994). Copyright © 1994 by the American Educational Research Association.

tune out signals from the state or federal levels. Teachers see their successes in terms of student learning or just getting through the day. The publicity surrounding the passage of an omnibus state or federal reform package is not central to teachers' lives. Consequently, intergovernmental policy has limited influence on classroom practice.

This ecology of different games of education policy is one appropriate concept for attempts by higher levels of government to leverage and change lower levels. It is easier to use state regulatory policies to influence administrators at the local level rather than to change classroom teaching. Some state policies employ mandates that outrun the state's existing technology and capacity at local classroom levels. For example, attempts to "tinker" (e.g., business-oriented budget systems, like Program Planning and Management by Objectives) have left scant residue at the local level.[14] In sum, each governmental level tries to maximize its sphere of influence by seizing opportunities or rejecting higher-level policies. It is in this larger political context that stasis and challenge interact in American education today within a complex intergovernmental system.

General Findings from a Decade of Research on Intergovernmental Relations

Over the last ten years, researchers have reached general conclusions about intergovernmental relations, of which four have major implications.

Not a Zero-Sum Game

Power and influence in education intergovernmental relations is *not* a zero-sum game whereby one level gains and another level loses the ability to influence policy.[15] Rather, the result may be an increased volume of policy at *all* levels. For example, state curricular frameworks can galvanize more local curriculum policymaking and leadership at the local level, so that the policymaking impact of all governance levels can increase simultaneously. For instance, state graduation standards in the 1980s became a required floor beyond which many local education agencies (LEAs) added courses. The dominant concept, then, is mutual influence among education policy levels, not zero-sum.

The interaction may take the form of state mandates; for example, requiring a semester of economics for high school students is strongly directive of local behavior. But mandates and rules have not been the main strategy for states to guide or influence local curricular content. California curricular policies in science and social studies, for example, are not mandates but provide a framework rather than prescribe a detailed list of content to be taught. Moreover, many local districts use the state curricular framework as a springboard for their solution to a particular local context. Much state policy is characterized by low enforcement, imprecise policy directives, and local initiatives. Many local districts not only complied with California's 1983 reform law (SB 813), but also were building on the state-based mandates to add new policies of their own.[16] In their study of six states (including California), researchers at the Consortium for Policy Analysis in Education found:

> Local activism in reform has been noted in several studies of the reform movement.... This local activism takes a variety of forms: staying ahead of the state and of peers by enacting policies in anticipation of higher state policies to meet specific needs, and using state policies as a catalyst for achieving district objectives.[17]

Limited Impact of Deregulation

Deregulation per se (perhaps even including abolishing state codes) does *not* result in widespread significant local policy change.[18] Additional policies and capacity building actually are needed to utilize the flexibility and creativity that deregulation may stimulate. This result implies that elimination of federal or state code sections should be supplemented with other policies such as technical assistance. Changes in state or federal regulatory policy interact with wide variations in local capacity and context. The impact of deregulation will vary depending on many local factors, and there may be no central tendency of local responses.

Different policy designs, however, can alter local responses.

For example, blanket waivers of state regulations have more potential impact than rule-by-rule waivers. Blanket waivers broaden the local horizon for change.[19] Often, LEAs are unaware that some desired local changes do not require a state waiver. In South Carolina, for example, one half of the changes undertaken in the wake of a flexibility program could have been implemented prior to new state deregulation.[20] However, automatic sweeping deregulation may stimulate change because it broadens the horizon for planning change, and removes constraints more thoroughly than rule-by-rule waivers.

States use differential regulatory strategies whereby some districts are granted more or less regulation depending on performance indicators and fiscal problems. The consequences of state differential treatment strategies are highly dependent on their designs and the local context. The less successful schools may be the most in need of deregulation, but some states restrict waivers only to high-performing schools.[21] The takeover of low-performing local districts by states has had little direct impact on schools.[22] The consequences of state takeover depend in part on the capacity of the state agency, and whether it can assist or broker meaningful help. State takeover of local school districts, like Jersey City, New Jersey, does provide better fiscal control and solvency in LEAs that have been near bankruptcy or using questionable fiscal practices. But unless the intervention is specifically designed to focus on instruction, the state presence is typically not felt beyond the central office. In sum, deregulation supporters assume particular types of local responses, but not much is known about the impact of large-scale bloc grants or massive repeal of state codes.

Sanctions, Incentives, and Knowledge Creep

No Child Left Behind uses sanctions and incentives to stimulate desired change or performance. But incentive systems are still in the trial-and-error stage. It is very difficult to obtain sufficient political support for sanctions on teachers or schools, such as decreasing teacher pay or removing categorical funds. Using federal assessment systems for rewards or sanctions at the school level has raised serious questions about their reliability and validity for such purposes.[23] Teacher salary schedules have not changed in decades and continue to include only academic credits beyond the B.A. and years of service. In sum, intergovernmental incentive systems are exceedingly complex to design if policymakers desire to have consistent effects on schools and students.[24] NCLB contains new incentives for low pupil test scores, such as choice, supplementary services, and school reconstitution. It is too early to assess the impact of these new incentives, but many schools and states are reporting reluctance to go along with federal rules.

Many recent curricular reforms (e.g., National Council of Teachers of Mathematics standards) are not clearly specified in terms of expected LEA and school implementation. Federal standards and frameworks have been promulgated in general terms with considerable local latitude (for example, see the standards statements under U.S. Department of Education grants). Though teachers may complain that such general policies fail to give sufficient guidance for instruction,[25] they still may have an effect on practice by shaping attitudes about content and performance. For example, state curricular policies can change the local discussion and inject new concepts and thinking into local policies. This is another example of how intergovernmental relations need *not* be a zero-sum game.

State policies can provide knowledge that creeps into local *practice* over time, such as the use of student portfolios in Vermont.[26] Curricular reform networks that are started and supported by government but are not part of government have changed classroom practice.[27] These reform networks, such as the California Science Improvement Network (CSIN), can build teacher capacity, reorient staff development, and seep into the classroom.[28] Policymakers get more impact by using "push" factors, like assessments and frameworks, *in conjunction* with "pull" factors, like incentives and demonstrations. Some package of these policies has more potential than stand-alone policies to help classroom practice.

The context of teachers is very different in reality from how many policymakers view intergovernmental impact on classroom practice.[29] Consequently, policy needs to be designed from a view inside the classroom looking outward rather than a view from top-down intergovernmental leaders. This classroom context-practice view indicates that capacity-building policies, such as staff development, are crucial if they provide teachers with coaching, follow up, and professional communities for mutual assistance.[30]

Organizational Capacity

State and local education agencies are slow to adapt to new federal policy goals. State education agencies (SEAs) are not well structured or well prepared to help implement and sustain federal reform.[31] Since the U.S. Department of Education has no regional offices, it relies heavily on state education agencies to implement NCLB. It is unclear whether SEAs can or will enforce NCLB choice, supplementary services, and school reconstitution requirements upon recalcitrant local schools. SEAs are organized primarily along categorical or special-purpose units that inhibit alignment among an array of policies and comprehensive approaches. These segmented state organizations could be recast into shared understandings, roles, and tasks that flatten the hierarchy. Comprehensive reform requires policy coherence and treatment of holistic problems, which means SEA teamwork and collaboration are crucial. Because even aligned federal and state policies cannot be expected to have consistent local effects, adjustments will be needed for diverse local contexts.

Most local central offices suffer from the same fragmented structural and operational problems as SEAs.[32] Until the effective schools movement in the 1970s, local central offices paid scant attention to curriculum and instruction. District structures resemble geological accretions of functions and special programs over many years and are not monolithic.[33]

Federal policymakers have devised techniques for their progress to attain their intended local purposes.[34] Such techniques included federal/state field audits; lawsuits; socialization of state and local administrators hired with categorical funds; and gradual infusion of categorical purposes within the standard operating procedures of schools. There developed a proliferation of federal regulations, rules, monitoring, and auditing. This trend periodically resulted in agitation for deregulation, waivers, and bloc grants.

As this categorical enforcement "success" was becoming more evident, concern shifted to the alleged negative, cumulative, and aggregative impact of the totality of categorical grants. But studies by Stanford Research Institute and others indicated that LEAs had become "accustomed" to handling the numerous federal categories and were not overburdened by regulations.[35] The Reagan administration attempted to consolidate most federal categoricals, but was rebuffed by the Democratic Congress, and ended up with only minor consolidations.[36]

Categorical issues and regulation then began to recede from the spotlight of intergovernmental politics around 1983, when state reforms turned to higher academic standards for all pupils, and to the core curriculum. Later in the 1980s categorical programs became a concern because they were not well integrated or aligned with high academic standards and systemic reform. Their restructuring and deregulation were a major focus of the 1994 ESEA reauthorization. NCLB has produced state and local complaints of underfunding and excessive federal regulation.

What enlightenment can research provide this political and conceptual debate? Categorical grants can have a lasting impact on local schools.[37] For example, policies can promote change in organizational structure including added personnel layers (e.g., vocational specialists or aides) or "pull-out" teaching structures under Title I. These instructional methods or organizational changes require a new layer of specialists that can be organized into a constituency for maintenance of the "program." Categorical grants also have a strong influence on pupil classification and the definition of specialties in teaching. For instance, certificates for teaching remedial reading or bilingual education differentiate the specialist from the regular classroom teacher. They are necessary to assure that federal funds are used for special programs and constituencies.

On the other extreme, categorical programs have little influence on the extent and nature of curricular coverage of specific topics or on teaching methods or strategies—such as individualization of instruction or inquiry methods. A study found that new math concepts and science inquiry methods promoted by the federal government in the 1960s had vanished from the vast majority of schools a decade later.[38] Teachers initiate most classroom talk and orchestrate classroom interaction around brief factual questions.[39]

These probable low-impact areas are the most difficult for federal and state governments to monitor or create political constituencies for program maintenance. Some tinkering such as federally sponsored in-service training could have some impact or leave a residue, and the Bush administration created a $1 billion reading program for teachers with explicit attention to phonics.

The school-level impact of bloc grants is more difficult to discern because unrestricted dollars cannot be easily identified. They become part of the general support base of an organization and will free up dollars for other purposes. In 1981 the Reagan administration succeeded in consolidating twenty-eight federal categorical programs into a Chapter 2 ESEA bloc grant. Field studies indicate that Chapter 2 was used for nonrecurring expenditures like computers that were not part of an articulated school improvement effort.[40] This small bloc grant ($800 million) did reduce local administrative burden, but local parents had less influence on spending decisions than under categorical grants, and the classroom impact is unknown. Studies suggest that increased local flexibility over small amounts of money not accompanied by local capacity building is unlikely to have much school or classroom impact. Larger bloc grants may have more potential for changing practice, but there are no data to support either a positive or negative case.

Overview

It is a long way from a federal or state grant to thousands of classrooms. Policies create a skeleton or shell within which classroom practice can change, but much more than policy is needed to alter instruction for most classes. Moreover, policies need to be much more robust and sophisticated than most traditional approaches that stress solely either regulation or deregulation and bloc grants. Policymakers must also not lose sight of the realities and context of the classroom teacher. Intergovernmental policies can help establish favorable conditions for teachers who are operating in their own varied contexts, but policy is only one of many influences on how teachers respond to students in their classrooms.

As the authors of a review of fifty states conclude, the states are

> all over the map, as they are reading the tea leaves and finding different answers. . . . There are fifty separate stories of interpretation and implementation. . . . The federal goal of creating single and "seamless" accountability systems that would apply equally to all states has not been realized.[41]

Clearly, this outcome runs up against the centrifugal tension of fifty state systems. State personnel may well accept these federal goals. However, working them out runs into the blocking brambles of state and local preferences, of diverse interpretation of the wording, or of inadequate fiscal resources to do very much. It is the case that different concepts of the value of efficiency, seen in measuring achievement in learning, complicate the matter far beyond any single national implementation.

Tensions and American Democracy

This picture of policy tensions is not unique for this law or for this modern era, for the issue is persistent in American history. Partly the tension is a struggle over power—Who should rule within the web of governments in this nation? Partly also, the tension is over our history of ideological debate about federal versus state authority. This tension underlies the origins of the Bill of Rights early in the Republic and in later Supreme Court decisions, in Andrew Jackson's struggle over internal improvements, in the dreadful abyss of the Civil War, in later efforts to regulate business, and in the current struggle over civil rights. For each of these issues, elaborate alliances have sprung up between policy adherents drawn from all levels of government.

For much of our history, though, the states and localities prevailed until the 1930s, even though most governments had done very little. Yet the course of the twentieth century brought the state and federal levels together in an expanded activity and in elaborate patterns of conflict and cooperation. In one sense, the debate over accountability involves conflict, as noted above, but also cooperation in trying to work out a common problem. The debate, as always, is over what the policy means and how to improve schooling. Note that the accountability conflict is over how to do it, and not over whether it should be done at all.

Across a broad front of education policy, then, officials at both levels are working policy out in this contemporary aspect of an historical struggle. The tension that arises naturally in this inter-action is ever present and will not disappear, given the vested interests at both levels in furthering the goals of schooling. Yet it is not all conflict; there is no firing on Fort Sumter every time a school issue arises. The larger picture today is that conflict may well yield to "mutual accommodation" between levels. In time, interests merge and policy practices become worked out together. Indeed, as he noted, some education policies may be better performed by an emphasis on the state level, while yet others on the federal level.[42]

In effect, as seen in this chapter, the tension of federalism remains and will continue. Clearly, it is a fitting policy for a complex and diverse country that Walt Whitman once called "a nation of nations."

NOTES

1. For an overview see Michael Timpane, ed., *The Federal Interest in Financing Education* (Cambridge, Mass.: Ballinger, 1979).

2. James Sundquist, *Politics and Policy* (Washington, D.C.: Brookings Institution, 1968), pp. 155–221.

3. Harold Howe, "National Policy for American Education" (speech to the Seventy-First Annual Convention of the National Congress of Parents and Teachers, Minneapolis, Minn., May 22, 1967).

4. U.S. Department of Education, *The Fiscal Year 1987 Budget* (Washington, D.C.: U.S. Department of Education, 1986).

5. Lorraine M. McDonnell and Milbrey McLaughlin, *Education Policy and the Role of the State* (Santa Monica, Calif.: Rand, 1982).

6. David Clark and Terry Astuto, "The Changing Structure of Education Policy in the 1980's," *Phi Delta Kappan* 55: 3 (1983): 188-193.

7. For an overview of the Clinton years, see Diane Ravitch, ed., *Education 2000* (Washington, D.C.: Brookings Institution, 2000).

8. See Michael Kirst and Richard Jung, "The Utility of a Longitudinal Approach in Assessing Implementation" in Walter Williams, ed., *Studying Implementation* (Chatham, N.J.: Chatham House/Longman, 1982).

9. Paul Hill, "The Federal Role in Education," in Ravitch, *Education 2000*, p. 19.

10. See David W. Brady and Craig Volden, *Revolving Gridlock* (Boulder, Colo.: Westview, 1998).

11. Dorothy Shipps and William Firestone essay in *Education Week* (June 18, 2003): 56; Bruce Fuller essay in *Education Week* (February 15, 2003): 44; *New York Times*, February 15, 2005.

12. Michael W. Kirst and Robert Jung, "Beyond Mutual Adaptation, into the Bully Pulpit," *Educational Administration Quarterly* (1986): 17–33.

13. William A. Firestone, "Education Policy as an Ecology of Games," *Educational Researcher* 18:7 (1989): 18–24. For an overview of the school finance game, see Kenneth K. Wong, *Funding Public Schools* (Lawrence: University of Kansas, 1999).

14. David Tyack and Larry Cuban, *Tinkering Toward Utopia* (Cambridge: Harvard University Press, 1995).

15. Richard F. Elmore and Susan H. Fuhrman, "Understanding Local Control in the Wake of State Education Reform," *Educational Evaluation and Policy Analysis* 12 (1990): 82–96.

16. Michael W. Kirst and Gary Yee, "An Examination of the Evolution of California State Education Reform, 1983–1993," in Diane Massell and Susan H. Fuhrman, eds., *Ten Years of State Education Reform* (New Brunswick, N.J.: Rutgers, Eagleton Institute of Politics: Consortium for Policy Research in Education, 1994), pp. 158–171.

17. Susan H. Fuhrman and Richard F. Elmore, "Understanding Local Control in the Wake of State Education Reform," *Educational Evaluation and Policy Analysis* 12 (1990): 82–96.

18. Susan H. Fuhrman and Richard F. Elmore, *Ruling Out Rules: The Evolution of Deregulation in State Education Policy* (New Brunswick, N.J.: Rutgers, Eagleton Institute of Politics: Consortium for Policy Research in Education, 1994).

19. Susan H. Fuhrman and Richard F. Elmore, *Takeover and Deregulation* (New Brunswick, N.J.: Rutgers, Eagleton Institute of Politics: Consortium for Policy Research in Education, 1992).

20. Consortium for Policy Research in Education, "Ten Lessons About Regulation and Schooling," *CPRE Policy Briefs* (New Brunswick, N.J.: Rutgers, Eagleton Institute of Politics, 1992).

21. Ibid.

22. Fuhrman and Elmore, *Takeover and Deregulation.*

23. Susan H. Fuhrman, ed., *Developing Accountability Systems for Education* (Philadelphia: CPRE, RB-38, 2003).

24. Consortium, "Ten Lessons."

25. Fuhrman, *Developing Accountability Systems.*

26. David K. Cohen and James P. Spillane, "Policy and Practice: The Relations Between Governance and Instruction," in Susan H. Fuhrman, ed., *Designing Coherent Education Policy: Improving the System* (San Francisco: Jossey-Bass, 1993).

27. Robert E. Floden, "Portfolios for Capacity Building: Systemic Reform in Vermont," in Margaret E. Goertz, Robert E. Floden, and Jennifer O'Day, eds., *Studies of Education Reform: Systemic Reform* (New Brunswick, N.J.: Rutgers, Eagleton Institute of Politics: Consortium for Policy Research in Education, 1995); Jennifer

O'Day, "Systemic Reform in California," in Goertz, Floden, and O'Day, *Studies of Education Reform*; Richard Murnane, "Teaching to New Standards," in Susan H. Fuhrman and Jennifer O'Day, eds.. *Rewards and Reform: Creating Educational Incentives that Work* (San Francisco: Jossey-Bass, 1997).

28. Consortium, "Ten Lessons"; Richard F. Elmore and Susan H. Fuhrman, eds., *The Governance of Curriculum* (Alexandria, Va.: Association for Supervision and Curriculum, 1994).

29. Milbrey McLaughlin and Joan Talbert, *Contexts that Matter for Teaching* (Stanford, Calif: Center for Research on the Context of Secondary School Teaching, 1993).

30. Ibid.

31. Susan Lusi, *Systemic Reform: Challenges Faced by State Departments of Education* (Washington, D.C.: ASCD Yearbook, 1994).

32. Richard F. Elmore, *The Role of Local School Districts in Instructional Improvement* (New Brunswick, N.J.: Rutgers, Eagleton Institute of Politics: Consortium for Policy Research in Education, 1991).

33. David Cohen, "Policy and Organization," *Harvard Education Review* 52, no. 4 (1982): 474–499.

34. Kirst and Jung, "Beyond Mutual Adaptation." A similar pattern emerged in other national policies; see Paul Peterson, *When Federalism Works* (Washington, D.C.: Brookings Institution, 1986).

35. Michael Knapp, *Cumulative Effects of Federal Education Policies on Schools and Districts* (Menlo Park, Calif.: SRI International, 1983).

36. Chester Finn, Jr., "Reflections on the 'Disassembly of the Federal Educational Role,'" *Education and Urban Society* 15: 3 (1983): 389–396.

37. Michael W. Kirst, "Teaching Policy and Federal Categorical Programs," in Lee Shulman and Gary Sykes, eds., *Handbook of Teaching and Policy* (New York: Longman, 1983), pp. 426–448; Richard F. Elmore and Susan H. Fuhrman, "The National Interest and Federal Role in Education," *Publius* 20 (1990): 149–163; Fuhrman and Elmore, "Understanding Local Control."

38. Robert Stake and James Easley, *Case Studies in Science Education* (Washington, D.C.: National Science Foundation, 1978).

39. John Goodlad, *A Place Called School* (New York: McGraw Hill, 1984).

40. Kirst and Jung, "Beyond Mutual Adaptation."

41. Margaret Goertz and Mark Duffy, *Assessment and Accountability in the 50 States* (Philadelphia: University of Pennsylvania, Consortium for Policy Research, 2001). Reviewed in *Education Week* (April 18, 2001): 60, 54–45. For NCLB see Center on Education Policy, *NCLB after the Second Year* (Washington, D.C.: CEP, 2004).

42. Paul Peterson, *The Price of Federalism* (Washington, D.C.: Brookings, 1996).

11

Federal Elections and Political Trends

CURRENT ISSUES

Historically, federal education policy played a small or no role in federal elections, largely because until the late 1950s federal education expenditures were 1 percent or less of total education spending. It was not until Lyndon Johnson's "Great Society" and "War on Poverty" in 1965 that education played a significant role in national political campaigns. This role has grown since 1965, and in 2000 the presidential election featured education policies. But in 2004, education was not a major issue, and was overshadowed by Iraq, the economy, and health care. The largest expansions in the federal role in education came from Texans—Johnson's Elementary and Secondary Education Act of 1965 and George W. Bush's No Child Left Behind legislation in 2001. Table 11.1 demonstrates the dramatic expansion in how often education was mentioned in presidential papers through the first Bush presidency.

However, whether education issues affect electoral outcomes and how elections change federal education policy, are open questions.[1] Education could be merely a symbolic issue that does

Table 11.1
Presidential Attention to Education

Years	President	Total Mentions of Education in Presidential Papers	Average Mentions per Year
1789–1913	Washington-Taft	226	2
1929–1833	Hoover	148	37
1933–1945	Roosevelt	382	29
1945–1953	Truman	667	74
1953–1961	Eisenhower	771	96
1961–1963	Kennedy	777	259
1963–1969	Johnson	3,104	621
1969–1974	Nixon	1,428	238
1974–1977	Ford	830	277
1977–1981	Carter	2,055	514
1981–1989	Reagan	2,497	312
1989–1992	Bush	2,657	664

Note: Table tallies the total mentions of the word *education* in the public papers of U.S. presidents through 1992.

Source: Frederick Hess and Patrick J. McGuinn, "Seeking the Mantle of Opportunity: Presidential Politics and the Educational Metaphor, 1964–2000," *Educational Policy* 16: 1 (January 2002): 77.

not change many votes. Candidates broaden their support by courting the "centrist" voter and downplaying extreme ideology. Education issues can increase voter turnout if education is one of the top national issues.[2] Republicans want voters to perceive Democrats as captives of teachers unions, and focus on accountability, school prayer, and "character" issues. Democrats support traditional categorical programs and want new ones. Party agreement in 2001 to pass No Child Left Behind (NCLB) was followed by party conflict over NCLB funding, implementation, and local consequences. As Table 11.2 indicates, from 1979 until the 2000 presidential election, the public thought Democrats addressed education issues better than did the Republicans. But President George W. Bush took the education issue advantage away from Democratic dominance in 2001 with the NCLB passage. But he was confronted in 2004 by a vociferous Democratic criticism that NCLB was underfunded and allowed excessive regulation of local schools by the U.S. Department of Education. In 2004 Democratic presidential candidate, Senator John Kerry, charged that

Table 11.2
Public Attitudes Toward the Ability of the Major Parties to Address Education, 1979–2000

Year	Democrats (%)	Republicans (%)	Advantage (%)
1979	25	16	Democrats +9
1984	37	19	Democrats +18
1988	55	22	Democrats +33
1992	42	17	Democrats +25
1996	59	30	Democrats +29
2000	44	41	Democrats +3

Source: Assorted polls from the Roper Center for Public Opinion Research at the University of Connecticut (n.d.).

Bush cut education aid in order to fund tax cuts for the wealthy. However, respondents to a Fall 2004 national poll rated the candidates even on whom they would support if they were voting solely on education issues.[3]

Another political issue is that who votes is a crucial determinant of the salience of education in national elections. Older white voters without children are less likely to care about education. For example, fewer Latinos and Asians than whites vote, which indicates racial inequality in voting participation.[4] The most consistent predictors of who votes are years of education, age, length of residence, and income. Whether gender, marital status, and organizational memberships affect voting participation is less clear.[5] "Soccer moms" and traditional Christians have been major symbols of swing voters in some, but not all, presidential election years. The 2004 Presidential election suggested that President Clinton "soccer moms" had been transformed into moral and martial moms. White married women increased their vote for Bush by 10 percent between 2000 and 2004.

The division of most of the country into likely Republican or Democratic states results in greater attention by candidates to swing states like Ohio, Pennsylvania, Wisconsin, and West Virginia. These swing states exert an exaggerated influence and receive disproportionate attention from presidential candidates. They also contain higher-than-average percentages of older voters without schoolchildren. Education was a key issue in some swing states (Illinois, Indiana, Minnesota, Wisconsin) in the 2000 presidential election.

From our analysis of the candidates' announcement and acceptance speeches, the debates, and press releases . . . it is clear that education policy did indeed play a central role in the 2000 presidential election. This is the case both because education was salient to the public, and because the candidates appear to have used education policy strategically to gain electoral support.[6]

By 2004, then, education was no longer a major campaign issue. What could account for the impact of educational policy on national elections? Education politics has gradually transformed from a local to a national issue, but education can be overwhelmed by big events like terrorism and economic recession. Nevertheless, education has become something that national politicians must address. Perhaps the power of ideas is important politically, starting in 1964 with a belief that education could reduce poverty and enhance civil rights. Education's importance intensified from 1980 to 2000 with an emphasis on education's potential to enhance U.S. economic growth and competition for jobs. One scholar calls this 1980–2000 focus on education, which emerged during the 1980–83 recession, a "new politics of education productivity." During those years, many jobs were allegedly lost to a better-educated Japanese workforce. Even though U.S. economic growth exceeded Japan's during 1990-2000, concern in the United States with productivity continued:

In short, this politics of productivity tends to favor macro-political groups, many of whom are critical of the performance of education systems. This is an ideological diverse set of interests that comprise centrist business groups like the Committee on Educational Development, libertarian groups on the right such as the Cato Institute, as well as those with liberal political leanings such as the Education Trust. Major foundations with national orientations are among the most prominent champions of this productivity orientation.[7]

In 2000 President Bush enlisted Sandy Kress, an attorney and former member of the Dallas School Board, to be his key White House negotiator to pass NCLB. The 2001 Democratically controlled Senate was the most difficult hurdle in the effort to pass this legislation. Senate Education Chair, Edward Kennedy, was pursuing two different goals—stop federal aid for vouchers and get more money for the schools. Bush put pressure on Kennedy to support NCLB by meeting with more moderate Democrats such as Senators Joseph Lieberman (D-Connecticut) and Evan Bayh (D-Indiana) in Austin, Texas. Kennedy feared that he could be left out of a winning coalition behind education policy. To encourage Kennedy's support, Bush pressed for disaggregating test scores by racial, economic, and ethnic subgroups. Kennedy and Bush agreed that the neediest children (e.g., Title I-eligible students) should get the most attention and money. A deal was made and NCLB passed in 2001, but Kennedy claims Bush reneged on promises for a large budget to fund NCLB requirements. Bush counters that funding for NCLB rose 42 percent, from nearly $8.8 billion in 2001 to $12.3 billion in 2004.

In 2004 public opinion on who would improve education was evenly divided between the parties at 46 percent for each.[8] Power in Washington, however, does not reflect this balance in public views. Republicans control the House, and can use their majorities to push through education legislation. Republican control of the Senate is less absolute, but effective for some education bills that do not risk a filibuster by the Democratic minority. A major Republican move to expand school choice would likely lead to a Democratic filibuster. Many business interests that used to give substantial amounts to each party are now overwhelmingly giving to the Republicans, which may help Republicans gain even more legislative seats.[9] NCLB passed with little influence exerted by teachers' unions or any other union.[10] Neither AFT nor NEA endorsed NCLB, and in 2004 NEA proposed a major overhaul of the act. This led Secretary of Education Paige to label NEA "a terrorist organization," which prompted the Bush White House to keep an even closer rein on Department of Education policies and public statements.[11] In 2005 President Bush replaced Paige with his White House domestic policy head and former Texas education advisor, Margaret Spellings.

Denunciations of NCLB and calls for major changes in the statute marked the 2004 Democratic presidential primaries. Some of this criticism reflected complaints by teacher unions and by principals that NCLB publicly identifies so many "failing schools" that the law seems in fact designed to enhance public support for vouchers. Twenty-three prominent business leaders countered that critics offer no real alternative and that NCLB is creating academic progress.[12] Senator Kerry, however, recommended mostly technical changes, and more NCLB funding. President Bush's 2004 election may provide a clearer political direction for federal education policy in the next few years. For example, Bush backed the Washington, D.C., demonstration voucher plan that passed Congress in 2004, but Senator Kennedy promised to repeal it. Bush wants to extend the K-8 testing focus of NCLB to high schools, called for early in 2005, and limit changes to the key NCLB accountability provisions.

HISTORICAL ISSUES

If we step back from the current conflicts, a clearer picture emerges over time of the role of federal politics in education. Christopher Cross' historical analysis of national policy and politics demonstrates that the primary federal role in education policy is to enhance equity.[13] During the past ten years federal policy focused more on changing classroom instruction for all pupils as a way to attain equity. Federal tactics have shifted from regulating school-site inputs and processes to demanding accountability for pupil outcomes. This policy change was produced by a loosely coupled Congressional process:

> Congress is organized as a system of committees and subcommittees that ensures that elementary and secondary education is never looked at as a whole. In the House, one subcommittee handles ESEA and vocational education, but never in the same year or in the same bill. Another subcommittee handles special education. The jurisdiction for preschool is split among committees and subcommittees, and yet another committee handles science and NSF. A similar pattern exists in the Senate. An entirely separate set of committees and subcommittees decides how much will be spent to operate programs and agencies, and communication between committees on these matters is rare. In fact, in the House, caucus rules prohibit a member from serving on both the education committee and the appropriations committee.[14]

Cross demonstrates that presidential leadership can be crucial but not essential in developing new education policy. For instance, the Education for All Handicapped Children law of 1975 was a breakthrough for equity, but it was passed after Nixon's Watergate problems crippled his leadership. Presidents Lyndon

Johnson and George W. Bush, on the other hand, are examples of the large difference presidential leadership can make, because their bills (ESEA and NCLB, respectively) created the largest increments in the federal role. Cross emphasizes that while it is relatively easy for an interest group to get a small categorical program enacted, it is much more difficult for interest groups to get new ideas passed like tough accountability and NCLB school-site sanctions. This usually requires a strong presidential push as evidenced by passage of NCLB.

The impact of Washington interest groups on education policy has been debated for several years. The biggest campaign donors represent teachers, administrators, and school boards (see Chapter 3). Their biggest victory was the creation of a federal Education Department in 1978. A categorical interest group, the Council for Exceptional Children, was a major force in passing the Education for all Handicapped Children Act of 1975. However, by the 1980s interest-group influence waned as members of Congress from "safe" districts with scant electoral challenge and low-budget campaigns became policy innovation leaders. For example, in 2001 George Miller (D-California), John Boehner (R-Ohio), and Edward Kennedy (D-Massachusetts) united to help pass NCLB. Moreover, the federal government pays more than half of staff salaries in state education agencies. So interest groups confront an organized base of state resistance in their attempts to change federal laws.

The most striking change in federal political influence in the last twenty years is the rise of "think tanks" and other education groups not linked to school system employees. But parents and students are not well organized and mostly rely on school employees and boards to advocate for them in Washington. The conflict between the producers of education (e.g., teacher unions) and the consumers of school instruction may widen in the future as right-leaning think tanks enhance their political effectiveness with the President and Congress. Public-opinion differences among parents, teachers, and business employers are large and fundamental, as Table 11.3 demonstrates. A study of how Reading First passed as part of NCLB concluded that a small network of people close to the Bush White House was crucial. Five key inside players dominated the legislative design. There

Table 11.3

Differences in the Beliefs of Parents, Teachers, and Employers about School Reform (by percentage)

	More Money	Higher Standards	Don't Know	Best Ways to Improve Local Schools High School Diploma Is No Guarantee of Mastering the Basics	Overhaul Persistently Failing Schools by Replacing Staff and Keeping Them Under Strict Observation	Tie Improvement in Student Performance to Financial Rewards for Teachers and Principals
Parents	61	35	5	31	62	59
Teachers	70	28	2	25	23	22
Employers	33	62	5	60	66	51

Source: Public Agenda (2000a, 2000e, 2000g, 2000k).

was scant or no influence on Reading First from the Department of Education, NEA, International Reading Association, or the National Council of Teachers of English.[15]

NCLB gives the nation until 2014 to render all students proficient in reading and math. It requires severe penalties for schools who fail to make annual progress on tests for two or more years. NCLB is a high-stakes accountability approach that rewards or sanctions educators. Sanctions include state takeover of schools, student choice of schools, and private tutoring services paid for with local school Title I funds. Political resistance is inevitable when stakes are high. In this case, resistance will try to undercut the coercion and sanctions in NCLB. Frederick Hess has identified four major groups who will resist NCLB high stakes such as choice, school closure, and tutoring:

1. Educators concerned about their professional autonomy and the specter of sanctions,
2. Ethnic and socioeconomic communities in which students are disproportionately sanctioned by tests,
3. Communities with well-regarded schools that resent the disruption or threat to their reputation because of testing, and
4. Those who find their moral or curricular preferences marginalized by the testing regime in question.[16]

In 2004 political controversy about amending or gutting NCLB was the predominant federal policy concern. By April 2004 twenty-three states had filed formal complaints with the U.S. Department of Education; by early 2005 the number was thirty-eight, and Utah legislatures insisted that state priorities override federal ones. If NCLB is gutted, the divisions between the parties are so deep that it is unlikely that a new coalition for a different federal approach can be formed. Most school districts did not pay much attention to NCLB until Fall 2003, so the Washington political battles have just begun. NCLB impacts most schools, unlike ESEA, which focused on 25 percent of the schools with large concentrations of low-income children. This large-scale NCLB impact on all schools provides a case for a much larger federal contribution to total education expenditures than does its 7.5 percent current allocation. But President Bush thinks that social security and health care are the top federal priorities now, and is less willing than Democrats to increase federal education aid. The key political issue is whether NCLB will provide the framework for many years of federal policy, or in the end will be an ephemeral initiative. The reelection of President Bush in 2004 shifts the odds greatly that NCLB will endure with only incremental change.

NOTES

1. See V. Darleen Opfer and Kenneth Wong, eds., "The Politics of Elections and Education," *Educational Policy* 16:1 (March 2002).

2. Diana Jean Schemo, "Kennedy Demands Full Funding for School Bill, *New York Times*, April 7, 2004, p. A18.

3. Lowell C. Rose and Alec M. Gallup, "Public Attitudes Toward Public Schools," *Phi Delta Kappan* (September 2004): 44.

4. A. Reynaldo Contreras, "Minority Voting Issues," in Opfer and Wong, "Politics of Education," pp. 56-69.

5. Contreras, "Minority Voting Issues," pp. 68-69.

6. Melissa J. Marshall and Robert McKee, "From Campaign Promises to Presidential Policy," in Opfer and Wong, "The Politics of Elections," p. 113.

7. James G. Cibulka, "The Changing Role of Interest Groups in Education," in Hanne Mawhenney and Catherine A. Lugg, eds., "Politics of Education Special Issue," *Educational Policy* 15: 1 (March 2001): 34.

8. Paul Starr, "The Republican Lock," *American Prospect* (February 2004): 3.

9. Starr, "The Republican Lock," p. 3.

10. *Education Week*, "Accountability Push in ESEA Debate Left Unions on Defensive" (November 6, 2002): 12.

11. Michelle R. Davis, "A Second Term for Paige Remains Uncertain," *Education Week* 24: 12 (November 17, 2004): 27.

12. For an overview of these contending forces, see Joel Spring, *Political Agendas for Education: From the Religious Right to the Green Party* (Mahwah, N.J.: Lawrence Erlbaum, 2002).

13. Christopher T. Cross, *Political Education* (New York: Teachers College Press, 2004).

14. Cross, *Political Education*, p. 170.

15. Cecil Miskel and Mengli Song, "Reading First: Prominence and Processes in an Elite Policy Network," *Educational Evaluation and Policy Analysis* 26: 2 (Summer 2004): 89-110.

16. Frederick Hess, "High-Stakes Accountability in the States," in Paul E. Peterson and Martin R. West, eds., *No Child Left Behind? The Politics and Practice of School Accountability* (Washington, D.C.: Brookings Institution, 2003), p. 61.

12

Court Functions amid Conflict over Change

Anyone who has participated in a ball game among youth without an umpire or referee knows how poorly the game progresses. Amid conflicts over base-running, there are cries of "Safe!" and "Out!" and nothing much gets done. As noted earlier, Americans' values and interests are diverse, and they often—but not always—conflict. When they do, the need for conflict resolution by a third or disinterested party is clearly necessary. That central function inheres in all courts in the nation when people and units of government fall into dispute, and someone must call somebody "Out" or "Safe."

We will start with placing courts within the systems analysis framework, then view their role in policy innovation and set out their primary functions. Special attention is given to how courts have been used to affect current challenges to the established system. In democracies, after all, any policy arena is open to challenge by the use of power, and courts are not different in this function. Even presidential elections (as in 2000) can bring the courts in so as to resolve conflict over vote totals.

For at least forty years schools have known this process of challenge and defense that is fought out within formal judicial

channels. Within the states, courts have also had major functions of legalizing established policies and often challenging them.
Not surprisingly, then, courts have served as another arena in
the current challenge to the steady-state qualities of American
schools.

COURTS AS A NEW POLICY AGENCY

The increased role that state and federal governments play in
the local schools comes in part from the judicial branch. Group
after group, frustrated by school policies, has turned to the state
and federal courts for relief. The courts thus became involved
not merely in settling disputes, but in confirming policy solutions to school problems and then overseeing their implementation. This chapter surveys this dual judicial role of innovation
and implementation that has affected all school districts in some
ways.

At first thought, courts seem an unlikely adjunct of schools
and an unlikely partner in policies. Yet the history of education
has been shaped by important court decisions on the duties and
responsibilities of school officials. Though trivial, the right of
students not to have their hair cut is just one of the latest of
many such contributions. At a more significant level, the United
States Supreme Court has been directly involved in the question
of religion in our schools, considering Bible reading, required
prayers, flag salutes, transportation and other expenses of parochial students, teaching of evolution, and vouchers. Court involvement can be as narrow as whether school lockers can be
searched (they can) or as extensive as whether schools can be
segregated by race (once no, but in the 2000s, probably). School
officials may react by massive noncompliance, as with the Bible
and prayer decisions, but they find that being indifferent to court
decisions is very difficult.

Court involvement in such matters may surprise only those
who view the bench as a political eunuch. Contemporary analysts of the judiciary look not only at its behavior but also at the
values that this behavior reflects. Judges are political because
they must choose between competing values brought before them

in a real conflict. As early as 1840, Alexis de Tocqueville noted that "scarcely any political question arises in the United States that is not resolved, sooner or later, into a judicial question." The reason for this is that when citizens differ in policy, the arena for resolution may be not in a legislature but in a court. The form and rules of judicial contests may differ from those in other arenas, but they remain essentially political. That is because in system theory terms, contenders are seeking the authority of the political system to command the distribution of resources—such as rights and property—that each wants. The allocation of resources to citizens that follows from a court mandate is just as effective as legislation.

What, then, are the relationships between the judiciary—part of the political system of the state—and the political system of the school? What are the constraints and strengths in this relationship? What are the accommodations and conflicts in the system aspects of the political process here? How does federalism filter the outcome? What values are reflected among participants?

THE FEDERAL JUDICIARY AS A SUBSYSTEM

Viewed theoretically, the judiciary is only one subsystem of the larger political system. The environment external to judges marches constantly into their chambers, sometimes unobtrusively and sometimes loudly, seeking the protection or enhancement of certain values. Earlier, we saw in state law that such forces underlie the four basic educational values of quality, equity, choice, and efficiency. However, the judge is not free to make such value choices alone, for there are limits. Thus, a constitution imposes certain constraints on what a judge may do. Further, professional canons have additional effects on who is selected or even considered to judge; institutional traditions also require procedures that shape the pace and division of labor. In addition, the partisanship of extramural party life has affected a judge's recruitment and deliberations in our past, and carries influence even today.[1]

Finally, changes in the social order outside the judicial chambers often bring conflict sweeping inside to the courts' domain where certain functions must be met. The value conflict thrust into the court seeks authoritative allocation of resources to implement those values. Consequently, federal courts have a *manifest* function of resolving conflict in accordance with special rules. Such decisions have an impact—not always favorable—on all branches of the national government and at all levels of government. For example, the reach of the *Brown* v. *Board of Education* decision on desegregation affected all these levels. This function means that federal courts affect the values underlying the conflict. As a result, the Supreme Court legitimizes some national policies and the values they reflect and, conversely, illegitimizes others. Illustrative are the reinforcement and later nonsupport given to desegregation by Court decisions in recent decades. The difficulty, of course, is for the Court to do this in such a way that support for the courts as an institution does not decrease, while their decisions are complied with. This is why the forefathers thought this branch the weakest, as it lacks legitimation through election.

Further, courts must maintain some kind of balance with other national subsystems in order to reduce conflict among them. In its own processes the judiciary provides signals to litigants, the general public, and other political actors (including their own local courts) as to the outputs that it will reinforce. Issuing such signals is not the same as their acceptance by others, however. Throughout its history, the Court has had to balance itself carefully at key intersections of a nationally separated government, a federally divided nation, and a diverse population.

Yet its policymaking has shown more consistency than one might expect because regular processes are at work. Thus, there is initiation of controversies, accommodation among contestants via out-of-court settlement, persuasion of judge or jury, decision making, implementation of decisions, and so on. Indeed, the nature of justice itself has always been determined by such procedures. Atop the entrance to the Greek temple of the U.S. Supreme Court there are these words: "Equal justice under the law." The courts reflect environmental demands, but their form and presentation differ here from that found in other institutions. The lobbyist gives way to the lawyer, buttonholing takes the form of law review articles, and publicity campaigns appear as litigants' briefs. The demands on a court are presented quite formally, dealing with matters of logic and legal precedent; however, research has stressed the independent role of a judge's values in the decisional process. Consequently, the outputs of courts result from the interplay of judicial values operating within the court procedures, with resulting political consequences for the environment.

However such decisions are derived, they constitute outputs into society. They instruct a wide circle of citizens as to the value norms that the courts seek to impose on the environment. However, what if no one notices or, if noticing, defies them or, if obeying, misinterprets them? When the Supreme Court confirms widely accepted social values, as with its nineteenth-century opposition to polygamy, then output and outcome are similar—compliance is very high. When, however, courts innovate in a direction contrary to accepted norms, some gap between output and outcome is to be expected, and compliance will be less. Despite the popular notion of a powerful Supreme Court, the conditions under which it can innovate are highly limited. Successful innovation could occur when (1) a majority of justices favor a change, (2) a national majority is also in agreement, and (3) the decision would not hurt the court in other areas of government. If the Supreme Court moves when conditions do not permit, though, considerable opposition can arise from other subsystems.

JUDICIAL FUNCTIONS IN SCHOOL POLICY

Courts have been an arena for the recently increased political challenge to the system of schools by introducing new substance and rules. Two functions of the court have been sought in new school policy—legalization and regulation. *Legalization* involves "establishing a system of decision making committed to rules, trafficking in rights rather than preferences or interests, and justifying outcomes with reasons." *Regulation* involves "efforts of one level of government to control the behavior of another level."[2] These activities of courts, legislatures, and bureaucracies have promoted educational programs such as desegregation and compensatory, special, and bilingual education. Most recently, a favorable court opinion on vouchers in Ohio (*Zelman* v. *Simmons-Harris*, 2002) was just such a stimulus. Such efforts, however, have been subjected to heavy criticism from school professionals and lower governmental officials who must live under these mandates. It is important to remember that this top-down policy movement pursues the value of equity in distributing school resources.

Two central legal concepts justified this legalization, namely, substantive and procedural rights. *Substantive rights* are advocated because students, educationally disadvantaged by the prevailing distribution of resources, had suffered a wrong inflicted on their constitutional rights. These rights were linked to the federal Constitution, particularly the equal protection clause of the Fourteenth Amendment. This process first appeared in *Brown* v. *The Board of Education of Topeka* in 1954, which evoked the right of equity for black segregated students. However, such a right could also be applied—and later was—to equity for handicapped, Hispanic, poor, and female students. Court decisions often stimulated major subsequent congressional action embodying equity rights with application to all school districts nationwide.[3] For example, a 1988 act of Congress said that discrimination in the use of federal funds in one part of an institution—say, a university—could bar such funds for all other parts.

A second aspect of rights in legalization was the emerging concept of *due process in schooling*. That is, students were held to have protections against how school policies were made and implemented; these procedures became fixed in federal law as a result of this judicial stimulus. This was a case of adult legal requirements that were applied to the young. An ancient concept, due process arose from protection in criminal law, rooted as far back as the Magna Carta of 1215 A.D. and in our own Fourteenth Amendment. The procedural protection was spread by litigation in the 1960s to welfare and public employment and in 1975 to education in the Supreme Court decision of *Goss* v. *Lopez*.

Congressional statutes thereupon provided education for handicapped children with explicit procedural protections in the individual education programs that required meetings, hearings, and appeals. Court-based protections against arbitrary suspensions and dismissals have also created elaborate procedural safeguards that school administrators must follow. For example, in many schools today there are many printed rules for expelling a student. In short, new judicial rules from higher courts that rested on student rights had built a new structure for defining school policy.

As the new legalization in education arose, implementing their rulings meant issuing more and more regulations. Officials in Washington and state capitals began by detailing what was required. Then they sought compliance by coercion through detailed oversight, reports, and threats of withdrawing funds. Behind this implementation was the potential threat of litigation if particular children were treated inequitably. Also, many states subsequently incorporated these programs into their own statutes (sometimes under federal stimulus) and thus sought compliance on their own by issuing even more regulations that thrust one more layer of mandates on local officials.

Education was not the only policy area where this centralization occurred; in fact, it was impacted less than others. Analysis of the origins of mandates for twelve different policy areas in the late 1970s found that states were issuing far more regulations than were "the feds." The ratio of state to federal mandates was higher in seven of these twelve areas than in education, with two state actions for every federal one.[4] Even critics of the excesses of legalization and regulation recognize its success. As one scholar notes,

> It bears remarking that the promise of legalization has been greatly fulfilled. The history of America generally and of the public schools in particular may be told as a tale of progressive inclusion in the polity, and in that telling the forms and values of law have a central place.[5]

If the interests of certain groups have been advanced in the name of equity, the interests of yet others have not. Certainly the claim of educational professionals that they provide quality has been challenged, as we have noted throughout this book. Further, the failure of states and local school boards to provide certain groups with access to decision making and district resources also brings into question their commitment to the democratic value of choice. Moreover, the costs—economic or otherwise—of regulations for the system of schooling have not been calculated against their alleged benefits. That is, the value of efficiency in various legal actions has not been much addressed. That charge of the costs of a heavy bureaucracy enforcing legalization became a central argument in reformers urging "choice" schools in the last two decades. They argued that to create a "market" solution to remedy school ills, parents should be free to choose, via voucher payments, schools that would better educate their children. This, they proposed, would eliminate much of the hand of bureaucracy.[6]

This call for reform came at the end of a decade of the Reagan administration trying to overturn many national regulations. "Deregulation" in this case meant federal education budgets being cut, and thirty small categorical grants were combined into a bloc grant with few regulations. Nevertheless, many of the regulations for bigger categorical programs still remained (e.g., compensatory, handicapped, and bilingual education). Also, while the Reagan administration withdrew from the plaintiff's side in desegregation cases, those cases continued, and the Supreme Court continued its support until the early 1990s when Reagan's appointees changed the Court's emphasis. However, the Reagan-sponsored voucher system of school funding got nowhere in Congress in that administration, and the U.S. Department of Education was not abolished. Yet its secretaries reduced some regulations, and its Office of Civil Rights stopped requiring reports on the amount of desegregation. Finally, the attempt of the Office of Management and the Budget to apply cost-benefit measurements to regulations in the area of handicapped education was stalled. That pattern of resistance to change ran through the presidencies of George Bush and William Clinton. Some reforms lost (e.g., desegregation in the Supreme Court), but some continued (e.g., vouchers in the second Bush presidency).

In short, the tenacity of regulation in education often blocked reform. Also, networks of pressure groups defended special programs before often-friendly legislative committees, and the courts were always available, too, as an option for asserting rights against unresponsive local administrators. Nor has federal deregulation down to local districts had much success at the state level, where state groups have closer contact and often greater strength with the formal agencies of state government.

Federal and state courts thus remain arenas for making decisions that may implement earlier legislation—or even overturn it. Notice the cross-currents of legalization's growth and challenge after 1980. The Reagan administration attempted not to enforce earlier laws granting rights or entitlements, but these were blocked by uncooperative federal courts. Nevertheless, parallel reform efforts in the states in this decade—the "top-down" addition of more course requirements—added even more regulations for local schooling. Under the first Bush and Clinton presidencies, efforts began to centralize once again with the effort to get professionals to set *national* schooling standards. The Supreme Court decided in the 1990s to forego desegregation unless there was evidence of official intention to remain segregated, in effect overturning the *Brown* v. *Topeka* decision of almost forty years earlier. After the 1994 congressional election, successful Republicans offered a "Contract for America" that sought to overturn national centralization by abolishing the Department of Education and sending funds back to the states. Years later that had not been done. Indeed, in the second Bush presidency, Department of Education budgets were increased.

The court role in another school reform of the 1990s—vouchers—is of interest. A later chapter evaluates its effects on schooling. The policy called for payment to parents to attend their choice of schools, public or private. Compared to the huge support in the 1980s for state top-down reforms for quality, very few districts or states have adopted vouchers. Thereafter, however, many states created permissive voucher laws or authorized charter schools. Politically the reform has drawn support from many conservative groups and some African American leaders. Teachers' organizations, however, have been firmly opposed, seeing it as a weakening of the public school system. The court role has been to support vouchers rather vaguely at first in only a few cases (e.g., Milwaukee). A 2002 Supreme Court case seemed to support use of public taxes to parents to support attendance at religious schools.

This quick sketch focuses again on the role of the judiciary as a policy arena and on its interactions not only with other federal and state agencies, but with the social environment of ideas about education. We next examine two large-scale examples of this political process in order to flesh out the forces of change and stasis. Desegregation and finance reform policies are illuminating.

THE DESEGREGATION EXPERIENCE

As noted earlier, the Supreme Court initiated and concluded a forty-year experiment in desegregating schools. Experiences in the South and North demonstrate somewhat different results, but the role of the judiciary was a constant in attempting to define this policy.

The Southern Experience

The Court in 1954 in the *Brown* decision overturned an historic Southern practice of legal discrimination of the races in schooling. Moreover, this case was a dramatic departure from the Court's sixty-year-old decisions that "separate but equal" education was constitutionally acceptable.[7] The new decision called for "all deliberate speed" to desegregate, but that was taken by Southern opponents as a signal for delay (although justices later said that "deliberate" had meant "thought out"). Almost forty years later in *Freeman* v. *Pitts* (1992), the Court reversed itself, saying that a court may determine that it will not order further remedies in the area of student assignments where racial imbalance is not traceable, in even a proximate way, to constitutional violations.

Earlier, in facing the *Brown* case but with no specific guidelines, the Southern states resisted for a decade or more by adopting evasive practices, especially "freedom of choice" plans that desegregated very little.[8] As a result, the Court began to insist on changes that would bring the two races together in schools, and a key was the busing of students to achieve that goal. Meanwhile, the administration of President Lyndon Johnson secured a new law providing federal aid to poor schools, but with a requirement that such funds were not available to segregated institutions. Both the judicial and legislative efforts put local districts between a rock and a hard place. Southerners could continue segregating but would lose much needed federal money; or they could attempt desegregation and get funds but would endure local and vocal—often violent—opposition.

Reluctantly, the South chose the latter course, while indignant white Southerners—if they could afford it—fled public schools to new "Christian academies." As early as 1972, the percentage of black students in formerly white schools had risen to 44 percent from 18 percent before desegregation. In the 1970s, however, this increase leveled off and held constant through the 1980s. The results were that the percentage of

- black students in mostly minority schools dropped from 81 to 57 percent,
- black students in heavily black schools dropped from 78 to 23 percent, and
- predominantly white schools fell to 43 percent of all schools.[9]

There was considerable variation among states, with the most desegregation in Kentucky and Florida but the least in Mississippi. The percentage of white students attending schools with blacks points to variation among Southern cities: 61 to 66 percent in Tampa, Louisville, and Greenville, but only 16 to 19 percent in Miami, Atlanta, New Orleans, Memphis, and Houston. On the other hand, no change in these numbers since the 1980s indicates a lack of national leadership to improve conditions. At the local level, then, a "New South" emerged in which there was more desegregation than in the past, with important consequences for the children of both races.[10]

What was occurring in these decades was the growing opposition of national institutions—presidents of both parties, majorities of Congress, and a new Supreme Court majority. In both regions a majority opinion of whites resisted further efforts to improve increasingly black schools and backed it up by increased "white flight" to the suburbs and "deseg academies."[11] Lacking political will by leaders and citizens, the reform went quite far but no further. By the time of the Supreme Court's 1992 opinion that if demography caused segregation, there was no constitutional barrier to its continuation. In that case, an *amicus curiae* brief by fifty-eight scholars of this field petitioned the Court that research had found that desegregation was no failure, as critics alleged—but the Court ignored it. Thereafter, many school districts—including Topeka in the *Brown* case—successfully sought to cast off earlier desegregation orders.

What are we to learn from this reform and counteraction in Court history? First, when forces such as Congress, the presidency, public opinion, and the national media supported desegregation, the Court moved in response. Such response was to overturn previous decades of court opinion and a regional history of racial violence. Second, however, when all those forces turned either indifferent or antagonistic, presidents could select justices who in turn found a means of not compelling desegregation.

Whatever one's views on this policy, or any other, the highest court comes close to following the old political saying that "the Court follows the elections." Given policy impulses from opinion and institutions at Time 1, the Court can innovate. However, given the opposite currents at Time 2, it will be shaped by them, as presidents appoint new members to alter or abolish an earlier policy. On the other hand, though, if all these opinions and institutions continue their support, the Court acts to sustain a policy. A clear case arises with voting rights that have been sustained by the Court. For education policy, then, these sequences illustrate the reality that courts are political institutions.

In the almost sixty years since the desegregation decision of *Brown* v. *Topeka,* its implementation has swung in the body politic from support to rejection. As a Harvard conference reported in late 2002, desegregation in the South at that time was less than that found in 1990, even though some Southern towns were more desegregated in housing. All but West Virginia of these states were less desegregated. That result was traceable to more Hispanics in school and to court decisions that ban use of race in student assignment, as noted earlier. Even teachers were flooding to own-race student bodies. As one scholar at this conference noted, one can't rely on the courts to lead the nation in civil rights on this policy.[12] In short, desegregation evaluation has gone through separate stages, as another analyst noted: from southern reaction to combined federal enforcement, to more conservative opposition by whites (and some black leaders), to a severe decline in students in desegregation schools. Maybe it is time to retire the meaning of this term to another—academic improvement.[13]

THE COURTS AND FINANCE REFORM

Earlier this book pointed out that a major aspect of the new school turbulence is found in efforts to reform the basis of school financing. As with desegregation, the judiciary played a key role in stimulating this effort by formulating a general constitutional wrong and by calling for a change in school policy. Unlike desegregation, though, most of this effort has been a product of the *states'* highest courts. By a narrow five to four majority in 1974, the Supreme Court refused to claim a constitutional safeguard against finance schemes that discriminated between rich and poor school districts. Note that school finances engage three of the four major education values—equity, quality, and efficiency. And if public school critics got their way with school vouchers, there would also be a choice value. Finance is also the issue that most engages legislators every year because it is the largest single expenditure in the state budget.[14] The finance issue is always current, controversial, and relevant to almost everything that schools do.

School finance reform began in California as a result of the stimulus of the state policy issue network cited in Chapter 8. That state's supreme court declared a new principle, in *Serrano* v. *Priest*, that the "quality of public education may not be a function of the wealth of . . . a pupil's parents and neighbors." Financing schemes had to possess "fiscal neutrality." Because California's did not, it offended the equal protection clause of the *state* constitution and so would have to undergo reform. This constitutional approach spread out over half of the state legislatures that faced similar challenges. By 2001 several dozen states had made changes, some minor but others major, to meet this new equity standard. The Kentucky case in the 1980s further expanded finance suits to cover the adequacy of funding as well as it equity.

More inequities than just those traceable to taxable wealth were under attack. Complex state financial formulas were introduced to adjust for such matters as adequacy, city cost overburdens, and special kinds of educational needs of handicapped and vocational programs and of other educationally needy children.[15] The degree of technicality now contemplated in the work of the courts generates serious problems. The courts are involved in areas that scholars debate—how to measure educational adequacy and how to relate finance to pupil attainment? It was much easier when the task was only to devise formulas so that equal property tax effort resulted in equal amounts of local school revenue. Such changes also require more state funds for low-wealth districts. Political limitations also emerge out of the effort to sustain a reform coalition when each partner worries about getting its own slice of limited resources.[16]

The initiative of the state courts thus generated a flurry of legislative actions, and both court and legislature were further stimulated by an elite of scholars and educational reformers. The reformers met with much success in many states, providing authorities with new knowledge and policy options, as noted earlier. If success is measured by the number of states addressing the problem of resource inequity, then the reform did well—over half of the states made changes. However, if success is measured by how much money actually got redistributed to improve the poor's schooling, the evidence is less certain. Certainly, reforms created school finance specialists, possessed of inventive minds, knowledge, and other resources needed to continue fighting. Note, however, that their source lay in the stimulus of state courts.

A second generation of lawsuits later arose claiming that state governments had not met the court requirements imposed from the 1970s. In New Jersey, for example, plaintiffs in 1995 were successful in asserting the problems of the low-property-wealth districts, or big cities. They had received state aid sufficient to close the spending gap with wealthy suburbs and thereby to neutralize the predominant effect of local property wealth on school spending. The *Serrano* case in California, initiated in 1969, was finally settled in 1993 on yet another appeal based on the same reasoning as the 1969 case. The plaintiffs in California and New Jersey acknowledge that each state has made some improvements in its finance formula; but claimants charged that they have not met the standards set by the initial court orders. While finance equity was not a highly publicized issue, it played a role in orienting how the states distributed the large increases voted to enhance academic "excellence."

The debate can never be completely resolved until the courts have heard arguments based on all major educational values. To date, plaintiffs have featured equity and adequacy as their key goal through the method of equalized, per-pupil spending. Often the state defendants have countered with arguments based on quality and efficiency. For example, state defendants claim that no strong correlation exists between per-pupil expenditures and education achievement, and that marginal increases in per-pupil spending are not strong determinants of educational outcomes. Also, defendants assert that waste and inefficiency occur in school spending, with too much money allocated to overhead costs that do not help teachers in the classroom. Voucher proponents contend, on the other hand, that choice should be the priority value by giving money directly to parents rather than to school districts. Parents could then choose which school they wanted, rather than being assigned a school by a public authority. These differing viewpoints will never be fully reconciled, and the courts will be just one of the arenas that the contestants will use to advance their specific values.

THE ROLE OF THE JUDICIARY IN TRADITIONAL AND REFORM LITIGATION

These accounts of two major educational reforms in which the judiciary played a major part do not exhaust either the impact of this process or the reforms; the latter are much too extensive for any but the briefest review. Rather, we now turn to the meaning of the courts in the political process when they deal with public policy.

Judicial and Legislative Policy Functions Compared

It would help first to be reminded that far more similarities exist between what courts and legislatures do than is popularly

known. Formal litigation seems different from the sweaty legislative committee rooms or boisterous chambers, but the differences are only matters of form. Also, some analysts have argued
that reform litigation differs basically from traditional litigation,
partaking more of the nature of legislation than do court decisions.

The distinctions emerge clearly between, on the one hand,
traditional litigation and, on the other, public law litigation and
legislation.[17] The first deals with only two interests of antago-
nists, it looks backward for experience, it provides relief for a
sharply defined violation and, finally, it involves a judge who is
passively unpartisan in the matter. However, public litigation and
legislation possess quite different qualities. They deal with multiple interests and look to future experiences for a "solution"
that will work. The relief sought must be modifiable and involve
many others. Also, the judge and legislators are partisan in the
sense of being policy advocates.

The implementation of decisions requires different behavior
by courts and legislators but both also take on other similarities.
Table 12.1 sets out different tasks that both undertake when they
seek to reform an institution, as was demonstrated in desegregation and finance policies noted above. Implementation breaks
down any time when even one of these tasks is not done. Note
the problems that arise in just one task, for example, "setting
intelligible standards" of compliance. In both policy cases the
highest courts—federal and state—failed in this task in their initial
decrees. When there was no supportive coalition to seek fuller
compliance in the state legislatures—as with desegregation—contending parties then had to go back to the courts to set standards drawn out of specific cases. Yet where there was support for
the court decision, as with financial reform, parties in each state
still had to work their way through the legislative labyrinth, in
which each member was vitally interested in the outcome for his
or her district. Nevertheless, in the finance case, despite its complexity, a more precise set of standards—such as various formulas of tax reform—resulted in the early stages than was the case
with desegregation.

Part of the problem is that actors in both arenas are necessarily vague in their pronouncements in court order or law. Why
should they be so vague? There are some major strategic advan-

Table 12.1

Structural Aspects of Traditional Litigation, Public Law Litigation, and Legislation

Structural Aspect	Traditional Litigation	Public Law Litigation	Legislation
Parties	Two, with mutually exclusive interests	Many with diverse interests—for example, amici in *Robinson v. Cahill*	Intervention by multiple interest groups is the rule
Fact-Finding	Retrospective and adjudicative (what happened, and so on)	Prospective and "functional"—what will work	Problem-solving approach is the norm
Relief	Coextensive with violation—nature of violation determines relief	Violation tells little about relief. New factors, like cost, enter in	Total pragmatism
	Relief closes transaction	Continuing jurisdiction, relief modifiable	Corrective amendments common
	Relief "nonintrusive," especially damages	Relief often entails running local governments	More detailed plans common
	Relief imposed and adjudicated (defendant has no role)	Formulation of decree involves negotiation, compromise	Social reform usually accommodates opposing interests
Decision Maker's Role	Judge is passive as to fact-finding, uninvolved with relief, no public identity	Judge must form court's position on facts, work out relief, and become identified with cause	Legislative fact-finding committees, work on specifics of bill, legislator identification with bill.

Source: William H. Clune with Robert E. Lindquist, "Understanding and Researching the Implementation of Education Laws: The Essential Characteristics of Implementation," Law, Governance, and Education Seminar, Institute for Research on Educational Finance and Governance, Stanford, February 1980, p. 31.

tages to ambiguity under some circumstances. One scholar noted about the Supreme Court on the early desegregation cases:

> Ambiguity may be, in part, a tactic to minimize the anger caused by the opinion. An unclear opinion leaves people puzzled and, consequently, less angry. Ambiguity also leaves the Court more room to maneuver in the future, to change directions as practical requirements arise which recommended such a change. Finally, ambiguity might be marked up to judicial uncertainty regarding its proper role without scheme of government . . . When doctrine is less clear, this leaves more room for the political process to have its way [as] choices can be left to the discretion of others.[18]

If there are change agents who are willing to seize on one aspect of the ambiguous goal that the court sets, as with finance reform, then the political process can be carried out. However, what if judicial vagueness has no decisive public support so that the normal political processes are blocked? That actually occurred in the South for more than a decade after the *Brown* decision and thereafter in the North as Congress and presidents backed off from enforcing both court orders and national law.[19]

Then the other tasks of implementation noted in Table 12.2—monitoring, dispute resolution, enforcement—fell into the laps of the judges. In this process, the highest court at first seeks to provide only broad guidelines, but these get more narrowly defined as more and more specific situations are brought to it on appeal. This means that the lower-level judges become increasingly embroiled in the implementation of desegregation. As a close study of the Boston case reveals, the monitoring judge can get involved in the innumerable minor details of school administration—boundary changes, personnel replacements, and so on—because the local school system ignores or resists the original order to desegregate.[20] Judges become increasingly faced by noncompliance with what for them is a constitutionally based order. They are compelled by their institutional responsibility to take on more of the implementation usually associated with administrative oversight.

An Evaluation of Judicial Action

Clearly, there are limits to what judges can do. Nor is it the case that judges should do nothing because no political support

Table 12.2
Judicial and Legislative Implementation Tasks

Courts	*Legislatures*

Decree formulation:
negotiations between plaintiffs and defendants, use of experts, concern with such factors as fiscal burden and personnel resentment, setting intelligible standards.

Monitoring
retention of jurisdiction and compliance reports, need for master or special experts to serve as unbiased ally of courts.

Dispute resolution:
application of standards to new facts, differing interpretations of standards.

Enforcement:
use of contempt power, brinkmanship, clarification of responsibilities, obtaining new resources, graduated sanctions.

Formation of legislation:
input from interested parties, expert testimony, budgetary role, setting intelligible standards.

Administrative monitoring:
compliance data, field offices, inspections, and so on.

Administrative dispute resolution:
negotiation when standards are unreasonable, appeal to administrative law judge, and so forth.

Enforcement:
continuum of harassment (extra reports, inspections), threatened fund cut-offs, actual cutoffs, and so on.

Source: Note, "Implementation Problems in Institutional Reform Litigation," *Harvard Law Review* 91 (December 1977): 428–63. Copyright © 1977 by the Harvard Law Review Association.

exists for correcting an unconstitutional situation. If this were the case, we could leave the interpretation of every law up to each citizen, an excellent formula for social anarchy and a major reason why we have rules of law in the first place. However, over four decades of judicial involvement in major educational reform and institutional changes, courts have been able to do some things better than others. While one may worry about the limits of legalism, the federal government can indeed provide national standards of service and behavior. However, settlement of the details is better attained by political agencies at all levels of government.[21] Yet, as desegregation demonstrates, what if those agencies not only do not act but even obstruct the national standard?

Judicial Activism and Its Effects

What are the consequences of judicial activism? "Activism" is often criticized by conservatives, who decry much policy change that eventuates. However, in the 1990s, activism took on a conservative stance (e.g., opposition to desegregation), which provoked no opposition from these groups. Let us trace some of the effects of activism in our two policies.

Besides having direct effects on groups of citizens (e.g., the Brown children in the *Topeka* case or Rodriguez in the *San Antonio* case), activism can affect other governmental institutions as well. In desegregation, there is a "ratcheting" effect, in which one court's determination that a particular school practice is discriminatory becomes an input to federal agencies; they then incorporate it into their regulations, which can later be used in other courts as litigation arises. Or courts may affect one another more directly. State supreme courts have been found to influence one another mutually in public policy initiatives, a form of "horizontal federalism," found in school finance reform.[22]

For example, complicated events in New Jersey over financial reform brought the state supreme court into conflict with the state legislature.[23] The latter's lack of guidelines for policy direction, as well as its mandate to correct the inadequacy of a financing law, threw the politics of that state into greater conflict for decades. However, the results did establish education adequacy standards that in turn set off challenges to finance adequacy in other states, just as the California decision in the *Serrano* case in the late 1960s set off a round of challenges elsewhere. A close analysis of the New Jersey controversy concluded that the results demonstrated that the judiciary's main role must be "agenda setting," not "decision making." That is, courts do their utmost when they raise policy issues that other government agencies must resolve but without the courts designating the actual process of solution.

Others have noted the broader policy roles of *state* supreme courts in our history. They have innovated in policymaking, complemented state legislative goals, elaborated the meaning of Supreme Court opinions (but also restricted the latter's opinions to protect their state's laws from invalidation), and lobbied in legislatures to maintain and develop their own institutions.[24] All of these court actions have consequences for public policy. They cause new policy issues to emerge, stimulating discussion of policy alternatives, authoritatively deciding the direction of new policies, and overseeing policy administration.

Judicial capacities are impressive because when undertaking implementation the judiciary possesses considerable authority, trust, and information. A judge is thus in a strategic position in policy conflict to assure that decisions are emphatically enforced. This presence changes the power quotient of the plaintiffs with court sanctions and information that can be added to their side. Policy goals thus can more easily be put into effect. That power combination is evident recently in the new conservative agenda before the Supreme Court in the 1990s. However, courts can also lag in such matters because they can also misconceive and misapply knowledge. As critics of regulation insist, courts can use sanctions that are too clumsy and actually counterproductive.[25] Then, as is true of other governmental agencies who fail in their political tasks, the policy results will not meet plaintiffs' needs and so may generate distrust of the courts.

The Judiciary in the World of School Policy

The judiciary has made its role much more evident in the arena of educational policies in the last four decades. When it *does not* act to define problems and needs, other agencies do so. When it *does* act, new distributions of resources and values usually emerge as educational policy. If both judicial inaction and action have policy consequences, then either condition makes the courts into policy actors. When the Supreme Court sidesteps a decision on the equity value in the finance reform case, then other levels of government feel free to seek their own solutions. However, when that same Court voids legal segregation or later accepts demographic segregation, it sets the scene for actions that effectively alter the practice. If, however, the Court is evasive in defining Northern segregation problems, then lower federal courts take on a much more active and determinative role.

The judiciary, however, cannot do everything, as the initial Southern rejection of the *Brown* decision demonstrated. Intervening between what the court seeks (outputs) and what eventuates (outcomes) are certain barriers. These are raised by group resistance based on other values, by popular ignorance, by communication failure, by information overload, and by other confounding aspects of social and policy conflict. A court mandate does not bring total or quick acceptance, does not provide sufficient resources for the resourceless, and does not teach us how to resolve conflict or to live with ambiguity. However, courts can create a new policy agenda that others in the political system can implement. Other persons and events must perform these tasks, even with a supportive judiciary. While the judiciary has been a major stimulus for educational innovation in the last four decades, it has also met with obstruction, misunderstanding, and uncertainty. The court is thus in the position that Shakespeare described in *Henry IV*, when one character proclaims, "I can call spirits from the vasty deeps," and Hotspur responds, "Why, so can I, or so can any man, but will they come when you do call for them?"

The supreme courts of state and nation have been evoked from their "vasty deeps" by citizens afflicted by racial and fiscal discrimination in education. Despite some reservations about how much courts can do in policy innovation, both judicial friend and foe would agree that little would have been changed without positive judicial response to such calls. That agreement marks the significant potential that inheres in these judicial "spirits." Even on its own, the judiciary can at least create a national dialogue about the standards of education that we will provide our children. In this way, the unthinkable of yesterday becomes in time the convention of today. Creating this flexibility of mind is a function that the judiciary and good teachers share equally.

NOTES

1. The intimate linkage of partisanship and judicial principles was at the core of the litigation over the 2000 presidential election.

2. David Kirp, "Introduction: The Fourth R: Reading, Writing, 'Rithmetic—and Rules," in David Kirp and Donald Jensen, eds., *School Days, Rule Days* (Philadelphia: Falmer, 1986), p. 12. This book is a thorough, often critical, view of these developments but with a balanced sense of what they have produced that is beneficial.

3. For a full review of these leading decisions, see Jay Herbert, ed., *Law and School Reform* (New Haven, Conn.: Yale University Press, 1998).

4. Catherine Lovell and Charles Tobin, "The Mandating Issue," *Public Administration Review* 41 (1981): 321; a recent review is Herbert, *Law and School Reform*, pp. 205–243.

5. Kirp, "Introduction," p. 6.

6. John Chubb and Terry Moe, *Politics, Markets, and America's Schools* (Washington, D.C.: Brookings, 1990).

7. Robert Kluger, *Simple Justice* (New York: Knopf, 1975) is an exhaustive account of this drama.

8. For a thorough coverage of the 1960s, see Gary Orfield, *The Reconstruction of Southern Education* (New York: Wiley, 1969). For the most comprehensive analysis of all phases of desegregation up to 1978, see Gary Orfield, *Must We Bus? Segregated Schools and National Policy* (Washington: Brookings Institution, 1978).

9. Data below from Gary Orfield, *Public School Desegregation in the United States, 1968–1980* (Washington, D.C.: Janet Carter for Political Studies, 1987). A conference of desegregation scholars in 2002 reported in the South less of it existed than before it began. Even teachers are flocking to own-race students. Much of the blame was laid on the courts. *Education Week*, October 11, 2002, p. 5.

10. For a detailed review of how that happened in one Mississippi county, over a quarter century, see Frederick Wirt, *We Ain't What We Was: Civil Rights in the New South* (Durham, N.C.: Duke University Press, 1997).

11. Earl Black and Merle Black, *Politics and Society in the South* (Cambridge, Mass.: Harvard University Press, 1987).

12. *Education Week*, October 11, 2002, p. 5.

13. James Guthrie and Matthew Springer, "Returning to Square One: From *Plessy* to *Brown* and Back to *Plessy*," *Peabody Journal of Education* (2004, in press).

14. Such was the finding in six states in the mid-1980s: Catherine Marshall, Douglas Mitchell, and Frederick Wirt, *Culture and Education Policy in The American States* (New York: Falmer, 1989).

15. A thorough examination is found in Walter Garms, James Guthrie, and Lawrence Pierce, *School Finance: The Economics and Politics of Education* (Englewood Cliffs, N.J.: Prentice-Hall, 1987) and successive editions; Herbert, *Law and School Reform*, 39–87.

16. Michael W. Kirst, "Coalition Building for School Finance Reform: The Case of California," *Journal of Education Finance* 4 (Summer 1978): 29–45.

17. William Clune with Robert Lindquist, "Understanding and Researching for the Implementation of Education Laws: The Essential Characteristics of Implementation" (Stanford, Calif.: Law, Governance, and Education Seminar, February 1980).

18. Herbert, *Law and School Reform*, 39–87.

19. Orfield, *Must We Bus?*, Pt. two.

20. See the details in Emmett H. Buell, Jr., *School Desegregation and Defended Neighborhoods: The Boston Controversy* (Lexington, Mass.: Lexington Books, 1981).

21. David L. Kirp, *Just Schools: The Idea of Racial Equality in American Education* (Berkeley: University of California Press, 1982).

22. In G. Alan Tarr and Mary C. Porter, "State Supreme Court Policymaking and Federalism" (paper presented to the American Political Science Convention, August 1980).

23. Richard Lehne, *The Quest for Justice* (New York: Longman, 1978).

24. Tarr and Porter, "State Supreme Court Policymaking."

25. For education, see Kirp and Jensen, *School Days*.

Part IV:

CURRENT POLITICAL
CONTROVERSIES

13 _____

The Politics of Education Standards

THE POLITICS OF APPROVING CURRICULUM CONTENT STANDARDS*

As the curriculum standards debate demonstrates, curriculum policymaking is essentially a political as well as a technical process. What decision rules will state and local standards bodies use to choose among competing standards alternatives? As noted, politics is the authoritative allocation of competing values. Disputes generated by issues such as AIDS education and creation science highlight the values conflict embedded in curriculum disputes.[1] Proposals to increase curricular scope have reached their logical (and absurd) conclusion when elementary teachers are expected to teach reading, writing, several varieties of arithmetic, geography, spelling, science, economics, music, art, foreign languages, and history. At the same time, they are helping

_____

*The section adapted from Michael Kirst, "The Politics of Nationalizing Curricular Content," *American Journal of Education* 102 (August 1994): 388–392. Copyright © 1994 by the University of Chicago Press.

children to develop physically, morally, and intellectually, and to be molded into good citizens. If the school were to take advantage of the millions of dollars invested in national curriculum development, each of these matters should be treated independently with specially trained teachers. Things are hardly less chaotic in secondary schools.

The oldest and simplest solution to this problem is to endow an individual or small group with the authority to make these decisions by exercising professional, and presumably expert, judgment. This decision-making body (e.g., a state school board or a national subject matter association) is linked to the community that gives it authority and power. This linkage provides the decision makers with a degree of autonomy that ranges from absolute responsiveness to virtual independence.

However, this only pushes our search one step further. What sort of decision procedures do curricular decision makers follow? Past procedures can best be described as following a strategy of *disjointed incrementalism,* that is, a strategy that simplifies complex problems.[2] The major features of disjointed incrementalism are (1) acceptance of the broad outlines of the existing situation with only marginal changes contemplated, (2) consideration of only a restricted variety of policy alternatives, excluding those entailing radical change, (3) consideration of only a restricted number of consequences for any given policy, (4) adjustment of objectives to politics as well as vice versa, (5) willingness to reformulate the problem as data become available, and (6) serial analysis and piecemeal alteration rather than a single comprehensive attack.

So many curricular decision makers have used pragmatic methods of decision making that result in minimal changes at the margin. Conflict can be avoided by using vague language concerning standards and covering so many topics that no major interest group feels left out. Content priority is sacrificed to the political necessity of breadth in coverage.

The push for state and national standards, however, proposes to change this disjointed incrementalism to a nonincremental and complete overhaul of subject matter standards and exams. Examples cited by national standards advocates include recent efforts by the National Council of Teachers of Mathematics

(NCTM) and the California History/Social Science State Framework. The politics of these efforts are complex, as one observer of the NCTM noted:

> Twin needs propelled the development of NCTM's standards for schools mathematics: the need to gain consensus and the need to promote change. On the one hand, if these standards were to stand as the banners of the community, then they had to reflect shared values and commitment. On the other hand, if change was desired, then these standards had to do more than reflect current practice. New ideas were needed, ideas that departed from extant assumptions and practices.[3]

Other curriculum formulation case studies evaluated NCTM, California and New York social studies, science curriculum reform in the 1960s, and the College Board's Advanced Placement Program.[4]

Some political dilemmas confronting policymakers based on these cases are presented below. The list is written from the vantage point of the decisions that will be faced by a state or local standards group when they consider certification of national content standards.

1. Who must be involved in the process to feel it is inclusive? Students? Business? If you exclude groups, this will lead to charges of bias. If you include every group that is suggested, this will lead to a cumbersome and slow process.
2. If you chose standards that achieve a broad consensus in the field, then the "leading edge thinkers" will object. You will be accused of certifying "what is" rather than "what ought."
3. If you chose a standard that achieves consensus in a field you will *not* be able to satisfy demands for "less is more" consensus expands topics rather than cutting them.
4. If you chose a standard that reflects current content consensus, this will lead to criticism that you have not sufficiently stressed interdisciplinary content. There is limited interdisciplinary content in any of the subject matter organizations like NCTM.
5. If you approve standards that are too general, or do not contain pedagogy, you will be criticized that there is insufficient instructional guidance for teachers, and the content

gaps will be filled by tests or assessment. If you do approve
pedagogy or detailed standards, you will be criticized because standards are too long and complex and overly control local practice.

6. If you do not hear appeals from the public for specific
content changes (e.g., inclusion of creation science) then
you will be criticized for not having public participation *at
the highest level* and for leaving crucial decisions to a technical panel of nonelected officials. If the state hears all these
protests it will become bogged down in time-consuming and
fractious disputes.

7. If you approve similar structure or dimensions for all subjects, you will be criticized for ignoring the big (structural)
differences between such fields as math, science, and social studies.

8. If you hear appeals from subject matter subspecialties (too
much physics, not enough biology), you will end up arbi-
trating balance among technical fields within a subject matter
area. If you do not hear these issues, you will be accused
of approving unbalanced standards within a subject area.
For example, there is too much physics and not enough
biology in science content standards.

In short, content standards require complex trade-offs, and
there is no way to avoid conflict and a sense of winners and
losers. Difficult choices must be made concerning content standards
and the procedures by which these standards are set. Merely
following the "right" procedural steps will not be sufficient.

For instance, one constraint is school time, because not everything that all content advocates want can be taught in 180 days
from 8:00 A.M. to 2:30 P.M. The history of curriculum politics
has been one of jockeying for priority in an overcrowded school
schedule. Some curricular priorities are politically organized into
the curriculum while others are neglected. Historically, organized interests like driver education and vocational education have
been more effective politically than have advocates for, say, music
education.[5] Curricular priorities compete for scarce school time,
and national content standards will be no exception. If states
approve multiple content proposals in a field like social studies,

will this provide sufficient local guidance concerning internationally competitive standards set by other countries? Changing concepts about content and new knowledge will make many of these standards quickly outdated. There needs to be a regular revision cycle such as the eight-year cycle for adopting statewide textbooks in California.

Organizations noted in an earlier chapter that favor a limited federal or state government role in school curriculum, such as the Eagle Forum (Phyllis Schafly) and conservative Christian churches, are being opposed by statewide big business groups such as the Washington Business Roundtable.[6] Business groups are concerned that local standards will not provide a well-prepared workforce.

THE FUTURE OF CONTENT STANDARDS

The currency of this debate ignores the fact that content standards and assessments constitute a long-running saga of U.S. curriculum politics. Decisions on what knowledge is most worth knowing are at the center of school politics, even though school finance usually attracts more media attention. National curricular standards are a crucial component of the overall vision of systemic reform.[8] Content standards are a beginning for subsequent state and local policy alignment of textbooks, assessment, staff development, categorical programs, and accreditation. All of these policy areas must be linked to teaching the content standards in America's classroom for systemic reform to succeed. Consequently, the centralization of curricular content at the state and district levels is high-stakes politics.

The future of standards-based reform is at a crossroads. On the one hand are many forces that have helped this reform grow and persist. Policymakers on both sides of the political aisle and across all levels of government (federal, state, and local) have broadly agreed on the merits and worth of this approach to school change, which has persisted despite substantial turnover in leadership. Further, the commitment of No Child Left Behind (NCLB) to this agenda has been remarkable and sustaining. NCLB set in motion a dense array of professional networks that are connecting and providing important support to teachers and school administrators. Many of the state academic content standards themselves have moved to the middle of the change spectrum, seeking a balance between forces calling for more far-reaching innovation and those calling for conserving traditional practices. This more moderate stance may help state standards move forward politically as well as operationally by allowing teachers to incorporate new practices gradually when they make sense both for them and their students.

On the other hand, while standards reforms have been maintained on the educational agenda and while this strategy is increasingly accepted and endorsed by local policymakers, the waters have become more politically turbulent and complex. The reasons are many. There are challenges that any initiative faces when it moves into the schools: untrained teachers, confused parents, and organizational structures that resist change. Given that standards reforms ask teachers to dramatically change their practice by moving beyond the status quo of teacher-talk and drill-and-practice memorization, to know their subjects more deeply, and to help all students master more challenging material, this process exponentially increases in difficulty.

All of these problems raise anew questions about what role administrators should play in standards reform (one not well addressed by state policy), what role a reduced state department staff can play, and how to achieve economies of scale. Is it efficient for each school to create the wheel of curriculum, instruction, and new standards instruction and try to measure up to the new standards on their own? What can districts do to facilitate exchanges, provide support, and fight the insularity that often plagues schools and teachers? Finally, state and district policymakers must learn how to listen to their publics but also teach them about their reform efforts. This requires well-articulated messages and long-term efforts.

Public support and understanding of standards-based reforms remain a major obstacle to the stability of state standards. All states have developed some mechanisms for professional and public feedback during the development of their standards. However, in practice these efforts were brief and looked like public-information campaigns rather than establishing ongoing dialogues for mutual understanding. While some LEAs attempted to mobilize local support for standards reform, these were often isolated efforts. However, most policymakers are at a loss as to know just how to go about creating real and sustained dialogue with the public; they tend to rely on polls for their information about broader public sentiment.[9] These polls have some important limitations, for opinions expressed about education in general can generate different reactions when it comes to one's own children or one's own community. But a Public Agenda poll in 2003 revealed that solid majorities of parents "strongly approve of policies that end social promotion, place low achievers for mandatory summer school, and require high school exit exams."[10] We now turn to a specific case of mathematics and science curriculum standards to elaborate the general issues analyzed above.

THE POLITICS OF DEVELOPING AND SUSTAINING MATHEMATICS AND SCIENCE CURRICULUM CONTENT STANDARDS*

Efforts to formulate curriculum standards have provoked concern over deciding what to teach. Authoritative allocation of highest priority curriculum content in these value conflicts is the essence of what we mean by the political process in curricular decision making. Should schools teach those things that are likely to be immediately useful in life outside the school or those things most fundamental to an understanding of organized knowledge? Should they emphasize the development of individuality or the transmission of a common cultural heritage? So long as people disagree on how to evaluate curriculum, they are bound to quarrel over its composition. The bases for this disagreement can be such things as social class or race.

*Adapted from Michael W. Kirst and Robin L. Bird, "The Politics of Developing and Sustaining Mathematics and Science Curriculum Content Standards," *Advances in Educational Administration*, 5 (1997): pp. 107–132.

Four broad bases for evaluating curricular elements emerge as salient: tradition, science, community, and individual judgment. These values cohere people's preferences, but their conflicting nature creates political stress and demands for curricular changes. They are neither mutually exclusive nor exhaustive, but they do represent major streams of thought and feeling among curricular constituencies. In short, they are ways of answering Herbert Spencer's question, "What knowledge is of most worth?"

The *appeal to tradition,* exemplified in recent times by the Great Books program and the Council for Basic Education, rests on the assumption that subjects of study that survive the test of time are in the long view most beneficial and, therefore, should receive the highest priority in the curriculum. The *appeal to science,* the newest basis for curricular decision making, has received strong support from many influential groups, including the National Science Foundation. This appeal rests on the assumption that educational and psychological research will reveal cognitive concepts that should guide teaching.

The *appeal to community* presupposes that every school is part of a community of association and interests, in which reside the ultimate criteria of usefulness, relevance, and benefit of any curricular element. Therefore, those matters that deserve first priority in the curriculum are to be determined by the community, either directly via its representatives, or indirectly by studies of the community. The *appeal to individual judgment* amounts to a skeptical denial of any rational value basis for curriculum making beyond the student's own values, needs, and desires as these are manifested in his own considered judgments. Adherents of this position argue that any basis for curriculum is doomed to failure if it purports to provide answers to Spencer's question.

Each of these values has its supporters and detractors who bolster their positions with techniques that we regard as political. Some schools stand primarily, and reasonably consistently, on only one of these bases. The curriculum of St. Johns University is based largely on the appeal to tradition, as are the curricula of a number of private "Latin" schools. A number of Christian groups advocate a traditional curriculum. By contrast, several schools embrace a scientific basis, such as constructivist pedagogy or stimulus and response psychological rewards. "Free" schools and "free" universities base their programs on free choices of individual students. Afro-centric schools are oriented to a community focus. By and large, however, U.S. public school programs are a heterogeneous mixture of these different bases. As such, they reflect the political compromises and diverse values found in any state or local district. Science and mathematics conflicts demonstrate these conflicting values over many years.

Recent History of Politics of Science and Math Reform

The political disputes of recent years were foreshadowed by post-World War II developments. Until the 1950s math and science curricula were selected by individual school systems in response to perceived desires of local communities. The successful launch of Sputnik I in 1957 created demands for stronger federal and state roles using two broad strategies: more math and science at all levels and different content and instructional foci.[11]

Nevertheless, there were strong demands for preserving local control on some traditional curriculum matters, and political conflict surrounding curriculum escalated in the 1970s.[12] Efforts to ban books doubled in the first five years of the 1970s over the last five of the 1960s. A 1974 book-banning crusade exploded into life-threatening violence in Kanawha County, West Virginia. The American Library Association reported three to five episodes a week in 1981 ranging from the Idaho Falls banning of *One Flew Over the Cuckoo's Nest* to Anaheim, California, excising Richard Wright's *Black Boy*. After the Warsaw, Indiana, school board banned forty copies of *Values Clarification*, the school board president posed the essential political question, "Who shall control the minds of the students?"[13]

One federal attempt to take a role in influencing local curriculum was rebuffed in the 1970s. Congress cut back the federal curriculum development role in large part because of a 1975 debate on the National Science Foundation's (NSF) proposed social curriculum, "Man: A Course of Study" (MACOS). Typical of this pressure was the charge of John Conlan (R., Arizona) that MACOS was a federal attempt to use classrooms for conditioning, to mold a new generation of Americans toward a repudiation of traditional values, behavior, and patriotic beliefs.[14] Twenty years earlier, however, the federal government had entered the curriculum and text development field because critics alleged that schoolbooks were outdated, inaccurate, dull, and lacking in diversity. Scholars and experts on whom federal and state governments rely have been criticized for trying to impose their own cosmopolitan and secular values upon diverse local communities. Curricular reform itself has been professionalized through government and foundation grants. No longer are perceived crises such as Sputnik required to generate curriculum change, because curricular change now has a self-starting capacity.

Curricular conflict has many roots. Military threats or changes in public sentiment, such as the women's movement, generate value conflict about curriculum, even though this is not why these events were initiated. Other forces, such as court decisions favoring bilingual education or the pronouncements of influential individuals, can change the curriculum orientation without the direct development of new materials. In order to incorporate all these influences, the process of new textbook creation is "managed," whereby a writing team prepares a series of texts. The actual author is frequently the publisher's internal editor, not the authors listed on the title page. Teachers are also contributors to textbook content through their instructional preferences.

These skeletal concepts can be brought to life by the flesh of reality provided in a specific education issue. The reform of the mathematics curriculum in this country from the mid-1950s to the late 1970s nicely illustrates these multiple influences. It also shows the essentially political nature of curriculum decision making, even though professionals often regard curriculum as apolitical and something to be shielded from gross political concerns.

The traditional methods of teaching mathematics in public schools are rooted in early-nineteenth-century pedagogy. For some time, however, mathematicians and math teachers had been discontented with these methods. During this private issue stage of policymaking, discontent was not sufficient to generate anything other than a scattered questioning of the old ways. Some university professors were experimenting with a new approach to math instruction—but there was no sense of urgency to act, and there were no resources to do so. The private-issue transformation stage of policymaking occurred at the confluence of several dramatic events in the late 1960s.

Politics of the New Math: 1960–1970.   Americans were enormously shocked in the late 1950s by the Russian success in orbiting the first space vehicle, the Sputnik. Critics of the American schools were already charging educators with poorly educating the modern generation; they seized on Sputnik as an illustration of how this American "defeat" was attributable to poor schools. Thus, external technological changes were used by reform groups who had been working for changes in math for many years.[15] The media appealed to university curriculum specialists for enlightenment, and parents made demands for action on state and national policymakers; the issue quickly became a public concern and was placed on the political agenda.

The crisis atmosphere of this issue's emergence illustrates how quickly a new national agenda can be created. Congress legislated and the U.S. Office of Education implemented a new law to provide funds for improving the quality of math and language training and for increasing the supply of such teachers. This National Defense Education Act (NDEA) of 1958 provided funds for developing new curricula in math, training employed teachers in the new math, and incorporating these changes into schools of education. In short, this policy output stage elevated the goal of providing students with better math training to national attention by redistributing federal money to teaching methods aimed at that goal.

The implementation stage was impressive in its thoroughness as federal agencies fastened on a particular strategy of raising students' math comprehension. This strategy involved a new way of thinking about math theoretically, which could be taught from the first grade onward by methods that students could easily grasp. There was an attempt to blend the traditional curriculum ladder (arithmetic, geometry, beginning and advanced algebra, trigonometry, and, in some schools, calculus) in many localities. Students were introduced sequentially to different levels and relevant applications of such concepts as set theory. Thus, to get across the concept of numbering, instead of using the traditional method of counting in the base of ten, students were taught to count in the base of seven or another number. The logic of numbering was sought rather than the rote learning of a multiplication table.

Federal funds underwrote eight- to ten-week summer training institutes for many teachers. Special text materials were devised and disseminated; later, computer usages became available. States endorsed these innovations, providing additional funds to incorporate the new into the old math curriculum. Administrative state agencies beefed up their curriculum divisions relevant to math programs and assisted in the implementation of the changes. Local school boards were encouraged to participate by releasing their teachers for summer instruction and to graft the new onto the old. In time, if one's school system did not enjoy the new math, one felt left out of a national tide of change. Recall that such retraining and materials were provided for every level of schooling, and public and parochial schools alike were enlisted in moving the reform into the system and onto the students. This was all done in a remarkably few years.

The program outcome stage produced several results, but one of them was unintended and eventually counterproductive. One goal was to improve math training, and millions of students had been exposed to the new math concepts and understood them reasonably well. Another goal was to institutionalize the reform, and there were thousands of local education agencies (LEAs) that had adopted the new curricular concept. Yet another goal was to prepare students for the application of mathematics to life, and some feedback developed that was quite critical. Parents (who often did not themselves understand the new math concepts despite efforts to give them a quick exposure) increasingly complained that their children could not use mathematics for everyday requirements, such as multiplying or adding in preparing a bill or grocery list.

So widespread did this negative feedback become by the opening of the 1970s that state laws and regulations were altered. State text adoptions returned to the old math, and state tests changed accordingly. Signs that teachers were also reverting to the old math contributed to this reversal. There was little evidence that students were learning mathematical principles any better. With the widespread decline in math and English test scores across the nation in the mid-1970s, few curricula could claim much success, and the new math had no strong constituency within school systems or lobby organizations other than federal leadership through the NSF. It was not easy to monitor whether teachers stressed the new math, and the new math did not stimulate any structural identity within the school bureaucracy. By the mid-1970s, new national priorities for the disadvantaged and the political feedback cycle resulted in a shift away from the new math with little permanent residue. Some teachers continued to partially implement their NSF summer-institute in new math skills, but hostile external forces gradually diminished such content.[16]

The Complexities of Systemic Change. Political developments in the twenty-first century underline the need to change the entire education system, but this strategy entails considerable political obstacles. The systemic reform strategy departs from the traditional practice of leaving content determination solely to individual teachers and local schools.[17] Frequent elections and turnover of key leaders make it very difficult for standards changes to persist long enough for systemwide implementation. The difficulty of re-electing federal and state leaders tends to preserve local control.

Historically, the educational system has not been designed for teaching a high-level curriculum. Federal and state policies have tended to reinforce the use of textbooks and low-level basic skills curricula that have become the *de facto* national curricula.[18] For example, it is typical for schools and teachers to make their decisions about what they will teach by deferring to textbook publishers' tables of contents and to let standardized tests required by states and districts define the skills children should learn.[19] Students are required by the state to take statewide multiple-choice tests and basic-skills examinations that typically emphasize single correct answers. They often do not adequately emphasize analysis, statistical inference, multistep mathematical problem solving, hands-on science, synthesis, expository writing, and complex reading.[20] Neither texts nor tests encourage the development of high-level skills.[21]

In addition, there are no high stakes for the students because teachers typically do not use students' scores on state assessments to determine grades. State tests are not used for college entrance, and employers rarely ask to see a high school transcript.[22] With the lack of explicit consensus about outcomes, low-level skills that are familiar and relatively easy to teach become the *de facto* curriculum.[23] Since the school system has no clear goals or directions, it cannot develop any authentic means by which to judge its progress, and thus, individual schools are left to use teacher grades.

Historically, policymakers have avoided making central determinations of outcome expectations because of support for local control. For the most part, educators have not tried to change the status quo, and many have argued against policy interference of this type in the past.[24] Educators have tended to be highly skeptical about policymakers' ability to develop ambitious and challenging standards for student achievement that can actually be carried out in the classroom. Their skepticism is based on the fact that it is easiest for politicians to set standards at levels that the current capacity can readily achieve. When standards are set too high, however, schools complain because they feel unfairly held to impossibly high standards.[25]

Since many educators do not believe that the government is able to make enlightened education policy using top-down reform, they have placed their hope for educational improvement on individual school (bottom-up) efforts.[26] As long as there is a school-based us-versus-them attitude at the policy level, systemic change may never be successfully achieved.

A third strategy integrates both top-down and bottom-up reform strategies, with both sides working together to help change the system. Project 2061 of the American Association for the Advancement of Science (AAAS),[27] is a good example of the complex politics of systemic reform, as will be elaborated next.

Project 2061: Science for All Americans (SFAA): Systemic Reform Politics

SFAA wrote, "Sweeping changes in the entire system from kindergarten through 12th grade will have to be made if the United States is to become a nation of scientifically literate citizens."[28] *SFAA*'s primary goal is to make every American student science literate by the time he or she graduates from high school.[29] Project 2061 completed Phase I in 1989 by forming literacy goals for science, mathematics, and technology; these are the understandings and habits of mind that the project felt are essential for all citizens in a scientifically literate society.[30] *SFAA* recommends that during students' elementary and secondary school careers, their science education should focus on the following ten themes, each of which includes several major subtopics:

- The Nature of Science
- The Nature of Mathematics
- The Nature of Technology
- The Physical Setting
- The Living Environment
- The Human Organism
- Human Society
- The Designed World
- The Mathematical World
- Historical Perspectives

By identifying these broad themes, Project 2061 differentiated itself from traditional science curricula. "The amount of detail that students are required to know, according to *SFAA*, is considerably less than in traditional science, mathematics, and technology courses. In order to provide a foundation for a lifetime of scientific understanding, ideas and thinking skills are emphasized in Project 2061 at the expense of specialized vocabulary and memorized procedures."[31]

In addition, although many of the topics recommended by *SFAA* are already taught in most schools, "*SFAA*'s recommendations differ from standard practice in their attempts to soften boundaries between traditional scientific and other academic disciplines, emphasizing connections instead." First of all, *SFAA* suggests that through students' academic careers, when they study the ten themes, their science education should revolve around six major organizing concepts: systems, models, constancy, patterns of change, evolution, and scale; students should also understand how these concepts cut across disciplinary boundaries. Second, *SFAA* aims to design a science framework that will lead students to develop three so-called "habits of mind": curiosity, openness to new ideas, and skepticism.[32]

Based on prior curriculum reform attempts, six controversial areas of *SFAA* appear to be:

> (a) interdisciplinary connections that include science, math, technology, and social studies; (b) less content coverage and more in-depth analytical learning; (c) more science in elementary school; (d) greater emphasis on real world application; (e) more math, science, and technology for non-college bound students; and (f) increased use of heterogeneous groups and decreased use of tracking.[33]

All of these components involve significant conflicts and resistance from organized groups. Math groups do not want to be subsumed within the science curriculum, and vocational educators are trying to feature technology education as their own, not as a part of science. The pressures for content coverage rather than in-depth topics are inherent in demands by university admissions and AP exams. The elementary school day is so crowded that some content or activity must be eliminated if science time is increased. Many attempts to detrack schools have caused resistance from parents of higher-achieving pupils.[34]

"Project 2061 has been a reform effort that prizes flexibility and openness in its developmental process" and "as a result, it is a growing organism continuously reshaping itself in response to new information."[35] When curriculum is more flexible and open-ended, however, teachers need to become more active decision makers in the curriculum process than they currently are.[36] But teaching for understanding requires teachers to teach in a way that they were seldom taught and frequently goes against the grain of school organization variables such as forty-five-minute periods.[37]

The Politics of Explicit Science and Math Standards

Today, math and science curriculum developers are bridging the gap between legislation and the classroom by specifying content and performance standards, while trying to give teachers and local school districts a meaningful zone of local discretion over how to achieve the goals of the legislation.[38] There are four main areas of political tension that make it difficult to develop a supportive coalition inside and outside the schools for new math and science curriculum standards: (a) tension between leadership and political consensus; (b) tension between flexible and specific standards; (c) tension between up-to-date, dynamic standards and reasonable expectations for change in the system; and (d) tension between professional leadership and public understanding of what new standards will entail.[39]

Tension Between Leadership and Political Consensus. Previous educational reform efforts, especially large-scale curriculum reforms, have often been criticized for ignoring the social, political, and technical realities of implementation in schools and classrooms.[40] The new mathematics and new science projects that were sponsored by the NSF from the 1950s to the 1970s are good examples of programs that were criticized because parents, teachers, community leaders, administrators, and others "had only limited, if any, involvement in the development of the new curriculum; were uninformed about the changes they were expected to make; and were ill-prepared to defend the reforms when challenges arose at the local levels."[41] Because of the failed reform efforts of the past, educators today are well aware of the types of problems that will arise if notions of change are not widely shared at the community level.[42] Thus, most of the standards projects today try to gather inverse input by engaging professional educators, community members, and others who have an interest in the standards. Gathering diverse input alone, however, will not achieve the development and implementation of leading-edge content standards, because leading-edge content standards are frequently at odds with reaching broad consensus. Many groups have tried to develop consensus around content standards for their field, and even the National Council of Teachers of Mathematics (NCTM), one of the most successful, has been recently subjected to intense disputes.

Nevertheless, NCTM has been fortunate enough to achieve a high degree of initial consensus around the content standards that it designed.[43] The following are some of the processes that NCTM used to enhance the impact of the standards:

1. A long period of preparation prior to convening the standards-writing committees to lay some of the intellectual groundwork for mathematics reform.
2. Broad involvement in the development process. In contrast to past large-scale curriculum reforms, NCTM engaged more educators as well as subject matter specialists on its drafting committees.
3. A far-reaching review and feedback. The organization embarked on an extensive consensus-building process that involved thousands of practitioners, academics, and other professionals as well as members of the lay public in different stages of setting the agenda. NCTM received the endorsement of major professional associations prior to the release of its standards document.
4. An extensive consensus and capacity-building effort after the standards were drafted.[44]

One should not be misled to think that science organizations will be successful at achieving content standards for their specific disciplines just by following the same steps that NCTM followed to formulate their standards.[45] Although the aforementioned processes do seem to have been critical for NCTM to achieve consensus during content standard formulation, there were also other factors that played an important role in NCTM's success, many of which are unique to the discipline of mathematics.[46]

Massell (1994b) describes the uniqueness of mathematics that seemed to aid NCTM in the formulation of its standards in the following manner:

> Mathematics, unlike science, is not fragmented into a large number of competitive sub-disciplines; furthermore, the sub-areas that do exist (i.e., geometry, algebra, calculus) share a common conceptual base and language that facilitates discussions across them and makes goals like "depth over breadth" more easily achieved. In contrast to science, mathematics does not tend to galvanize debate on pressing social issues or political concerns. The mathematics community has relatively few national organizations, and many have overlapping membership. These elements strengthen communication and provide a more solid foundation for consensus.[47]

The less turbulent political atmosphere in regard to standards at the time when NCTM developed its standards in 1988, compared to 1995, also facilitated its success. In fact, NCTM had to use its own resources to produce the standards because "federal and foundation actors did not think a national curriculum document was a good idea."[48] Since NCTM had no external support, it had to construct support for the standards project from within its membership. NCTM was also able to take its time (seven to nine years, depending on how you count) to develop its standards; a luxury today's standards developers do not have.

Although NCTM, by having many factors in its favor and by following the processes it did, was able to achieve a degree of consensus around the content standards it designed, one cannot ignore the fact that there were professional disputes that arose during the formulation process that still linger today. For example, NCTM members have paradigmatic arguments about how basic skills content should be taught along with disagreements over when problem solving should be introduced.[49]

Members who took a behavioral approach argued for a teacher-centered direct instructional method stressing memorization. Behaviorists also argued: You have to crawl/walk before you can run. If formulas aren't memorized, there will be no basis for the mathematical reasoning. If there is no mechanistic answer finding, there will be no conjecturing, inventing, and problem solving. If you don't know a body of so-called isolated concepts and procedures, there won't be any connecting mathematics and its applications. Judicious use of old-fashioned rote memory and drill are as necessary today as they were in generations past.[50]

Other NCTM members thought that classrooms should be student centered with emphasis on mathematical reasoning learned through constructing and solving problems. Their timing argument, and the one that NCTM accepts, is that skills and concepts can and do emerge during the process of problem solving and should proceed in tandem.[51] The *Curriculum and Evaluation Standards* states:

Two general principles have guided our descriptions [of students' activities related to math]: First, activities should grow out of problem situations; and second, learning occurs through active as well as passive involvement with mathematics. Traditional teaching emphases on practice in manipulating expressions and practicing algorithms as a precursor to solving problems ignore the fact that knowledge often emerges from the problems. This suggests that instead of the expectation that skill in computation should precede word problems, experience with problems helps develop the ability to compute.[52]

Even if current science standards developers follow the processes that NCTM used and are aware of paradigmatic conflicts that may arise within their discipline, diverse fields like science did not try to develop standards in the same way as NCTM did.[53] Current science standards developers were not afforded the time they need to build discussion and agreement among their diverse members. When NCTM developed their standards, there were no political or time pressures under which they had to work. Science standards projects, like most other standards projects today, do not have the luxury of taking seven to nine years to achieve initial consensus, but rather are forced to adhere to strict and short timelines. NCTM standards are under widespread political attack for their alleged emphasis upon using calculators and not providing enough training in logic and accuracy. Moreover, parents, employers, colleges, and vocational educators all have conflicting views about math content priorities.

Realizing the improbability of quick consensus among their diverse members and the fact that the high-stakes marketplace of public ideas, professional status, and dollars may make dialogue and consensus a more difficult challenge, some of the current initiatives

have set out to develop national standards in their field without widespread agreement among their members. The actions of these standards initiatives can provide the various fields with a wonderful opportunity for broad-based discussions that may help to clarify the goals and purposes of the fields being discussed. With this in mind, future math and science standards developers may find it necessary to approve standards that not everyone will support in order to achieve the goal of producing leadership in the field; they may even find that they must compromise certain aspects of the standards they want in order to survive political challenges.[54]

Tension Between Flexible and Specific Standards. Historically, the United States has moved from local control of curriculum to increased roles for state and federal governments. Thus, for national standards in math and science to be accepted, the people of this nation must want to have them, and the standards must be flexible enough to allow for local elaboration and variation. Keeping this in mind, Marshall Smith and Jennifer O'Day propose simultaneously to

> increase coherence in the system through centralized coordination and increase professional discretion at the school site. Thus while schools have the ultimate responsibility to educate thoughtful, competent, and responsible citizens, the state—representing the public—has the responsibility to define what 'thoughtful, competent, and responsible citizens' will mean in the coming decade and century.[55]

Today, the term *standard* is typically used as a sort of flag that reflects the valued goals around which educators can rally and decide for themselves how the objectives of the standards will be accomplished in their schools and classrooms.[56] Thus, the new standards developers for math and science may find it undesirable to enforce a particular set of practices or materials. Rather, math and science standards could be designed to direct and guide local choice instead of determining and prescribing practice and teaching. No rigid or specific implications for practice would be inferred from standards.[57]

By being this flexible, math and science standards developers may run into the problem of not knowing when their standards have become so flexible that they can no longer provide leadership.[58] The same concern over flexibility emerged among experts who were trying to design teacher knowledge assessments for the National Board for Professional Teaching Standards:

> By not creating standards at what we would call a fine-grained level . . . standard writers leave the critical work of operationalizing standards for exercises and judging to the assessment developers. We, not the standards committee, . . . imagined the vignettes or examples of accomplished teaching, we attempted to ground the standards in research, and we think the standards committee should have been involved in the assessment effort to operationalize standards.[59]

Therefore, "a certain level of detail in the content standard is necessary to guide the construction of performance standards,

which will then guide test specifications, and finally the development of the tests themselves."[60] If the math and science content
standards do not provide sufficient detail, then they will not pave
the way for "other policy components such as assessment and
instructional materials"; this is the same problem math and science frameworks are struggling with today.[61] Thus, the national
debate on math and science standards

> must go beyond generally worded standards to include the development of
> curricula specific enough to guide teaching and assessment. These must be
> the first steps; a syllabus-based examination system will have to wait until
> standards are established, because we cannot insure that students have a
> fair chance to learn what is tested until we have a curriculum in place.[62]

But with more specificity comes less flexibility for people at
various levels in the system and more political objections to
policymakers who do not work in classrooms, telling teachers
what to teach. Developing numerous, relatively detailed, and precise
strands of content keyed to a common set of standards is a possible resolution to the flexibility/specificity dilemma.

*Tension Between Up-to-Date, Dynamic Standards and Reasonable
Expectations for Change in the System.*   In its 1992 report, "the National Committee on Educational Standards and Testing called
for dynamic content standards, that is, standards that are continuously updated to reflect advances in scholarship."[63] But, how
often should standards be revised? We already know how difficult it is to develop standards, and with all the interlocking systemic components like teacher repertoires, instructional materials,
and assessments that take time and significant resources to develop, frequent revisions are not practical. California currently
revises its curriculum frameworks in a subject area on a staggered, eight-year schedule. That is, one particular content area
framework is reviewed every eight years, with a new subject being addressed each year by the state policymakers. Eight years
may seem like a long time, but breaking the process up into the
time it takes to complete each step demonstrates that eight years
can become a very short time. For example, it takes approximately
two years to revise the curriculum framework, and then publish-

ers must be given enough time to align their texts accordingly. Furthermore, staff development, assessment, and other facets of the system must be constructed and implemented in the schools.

California has been frequently criticized for having its frameworks and assessments ready before the staff development and curriculum materials were in place.[64] Although the staggered schedule does not present a great burden of change on junior high, middle school, and high school teachers, it does for elementary teachers because they are responsible for a whole range of subjects and, therefore, have to reassess a key component of their curriculum every year;[65] district curriculum supervisors have the same problem.[66] Thus, math and science standards developers must keep in mind a practicality and feasibility timeline; revised standards do nothing to help educate students if educational resources and systems cannot keep up with them.

Many educational frameworks, standards, and materials for mathematics, science, and other disciplines are also criticized because they tend to cover a wide range of material superficially instead of emphasizing in-depth learning of key concepts. Typically, such broad and vague frameworks do not push publishers to develop high-quality material, have little impact in the classroom, and are "seen as little more than 'good doorstops.'"[67] When they are provided to districts, schools, and teachers, they have little effect because of their intentionally vague language.

The politics that emerge between and among discipline members is a large factor that leads developers to focus on breadth rather than depth. For example, when frameworks and standards are being developed for a field such as science, which has various subareas (e.g., biology, chemistry, physics), it is hard to get developers to reach a consensus concerning what should be covered in depth.[68] Instead of working together and compromising so as to develop in-depth coverage of a few key topics, developers tend to include everything. By using broad and vague terms the developed subareas (like physics or biology) do not offend, because topics from one area do not get emphasized more than another.

Tension Between Professional Leadership and Public Understanding of What New Standards Will Entail. Parents, religious groups, and other factions in society will continue to have an effect on the wording and contents of standards documents and on what teachers choose to teach in their classrooms. Challenges to public school programs and materials are nothing new in America. As Martha McCarthy notes:

> For decades civil rights groups have been challenging materials as racist or sexist or as curtailing free speech; consumer groups have been contesting materials that promote bad health habits; environmentalists have been critical of texts that do not encourage global responsibility; and parents and religious groups have objected to the language and orientation of particular books, courses, and activities.[69]

Recent disputes, however, are different from the above-mentioned challenges in many ways. In the 1960s and 1970s "the most vociferous critics of public education usually came from the political left."[70] Since the 1980s, however, more and more critics of public education have come from conservative citizen groups; the groups have been labeled the "new right." Also, the number of challenges has increased dramatically, and the central focus of the challenges has broadened from single books to entire programs and strategies to redesign schooling.[71] In addition, the disputes have galvanized considerable media coverage. "Battle lines are clearly drawn, misinformation abounds, vicious accusations are being hurled, logic is often replaced by emotion, and there seems to be little desire to compromise."[72]

The conflicts today seem to reflect the different values and world views of educators, parents, business leaders, and policymakers in regard to not only the purpose of schooling, but also the relationship between individual and societal interests in a democratic society.[73]

Local and State Policy Influentials in Standard Setting

Math and science political conflicts must be decided by some authoritative political body (e.g., state or local government entities), if they are to become official policy. The critical state decision makers for math and science standards will be different from those for policy in general and dependent on the political traditions within a particular state and local context. To understand the politics of policymaking, it is necessary to highlight

Table 13.1
Ranking of Science Curriculum Influentials

State Level

Insiders

Professional associations in science, math, and social studies, NSTA, AAAS, American Chemical Society, etc.

Higher education policymakers and professors in science and related disciplines.

State curriculum framework policy makers.

Textbook publishers/testing agencies (private industry).

NSF Curriculum Development

National Research Council.

Leaders in education policy in the legislature.

Near Circle

State Board of Education (Text Adoption States)

Teacher preparation institutions + teacher certification, National Council for Accreditation of Teacher Education, National Board for Professional Teaching Standards, and American Association for Teacher Education.

Ideological interest groups (e.g., creationists).

U.S. Department of Education No Child Left Behind)

Far Circle

Organizations of state officials, National Governors' Association, Education Commission of the States.

Council of Chief State School Officers.

Sometimes Players

School accrediting agencies (e.g., North Central).

Business organizations, minority organizations.

Notes: Categories adapted from Mitchell, Marshall, and Wirt, *Culture and Education Policy in the American States* (London: Falmer, 1984). Rankings based on review of literature concerning the politics of curriculum policymaking.

the key actors. For example, many insiders and crucial players for science standards are "sometimes players" in general state policy analysis. Our rankings for science curriculum influentials at the state level is presented in Table 13.1. The ordering is from the most to least influential in terms of being able to help determine state and local science policies.

Table 13.1 suggests science standards reformers should focus on the insiders and the near circle and devote less attention to the far circle and sometimes players. The No Child Left Behind requirement to include science in state accountability testing in

2007 creates more federal influence. There is considerable conflict over whether these state tests should focus on direct instruction, or on more laboratory and exploratory skills. Business
groups, however, can be mobilized behind science/math reform
and are quite influential. There are also many crucial players at
the local level that will help determine the success or failure of
any standards proposal:

- Local School Boards
- Teacher Unions
- Administrators
- Parent Organizations
- LEA Curriculum Supervisors
- Department Chairs

Some of the key local influentials are not organized in any
way above the school or school district level (e.g., department
chairs). They can be crucial in a specific locality, but they are
very difficult to target in a general reform strategy.

Final Thoughts on Math and Science Standards

Math and science content standards and exams are another
chapter in the long-running saga of U.S. curriculum politics.
Decisions on what knowledge is most worth knowing are at the
center of school politics, even though school finance usually attracts more media attention. Curricular standards are the crucial component of the overall vision of systemic reform.[74] Content
standards are a beginning for subsequent state and local policy
alignment of textbooks, assessment, staff development, categorical programs, and accreditation. All of these policy areas must
be linked to teaching the national content standards in America's classrooms for systemic reform to succeed. Consequently,
standards for math and science content are high-stakes politics.

Some potentially useful political strategies for math and science curriculum developers include better public engagement
and parent involvement; coalition building with business, higher
education, vocational education, and teacher organizations; and
a recognition that some value conflicts are so deep that no reason-

able compromise is possible. But these curriculum wars have been going on since the eighteenth century, as the losers fight to overcome their losses. The recent trend has been declining influence of professional educators and disciplinary scholars.[75]

NOTES

1. Frederick Wirt and Michael Kirst, *Schools in Conflict* (Richmond, Calif.: McCutchan, 1992).

2. Charles Lindblom and David Braybrooke, *A Strategy of Decision* (New York: Free Press, 1963).

3. Deborah L. Ball, *Implementing the NCTM Standards: Hopes and Hurdles* (East Landing, Mich.: National Center for Research on Teacher Learning, 1992), pp. 2–3. For an overview of mathematics politics in California, see Suzanne Wilson, *California Dreaming: Reforming Mathematics Education* (New Haven, Conn.: Yale University Press, 2003).

4. Diane Massell and Michael Kirst, "Formulating National Content Standards," *Education and Urban Society* 26: 2 (February 1994). See also Jo M. Fraatz, *The Politics of Reading* (New York: Teachers College, 1987).

5. Wirt and Kirst, *Schools in Conflict.*

6. Julie E. McDaniel et al., "The National Reading Policy Arena," *Educational Policy* 15: 1 (March 2001): 92-114.

7. Douglas E. Mitchell and William Boyd, "Curriculum Politics in Global Perspective," *Educational Policy* 15: 1 (March 2001): 58-75.

8. Marshall Smith and Jennifer O'Day, "System School Reform," in Susan Fuhrman and Betty Malen, eds., *The Politics of Curriculum and Testing* (New York: Taylor and Francis, 1991), pp. 223–267.

9. Diane Massell, Michael Kirst, and Peg Hoppe, "Persistence and Change in State Education Reform" (paper presented to the 1996 annual meeting of the American Education Research Association, New York, April 1996).

10. Jean Johnson and Ann Duffett, *Where Are We Now?* (New York: Public Agenda, 2003). For more depth see Lorraine McDonnell, "Assessment Policy as Persuasion and Regulation," *American Journal of Education* 102: 4 (August 1994): 394–420. See also Mary Lee Smith, Walter Nernecke, and Audrey Noble, "Assessment Policy and Political Spectacle," *Teachers College Record* 101: 2 (Winter 1999): 157–191.

11. Gary Yee and Michael Kirst, "Lessons from the New Science Curriculum of the 1950s and 1960s," *Education and Urban Society* 26 (1994): 158–171.

12. Peter B. Dow, *Schoolhouse Politics: Lessons from the Sputnik Era* (Cambridge, Mass.: Harvard University Press), 1991.

13. Wirt and Kirst, *Schools in Conflict.*

14. Ibid.

15. Dow, *Schoolhouse Politics.*

16. Ibid.

17. Susan Fuhrman, "Politics of Coherence," in Fuhrman, ed., *Designing Coherent Policy: Improving the System* (San Francisco: Jossey-Bass, 1993), pp. 1–34. See also Tom Loveless, ed., *Curriculum Wars* (Washington, D.C.: Brookings Institute, 2001).

18. Richard Elmore and Susan Fuhrman, *The Governance of Curriculum* (Alexandria, Va.: Association for Supervision and Curriculum Development, 1994). For a recent view see A. J. Binder, *Contentious Curricula* (Princeton, N.J.: Princeton University Press, 2002).

19. Ibid.

20. Michael Kirst, "The Politics of Nationalizing Curricular Content," *American Journal of Education* 102 (August 1994): 383–393.

21. Doug A. Archbald and Fred Newman, *Beyond Standardized Testing: Assessing Authentic Academic Achievement in Secondary School* (Reston, Va.: National Association of Secondary School Principals, 1988); Norah Frederickson, "The Real Test Bias: Influences of Testing on Teaching and Learning," *American Psychologist* 39 (1984): 193–202; Fuhrman, "Politics of Coherence"; Harriet Tyson-Bernstein, "The Academy's Contribution to the Impoverishment of American Textbooks," *Phi Delta Kappan* 70 (1988): 193–198.

22. Kirst, "Politics of Nationalizing Curricular Content."

23. Fuhrman, "Politics of Coherence"; Smith and O'Day, "System School Reform."

24. Fuhrman, "Politics of Coherence."

25. Diane Ravitch, *National Standards in American Education* (Washington, D.C.: Brookings Institute, 1995).

26. Michael Cohen, "Instructional Management and Social Conditions in Effective Schools," in Allan Odden and L. Dean Webb, eds., *School Finance and School Improvement Linkage for the 1980s* (Cambridge, Mass.: Ballinger), 1983; Larry Cuban, "School Reform by Remote Control: SB813 in California," *Phi Delta Kappan* 66 (1984): 213–215; Richard Elmore, "The Development and Implementation of Large-Scale Curriculum Reforms" (background paper prepared for the American Association for the Advancement of Science, 1993); Fuhrman, "Politics of Coherence"; Stewart C. Purkey and M. Smith, "School Reform: The District Policy Implications of the Effective Schools Literature," *Elementary School Journal* 85: 4 (1983): 358-389.

27. American Association for the Advancement of Science, *Project 2061: Science for All Americans* (Washington, D.C.: Author, 1990).

28. Cited in Diane Massell and Margaret Goertz, *2061 POLICYBlueprint* (unpublished manuscript prepared for the American Association for the Advancement of Science, Washington, D.C., October 1993).

29. Michael Kirst, B. Anhalt, and R. Marine, "Politics of Science Education Standards," *The Elementary School Journal* 96 (Winter, 1997).

30. American Association for the Advancement of Science, *Project 2061.*

31. Ibid., p. 5.

32. Ibid., p. 6

33. David Tyack and Larry Cuban, *Tinkering Toward Utopia* (Cambridge, Mass.: Hanan, 1996); Kirst, Anhalt, and Marine, "Politics of Science Education Standards."

34. Kirst, Anhalt, and Marine, "Politics of Science Education Standards."

35. Massell and Goertz, *2061 POLICYBlueprint*, p. 2.

36. Ibid.

37. Elmore, *Large-Scale Curriculum Reforms*; Massell and Goertz, *2061 POLICYBlueprint*, p. 30.

38. Elmore and Fuhrman, *The Governance of the Curriculum*; Jennifer O'Day and Marshall Smith, "Systemic Reform and Educational Opportunity," in Fuhrman, ed, *Designing Coherent Education Policy*; Smith and O'Day, "Systemic School Reform."

39. Diane Massell, "Setting Standards in Mathematics and Social Studies," *Education and Urban Society* 26 (1994): 118–140.

40. Dow, *Schoolhouse Politics*; Milbrey McLaughlin, "The RAND Change Agent Study: Ten Years Later," in Allan Odden, ed., *Education Policy Implementation* (Albany: State University of New York Press, 1991); Yee and Kirst, "Lessons from the New Science Curriculum."

41. Diane Massell, "Three Challenges for National Content Standards," *Education and Urban Society* 26 (1994): 185–195.

42. C.G. Carlson, "The Metamorphosis of Mathematics Education," *Focus* 27 (Princeton, N.J.: Education Testing Service, 1995).

43. Massell, "Three Challenges."

44. Massell, "Setting Standards," and "Three Challenges."

45. A. Collins, "National Science Education Standards in the U.S.: A Process and Product," *Studies in Education Science* 26 (1995): 7–37.

46. Massell, "Three Challenges."

47. Ibid., p. 188.

48. Ibid.

49. Massell, "Setting Standards."

50. Carlson, "The Metamorphosis of Mathematics Education."

51. Massell, "Setting Standards."

52. National Council of Teachers of Mathematics, *Curriculum and Evaluation Standards for School Mathematics.* (Reston, Va.: Author, 1989), p. 254.

53. Collins, "National Science Education Standards."

54. Massell, Three Challenges," p. 189.

55. Smith and O'Day, "Systemic School Reform."

56. Ravitch, "National Standards."

57. Ball, *Implementing the NCTM Standards*; Miles Myers, "Problems and Issues Facing the National Standards Project in English," *Education and Urban Society* 26 (1994): 141–157; Gary Sykes and Peter Plastrik, *Standard-setting as Educational Reform* (paper prepared for the National Council on Accreditation of Teacher Education, Washington, D.C., 1992).

58. Massell, "Three Challenges."

59. P. Pence and Anthony Petrosky, "Defining Performance Standards and Developing an Assessment for Accomplished English Language Arts Teaching of Young Adolescents (paper presented at the annual meeting of the National Council on Measurement Education, San Francisco, April 1992).

60. Massell, "Three Challenges," p. 192.

61. Ibid.

62. D.M. Korertz, George Madaus, Elizabeth Haertel, and Albert Beaton, *National Educational Standards and Testing: A Response to the Recommendations of the National Council on Educational Standards and Testing* (Santa Monica, Calif.: RAND, 1992).

63. Massell, "Three Challenges," p. 193.

64. Massell, "Three Challenges."

65. Ibid.

66. D.D. Marsh and Allan Odden, "Implementation of the California Mathematics and Science Curriculum Frameworks," in Odden, ed., *Education Policy Implementation*, pp. 219–240.

67. Massell, "Setting Standards," p. 119.

68. Collins, "National Science Standards."

69. Martha McCarthy, "Challenges to the Public School Curriculum: New Targets and Strategies," *Phi Delta Kapan* 75 (1993): 55–60.

70. Geoff Whitty, "The Privatization of Education," *Educational Leadership* 41, no. 7 (1984): 51–54, p. 52.

71. McCarthy, "Challenges to the Public School Curriculum." See also Jonathan Zimmerman, *Whose America? Culture Wars in the Public Schools* (Cambridge, Mass.: Harvard University Press, 2002).

72. Ibid., p. 55.

73. Ibid.; Robert J. Marzano, "When Two World Views Collide," *Educational Leadership* 15: 4 (1993–1994): 18–19.

74. Smith and O'Day, "Systemic School Reform."

75. Peter Schrag, "The New School Wars: How Outcomes Education Blew Up," *The American Prospect* (Winter 1995): 53–62; Fraatz, *The Politics of Reading.*

14

Policy Evaluation: The Case of Choice Schools

The education policies described in this book each face at the end a common query—Did the policy work? That is, did the policy accomplish its intended goals? If not, what then? This phase of policy studies is called "evaluation" It has a temporal dimension, that is, *the study of policy effects must be over time.*

Much of policy analysis rests on data in government reports, journals, or even books. However, such sources describe only short time periods, for example, a year or perhaps five years. Very little analysis looks at data over longer periods, say, two to five decades. An example of a long-run analysis of educational policy is the earlier chapter's evaluation of Southern school desegregation that reviews thirty years of data. Another long-run analysis looked at over fifty years of data on the education provisions of the 1944 GI Bill of Rights.[1] In this chapter we will focus on one example of short-run analysis, choice schools, because of the practical and analytical benefits of such evaluation.

THE BENEFITS OF SHORT-RUN POLICY ANALYSIS

One practical benefit of short-run analysis is that it always requires fewer resources for research than do evaluations of policy far into the future. As we will discuss, down that long road there are effects that may be harder to trace. We can understand this benefit of short-run analysis if we understand the audience for the products of such research. These are private groups and public officials who oversee a policy's implementation, or who benefit from it. Short-run research, often termed "formative evaluation," can influence subsequent implementation of a policy. Many of these participants know that research may stimulate immediate political pressures on the policy's implementation. That awareness gives rise to a continuing quality of evaluation, namely, the *problem of immediacy in the policy world*. That short-run context shapes policy officials' focus on the present as well as their lack of interest in the long-run impact, often termed "summative evaluation."

This point needs emphasis. Short-term evaluation arises and operates within layers of, first, policymakers (who are often elected) and, second, policy beneficiaries. In their immediate world, policy actors operate among what one scholar terms different "streams" of problems, policies, and politics with which they must cope.[2] That is particularly so when these streams combine to place new ideas on what the policy should be, that is, the government agenda. The policymakers are most often involved in ongoing policy conflict that may connect to the next election. For this group, an important consequence is the upcoming election.

Short-run judgments of policy effects can help or hinder a policy's success. Similarly, for the appointed policy administrators, evaluation of a policy's recent effects can influence their next budget requests to the legislature. After all, the policy context is primarily relevant to officials who see themselves as responsive and responsible to the *contemporary* political scene—but not to one that lies far down the road. In short, the officials' concerns with policy analysis is most often focused on the near future in order to enhance their status or power. Interest groups form around new programs and will react to short-term evaluation. For example, charter school operators are vigilant about positive or negative short-run research that compares their achievements with that of non-charter schools.

On the other hand, research into long-range effects may well not influence—indeed may even weaken—the efforts of policy officials to implement a certain program. That is, research may show that over time the policy could possibly be injurious in some way. For example, southern Democrats in the mid-1930s voted to support a federal law to assist poor farmers to purchase land. These leaders thought *white* farmers would use this aid. Yet within a year, black farmers had used it frequently, and as a consequence southerners killed the law the next year. The law not only resulted in unintended short-run consequences for this segregationist group of white officials, but decades later these independent black farmers formed one major group in support of civil rights changes.[3] In effect, if in the short run the results are shown to be negative, then officials are reluctant to look any further for their political survival. Policy officials, then, may support the truth of Samuel Johnson's adage, "The future is purchased by the present."

There is also another benefit in short-run policy research— namely, it avoids problems arising from the uncertainty of measuring causation over a long period. This *problem of infinite causation* causes many scholars and policymakers to focus on the near past and the short future. They would call these qualities "realities," which are much easier to deal with than the uncertain "possibilities" that lie much farther ahead. After all, "long term" implies there may arise new causes and new effects that may be threatening to one's program. The reverse is also true. Those seeking *prior* explanations for current policy effects can lead themselves backwards to an infinite set of explanations that become increasingly fuzzy about what had caused what.[4] For example, did World War II veterans achieve postwar economic success due to the use of the GI Bill of Rights? Or was success caused by a nationwide prosperity that benefited everyone, regardless of education?

Another reason for support of short-term analysis lies with the *problem of actually measuring long-run effects*. To measure recent effects of a policy one may ask those who are the target of the policy. That is relatively easy to do; for example, many major cities now conduct citizen consumer surveys to test their agencies' responses to local services. However, data on long-term effects are much more difficult to obtain. The data on schooling over past years rest with the federal government's National Center for Education Statistics. For many scholars these data look "hard" and thus reliable. Even better, data can be traced back a few years to measure effects. However, what if one wants to test a policy's effects for, say, ten, twenty, or fifty years? A problem may be that the data may well appear incomplete if the same measurement term is not used every year or if common terminology is not used at all. Or the *policy* may be worded differently at different times. In short, long-run research may find objective data harder to obtain and more difficult to measure, especially when unexpected future effects may arise.

In contrast, short-run research is highly useful for informing the ongoing debates over expanding or contracting policy services. One widespread example is seen in the annual debates over budgets, say, those for schools. There is a high and very significant correlation between the amount spent in the last year and the one sought for the next year. One reason for this correlation is that it is easier for all parties to deal only with marginal changes in the year ahead. That political condition accounts for the heavy reliance of public policy on *incrementalism*, namely, growth through only minor changes over time. Moreover, large changes worry policymakers who become fearful of the effects of such big, nonincremental change on their status, power, and constituents. Given that fear, it is easier to make small changes with small budget increases. Note, though, that small changes have a curious effect; they can produce major changes if sustained over time. One illustration is the increased proportion of those attending schools in the last century. In 1900 students attended school an average of eight years; in the 1990s it was twelve and a half years. Over the decades no big jump occurred, but gradual increments made this large increase possible.

Given these common forces working within policy of any type, it is not surprising that there is no incentive for any policy actors to take the long view of their work. Yet the short run may have good effects, as we will see in the recent education reform of choice schools.

SHORT-RUN ANALYSIS OF SCHOOL CHOICE REFORMS

How well students are taught is a major criterion for judging public education. Since the end of the nineteenth century, meeting this criterion has rested with school professionals, as set out in earlier chapters here. Their profession worked to institutionalize across the nation a large set of requirements such as higher quality in teaching, improved curricula, and more testing. Moreover, both educators and lawmakers shared a belief, which intensified from 1900 to 1920, that education professionals knew best what to teach and how to measure it.

Of course, the complaints regularly heard from parents might have indicated that not all students were taught effectively. These complaints grew after World War II, and the national reform movements noted earlier in this book were shaped by these complaints:

- In the 1950s it was that "Johnny can't read."
- In the 1960s it was that we lacked scientific training to counter the Russian threat in space.
- After 1960 it was that schools discriminated against minorities.
- In the 1980s it was that our economy was lagging behind other countries like Japan due to inadequate K-12 education.

In keeping with the dissatisfaction theory of democracy set out in earlier chapters, some complaints, often heard from critics across the nation, generated new laws to improve the effectiveness of schooling. However, the impact of state or federal laws on local schooling (other than to require more reports) is unclear, to judge from the previous chapter. The problem is that detailed analysis of such effects is missing, although there is evidence of increased state impact on curricula and local testing that, as a scholar has noted, "may be influencing local schools in potentially powerful ways that have not been broadly recognized."[5] Over the last three decades there has been an increased role of states and Washington in seeking to remedy some dissatisfaction with local school effectiveness, including a huge increase in state and local laws.

In the 1990s, however, wide dissatisfaction with public schools led to a systemwide reform *outside* the traditional public schools.

This reform adopted a new concept of schooling as constituting a "market." The concept was to create alternative schools to compete with traditional public schools, which would improve the effectiveness of both. While the movement by the early 2000s affected only a small minority of school buildings or school districts, the attendant publicity by scholars, practitioners, and lawmakers was huge. This push for choice alternatives has clearly reflected a deep dissatisfaction with previous education policy. In addition, we will see that this reform has followed a typical policy cycle where reform leads to more policy conflict, which in turn leads to more politicization and more laws.

Definitions and Justifications for School Choice

The fundamental thesis, fully set out by the reform's intellectual godfathers, John Chubb and Terry Moe,[6] is that public schools lack competition, which leads to a monopoly of educational services, to a centralized bureaucracy that resists challenge to individual decisions, and to a lack of outreach to the parents and the community. It is these alleged conditions that create not only a monopoly but also a lack of democracy in public schools that contributes to parents' increasing dissatisfaction with those schools. As a remedy, reformers advocate creating alternative schools that would generate competition, which would in turn cause public schools to focus on customer satisfaction, much like other private businesses do in the marketplace. That is, schools must satisfy the consumers or go out of business. Moreover, to succeed in a competitive market, public schools must reform their own policies and attitudes in order to meet the public's demands. In short, competition could act to modify and improve both alternative choices and the traditional public schools.[7]

The choice reform takes primarily two modes—vouchers and public charter schools—both of which rely on changing the funding and structure of public schools. The voucher reform, in its simplest form, involves parents receiving public money to move their children either to new schools in the public system or to private schools. Despite some variation in this system (for example, the dollar amount of the voucher), this reform seeks an alternative educational system funded through vouchers. The public charter school reform enables certain groups (teachers, administrators, private parties) to create their own schools. These schools are removed from the constraints of many—but not all—state and local regulations, which allows for the development of non-standard educational approaches. The voucher reform takes money from the public schools by using the public taxing system for alternatives, and the charter school reform creates schools that may operate with reduced or no state regulations.

Table 14.1 outlines the significant differences in these two reforms. This brief description cannot, however, address the considerable complexity of how such reforms have been implemented in the fifty states. This variety was illustrated in a study in the 1990s of how four states worked to build charter school systems against opposition, as the reform quickly became a political and partisan issue.[8] The analysis found conceptual variations among the states' charter schools that arose from the role of governors, partisan control of the legislature, and the influence of teacher unions. There is variety in the meaning of the basic term "authorization" of a school found in the charter school laws of twenty states. For example, there might, or might not, be limits on charter authorization, on who may start one, on the independence from the local school board, on exemptions from existing school law, and on how many schools may open in a state. Consequently, the simple outline of Table 14.1, while useful in clearly presenting the major differences in these reforms, ignores the great complexity of choice reforms that now exist among the American states.

Table 14.1
Differences between Voucher and Charter Systems

Subject	Charter Public Schools	Voucher (unregulated)
Access: Admission Standards	May not impose academic or athletic admission standards; oversubscribed schools may select students by lottery.	May impose whatever constitutional admissions standards they see fit.
Tuition	May not charge tuition or fees.	May charge tuition or fees.

Accountability:

Authorization	Must obtain charters from public bodies in order to receive public funds	Must meet only minimal (procedural) requirements to receive public funds.
Performance Contracts	Failing to meet contractual performance targets can lose charter.	Do not sign performance contracts.
Religion	May not provide religious instruction or affiliate with religious institutions.	May provide religious instruction and/or affiliate with religious institutions.

Source: Bryan Hassel, "The Case for Charter Schools," in Paul Peterson and Bryan Hassell, eds. *Learning from School Choice.* (Washington, D.C.: Brookings, 1998), p. 38.

Patterns of Reform Adoption in the 1990s

Amid such conflict, some states such as Florida developed both charters and vouchers, and states' adoptions grew after the early 1990s. As we will see, though, there is a contrast to be found between the proclaimed support that is drawn from these increasing numbers and the actual impact of these reforms on the nation's public school system.

Charter Schools. After at least a decade of reform, in the 2001-2002 school year 2,400 charter schools were in business, up from just three, as Table 14.2 shows.[9] These charters vary in such matters as enrollment, costs, teachers, and what agency authorizes the charter contracts (e.g., local or state boards, universities, and even city officials). In addition, while laws in thirty-nine states and the District of Columbia allow for charter schools, twenty-one states have actually adopted them. The number of charter schools in each state ran from 451 (Arizona) to 7 (Oklahoma); many schools had waiting lists of parents seeking placement from public schools.[10] Many charter schools are located in big-city districts, and hence they enroll a large number of minority students.[11]

Table 14.2
Charter School Increases, 1992-2001

Year Beginning	Number of Schools
1992	3
1993	42
1994	106
1995	254
1996	431
1997	712
1998	1,172
1999	1,689
2000	2,069
2001	2,400

Source: Center for Education Reform, cited in Charles Ridenour, Thomas Lasley, and William Bainbridge, "The Impact of Emerging Market-Based Public Policy on Urban Schools and A Democracy," *Education and Urban Society* 34:1 (November 2001): 69.

This brief summary of charter adoptions does not ignore the fact that some charter schools have had problems. This reform began with the idea that persons with an idea about how to provide education could open a school and manage it, but it said little on actually how to carry out this task. Some schools had management problems, including financial. Also, there quickly developed a new set of school stakeholders, namely, "for-profit" education management systems, as shown in Table 14.3.

Vouchers. Many early supporters of school vouchers thought this was an original idea to give government funds to students to attend schools of their own choice. However, over fifty years before this reform there was a pioneer postsecondary voucher policy, part of the 1944 GI Bill of Rights, that provided federal funds to World War II veterans for higher education. There resulted an enormous financial impact of these reforms on institutions, including education, and on improved personal lifestyles for millions. Moreover, these veterans with higher education later shaped new social institutions and generated for one matter the postwar expansion of the American economy.[12]

In the application of vouchers to public schooling decades later, then, the idea of tax-funded grants to parents had originated in early discussions by scholars,[13] which led in time to recommend public policy. In Minnesota a 1997 law provided a tax deduction to middle-income taxpayers and tax credits of up to $1,000 annually if the money was spent for the schooling of one's children. In another model, Arizona gave tax credits to those donating to private foundations that provided private scholarships. Ohio provided $2,250 scholarships for 1,500 students chosen by lottery; one-half of these scholarships were designated for children in private schools. However, the state subsequently cut that dollar amount down to 25 percent and focused on children of poor families.[14]

Table 14.3
Rise of For-Profit Managers of Charter Schools

Company	Number of Schools	Number of Students
Chancellor Beacon Academies Inc. Coconut Grove, Florida	76	18,500
Edison Schools Inc. New York City	53	21,500
Mosaica Education Inc. New York City	37	10,000
The Leona Schools, Inc. East Lansing, Michigan	33	12,000
National Heritage Academies Inc. Grand Rapids, Michigan	28	14,000
Charter Schools USA Inc. Southfield, Michigan	20	7,500
Charter School Administrative Services* Southfield, Michigan	18	8,000
White Hat Ventures LLC Akron, Ohio	16	6,000
Helicon Associates Inc. Trenton Michigan	9	3,500
Excel Education Centers Inc.	7	700

*Figures derived from other sources than corporation letter.

Source: Education Week (May 22, 2002): 12.

EVALUATION OF EFFECTS ON STUDENT LEARNING

As with any policy, there are many outcomes of choice reforms that one may evaluate. However, the evaluation of school choice is limited by the relatively short period of reform implementation.[15] Thus, in 2005 we have only short-run research results.

While the time period of research results is limited, the effects of school choice reforms are not multiple; that is, policy touches on the values of many stakeholders, who include students, parents, teachers, administrators, school board members, and state and federal officers. The guiding theory behind choice in local schooling is two-fold. Market competition among public and private schools, generated by offering vouchers or charter schools, will diversify and improve schooling, and will benefit both the children enrolled in the alternative schools as well as those in traditional public schools. Managers of the latter would have to alter their own practices in order to compete with the alleged benefits of choice schools. The key in the evaluation of choice reforms, then, is measuring benefits for children, and the most common measure would be student test scores, especially for mathematics and reading. A focus on test scores is justified in part because underlying the theory that school choice improves education is a basic belief that achievement will increase from competitive markets. Moreover, this focus supports evaluating change over time.

Another gross measure might be seen in the number of students using vouchers or attending charter schools; those data seem to indicate success for a few students (see Table 14.1). Yet another measure of the success of these reforms lies in the adoption rate of publicly financed and independent schools. For example, in late 2002 there were thirty-nine states and the District of Columbia that had adopted "permissive" choice laws that permitted but did not compel school districts to adopt these reforms.[16] Of course, as shown in the previous section, there has been great variation in policy matters such as who authorizes contracts for these schools (state agencies or local school boards, for example) or who makes contracts for such schools (a wide range exists).

These numbers are impressive, but they are still minor when measured against the *total* school buildings or students in the public system. For example, Table 14.1 notes a total of 2,400 *buildings* with charter schools, but compare that number with the 15,000 school *districts* multiplied by the average number of buildings in each district. For example, in Ohio in mid-2002, there were 95 charter schools in buildings, but there were 3,700 buildings in the state's public schools. Clearly, choice reform changes are proportionately quite small, but reformers' enthusiasm and financial support have generated impressive publicity about these reforms and their adoption rates. However, not only is a small portion of American schooling affected by these reforms, but little choice is available outside big cities.

A longer-term evaluation, however, may lead to one of several possible outcomes. That is, growth in student enrollment in choice schools may

- stabilize at about the level of the early 2000s,
- expand enormously, approaching the number of students in public schools, or
- fade away to even less than that found in 2005.

Another way to evaluate reform would be to look at the attitudes of parents and other stakeholders who are experiencing these reforms. Research findings reveal that these stakeholders are intensely excited about the reforms; that is, the emotional component of reform support is quite strong. This finding appears regardless of what is studied—voucher or charter reform, parent or teacher, level of grade, and so on. This measure shows high satisfaction with reform schools compared to satisfaction with previous experiences in public schools. A typical finding of stakeholders' attitudes is seen in a study of fifty charter schools where the data were stakeholders' self-reports on degree of satisfaction with the reform.[17] Students, teachers, and parents found charters much better than public schools; this high regard was especially true among minority students. The enthusiastic response to choice schools seems to be particularly strong among less-advantaged families. If such results are found consistently in other research over time, this outcome would clearly be a major improvement of public support in American schooling.

Choice and Learning: Early Studies

Shortly behind the spread of this school reform came schol-arly reviews of its effectiveness. As shown, stakeholders in choice systems are enthusiastic, and preliminary studies show somewhat improved student test scores. Of course, most of this is short-term research, but it substantiates what was said earlier about the benefits of the short run in evaluation. We may only summa-rize here these findings, but there were several studies in the 1990s and early 2000s. Early research indicates that the test scores of minority students enrolled in choice schools improve even more than those of white students. That finding is especially sig-nificant for poor children using vouchers by attending religious schools. A 2002 longitudinal study found that disadvantaged stu-dents enrolled in religious schools did better academically than children from low-income families who attended nonreligious schools.[18] Similar results were found in the same year among California's poor children; indeed, a larger percentage of poor children in this state were found in charter schools than in pub-lic schools.[19] Also, a 2002 U.S. Supreme Court decision (*Zelman* v. *Simmons-Harris*) found that most students in Cleveland, Ohio, used state vouchers for parents to have their children attend mostly black religious schools, and had reported improved scores.

Table 14.4 presents broad components of effects on student learning from data before 2000 that were reported in a recent anthology on school choice.[20] The brevity of this table conceals the richness of these studies, which set out complex theories, employ large data sets, and seek meanings in the data. Table 14.4 does, however, make some important points about evalua-tion in the short term of this reform. There is a great diversity among researchers' judgments of what happened in the 1990s to students' learning concerning choice. Thus, these studies in-volve students in different samples—a few big-city school systems, metropolitan areas, and a national sample. There are also dif-ferences in which grades were studied. In addition, analysts also used novel sets of questions and explored different ways of esti-mating the effectiveness of choice schools.

While the findings differ in some ways, they also agree on several others, including slightly improved test scores in and stakeholder satisfaction with these new schools. This satisfaction

Table 14.4
Reviews of Learning in Choice Schools Before 2000

Scholar*	Year of Data	Grades Tested	Subject Tested**	Improved Scores	Satisfaction			Unit of Analysis
					Parent	Child	Teacher	
1	1990s	General	M, R	Yes	High	NA***	NA	Milwaukee (and 3 other cities)
4	1992	1-12	R	Yes	NA	NA	NA	National sample
6	1990	General	M, R	Yes	High	NA	NA	SMSAs
8	1996-97	5	—	Yes	High	High	High	Choice schools (used self-reports)
9	1996-97	K-2	R	Yes	High	High	High	Charter schools
8	1992	3-11	M, R	Yes	High	NA	NA	San Antonio
12	1991-93	2-8	M, R	Yes	High	NA	NA	Indianapolis
13	—	K-12	M, R	Yes	NA	NA	NA	Milwaukee (used randomized experiment)
14	1997	K-3	—	Yes	High	NA	NA	Cleveland

Source: These reviews are in Paul Peterson and Bryan Hassel, eds. *Learning from School Choice* (Washington, DC.: Brookings, 1998).

*The numbers on the left refer to the chapters found In Peterson and Hassel: 1-Paul Peterson; 4-Jay Greene; 6-Caroline Hoxby; 8-Gregg Vanourek et al.; 9-John Chubb; 11-R. Kenneth Godwin et al.; 12-David Weinschrott and Sally Kilgore; 13-Jay Greene et al.; 14-Jay Greene et al.

**M=mathematics; R=reading

***Indicates not in study (not applicable)

with the reform came not only from parents but also in some cases from students and teachers. Second, there were differences in learning as defined by more improved test scores in choice schools than in public schools. Table 14.4 shows that, without exception, test scores for reading and math slightly improved in either charter or voucher systems. Although the research found that the improvements were relatively minor, the scholars expressed hope that test scores would continue to increase.

The analysis behind these reports is complex. For example, few of the researchers agreed on what students were being compared to other students, for the focus was only on whether they were enrolled in choice or in public schools. Do we compare students in choice schools with similar students in public schools? Or compare those in choice schools, private schools, and all public schools? Or public school students living near the choice schools? Or those students with or without financial support? Can differences be linked to different socioeconomic variables like race, income, parents' education, and so on? Or can differences be linked to the size of the school district?

In short, the problem of causality in evaluation, noted earlier, leads to different explorations that may mask any relationships in the overall success of the reform. Through that web of causal relationships tested before 2000, though, these analysts found some improvements in learning, but even greater was the satisfaction of stakeholders. Finally, though, choice schools have such different objectives and populations that lumping them together masks important variations. Removing those masks is likely the next large step in research.

Choice and Learning: Recent Studies

As analysts continued to study comparative results on student learning, there were clearly two camps of researchers that emerged in the later 1990s and continued into the 2000s. One group concluded that research showed more learning through choice schools, while another group challenged that finding based on the methods employed. Like other studies in the politics of education, these were conducted by scholars whose research was used in the decision making of local, state, and federal bodies.

Let us review these two research lines. The first group, having found modest or mixed results in the early stages, consistently continued support for the reform.[21] For example, one team in this group found that voucher programs in New York City, Washington, and Dayton had shown some improvement in test scores, especially for African Americans in New York. One reviewer in this study noted in 1998 that "the voucher experience clearly is having positive effects on average, but the results to date are not spectacular as to convince skeptics."[22] A summary of such research from the early 2000s, like that for the 1990s in Table 14.4, would find not only increasingly sophisticated research techniques but a similar pattern of limited or mixed gains for students. Thus, one review of choice schools in ten states that related different types of choice students to their scores found some consistent benefits across all the cities studied.[23] However, it became clear, as noted earlier, that these reforms especially benefited poor children. Many supporters for vouchers had pushed to apply for tuition at small, often religious, private schools. A two-year study of California schools reported in early 2002 that low-income students enrolled in charter schools increased their test scores by over one-quarter more than other students in the charter schools. When the low-income group was compared to poor children in public schools, the charter scores were better, but not significantly.[24]

Criticism by other analysts arose over such findings and their methodologies. Some critics questioned the design of contracting charters and dispensing vouchers. In that post-2000 period, then, basic questions about choice reforms needed to be answered before claiming success.[25] For example, a focus on only choice students and those in public schools ignores the possibility that little difference exists among them and other private school students, which would challenge the "market" thesis of reformers that assumes differences among them.[26] Some analysts seriously question the reports of increased scores by challenging the methodology used to obtain them. Others question whether charter schools may work but only for small classes,[27] and some found that, in all but one of ten states studied, students in choice schools had test scores *below* those in public schools. It may be that these differences in results lie not in a school's structure (private versus public) but in the status differences of the students. That is, schools enrolling mainly low-income students have poor results due not to organization but to the effects of other variables, such as parental support of teachers.

In effect, analyst has tangled with analyst, sometimes over the same data. Thus, one group found that school vouchers had improved test scores of African Americans in New York City but not those of whites; another group, however, questioned those findings due to problems in the sample used.[28] Scholars from Stanford and Arizona universities disagreed over improvements reported on tests from charter schools in Arizona, the state with the most charter schools.[29] Conflicting reinterpretations also followed a favorable report on test scores of children in Edison Schools (see below). Analysts from the American Federation of Teachers (AFT) found modest improvements in these data that occurred only from when charter schools first opened but not later. Is it the case that accountability efforts, noted in an earlier chapter, improve test scores? One leading analyst reports "Yes," but another reports "No."[30]

The technical details of this controversy aside, however, it seems charter schools and vouchers have had some success but also some problems. Some charter schools perform much better than others; since these results cancel each other, the averaged findings were not conclusive in the public mind, despite support by stakeholders. In time, state governments became involved with how the reforms were working. While better than half the states adopted such laws, not all pursued them fully because some were weak laws.[31] For example, Illinois in 2002 found test scores for charter schools were much *below* the state averages for all school grades.[32] Some states challenged choice schools for lack of accountability, a matter much debated in this policy conflict.[33] To complicate matters in Illinois, 44 percent of public schools had not passed the tests required in the first round of the No Child Left Behind law of the Bush Administration.

The citizens of some states, including California, used statewide referenda to reject such reform. Later, one state (Colorado), defeated choice in referenda, but a later governor and legislature, both Republican, pushed through such a law. This Colorado law has been overturned by the state courts. Other states questioned the lack of resources for adopting such reforms, noting that they failed to obtain federal grants for low-income children.[34] Finally, a few charter schools failed and were closed by the states. Critics saw this as another sign of an imperfect market for these reforms, noting that students in choice schools were dropping out.[35]

Amid the conflicting short-run research results on learning in choice schools are balanced reviews that found positive but also negative aspects in the reforms at that time. For example, in 2002 the RAND Corporation found there was no continuing evidence for conclusive judgments on the success of choice reforms. This analysis is particularly impressive as it was a meta-study, that is, a review of other studies testing short-run effects, and thus this judgment of inconclusive evidence may well be the answer at this time.[36] In a similar vein, another observer noted of the research on vouchers that unions and others "who distrust the motives of choice advocates, or who staunchly believe that the public's children should be educated in government-run schools, will not change their minds in light of the available evidence."[37]

Despite the conflicting research results on choice systems, public support for this reform grew. Gallup poll response to the question of "paying students to attend private schools" shows this increase—from 2001 to 2002 the support rose from 34 to 46 percent. For another question, "If government paid all or part of the tuition," there was 52 percent approval while opposition to it dropped from 63 to 52 percent. But one pro-voucher group found even higher support—63 percent nationally—and challenged Gallup for using "negative questions." This criticism was perhaps based on Gallup's question about whether parents would want to send their oldest child to public schools; 71 percent answered "Yes."[38] Different wording of poll questions results in different levels of support for school choice.

In summary of this evaluation of short-run effects of choice schools, analysts' opinion was divided but also found some reason for improvement in learning, especially for poor children. Moreover, those involved in the choice schools, such as parents and teachers, were highly supportive. Even farther ahead, though, is the question of evaluating whether choice reforms will end up substituting for public schools or improving public schools by competing with them. While these objectives were the major aims of many choice reform advocates, they are open questions at this time to be answered in the long run.

THE POLITICS OF SCHOOL CHOICE

There is a *political* context to this dispute over the effects of choice reforms on test scores. Supporters of choice are vocal and publicized, and they are organized locally and nationally. A 2003 analysis by the American Association of School Administrators listed the individuals, corporations, and foundations that support, either fully or in part, some aspect of choice schools, as shown in Table 14.5. Their assets are considerable, and they fund research, lobbying, and legal fees. National publicity groups, such as the National Charter School Alliance, founded in 2003, are organized to project favorable news of choice reforms. The opponents of reform, including the Washington, D.C., groups opposed to vouchers (listed in Table 3.2), involve a wide range of interests, not just teachers' unions. Earlier, however, we saw how powerful teachers' unions were in local elections. Their critiques are several:

Table 14.5
Financial Supporters of Choice Reforms, 2003

Contributors

John Walton (Wal-Mart), individual, corporate, foundation

American Education Reform Foundation ($300,000)

Center for Education Reform ($660,460)

Black Alliance for Educational Options ($900,000, Walton + 8 Foundations

Institute for Transformational Learning (25 foundations [Walton] 2 individuals)

Greater Educational Opportunities Foundation 3 foundations + 4 individuals [Walton]

Henry Hazlitt Foundation

Heartland Institute ($442,578)

SchoolReformers.com (7 foundations)

Children First ($590,000, chaired by former Wal-Mart executive)

Parents in Charge (includes conservative and liberal board members, funded by one man)

Heritage Foundation (originated with funding from Joseph Coors and
    Richard Mellon-Scaife. 6 grants of 1,000,000 or more, and 9 grants of
    $100,000 or more—including Walton family)
Institute for Justice ($2.8 million)

Foundations (choice only one of other policies supported)
Helen Bader ($2,189,000)
Bradley ($700,000)
Milton and Rose Friedman (school choice only) Unknown assets but
    received grants from Walton Family Foundation ($100,000), Scaife Foun-
    dation ($300,000), and Bradley Foundation ($1,250)
Grover Hermann ($14,900,000. Had grants of $7,224,000 in 1998.)
Koch Family foundations (4 foundations) ($62,000,000 but 2 foundations
    not listed)
John Olin ($109 million and 1999 grants of $19 million
Scaife Family ($240 million and grants of $7.7 million)
Walton Family ($987 million and 1999 grants $66 million)

Source: Nicholas Penning, *Vouchers: Who's Behind It All?* (Arlington, Va.: American Association of School Administrators, 2003).

- The use of vouchers will weaken public schools if widely
  adopted.
- By diverting public dollars to finance vouchers or charter
  schools, choice policies weaken public support to fix existing problems in public schools.
- By financing schools with a homogenous ethnic base, the
  reforms increase racial segregation. (Many schools with a
  large African American student base, however, have leaders
  who support choice.)
- Segregation will result from public support of religious schools
  (85 percent of private schools are religious) so that both
  racial and religious conflicts would lead to societal divisions.
- The above consequences will weaken a commitment of over
  150 years to a democratic, secular, and, indeed, common
  school.

In this last argument and behind these three terms—democratic, secular, and common—there is an extensive ideological
underpinning for a policy concept, which is support for the *public* schools to which most teachers and administrators have dedicated their lives for generations.[39]

Teacher unions use their own research into the effects of these reforms, and all of it is critical. A report in 2002 by the AFT on the existing research rejected most charter schools as just "experiments."[40] Relying on state data, the AFT reported that the promise of choice schools had not been met. In comparing student scores in these choice schools with those of students from public schools, the AFT reported that choice schools had no better student achievement and were no better in changing school instruction. Moreover, the AFT also found evidence that in charter schools there was more student isolation based on race and class, less financial accountability, and failure to educate students with special needs. When a report from the Edison Schools spoke well of its success in its managed schools, the AFT responded with an analysis that found only modest success; both sides challenged the other's research designs.[41]

Besides teacher groups, other organizations use research to challenge choice reforms. The Center for Policy Research in North Carolina found that students in charter schools did not do as well as those in public schools on writing and mathematics tests. In addition, the charter schools lacked racial balance and had financial problems.[42] Another center in California, using census data on principals and teachers, found that charter schools lacked resources compared to public schools. For example, they did not secure federal grants for low-income students, their teachers lacked credentials, and their per-pupil expenditures were lower.[43]

Supported by this research, unions lobbied state legislatures to reject choice laws or to weaken them.[44] As we saw in earlier chapters, the unions have become potent in affecting school policies in recent decades.[45] Here their focus was on teacher bargaining because they claimed that many charter schools had no union contracts and were exempt from state laws that unions had fought for, such as teacher certification. In a balanced review, one study of state adoption of charter schools pointed out that states varied in how fully such laws were adopted. Teacher unions were at the center of all legislative contests in which governors, political parties, and other pressure groups contended. That is why so few states adopted effective voucher laws, although over one-half the states had adopted some kind of permissive charter laws. When such laws permitted districts to approve school

charter contracts, localities resisted approval of such schools under
pressure from local teacher unions. At the state level, note the
challenges in Texas in 2003 to creating a voucher system: All
state leaders were Republican and outspoken in support of the
choice, while opponents to vouchers formed a Coalition for Public
Schools with thirty-five groups.[46]

The local or state influence of teacher unions failed, however,
when the policy focus shifted to the national level. Note that
choice was instigated at the state level and often fought at the
local level, but in Washington the Bush Administration passed a
voucher experiment for the District of Columbia in 2004. The
emergence of the Republican party in the early 2000s in both
the White House and Congress brought eager supporters of choice
laws. They sought laws and administrative effort for voucher systems, noted in earlier chapters, but Congress did not support
vouchers. However,

- President George Bush proclaimed support in major speeches,
- Congressional committees considered such laws (but rarely
  passed them), and
- the U.S. Department of Education created a subagency to
  support vouchers.

However, as teacher groups were overwhelming Democratic
(the NEA and AFT supported Al Gore in 2000 and John Kerry
in 2004), their opposition in Washington in a Republican atmosphere was not surprising. However, they were able to gather
support to defeat voucher laws until 2004. On the other hand,
though, when the No Child Left Behind legislation was under
consideration in Congress, representatives of teacher unions were
called to testify but their arguments went unheeded.[47]

CONCLUSION

Reviewing the choice school movement in 2004, there are signs
of support and challenge, but its outcome is still uncertain. Large-
scale studies of these reforms still leave questions. A review of
charter schools examines management details of such schools

and compares students in for-profit and public schools[48] Internal dissent within a major foundation for these schools found the Walton Family challenged for "taking control of the issue."[49] Also, problems of accountability with voucher schools in Florida caused the state to close fourteen schools by stopping payments.[50] A seven-year study of Milwaukee vouchers found little parent-driven accountability, a central hope of reformers.[51] Despite the Supreme Court's recent upholding of the voucher principle used in Cleveland, critics are deeply concerned about the sectarian nature of this reform.[52] Indeed, a report of over four years of Cleveland's reform found that students using vouchers did about the same on standardized tests as students in public schools.[53]

The analysis of choice policy in this chapter was designed to demonstrate one form of evaluation—the short run. We have shown how the first evaluations fed the interests of choice supporters, even though the results were not overwhelmingly positive by any measure. The reason that such findings did not constitute a setback for the reformers was the great enthusiasm for it by all involved—except teachers.

Indeed, policymakers might discount as not relevant the division of policy analysts on choice, given widespread acceptance by parents in choice schools. That reformers did not wait for a long-run analysis or achievement benefit was discounted by the well-organized choice lobbies. Word of problems with choice schools elsewhere—failed charter schools, donations to religion through vouchers, and other elements noted in this chapter—was probably not known to policymakers caught up in creating choice programs. For many supporters, research that showed improvement in test scores, no matter how minor, reinforced the correctness of choice. The hope was that small gains at first might we lead to greater gains later. No long-run research demonstrates what choice might create, but a research center at the University of Washington is undertaking a large meta-analysis of assessing performance of charter schools.

Part of the problem in evaluating choice research lies in the fact that "choice" comes in different packages. Research on one form in one state, or even a national sample of one approach, tells us little about the effects of other forms. As one analyst noted recently about charter schools:

398 CURRENT POLITICAL CONTROVERSIES

> The learning model adopted is a school-level decision. Some schools will
> use a proven model; some will try a new model. Some have teachers are
> talking to kids in groups; some use project-based learning. Some are high
> technology; some low-technology. Some are small; some are not small. In
> some, kids dress as they choose; in others, they wear uniforms. . . .[54]

Such diversity is further complicated by differing methodologies in measuring student test scores. A particular problem is what, exactly, is being measured. Is it grade-level organization, student backgrounds, teaching techniques, governance, test scores, and so on? As of now, that kind of comparison of types of choice schools does not exist, and without it we cannot be sure what—if anything—is causing a change. If research consensus shows that choice does work, it will give a major stimulus to even wider choice reform. If not, however, it can stop its growth.

It is clear from this chapter that there exists a "lag effect" between recognizing that a problem exists, to meeting it.[55] There are numerous lags of time in this process. The public's general concern over a problem takes time to build into a coalition of reform. Time for policy action constitutes a legislative lag, and this sequence is followed by a policy selection lag on what program to adopt. From this decision, flow administrative and regulatory lags as the policy gets organized to deliver services. Of course, a litigation lag can arise from those unhappy with the policy, which adds even more time. Then, those whom the policy is to change must learn how to adapt—thus a learning lag. Finally, there is an evaluation lag that takes more time. This lag involves measurement and reporting on results, which is entangled in a methodological lag.

From that theoretical approach, this chapter has shown that the choice school reform is likely still deeply involved in the evaluation lag. The point, however, is that the policy process takes time and is more aligned to adopting what is known and familiar (the incremental approach), rather than moving quickly and in large scale to deal with a problem. Making evaluation even more complicated is the reality that multiple reforms face American schools, so that it is difficult to isolate the independent effects of a given policy.

The policy concerns aside, however, this analysis points to the political aspects of evaluation. It touches on several basic themes found throughout this book. Clearly, the possibility of using choice schools generates a conflict of values. Clearly it also demonstrates how dissatisfaction with schools generates a response through all the forms of political conflicts and levels of government. Curiously, whether the reform works or not in the long run, its progress clearly illuminates the role of policy in a democracy. We are certainly a long way from the professional dominance of school policy and politics that had been the norm until a half-century ago.

Within the political stimuli discussed in this book, American schools today are permeated by professionals' awareness of the need to incorporate parental and community concerns. Dissatisfaction with some part of schooling can generate a wide range of political actions and policies. Nevertheless, the steady state of American schooling operates alongside these dynamics of political change. Lesson plans are generated by professionals, instruction provided and results measured, as administrators do their part to hold the system together. It is this tension and steadiness that are the hallmarks of American education politics today.

NOTES

1. Frederick Wirt, *We Aint' What We Was: Civil Rights and the New South* (Durham, N.C.: Duke University Press, 1997), and Wirt, *The GI Generation: Postwar Veterans and American Society* (forthcoming).

2. John Kingdon, *Agendas, Alternatives, and Public Policies* (Boston: Little, Brown, 1984).

3. Lester Salamon, "Follow-ups, Letdowns, and Sleepers: The Time Dimension in Policy Evaluation," in Charles Jones and Robert Thomas, eds., *Public Policy Making in a Federal System* (Beverly Hills, Calif.: Sage, 1976), pp. 257-284.

4. Kingdon, *Agendas, Alternatives,* chapter 1.

5. Betty Malen, "Tightening the Grip? The Impact of State Activism on Local School Systems," *Education Policy* 17:2 (2003): 195-216.

6. John Chubb and Terry Moe, *Politics, Markets, and American Schools* (Washington, D.C.: Brookings, 1990).

7. Besides the seminal analysis found in footnote 1, almost any writing on this topic, for or against, set out this fundamental thesis. For supporters, see articles in Paul Peterson and Bryan Hassell, eds., *Learning from School Choice* (Washington, D.C.: Brookings, 1998); and Peterson and David Campbell, eds., *Charters, Vouchers, and Public Education* (Washington, D.C.: Brookings, 2001). For one of many critiques, see Seymour Sarason, *Questions You Should Ask*

About Charter Schools and Vouchers (Portsmouth, N.H.: Heinemann, 2002), and Bruce Fuller, ed., *Inside Charter Schools* (Cambridge, Mass.: Harvard University Press).

8. Bryan Hassel, *The Charter School Challenge* (Washington, D.C.: Brookings, 1999).

9. Cited from Washington Center for Education reform in Tom Loveless, *How Well Are American Students Learning?* (Washington, D.C.: Brookings, 2002 Brown Center Report), p. 30.

10. Washington Center for Education Reform, cited in source for Table 14.2; *Education Week*, November 20, 2002, p. 12

11. Paul Peterson, "School Choice: A Report Card," in Peterson and Hassell, *Learning from School Choice*, pp. 112-117.

12. Wirt, *The GI Generation.*

13. Chubb and Moe, *Politics, Markets.*

14. For accounts of later developments for Milwaukee and Cleveland, see authors supportive of such reforms in Peterson and Hassell, *Learning from School Choice*, chapter 13 and 14.

15. For example, Peterson and Hassell, *Learning from School Choice.*

16. Washington Center for Education Reform statistics cited in *Education Week*, November 20, 2002.

17. Greg Vanourek, Bruno Manno, Chester Finn, Jr., and Louann Bierlin, "Charter Schools as Seen by Students, Teachers, and Parents," in Peterson and Hassell, *Learning from School Choice*, pp. 187-211.

18. William Jeynes, "Educational Policy and the Effects of Attending a Religious School on the Academic Achievement of Children," *Educational Policy* 16:3 (July 2002): 406-424.

19. Simeon Slovacek and Anthony Kunnan, "California Charter Schools Serving Low-SES Students: Analysis of the Academic Performance Index," School of Education, California State University, Los Angeles, 2002.

20. Peterson and Hassell, *Learning from School Choice.*

21. For example, see contributors in Paul Peterson and David Campbell, eds., *Charters, Vouchers, and Public Education* (Washington, D.C.: Brookings, 2001).

22. William Howell, Patrick Wolf, Paul Peterson, and David Campbell, "Effects of School Vouchers on Student Test Scores," in Peterson and Campbell, *Charters, Vouchers, and Public Education*, chapter 8; commentary is from the same source in Paul Hill, "Reflections on the School Choice Debate," p. 294.

23. Jay Greene, "The Hidden Research Consensus for School Choice," in Peterson and Campbell, *Charters, Vouchers, and Public Education*, chapter 5.

24. Slovacek and Kunnan, "California Charter Schools," cited in *Education Week*, March 13, 2002.

25. For example, Sarason, *Questions You Should Ask.*

26. That conclusion was reached in analysis in Luis Benveniste, Martin Canoy, and Richard Rothstein, *All Else Equal* (New York: Rutledge Falmer, 2003).

27. Sarason, *Questions You Should Ask.*

28. This dispute is reviewed in *Education Week* for the challenge to Paul Peterson in February 2, 2003, and his rebuttal in June 18, 2003.

29. *Education Week*, February 4, 2003

30. Cited in *Education Week,* March 5, 2003.

31. Hassel, *The Charter School Challenge.*

32. *Chicago Tribune,* November 16, 2002, p. 6.

33. Reviewed in *Education Week,* April 30, 2003, and June 19, 2002.

34. A review appears in *Education Week,* November 20, 2002; March 5, 2003; and April 16, 2003.

35. Reviewed in *Education Week,* November 20, 2002.

36. Rand Corporation, *Rhetoric v. Reality* (Santa Monica, Calif.: Rand, 2002).

37. Paul Hill, "Reflections on the School Choice Debate," in Peterson and Campbell, *Charters, Vouchers, and Public Education,* pp. 294-295.

38. Gallup Poll cited in *Education Week,* September 4, 2002. See also Terry M. Moe, *Schools, Vouchers, and the American Public* (Washington, D.C., 2001).

39. For a fuller review of these points, see any teacher union's study of choice systems, for example, *Education Week,* October 23, 2002.

40. American Federation of Teachers, "Do Charter Schools Measure Up? The Charter School Experiment," cited in *Education Week,* August 7, 2002.

41. Both studies reviewed in *Education Week,* March 5, 2003.

42. North Carolina Center for Public Policy Research, *Education Week,* August 7, 2002.

43. Policy Analysis for California Education, "Charter Schools and Inequality," cited in *Education Week,* April 16, 2003.

44. That process is reviewed in Fuller, *The Charter School Challenge.*

45. See state data in Catherine Marshall, Douglas Mitchell, and Frederick Wirt, *Culture and Education Policy in the American States* (Philadelphia: Falmer, 1989), pp. 234-235.

46. *Education Week,* March 26, 2003, p. 16.

47. For an analysis of what unions did in the Leave No Child Behind legislation, see *Education Week,* November 6, 2002, p. 1.

48. Katrina Bulkley and Priscilla Wohlstetter, *Taking Account of Charter Schools* (New York: Teachers College Press, 2003).

49. Summarized in *Education Week,* December 10, 2003, p. 10.

50. *Education Week,* November 26, 2003, p. 14.

51. Emil Van Dunk and Anniliese Dickman, *School Choice and the Question of Accountability* (New Haven, Conn.: Yale University Press, 2004).

52. Richard Kahlenberg, ed., *Public School Choice vs. Private School Voucher* (New York: Century Foundation Press, 2003).

53. "Evaluation of the Cleveland Scholarship and Tutoring Program" (Bloomington: Indiana Center for Evaluation, 2003).

54. Essay by Ted Kolderie in *Education Week,* October 8, 2003, p. 30.

55. Lewis Solmon, "Education Policy 'Lag Time,'" *Education Week,* December 12, 2003, p. 34.

Subject Index

Author Index